WS-BPEL 2.0 Beginner's Guide

Design and develop WS-BPEL executable business processes using Oracle SOA Suite 12*c*

Matjaz B. Juric

Denis Weerasiri

BIRMINGHAM - MUMBAI

WS-BPEL 2.0 Beginner's Guide

First published: September 2014

Production reference: 1180914

Published by Packt Publishing Ltd.
Livery Place
35 Livery Street
Birmingham B3 2PB, UK.

ISBN 978-1-84968-896-3

www.packtpub.com

Cover image by Karl Moore (karl@karlmoore.co.uk)

Credits

Authors
Matjaz B. Juric
Denis Weerasiri

Reviewers
Tolulope Ayodele Adeniji
Prudhvi Avuthu
Gyan Darpan
Hans Forbrich
John K. Murphy
Prakash Jeya Prakash
Arun Ramesh
Dimitrios Stasinopoulos

Acquisition Editor
Richard Harvey

Content Development Editor
Azharuddin Sheikh

Technical Editors
Manan Badani
Madhuri Das
Shiny Poojari

Copy Editors
Janbal Dharmaraj
Sayanee Mukherjee
Alfida Paiva
Laxmi Subramanian

Project Coordinator
Sanchita Mandal

Proofreaders
Ameesha Green
Samantha Lyon
Bernadette Watkins

Indexer
Monica Ajmera Mehta

Graphics
Abhinash Sahu

Production Coordinators
Aparna Bhagat
Manu Joseph

Cover Work
Aparna Bhagat

About the Authors

Matjaz B. Juric holds a PhD in Computer and Information Science. He is a full-time professor at the University of Ljubljana and the Head of the Cloud Computing and SOA Competency Centre (`www.soa.si`). Matjaz is an Oracle ACE Director, a Java Champion, and an IBM Champion. He has more than 20 years of work experience. He has authored/coauthored *Do More with SOA Integration, WS-BPEL 2.0 for SOA Composite Applications, Oracle Fusion Middleware Patterns, Business Process Driven SOA using BPMN and BPEL, Business Process Execution Language for Web Services* (English and French editions), *BPEL Cookbook: Best Practices for SOA-based integration and composite applications development* (awarded the best SOA book in 2007 by SOA World Journal), *SOA Approach to Integration*, all by Packt Publishing.

He has also worked on *Professional J2EE EAI, Professional EJB, J2EE Design Patterns Applied*, and *Visual Basic .NET Serialization Handbook*, all by WROX Press Ltd. He has published chapters in *More Java Gems, Cambridge University Press*, and in *Technology Supporting Business Solutions, Nova Science Publishers, Inc.* He has also published articles in several journals and magazines and presented at conferences. Matjaz has been involved in several large-scale projects. In cooperation with IBM Java Technology Centre, he worked on performance analysis and optimization of RMI-IIOP, an integral part of the Java platform.

My beautiful daughter Ela and my wonderful Eva, this book is dedicated to you. Without your support, this book would not be possible.

Big thanks to my mother and my grandmother (R.I.P.). Special thanks to my colleagues and friends at the University of Ljubljana and Packt Publishing, particularly to Rok Povse and Pece Adzievski, who have helped with code samples, screenshots, and installation.

Denis Weerasiri is a Computer Science and Engineering student, pursuing his PhD at the University of New South Wales. Before this, he worked as a senior software engineer for WSO2, an open source SOA company. He obtained his BSc Engineering degree with first class honors in the year 2010 from the Department of Computer Science and Engineering, University of Moratuwa, Sri Lanka. His research interests are distributed systems, cloud resource configuration management, and business process management.

I would like to thank my father, Mr. Alfrad Weerasiri, my mother, Mrs. Chandra Pathirana, and my family for standing beside me throughout my life.

I would also like to specifically thank some of my mentors, Mr. Milinda Pathirage, Mr. Waruna Ranasinghe, Dr. Srinath Perera, Dr. Sanjiva Weerawarane, Mr. Samisa Abeysinghe, Mr. Prabath Siriwardena, Mr. Sumedha Rubasinghe, Professor Boualem Benatallah, and all of my colleagues who have provided invaluable opportunities for me to extend my knowledge and shape my career.

I would also like to mention the team from Packt Publishing who contributed to this book in many ways.

About the Reviewers

Tolulope Ayodele Adeniji is a seasoned Oracle Fusion Middleware consultant with specific expertise in integration, using JEE technologies and Oracle SOA Suite products. He has over 8 years of experience in the design, development, deployment, and administration of JEE-based applications and SOA-based systems in a mission-critical enterprise environment. He has been involved in several major integration projects in the telecoms domain. Tolulope is currently a senior consultant at Falcorp Technologies (Pty) Ltd, South Africa.

> I would like to appreciate my family, especially my wife, for bearing with me during those odd evenings when I got glued to my computer and didn't participate in their conversations so that I could focus on reviewing this book.

Prudhvi Avuthu is very passionate about teaching and learning new technologies. Currently, he runs his own firm, erpSchools Inc, which provides online education on ERP technologies.

Prudhvi holds a Master's degree in Computer Science from Illinois Institute of Technology, Chicago. After graduation, he worked in the US for various clients such as American Bar Association, Fellowes, Ventana Medical Systems, Roche, Bechtel, and Deloitte. Having worked in various roles, ranging from a consultant to a solution architect in Oracle ERP, Prudhvi moved back to India to accept a much more challenging role, project manager, in Zensar Technologies. After 3 years of work as a project manager in India, he moved on to become an entrepreneur by converting his online education portal, `www.erpschools.com`, founded in 2007, into a US-registered firm, erpSchools Inc, in 2013.

> I would like to thank my wife, Haritha Gogineni, who happens to work in the same Oracle ERP technology, for sharing my regular work and thereby giving me ample time to review this book. I would also like to thank my uncle, Srinivas Bonthu, who has given me enough motivation to take bold steps in my career.

Gyan Darpan is a senior Oracle consultant, focusing on Oracle E-Business Suite and Oracle Fusion Middleware technologies. He has completed his Master's in Computer Applications as a topper from New Horizon College of Engineering, Bangalore, India. He is passionate about exploring new technologies, training, and mentoring. At present, he is based in Australia and is working for NEC, Australia. Prior to this, he worked for Polaris Software, EXL Services, Espire Infolab, Sapient Consulting, and Path Infotech. He started his career as a Java developer and moved to Oracle Stack. His expertise lies in Oracle SOA, Oracle ADF, OBIEE, ODI, Oracle E-Business Suite, OAF, and Java.

He is also the founder of the web startup, Querent Technologies (`www.querenttech.com`), which deals with software consulting, outsourcing, implementation, support, and training.

Gyan is actively involved in large implementations of next-generation enterprise applications, utilizing Oracle's JDeveloper, Application Development Framework (ADF), and SOA technologies. He has rich implementation expertise in EAI/SOA integrations, and has worked on some challenging projects across different verticals. He has strong team lead and communication skills and a deep technical knowledge covering both Oracle and Java.

Gyan is also an active member of OTN and is known as the Oracle Guru for his work on Oracle Technologies.

He can be contacted at his personal e-mail address at `gyan.ebs@gmail.com`.

You can also visit his LinkedIn profile at `https://au.linkedin.com/pub/gyan-darpan-yadav/21/996/b30`.

He likes to share his experiences by blogging on `http://oraclefusionmate.blogspot.com`.

I would like to specially thank my family and friends for their unconditional love and support.

I would also like to thank my managers who, throughout the years, have provided me with opportunities to work on new technologies and projects and take on challenging tasks.

Hans Forbrich is an Oracle ACE Director and the owner of Forbrich Consulting Ltd., an international Oracle partner and consultancy based in Alberta, Canada, since 2002. Hans has been using, administering, developing with, and consulting on Oracle products since 1984. As an Oracle University partner, he has been training organizations on the Oracle SOA Suite since 2008.

Hans has reviewed several SOA Suite books from Packt Publishing as well as a number of database-related books, and he is pleased to have been involved with this project.

John K. Murphy lives in the US and is a software industry veteran with more than 30 years of experience as a programmer and database administrator. A graduate from the University of West Virginia, he began writing computer games in the 1980s before pursuing a career as a computer consultant. Over the years, he has enjoyed developing software in most of the major languages for a wide variety of industries while striving to keep up with all the new technologies.

John has reviewed several books for Packt Publishing and is the author of *DotNetNuke 5.4 Cookbook, Packt Publishing*.

Prakash Jeya Prakash is an experienced middleware specialist with more than 10 years of experience in the middleware and integration space. He is currently a lead SOA architect working for a global consulting organization in the UK. Prakash holds a Master of Science degree in Software Engineering from BITS Pilani, Rajasthan, and he is also an Oracle certified SOA architect. He can be contacted via LinkedIn at `http://uk.linkedin.com/in/prakashjeya/`.

Thanks to my wife, Srividya Nambiar, who supported me in taking time off from our holidays to review a few chapters of this book.

Arun Ramesh has more than 9 years of IT experience and has been a forerunner in providing SOA-based integration solutions to customers across industries. He has been a part of some major IT consulting giants, globally. He has a niche portfolio of skills in integration-related technologies from multiple vendors. He is currently a solution architect specializing in SOA-based integrations using Oracle Fusion Middleware. He has been a part of major pioneering implementation milestones using Oracle Fusion Middleware, Oracle MDM, and Oracle AIA. He has also been instrumental in implementations using the Oracle stack, with the integration layer being Oracle AIA. He is an expert in complex and very large customizations in AIA PIPs and has been a frontrunner for one such challenging engagement for a telecoms major in Europe.

He has been a reviewer for various books on Oracle Fusion Middleware and Oracle BPM. He is well known in the public domain for his technology blog on Oracle Fusion Middleware and Oracle AIA, which provide numerous technical tips, product reviews, code snippets, and solutions to other blogger queries.

I would like to take this opportunity to thank my wife, Aparna, who supported and encouraged me in this effort, in spite of all the times that it took me away from the family.

I would also like to thank all those who have helped me in some way to complete the review of this book and whose names I have failed to mention.

Dimitrios Stasinopoulos is a certified Application Development Framework Implementation specialist with more than 7 years of experience in Oracle Fusion Middleware. He currently works as an Oracle Fusion Middleware consultant. In his spare time, he maintains a blog, `dstas.blogspot.com`, where he posts his findings and ideas. Dimitrios holds a BSc degree in Computer Science from Technological Educational Institution of Larissa, Greece.

www.PacktPub.com

Support files, eBooks, discount offers, and more

You might want to visit www.PacktPub.com for support files and downloads related to your book.

Did you know that Packt offers eBook versions of every book published, with PDF and ePub files available? You can upgrade to the eBook version at www.PacktPub.com and as a print book customer, you are entitled to a discount on the eBook copy. Get in touch with us at service@packtpub.com for more details.

At www.PacktPub.com, you can also read a collection of free technical articles, sign up for a range of free newsletters and receive exclusive discounts and offers on Packt books and eBooks.

http://PacktLib.PacktPub.com

Do you need instant solutions to your IT questions? PacktLib is Packt's online digital book library. Here, you can access, read and search across Packt's entire library of books.

Why subscribe?

- Fully searchable across every book published by Packt
- Copy and paste, print and bookmark content
- On demand and accessible via web browser

Free access for Packt account holders

If you have an account with Packt at www.PacktPub.com, you can use this to access PacktLib today and view nine entirely free books. Simply use your login credentials for immediate access.

Instant updates on new Packt books

Get notified! Find out when new books are published by following @PacktEnterprise on Twitter, or the *Packt Enterprise* Facebook page.

Table of Contents

Preface

WS-BPEL 2.0 (Business Process Execution Language for Web Services, also BPEL or BPEL4WS) has become the industry standard for orchestration of services, implementation of business processes, and development of composite applications. BPEL provides a rich vocabulary for expressing the behavior of business processes and composites. Although it looks quite simple at first sight, BPEL provides a rich set of operations (called activities) to model the process flows of composite applications, such as asynchronous and parallel invocation of services, correlation, event, fault, compensation and termination handlers, scopes, source and destination links, and so on.

BPEL is an OASIS specification. It is not owned by a specific vendor or company. This means that using BPEL leads to the development of portable, vendor-agnostic solutions. BPEL is also supported by major BPM/SOA-development platforms, including most important commercial platforms such as Oracle SOA Suite and Oracle JDeveloper, IBM WebSphereBPM, and so on, and open source tools and servers, such as JBoss, Eclipse, and so on.

Although BPEL is widely used, studies have shown that most software architects and developers do not have an in-depth familiarity with the BPEL language. The majority of them are familiar only with the basics, which is also reflected in BPEL code that in most cases includes only the most straightforward activities. An in-depth familiarity with BPEL is essential to unleash its full potential. Therefore, it makes sense to publish a book that covers BPEL functionality for beginners, showing step-by-step how to use BPEL from the most straightforward to the more complex scenarios.

This book will guide software architects and developers through the BPEL language and teach them the various activities, use-cases, and scenarios that can be developed in BPEL. The book will be a beginner's guide, starting with the basics and advancing through different increasingly complex scenarios. The book will be tool-independent, but will show how to use BPEL with most popular tools, such as JDeveloper, SOA Suite (from Oracle), and so on.

What this book covers

Chapter 1, Hello BPEL, provides a basic understanding of BPEL. We will see that BPEL is an important part of Service Oriented Architecture (SOA). It is a language for service orchestration and uses the XML syntax. Usually, it is represented graphically for easier development. We will learn how to install Oracle JDeveloper and SOA Suite, how to create a domain on the SOA Suite server, and how to use JDeveloper to develop BPEL. We will develop two simple BPEL processes. The first one will be a very simple process returning the stock quantity of a book as a hardcoded constant. The second BPEL process will be a little more sophisticated and return the quantity depending on the ISSN number. In addition to understanding the BPEL source code, we will get an understanding of the `<assign>` and `<if>` activities as well. We will also learn how to deploy a BPEL process to the SOA Suite server and how to use the Enterprise Manage console to test the BPEL processes.

Chapter 2, Service Invocation, explains how to invoke and orchestrate services. We will explain the primary mission of BPEL—service orchestration. It follows the concept of programming-in-the-large. We will develop a BPEL process, which will invoke two services and orchestrate them. We will become familiar with the `<invoke>` activity and understand the service invocations background, particularly partner links and partner link types. We will also learn from BPEL that it is very easy to invoke services in parallel. To achieve this, we will use the `<flow>` activity. Within `<flow>`, we can nest several `<invoke>` activities, but also other BPEL activities.

Chapter 3, Variables, Data Manipulation, and Expressions, explains how to use variables in BPEL and how to manipulate data. We will explain that in BPEL all variables store XML. They are used to hold the requests and responses for invoked services (partner links), and also to store other data related to the process state. We will see that we can declare variables of three different types, message types, elements, and simple types. To manipulate data, we will use the `<assign>` activity. We will become familiar with the `<assign>` activity and learn how to use different possibilities when copying data. Probably, the most commonly used are expressions, which are written in XPath. We will also learn how to access variables from the expressions, how to validate variables, and how to use XSLT transformations to transform the data.

Chapter 4, Conditions and Loops, covers the conditions in BPEL processes. We will discuss the syntax of the `<if>`, `<elseif>`, and `<else>` activities and see an example on how to implement conditions. We will also take a close look at the loops. We will learn about the three types of loops that BPEL provides: `<while>`, `<repeatUntil>`, and `<forEach>`. The `<forEach>` loop also provides the ability to execute the loop instances in parallel. We will implement the `<while>` and `<forEach>` loops, the latter in a sequential and parallel way. We will also get familiar with delays, which can be useful in loops. With delays, we can specify a certain deadline or duration. We will learn how to specify both. Finally, we will see how to end a BPEL process with the `<exit>` activity and why and when to use `<empty>` activities.

Chapter 5, Interaction Patterns in BPEL, covers how to communicate with external web services in an asynchronous manner and also we will learn how invoke an asynchronous BPEL process. This chapter is important as asynchronous communication is essential in real-world, long-running business processes where the request response time is undeterministic for a particular external web service invocation. Also, there are circumstances where the endpoints defined for the response and for the particular request are exposed by different web services. As an example, a business process can invoke its purchase service. However, the confirmation response to that particular request actually comes from the shipping process. So, in such scenarios, asynchronous communication is inevitable. The concepts we learn in this chapter are useful in real-world business process developments.

Chapter 6, Fault Handling and Signaling, first explains some of the faults that could be generated within a business process. Then we discuss what a fault handler is. We move on to a sample that covers these aspects and we explain how the BPEL 2.0 specification models the aforementioned faults. We categorize these faults into three groups as follows:

- Modeling execution errors with BPEL 2.0 Standard Faults
- Modeling logical (explicit) errors with the `<throw>` activity
- Modeling errors propagated from external web services

We describe how logical (explicit) faults are signaled within the business process definition, and then we will explain how a signaled fault is propagated back to the client of the business process. So at the end of this chapter, the reader will be capable of declaring fault handling behaviors to a business process.

Chapter 7, Working with Scopes, introduces the concept of the `<scope>` activity and describes the advantages of it. We will see how to add `<scope>` activities to hierarchically organize the Book Warehousing sample. Some between the differences of the `<scope>` activity and other activities such as `<process>`, `<sequence>`, and `<flow>` are explained. Then we will see how to add a fault handler and a termination handler to a `<scope>` activity. Finally, we will introduce the concept of isolated scopes.

So at the end of this chapter, the reader will be capable of declaring the `<scope>` activity to organize a BPEL 2.0 process hierarchically.

Chapter 8, Dynamic Parallel Invocations, explains the `<forEach>` activity in detail. It lets us define repetitive tasks in a sequential or in a parallel manner. First, we will learn a practical use-case of the `<forEach>` activity by trying out an example. Then, we will see how to configure a `<forEach>` activity step by step. During this exercise, we will also learn about dynamic partner links as a requirement to invoke different end points within the `<forEach>` activity in parallel. After that exercise, we will explain each configuration within the `<forEach>` activity that determines the repetitive and parallel behavior. So, at the end of this chapter, the reader will be capable of declaring the `<forEach>` activity to define repetitive tasks in sequence or in parallel.

Chapter 9, Human Tasks, introduces the concept of human interactions in BPEL 2.0 processes. We will first learn how human interactions work. Then, we will go on to develop human task definitions and configure them with assignments, deadlines, notifications, and other important properties. We will continue with invoking a human task from the BPEL process and receiving the human task outcomes. You can make use of the concepts we learn in this chapter in real-world scenarios to model business processes with human user interactions.

Chapter 10, Events and Event Handlers, discusses how event handlers provide a mechanism for running business processes to react to events that can be triggered, without interfering with the main flow of the process. In this chapter, we will take a brief look at Event Driven Architecture (EDA). We will explain how a BPEL process can react on events. We will get familiar with business, message, and alarm events, and understand the difference between deadlines and durations. We will learn how to develop event-driven BPEL processes and how to invoke events from BPEL processes. We will also learn how to use the `<pick>` activity and `<eventHandlers>` at either the scope or process level. Furthermore, we will explain `<onEvent>` for triggering events by incoming messages that correspond to operations in WSDLs and `<onAlarm>`, which needs to be triggered when a deadline is reached or after a specified period. By following this chapter to add the event handlers and event-related activities for the BPEL sample, the reader gains the capability to model BPEL 2.0 processes to accept requests that arrive in parallel to its normal flow of control.

Chapter 11, Compensations, discusses the backward recovery or rollback mechanism for BPEL 2.0 processes. Here, for achieving compensation, we will learn how to use `<compensationHandler>`, then `<compensate>`, and `<compensateScope>` activities. Later, we will extend our sample to include a compensation that reverses the effects of activities which were completed up until a fault occurred in the process. After reading this chapter, you will have a clear understanding of how to undo previous operations, using compensation to get back to a consistent state.

Appendix B, BPEL Syntax Reference, provides a lot of useful syntax references for the WS-BPEL Web Services Business Process Execution Language. The complete appendix can be found online at `https://www.packtpub.com/sites/default/files/downloads/8963EN_Appendix_B.pdf`.

What you need for this book

In order to develop the examples in this chapter, we need to install the integrated development environment and the process server on which the BPEL processes will execute. To develop BPEL processes, we will use the Oracle JDeveloper 12*c* 12.1.3. To execute the BPEL processes, we will use the Oracle SOA Suite 12*c* 12.1.3.

The installation will consist of the following steps:

1. We need to install Java Development Kit (JDK) and set the environment.
2. We need to install the SOA Suite 12*c* with JDeveloper.
3. We need to create the default domain.

Detailed instructions on how to install JDK, SOA Suite 12*c*, JDeveloper, and how to create the domain are provided in *Chapter 1, Hello BPEL*.

Who this book is for

The target audiences for this book are software architects and designers, software developers, SOA and BPM architects and project managers, and business process analysts, who are responsible for the design and development of business processes, composite applications, and BPM/SOA solutions. This book provides in-depth coverage of WS-BPEL 2.0, and gives practical development examples on how to move from simple to more complex BPEL applications.

Conventions

In this book, you will find several headings appearing frequently.

To give clear instructions of how to complete a procedure or task, we use:

Time for action – heading

1. Action 1
2. Action 2
3. Action 3

Instructions often need some extra explanation so that they make sense, so they are followed with:

What just happened?

This heading explains the working of tasks or instructions that you have just completed.

You will also find some other learning aids in the book, including:

Pop quiz – heading

These are short multiple-choice questions intended to help you test your own understanding.

Have a go hero – heading

These practical challenges give you ideas for experimenting with what you have learned.

You will also find a number of styles of text that distinguish between different kinds of information. Here are some examples of these styles, and an explanation of their meaning.

Code words in text, database table names, folder names, filenames, file extensions, pathnames, dummy URLs, user input, and Twitter handles are shown as follows: "Finally, we need to set the `JAVA_HOME` and `ORACLE_HOME` environment variables."

A block of code is set as follows:

```
<process ...>
  ...
  <sequence>

    <!-- Wait for the incoming request to start the process -->
    <receive ... />

    <!-- Perform some activities -->
    ...

    <!-- Return the response -->
    <reply ... />
  </sequence>
</process>
```

When we wish to draw your attention to a particular part of a code block, the relevant lines or items are set in bold:

```
<process ...>
   ...
   <sequence>
      <!-- Wait for the incoming request to start the process -->
      <receive ... />
      ...
   </sequence>
</process>
```

Any command-line input or output is written as follows:

```
SET JAVA_HOME=%USERPROFILE%\top_level_folder_jdkversion
SET ORACLE_HOME=%USERPROFILE%\Oracle\Middleware\Oracle_Home
```

New terms and **important words** are shown in bold. Words that you see on the screen, in menus or dialog boxes for example, appear in the text like this: "The first step is the **Welcome** screen, where we only need to click on the **Next** button."

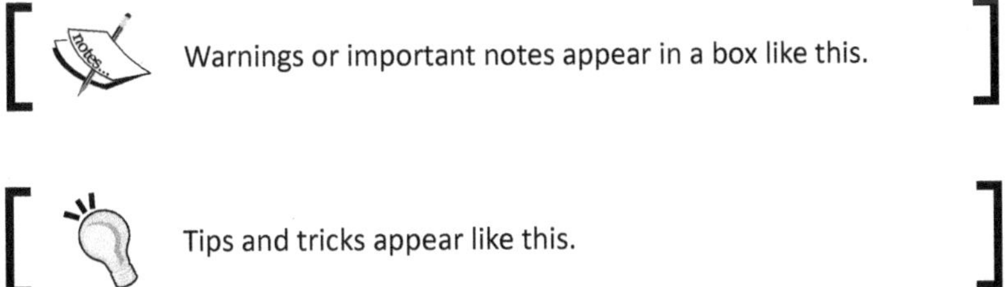

Warnings or important notes appear in a box like this.
Tips and tricks appear like this.

Reader feedback

Feedback from our readers is always welcome. Let us know what you think about this book—what you liked or may have disliked. Reader feedback is important for us to develop titles that you really get the most out of.

To send us general feedback, simply send an e-mail to `feedback@packtpub.com`, and mention the book title through the subject of your message.

If there is a topic that you have expertise in and you are interested in either writing or contributing to a book, see our author guide on `www.packtpub.com/authors`.

Customer support

Now that you are the proud owner of a Packt book, we have a number of things to help you to get the most from your purchase.

Downloading the example code

You can download the example code files for all Packt books you have purchased from your account at `http://www.packtpub.com`. If you purchased this book elsewhere, you can visit `http://www.packtpub.com/support` and register to have the files e-mailed directly to you.

Errata

Although we have taken every care to ensure the accuracy of our content, mistakes do happen. If you find a mistake in one of our books—maybe a mistake in the text or the code—we would be grateful if you would report this to us. By doing so, you can save other readers from frustration and help us improve subsequent versions of this book. If you find any errata, please report them by visiting `http://www.packtpub.com/submit-errata`, selecting your book, clicking on the **errata submission form** link, and entering the details of your errata. Once your errata are verified, your submission will be accepted and the errata will be uploaded to our website, or added to any list of existing errata, under the Errata section of that title.

Piracy

Piracy of copyright material on the Internet is an ongoing problem across all media. At Packt, we take the protection of our copyright and licenses very seriously. If you come across any illegal copies of our works, in any form, on the Internet, please provide us with the location address or website name immediately so that we can pursue a remedy.

Please contact us at `copyright@packtpub.com` with a link to the suspected pirated material.

We appreciate your help in protecting our authors, and our ability to bring you valuable content.

Questions

You can contact us at `questions@packtpub.com` if you are having a problem with any aspect of the book, and we will do our best to address it.

1
Hello BPEL

Web Services Business Process Execution Language *(***WS-BPEL***), also BPEL or BPEL4WS, is an orchestration language for composition, orchestration, and coordination of services. BPEL is not used for actual programming of functionalities. Rather, it is used to orchestrate and compose functionalities, exposed through services, into larger units and composite applications.*

Composition or orchestration usually follows a certain order of activities; it forms a process. Therefore, this language is called business process execution language. Particularly in information systems, BPEL has an important role. It is used to orchestrate business processes which consists of several activities. Some of them are automated, some are not. For automated activities, a BPEL process would invoke a specific service that provides the corresponding operation. For manual activities, a BPEL process would call a human task. We will explain human tasks later in this book.

As BPEL is not suitable for actual programming of functionalities, it is much easier to learn and understand than traditional languages, such as Java, C#, or C++. However, BPEL still provides a rich vocabulary for expressing the behavior of business processes. In BPEL, it is much easier to implement specifics of business processes, such as parallel or asynchronous invocations of activities, fault handling, and compensations.

BPEL is usually considered as a part of **Business Process Management** *(***BPM***) with* **Service Oriented Architecture** *(***SOA***). It is used to weave the bits and pieces of the SOA technology together into a more useful and business-friendly whole. BPEL is as important for SOA as SQL is for relational databases.*

In this chapter, we will get familiar with the basic concepts and develop our first Hello BPEL process. We will cover the following topics:

- Understanding what BPEL is and how it differs from traditional languages
- Learning how to install Oracle JDeveloper and SOA Suite
- Creating a domain on the SOA Suite server
- Developing a simple BPEL processes
- Having an understanding of the BPEL source code
- Understanding some of the basic construct of BPEL
- Deploying the BPEL processes to the SOA Suite server
- Using the Enterprise Manage console to test the BPEL processes

Let's get started...

Introduction to BPEL

Business Process Execution Language (**BPEL**) is a language for composing, orchestrating, and coordinating the flow of services. BPEL is a programming-in-the-large language, used for service composition. It differs from programming-in-the-small languages, such as Java, C#, or C++, which are used to implement specific functionalities. BPEL is used to compose (orchestrate) functionalities exposed through services (service interfaces) into composite applications.

For example, let's consider that we have a bookstore. In this bookstore, we have an application that provides support for the bookstore operations, among them the stock management. Let's assume that this application provides a web service interface through which we can query the number of books in stock. If the number of books in stock is lower than anticipated, our bookstore would need to buy more books. It would need to make the purchase order with the book publisher. Again, let's assume that the publisher provides a web service through which the bookstore can make the purchase order.

BPEL allows us to implement the previously-mentioned process in an easy and straightforward way, as we will see very shortly. BPEL is a language specialized for process orchestrations; it provides specific language constructs for business processes. BPEL, therefore, provides several important advantages as follows:

- Implementing business processes with BPEL is easier and more straightforward when compared to traditional programming languages.
- Business processes implemented with BPEL still look like processes. Maintaining, updating, and modifying them in the future will be much easier when compared to using traditional programming languages.

- BPEL tends to bridge the huge gap between business executives and software developers, as business people can visually comprehend what goes on in the business processes.
- BPEL separates defining business process from coding the actual functionality in programming language thereby leading developers to use the same code for multiple processes. In other words, it promotes reuse.

There are two ways we can write the BPEL code. One is to write the code directly. BPEL uses an XML-based vocabulary that allows us to specify and describe business processes. Writing the BPEL XML code directly requires quite a lot of knowledge. The other simpler approach is to use a visual editor. Using an editor allows us to construct the BPEL processes using a drag-and-drop approach where we select the appropriate BPEL activity and drop it to the process flow. BPEL is today widely supported in development environments, such as JDeveloper, WebSphere Integration Designer, or Eclipse. Visual editors in these tools might differ. However, the BPEL code generated by all **Integrated Development Environments** (**IDEs**) is the same. This is because BPEL is an industry standard and is defined as OASIS specification (`https://www.oasis-open.org/`). The current version of BPEL is 2.0, although the previous version BPEL 1.1 is still widely used. As long as we stick with the standard BPEL without vendor-specific extensions, BPEL code is portable between different environments.

To execute a BPEL process, we need a **process server**. There are several commercial and open source BPEL process servers available. Most well-known are Oracle SOA Suite, IBM WebSphere BPM, ActiveVOS, and Apache ODE.

In this book, we will develop examples using Oracle JDeveloper 12*c* and Oracle SOA Suite 12*c*. However, please bear in mind that the BPEL code is universally portable to other tools and environments.

Installing Oracle JDeveloper and SOA Suite

In order to develop the examples in this chapter, we need to install IDE and the process server on which the BPEL processes will execute. To develop the BPEL processes, we will use Oracle JDeveloper 12*c* 12.1.3. To execute the BPEL processes, we will use the runtime environment of the Oracle SOA Suite 12*c* 12.1.3.

The installation will consist of the following steps:

1. Install the **Java Development Kit** (**JDK**) and set the environment
2. Install SOA Suite 12*c* with JDeveloper
3. Create the default domain

Installing the JDK and setting environment

A prerequisite for installing and running JDeveloper and SOA Suite is the JDK. We will install the latest JDK Version 7. Currently, SOA Suite 12*c* required Java SE 7 and has not been certified to work with Java SE 8 yet. However, this might change with newer versions.

Time for action – installing the JDK and setting environment

Perform the following steps to download and install the JDK:

1. Go to `http://www.oracle.com/technetwork/java/javase/downloads/index.html` and download and install the latest version of Java SE 7 Java Platform, Standard Edition. Currently, this is Java SE 7u60. You need to download the JDK (and not JRE or Server JRE).

2. Install the JDK. On Windows, you will need to double-click on the installation file and you will be guided through the install process. On Linux, you will have to execute the install from the command shell, as shown in the following screenshot:

```
oracle@soa-12c-linux:/home/oracle/Desktop
File  Edit  View  Search  Terminal  Help
[oracle@soa-12c-linux Desktop]$ su
Password:
[root@soa-12c-linux Desktop]# ls
gnome-terminal.desktop  jdk-7u60-linux-x64.rpm
[root@soa-12c-linux Desktop]# chmod +x jdk-7u60-linux-x64.rpm
[root@soa-12c-linux Desktop]# rpm -i ./jdk-7u60-linux-x64.rpm
Unpacking JAR files...
        rt.jar...
        jsse.jar...
        charsets.jar...
        tools.jar...
        localedata.jar...
        jfxrt.jar...
[root@soa-12c-linux Desktop]#
```

3. Finally, we need to set the `JAVA_HOME` and `ORACLE_HOME` environment variables. On Linux, you need to write the following command:

```
JAVA_HOME=$HOME/top_level_folder_jdkversion
export JAVA_HOME
ORACLE_HOME=%HOME/Oracle/Middleware/Oracle_Home
export ORACLE_HOME
```

On Windows, write the following command:

```
SET JAVA_HOME=%USERPROFILE%\top_level_folder_jdkversion
SET ORACLE_HOME=%USERPROFILE%\Oracle\Middleware\Oracle_Home
```

What just happened?

We installed the JDK and set the environment variables, `JAVA_HOME` and `ORACLE_HOME`, which are required for the JDK and SOA Suite.

You can check the JDK installation with a simple `java -version` command, which will print the JDK version and the virtual machine version:

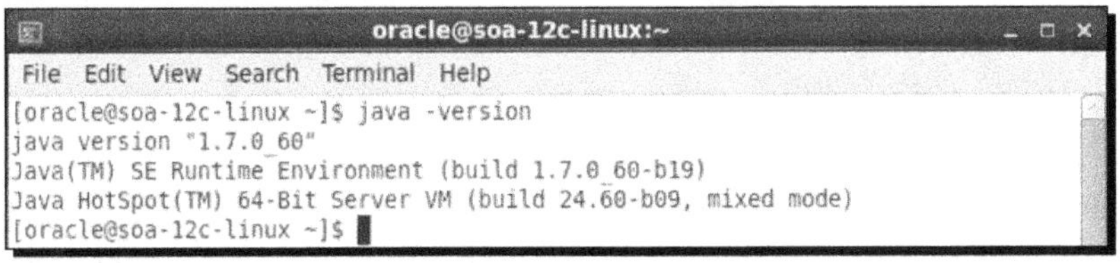

```
oracle@soa-12c-linux:~
File Edit View Search Terminal Help
[oracle@soa-12c-linux ~]$ java -version
java version "1.7.0_60"
Java(TM) SE Runtime Environment (build 1.7.0_60-b19)
Java HotSpot(TM) 64-Bit Server VM (build 24.60-b09, mixed mode)
[oracle@soa-12c-linux ~]$
```

Installing SOA Suite with JDeveloper

The easiest way to start using both products is to download a free SOA Suite 12*c* installation available at `http://www.oracle.com/technetwork/middleware/soasuite/downloads/index.html`.

We will use a quick-start installation. The quick-start installation will contain all the following software required for a development environment on a single host:

- JDeveloper with SOA IDE extensions
- BPEL Process Manager
- Human Workflow
- Business Rules
- Mediator
- Service Bus
- Technology Adapters
- Enterprise Scheduler
- SOA Spring Component
- Enterprise Manager Fusion Middleware Control
- Integrated WebLogic Server
- Java DB

The quick-start installation is the quickest way to start developing and testing the BPEL processes using SOA Suite and JDeveloper and exactly what most developers need (and what we need for this book).

Please note that the quick-start installation is limited to one server and cannot be upgraded to a production environment. A production environment requires a much more complex installation, described at `http://docs.oracle.com/middleware/1213/core/INSOA/planning.htm`.

Time for action – installing JDeveloper and SOA Suite

Perform the following steps to download and install Oracle SOA Suite 12*c* with JDeveloper using the quick-start installation:

1. Go to `http://www.oracle.com/technetwork/middleware/soasuite/downloads/index.html` and download the free SOA Suite 12*c* installation. You can choose between a **Microsoft Windows 64 bit JVM** installation and **All Platforms Generic 64 bit JVM** installation. Select **SOA Suite Quick Start Installer** of SOA Suite 12.1.3. You don't need any **Additional Components** for this book.
2. Once downloaded, unzip the content into the same directory. Two `.jar` files will unzip, as shown in the following screenshot:

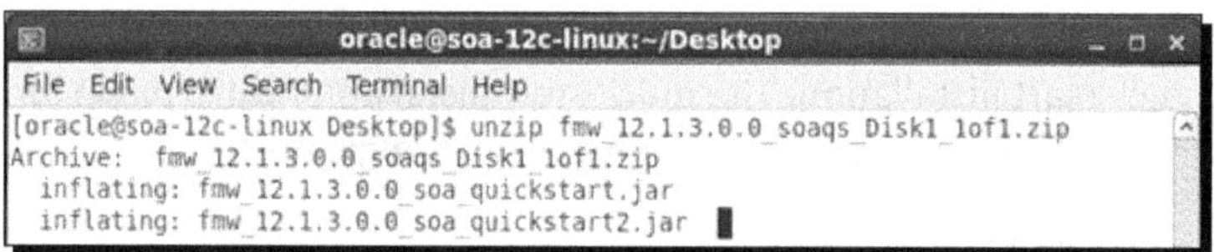

3. We need to execute the `fmw_12.1.3.0.0_soa_quickstart.jar` file, which will launch the installation wizard, as shown in the following screenshot:

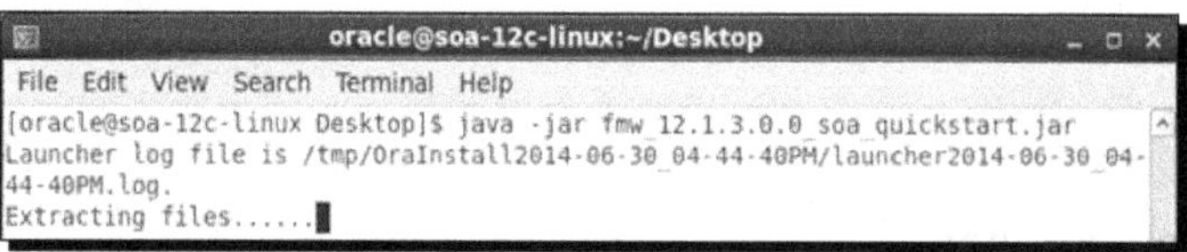

oracle@soa-12c-linux:~/Desktop
File Edit View Search Terminal Help
[oracle@soa-12c-linux Desktop]$ java -jar fmw_12.1.3.0.0_soa_quickstart.jar
Launcher log file is /tmp/OraInstall2014-06-30_04-44-40PM/launcher2014-06-30_04-44-40PM.log.
Extracting files......

4. The installation wizard will appear, guiding you through several steps. First, we need to specify the **Central Inventory** installation directory. Specify `/home/oracle/oraInventory`. We also need to specify **Operating System Group**. This is the group with write permissions to the inventory directory. Use the `oracle` group:

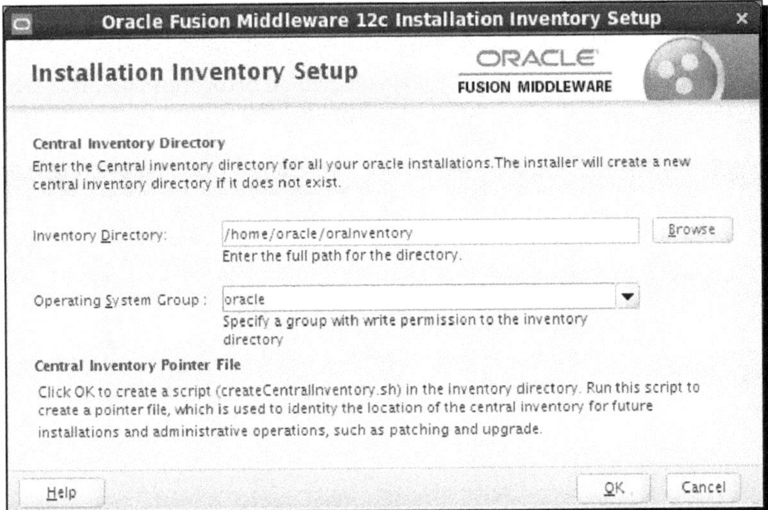

5. Next, the quick-start installer will appear, guiding you through the six steps. The first step is the **Welcome** screen, where we only need to click on the **Next** button:

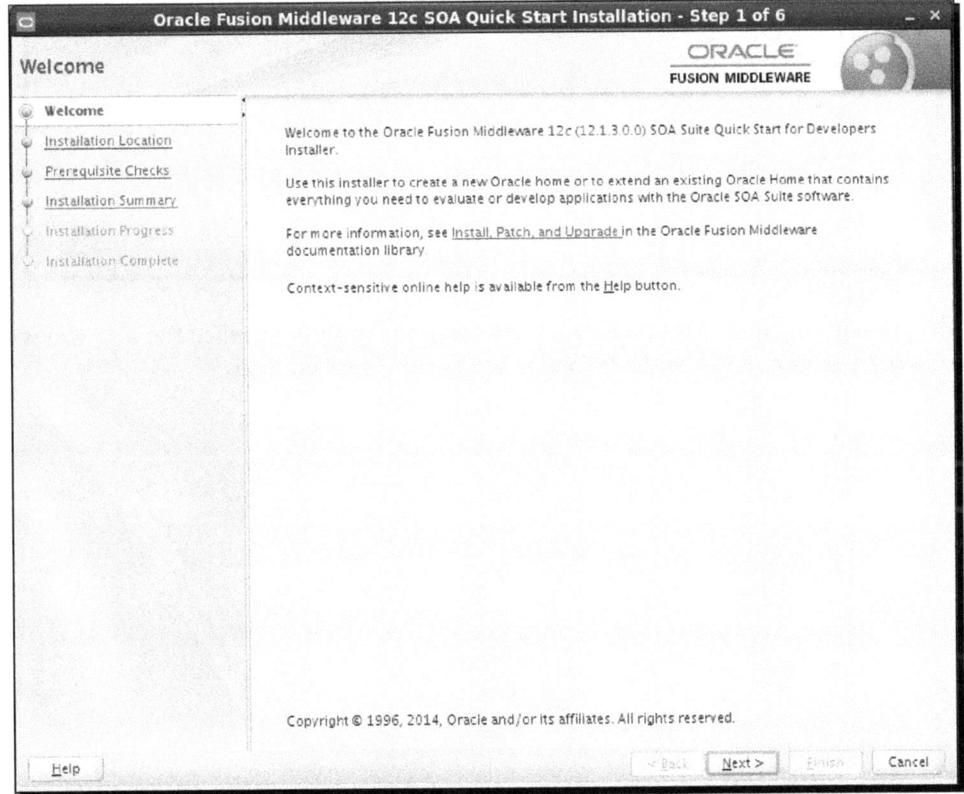

6. In the next step, we need to specify the location where we would like to install SOA Suite and all the related components. This is called **Oracle Home**. This directory must be empty, otherwise the wizard will give an error message. Use the default path, `/home/oracle/Oracle/Middleware/Oracle_Home`:

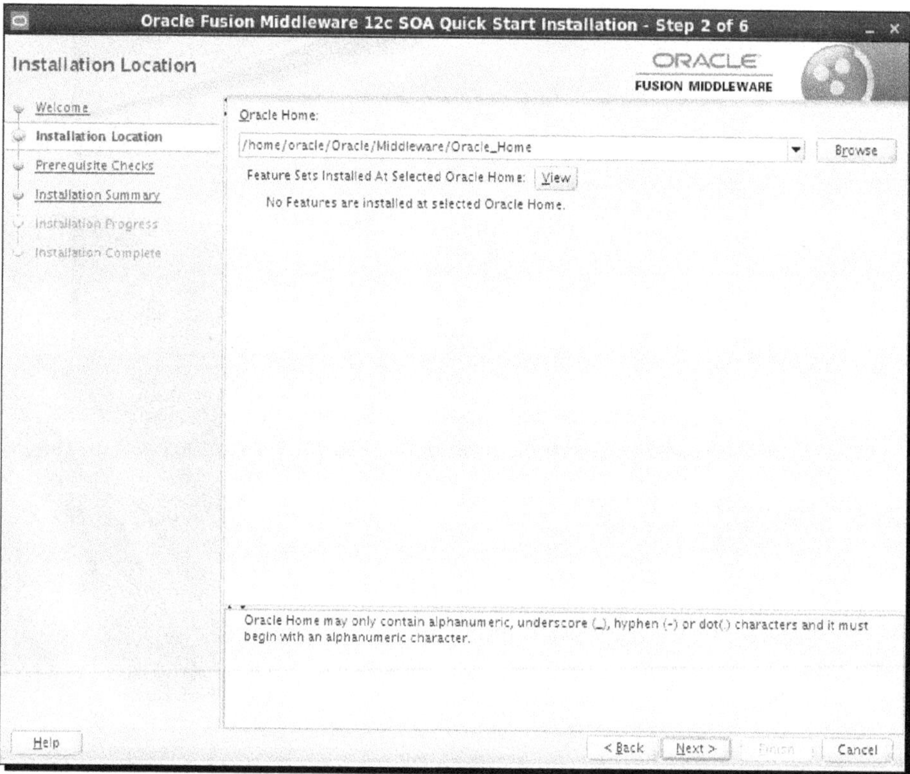

7. The prerequisite checks will run. If you have successfully installed the JDK, you will see a screen shown in the following screenshot; click on **Next**:

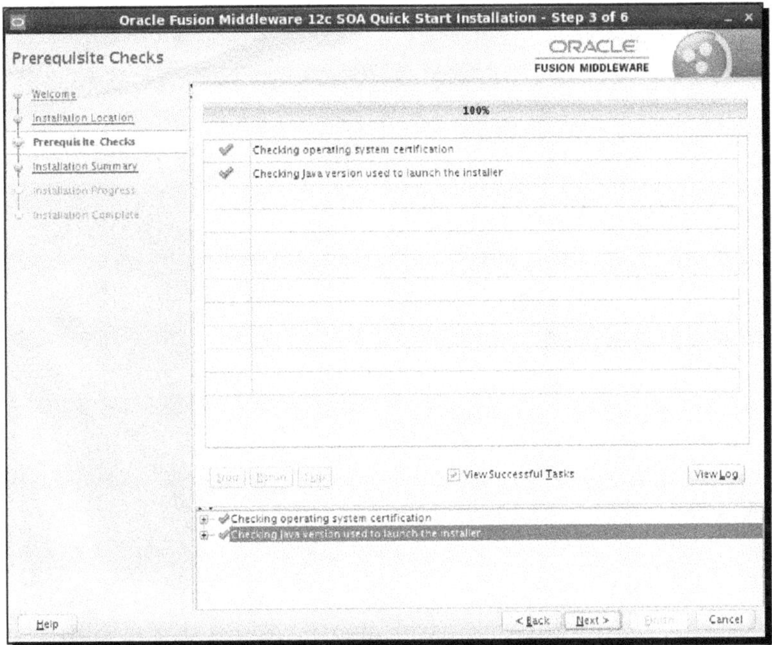

8. The installation procedure will show the installation summary. Check the installation location once again and look at the feature sets to be installed. Click on **Install** to proceed with the installation:

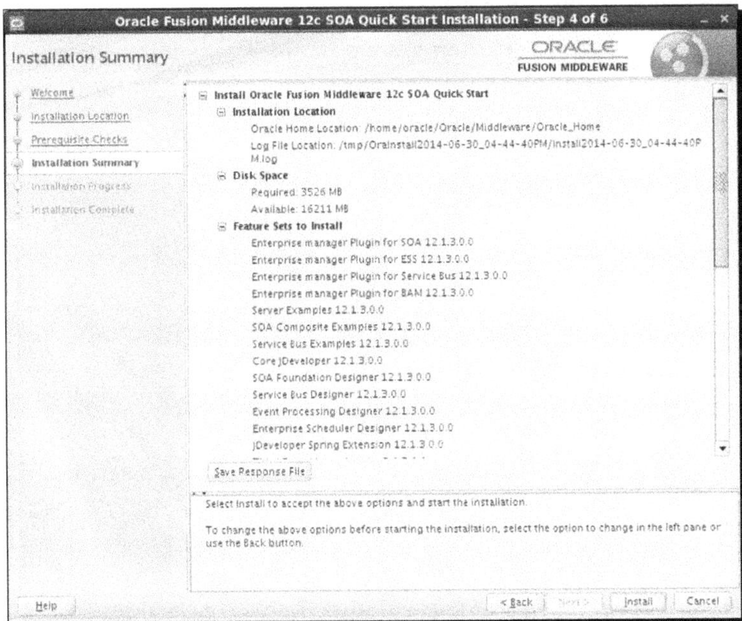

9. Monitor the installation progress and click on **Next**:

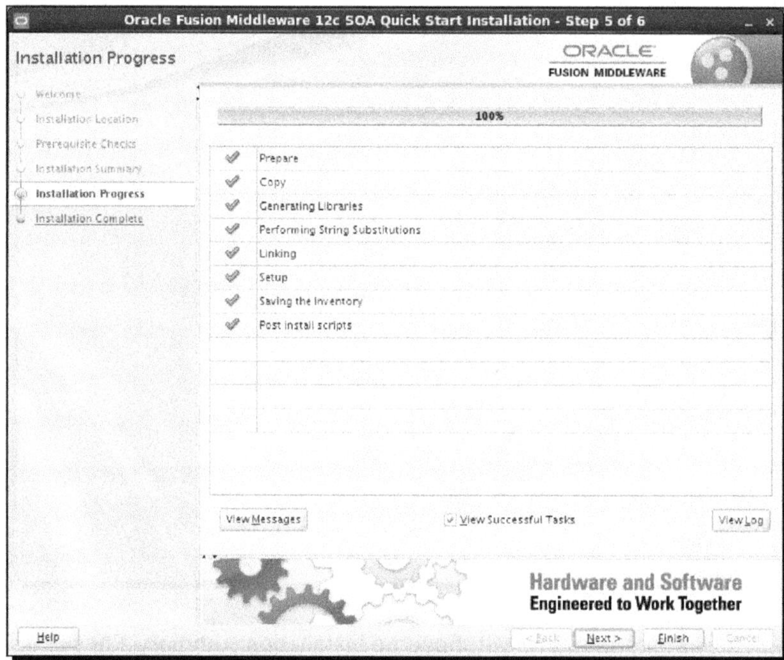

10. Finally, we will see the **Installation Complete** screen. Please notice that the checkbox for **Start JDeveloper** should be checked:

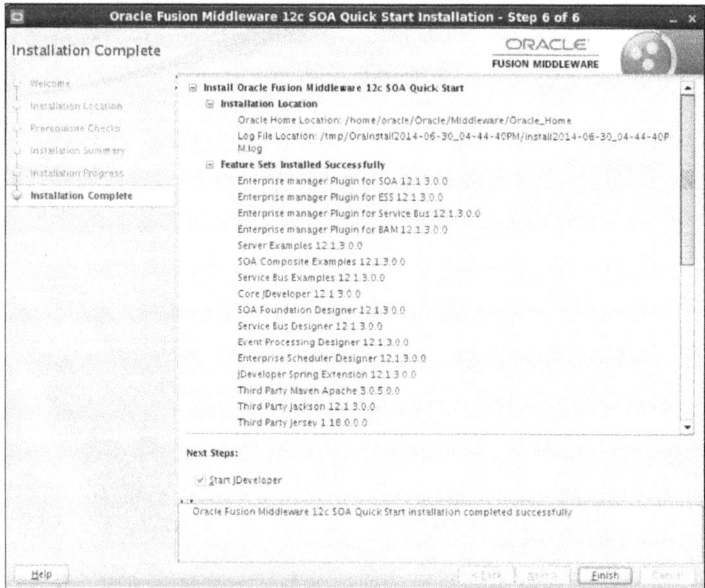

11. Clicking on the **Finish** button will launch JDeveloper. On the first screen, select the **Studio Developer (All Features)** role, which we will be using throughout the book:

12. After this, JDeveloper will launch and we will see the JDeveloper desktop.

What just happened?

We installed SOA Suite 12*c* with bundled JDeveloper. Before we can start using SOA Suite, we need to create the domain and verify the installation.

Creating a default domain

SOA Suite runs on top of Oracle WebLogic Server. A domain is the basic administration unit for the WebLogic Server instances. The easiest way is to create the default domain within Integrated WebLogic Server, which is bundled with JDeveloper. We will use this option.

Alternatively, you can configure a standalone domain or a compact domain. For more information, refer to `http://docs.oracle.com/middleware/1213/core/SOAQS/integrated.htm`.

Time for action – creating a default domain

To create the default domain, perform the following steps:

1. In JDeveloper, start the integrated WebLogic Server. Choose the **Run** menu and select the **Start Server Instance** option:

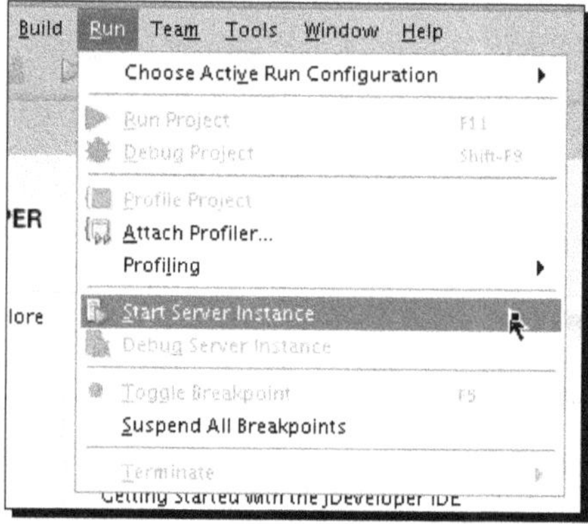

2. A dialog box will open where you need to enter **Administrator ID** and **Password**. Use `weblogic` for **Administrator ID** and `welcome1` for **Password**:

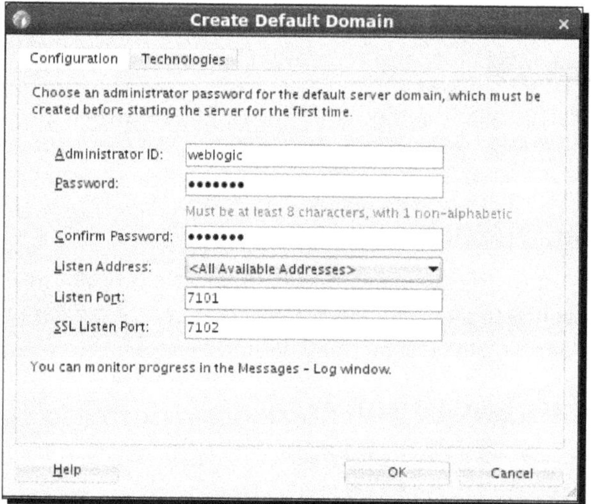

> Be sure to write down your administrator ID and the password as you will need it to log in to different components of SOA Suite.

3. The creation of the default domain will start. It might take a half hour or more, depending on the performance of your computer, so be patient. Once you see the following messages in the log window, you know that the domain has been created and the server is running: **SOA Platform is running and accepting requests and IntegratedWebLogicServer started**.

What just happened?

We created the default domain, which is required to deploy and execute SOA composite applications (which include the BPEL processes).

To verify that the SOA Suite server is running, we will use the Enterprise Manager console. We will access it through the Web browser. Therefore, let's now start the Web browser and enter the following address: `http://localhost:7101/em/`

We will log in with the `weblogic` username and `welcome1` password and will see the Enterprise Manager console:

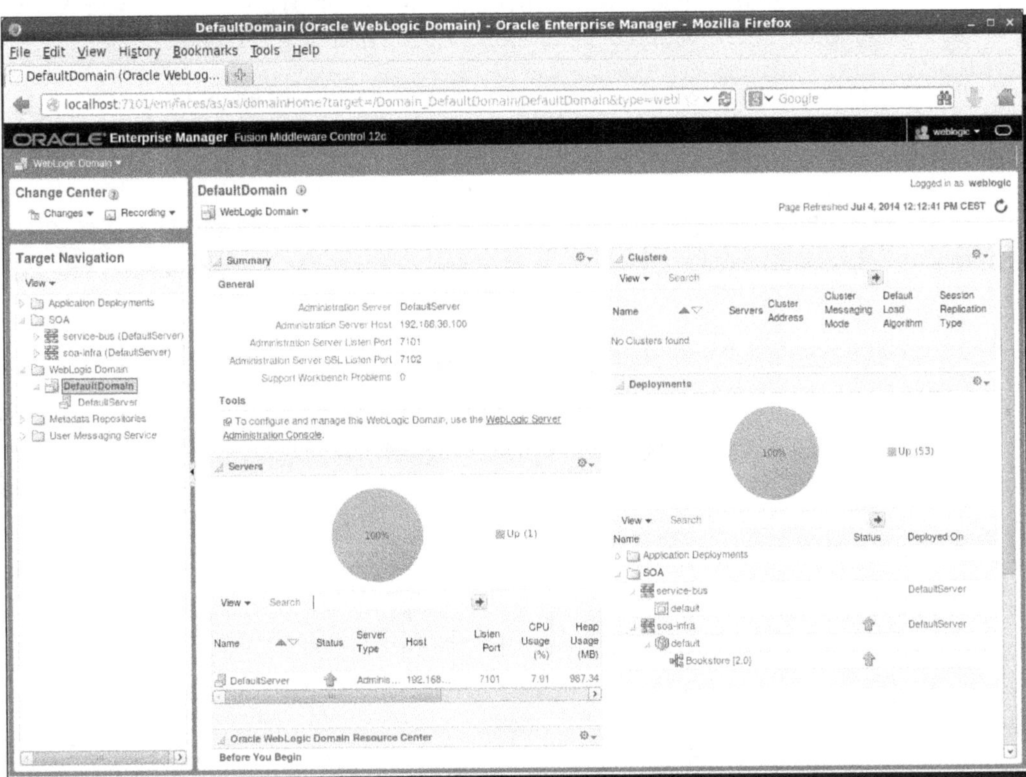

With this, we have successfully finished the installation and creation of the domain and are ready to develop our first BPEL process, which we will do in the next section.

Developing our first BPEL process

In this section, we will develop our first BPEL process. We will start with a simple BPEL process to get things rolling. Earlier in this chapter, we explained that BPEL is usually used to orchestrate services. This is true. However, in our first BPEL process, we will not be able to orchestrate services, as we do not have any. Rather, we will create a very simple BPEL process, which will return the number of books in stock.

Before we start, let's have a brief look at the artifacts that need to be created. Each BPEL process is part of the SOA composite. SOA composite shows all components, relations between components, service interfaces, and links to external services (external references). In addition to the BPEL processes, an SOA composite can include human tasks, business rules, mediators, adapters, and other components. Our first step will be the creation of an SOA composite.

Each BPEL process also consists of several artifacts. The most important is the BPEL code, which uses XML representation. Each BPEL process also has a WSDL interface, through which it can be invoked. The third artifact is **XML Schema Definition** (**XSD**) used by BPEL and WSDL. Our second step will be the creation of BPEL with the corresponding XSD and WSDL.

We will proceed in two steps. First, we will create the SOA composite application. Then, we will add the BPEL process with the corresponding XSD and WSDL (first, we will create the XML Schema, then WSDL, and then we will implement the BPEL process).

Time for action – creating the SOA composite application

Let's start. To create the SOA composite application, we will perform the following steps:

1. First, create a new application. Select the **New Application...** option in the **Applications** window:

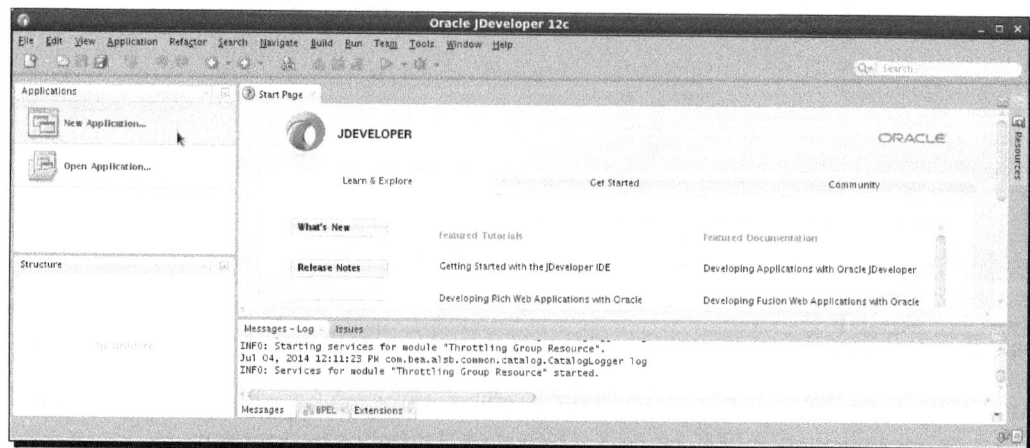

2. Next, select **SOA Application**:

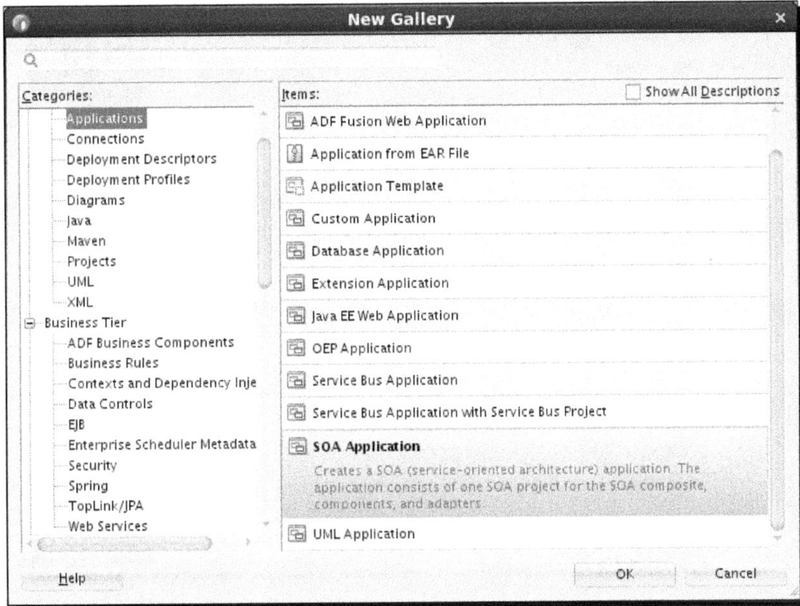

3. Name the application `Chapter1`, as shown in the following screenshot. Use the default directory and click on **Next** to proceed:

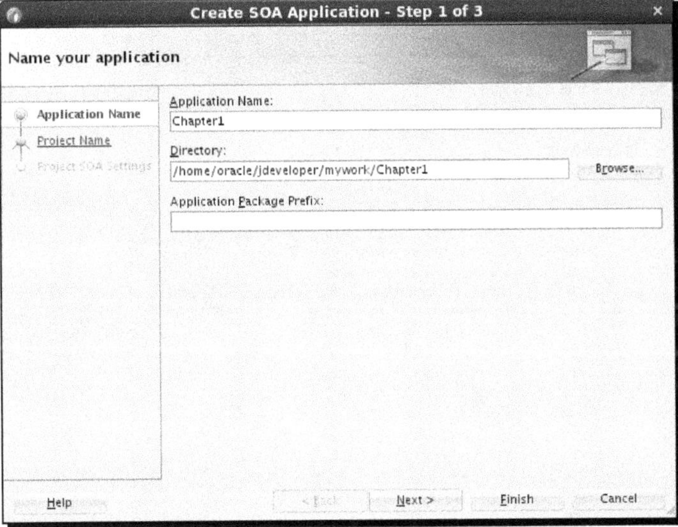

4. Next, create a project and name it `Bookstore`. Use the default directory again:

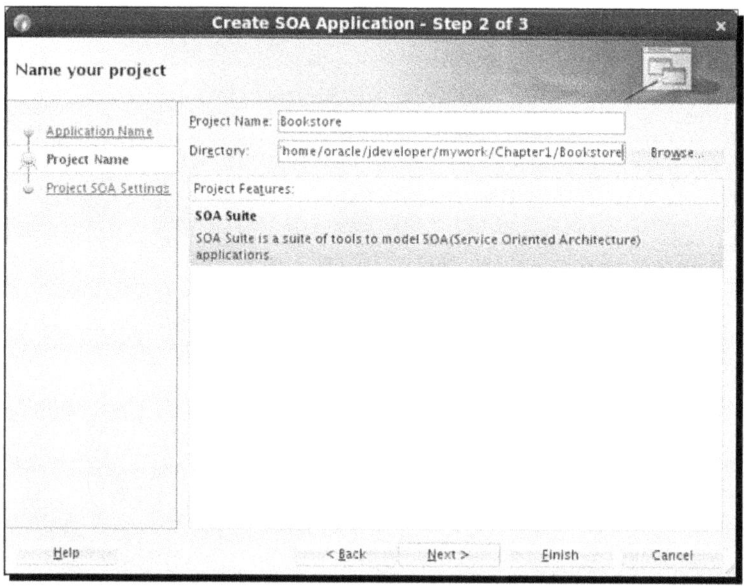

5. After clicking on **Next**, we are asked what type of composite template we would like to use. We will start from a **Standard Composite** template. Select the **Composite WithBPEL Process** option and click on **Finish**. Alternatively, we can select **Empty Composite** and add the BPEL process later.

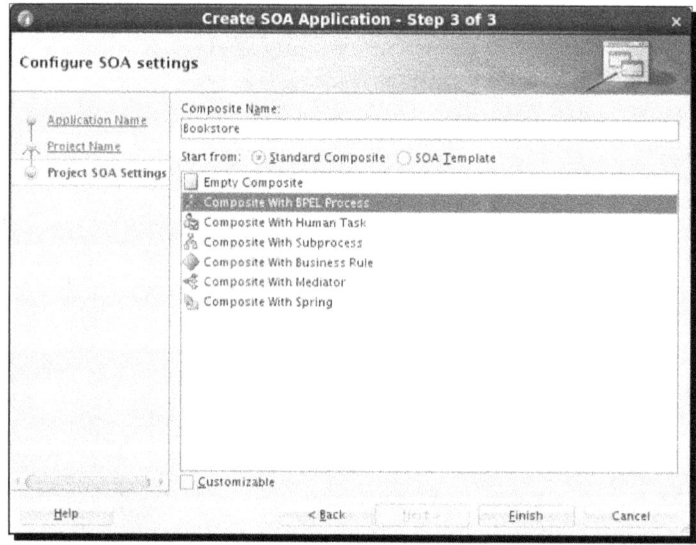

6. Clicking on **Finish** brings us to the **Create BPEL Process** wizard. Here we have the option to select the BPEL version, name the process, and specify the BPEL XML namespace. Each BPEL process is uniquely identified by `QName`. Thus, a namespace and a process name are needed. We also need to select the process template and define the service name. We will expose the BPEL process as a SOAP web service, therefore we should leave the **Expose as a SOAP service** checkbox selected.

   We will use BPEL 2.0 specification, name the process as `BookstoreABPEL`, add the namespace `http://packtpub.com/Bookstore/BooksotreABPEL`, and select the **Synchronous BPEL Process** template. We leave default values for **Transaction**, **Input**, and **Output**, and click on **OK**, as shown on the following screenshot:

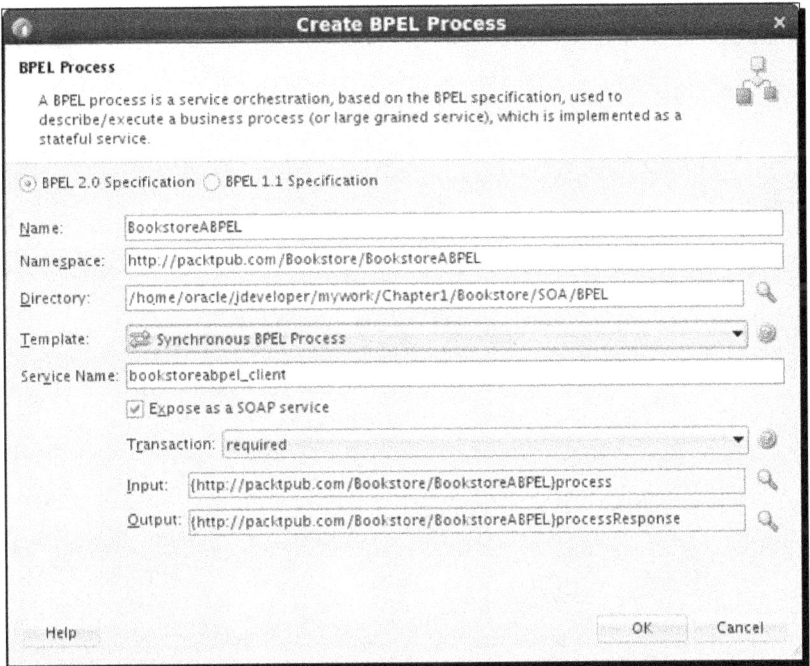

What just happened?

We created an SOA composite application with the BPEL process. We can see the composite view already opened under the **BookstoreA** tab. A composite application usually consists of several service components. The BPEL process is just one component type. The others include human tasks, business rules, mediators, adapters, and Spring components.

The SOA composite view has three sections. The middle part shows all **Components**, which are part of the composite. In our case, this is the `BookstoreABPEL` process. In following chapters, we will add more components to the composite. The left part shows **Exposed Services**. Exposed services are service interfaces exposed to other service consumers. Usually, these are WSDL interfaces (but can also be REST interfaces or events). In our example, the `BookstoreABPEL` process is exposed through the `bookstoreabpel_client` WSDL interface, which has one operation named `process`. The right-hand side shows **External References**. External references are external services used by our composite. External services are not part of our project. We only use them by referencing their WSDL interface. In our example, we do not have any external references yet. The composite design view is shown in the following screenshot:

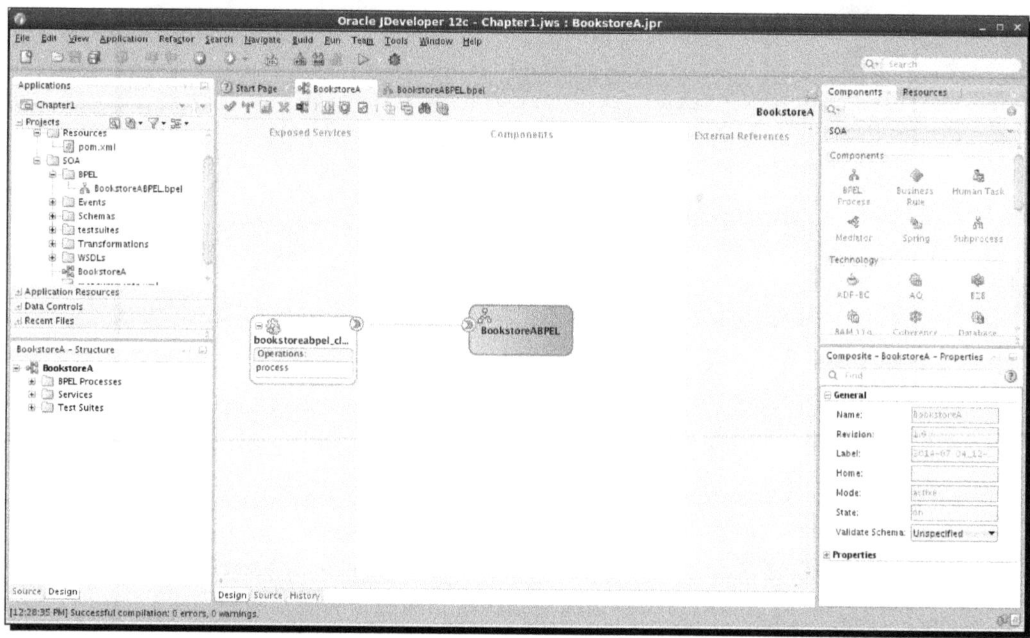

We also created the BPEL process. Let's have a closer look. To open the BPEL process, we have to select the already opened **BookstoreABPEL.bpel** tab. Alternatively, we can double-click on the `BookstoreABPEL` component on the composite design view (the blue-colored component in the middle of the screen) or double-click on the `BookstoreABPEL.bpel` file from the project tree in the left-hand side window. This brings us into the BPEL designer:

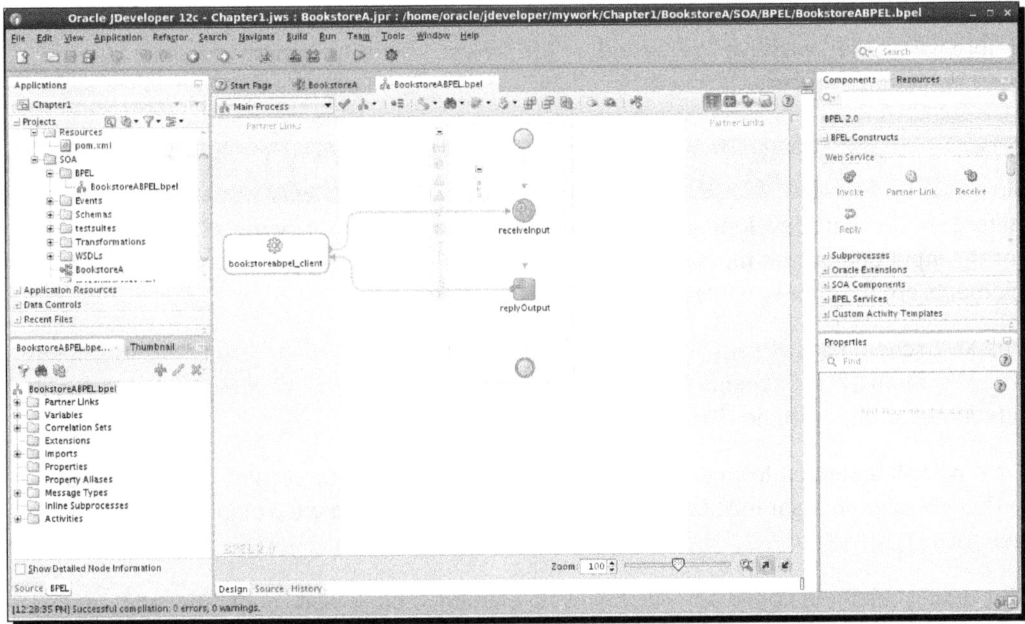

Each BPEL process consists of a receive activity, which is supposed to receive the initial request. This means that once the service consumer (client) will invoke the `process` operation on the WSDL interface of the BPEL process, the **receiveInput** receive activity will receive the request. This request will be a WSDL message, as we will see later in this section.

The other essential part of a BPEL process is the reply activity, which is used by the BPEL process to return the response to the service consumer (client). Remember that we have selected a synchronous BPEL process, which follows the request and response message exchange pattern. Therefore, in the **replyOutput** activity, the BPEL process will return the response to the client.

The BPEL processes can be **synchronous** or **asynchronous**. The synchronous BPEL processes follow the request and response semantics. A service consumer, which invokes a synchronous BPEL process will wait until the process finishes and will receive a reply from the process. This assumes that the BPEL process will finish in a reasonable time and that it will cutely return a response.

The BPEL processes can also be asynchronous. A service consumer, which invokes an asynchronous BPEL process, will not wait for the response. An asynchronous BPEL process might not return any response, or it might use a callback for the response. We will explain the asynchronous BPEL processes in *Chapter 5, Interaction Patterns in BPEL*.

We will put the BPEL process logic between the initial receive and the final reply activities. Before we do that, we have to create the XML Schemas for the elements and messages used in the BPEL process.

Time for action – creating XML Schema for the BPEL process

Before we can start developing our BPEL process, we have to specify the XSD elements used for the input and output messages (for the request and the response message). Also, the XSD elements are used for variables within the BPEL process.

The XML schema has already been created and can be found in the `BookstoreABPEL.xsd` file. The default XSD elements for request and response contain only strings, which are not adequate for our example. Therefore, we will modify it.

First, we will rename it from `BookstoreABPEL.xsd` to `BookstoreBPEL.xsd`. The reason is that we might use same XSD for more than one bookstore, so we would like to have a generic XSD filename.

Our request element consists of the following elements: book ISSN, book title, edition, and date of publishing. The response element consists of the following elements: book ISSN and stock quantity.

We will perform the following steps:

1. To rename XSD, right-click on the `BookstoreABPEL.xsd` file in the project tree, select **Refactor**, and then **Rename**:

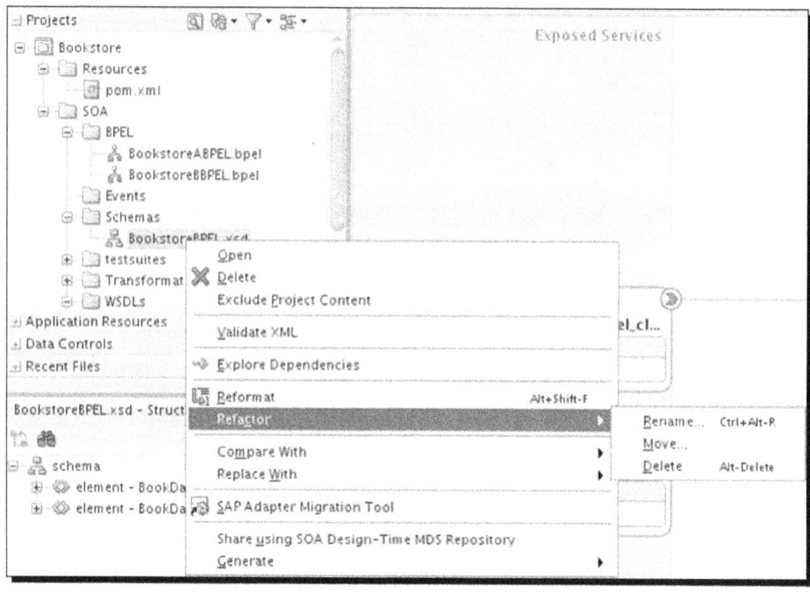

2. In the dialog box, enter the new name, `BookstoreBPEL.xsd`.
3. Double-click on the `BookstoreBPEL.xsd` file in the `Schemas` folder and switch to source view.
4. We have to define two complex elements. First, edit the existing `process` element, rename it to the `BookData` element, and enter the code shown in the following screenshot:

```
<element name="BookData">
        <complexType>
                <sequence>
                        <element name="BookISSN" type="string"/>
                        <element name="Title" type="string"/>
                        <element name="Edition" type="string"/>
                        <element name="PublishingYear" type="date"/>
                </sequence>
        </complexType>
</element>
```

5. Next, define the content of the `processResponse` element, which we will rename to `BookDataResponse` and add the two elements shown in the following screenshot:

```
<element name="BookDataResponse">
        <complexType>
                <sequence>
                        <element name="BookISSN" type="string"/>
                        <element name="StockQuantity" type="int"/>
                </sequence>
        </complexType>
</element>
```

Before we continue, let's save the XSD file.

What just happened?

We created the XSD elements used by the BPEL process. To be more accurate, we modified the autogenerated XSD file and specified the request element (`BookData`) and the response element (`BookDataReponse`).

The request element (`BookData`) is used as the input for the initial receive activity (**receiveInput**). The response element (`BookDataReponse`) is used by the final reply activity (**replyOutput**).

This is specified in the autogenerated WSDL file, which you can find in the `WSDLs` folder. It is named `BookstoreABPEL.wsdl`. Let's have a look at it.

Time for action – modifying WSDL

WSDL specifies the web service interface, which is used to invoke the BPEL process. When creating the BPEL process, the corresponding WSDL has been generated in the `WSDLs` folder of the project tree. It is named `BookstoreABPEL.wsdl`.

By default, WSDL contains a single operation named `process`. We will modify the default WSDL and rename the operation name from `process` to `getBookData`. This name denotes the purposed of the operation more precisely. We will also modify WSDL to include the XSD elements, which we created in the previous section.

To achieve this, let's perform the following steps:

1. Double-click on the `BookstoreABPEL.wsdl` file in the `WSDLs` folder and switch to the source view.
2. In the `<portType>` section, rename the operation name from `process` to `getBookData`:

```
<!-- portType implemented by the BookstoreABPEL BPEL process -->
<wsdl:portType name="BookstoreABPEL">
        <wsdl:operation name="getBookData">
                <wsdl:input  message="client:BookstoreABPELRequestMessage" />
                <wsdl:output message="client:BookstoreABPELResponseMessage"/>
        </wsdl:operation>
</wsdl:portType>
```

3. In the `<message>` section, change the element names of both messages to `BookData` and `BookDataResponse` respectively. This way, we will reference the changes that we made in the XSD:

```
<!--~~~~~~~~~~~~~~~~~~~~~~~~~~~~~~~~~~~~~~~~~~~~~~~~~~~~~~~~~~~~~~~~~~~~~~
MESSAGE TYPE DEFINITION - Definition of the message types used as
part of the port type defintions
~~~~~~~~~~~~~~~~~~~~~~~~~~~~~~~~~~~~~~~~~~~~~~~~~~~~~~~~~~~~~~~~~~~~~~-->
<wsdl:message name="BookstoreABPELRequestMessage">
        <wsdl:part name="payload" element="clientBPEL:BookData"/>
</wsdl:message>
<wsdl:message name="BookstoreABPELResponseMessage">
        <wsdl:part name="payload" element="clientBPEL:BookDataResponse"/>
</wsdl:message>
```

4. Finally, change the name of the included schema file from `BookstoreABPEL.xsd` to `BookstoreBPEL.xsd`, as shown in the following screenshot:

```
<wsdl:types>
        <schema xmlns="http://www.w3.org/2001/XMLSchema">
                <import namespace="http://packtpub.com/Bookstore/BookstoreBPEL"
                schemaLocation="../Schemas/BookstoreBPEL.xsd" />
        </schema>
</wsdl:types>
```

What just happened?

We looked at WSDL for the BPEL process and modified the operation name. Instead of using the default `process` name, we renamed it to `getBookData`. We also modified WSDL to reflect the XSD elements that we defined. Finally, we modified the XSD filename, which we renamed previously.

This way we have become familiar with WSDL, which is generated for each BPEL process. We are now ready to implement the BPEL process.

Time for action – implementing the BPEL process

In this step, we will implement the BPEL process itself. The goal is to return the book data, including the stock quantity. For this, we would usually need to access the database to query for the stock of the specified book. In our case, we do not want to complicate the example, so we will simply return a fixed value.

To achieve this, we will use the **Assign** activity to assign a fixed value to a BPEL variable. **Assign** is one of the basic BPEL activities. We will explain the BPEL language later in this chapter.

For now, let's perform the following steps. First, we will copy `BookISSN` from request `inputVariable` to response `outputVariable`. Second, we will copy a number `5` to the `StockQuantity` element of the output message:

1. Open our `BookstoreABPEL` process by selecting the already opened **BookstoreABPEL.bpel** tab. Alternatively, you can double-click on the `BookstoreABPEL` component on the composite design view or double-click on the `BookstoreABPEL.bpel` file from the project tree on the left-hand side window.

2. Drag-and-drop the **Assign** activity from the right-hand component palette to the BPEL process in the middle between the **receiveInput** and **replyOutput** activities, as shown in the following screenshot:

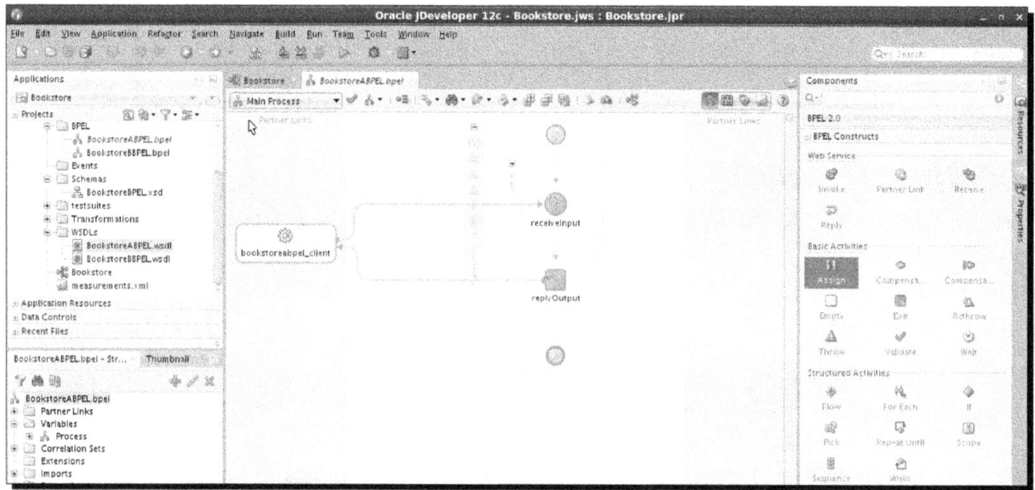

3. Double-click on the **Assign** activity and set the parameters. Name the activity as `DetermineStockQuantity`. Copy `BookISSN` from `inputVariable` to `outputVariable` by dragging `BookISSN` from `inputVariable` and dropping it on `BookISSN` in `outputVariable`, as shown in the following screenshot:

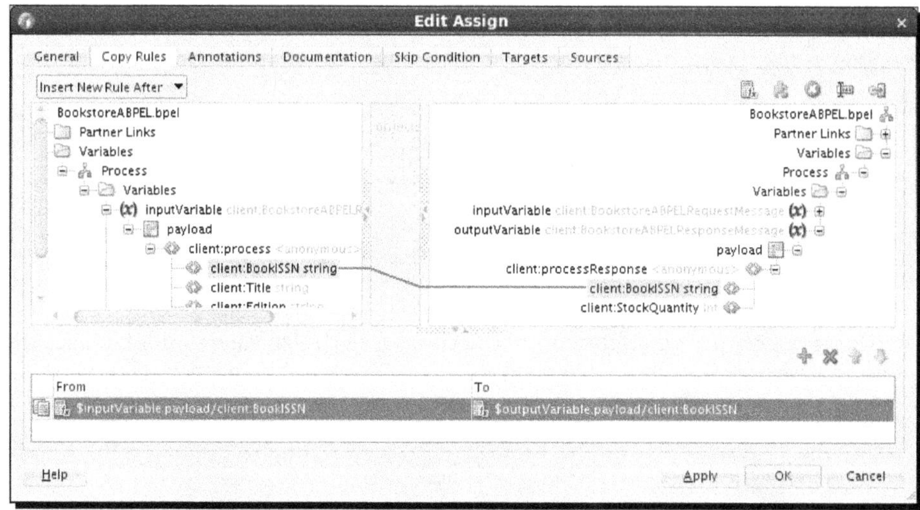

4. To set the `StockQuantity` element of the output message, we will need to use an expression. Drag-and-drop **Expression** from the upper-right corner of the window to the `StockQuantity` element. Doing this, the **Expression Builder** window will appear.
5. Click on the **Conversion Functions** tab and select the **n()number** function. Let's assume that we will return stock quantity of `5`. This means we need to write `number(5)`:

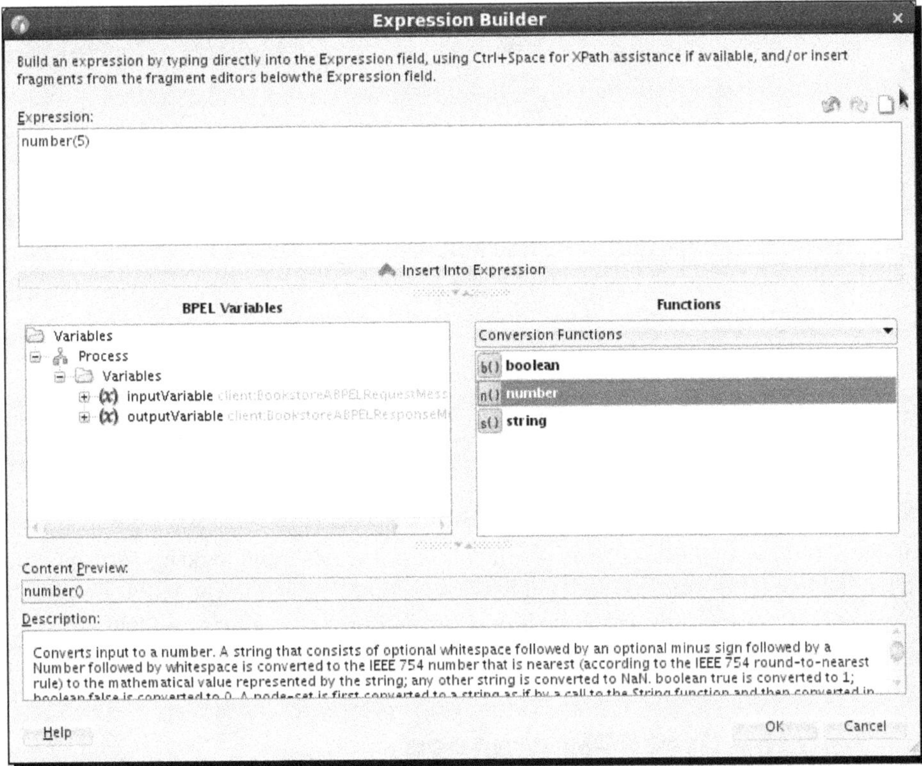

6. Clicking on **OK** twice and saving all we have performed brings us to the following screenshot:

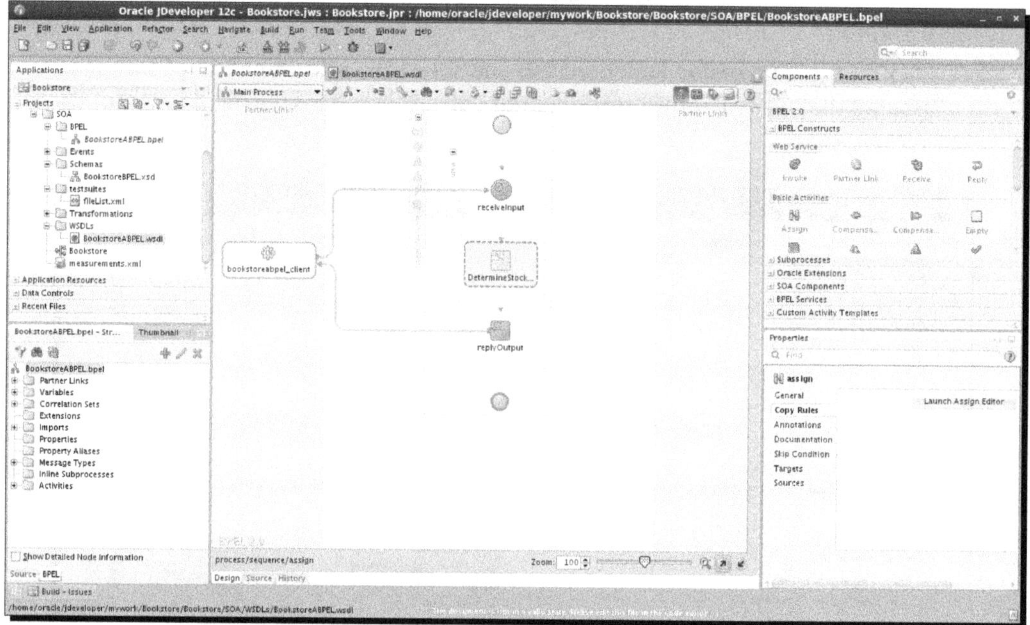

What just happened?

We implemented our first BPEL processes. It contains a very simple logic for returning the book data, including the stock quantity. It assigns the book ISSN and the stock quantity to the constant value of `5`. Obviously, this is an oversimplified process, but it is sufficient for our first example and to get a feeling about BPEL. Next, we will try to deploy the BPEL process.

Deploying the first BPEL process

We are now ready to deploy the process to the SOA Suite process server and test it. To deploy an SOA composite, several options exist. We will deploy our application directly to the server.

Time for action – deploying the BPEL process

To deploy the process, perform the following steps:

1. Right-click on the **BookstoreA** project and click on the **Deploy** submenu. Select **BookstoreA** from the option.

2. Select **Deploy to Application Server**:

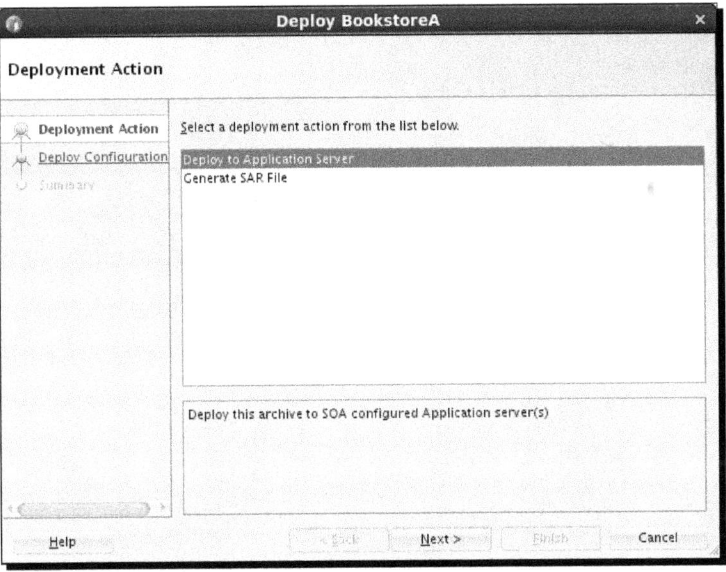

3. We can specify the deployment configuration. For this time, we will use the default values. Please note that the most important is to specify **New Revision ID**, which denotes the revision (or version) number of your composite application. Also note **Overwrite any existing composites with the same revision ID**; this has to be checked if you want to redeploy a composite application with the same revision ID:

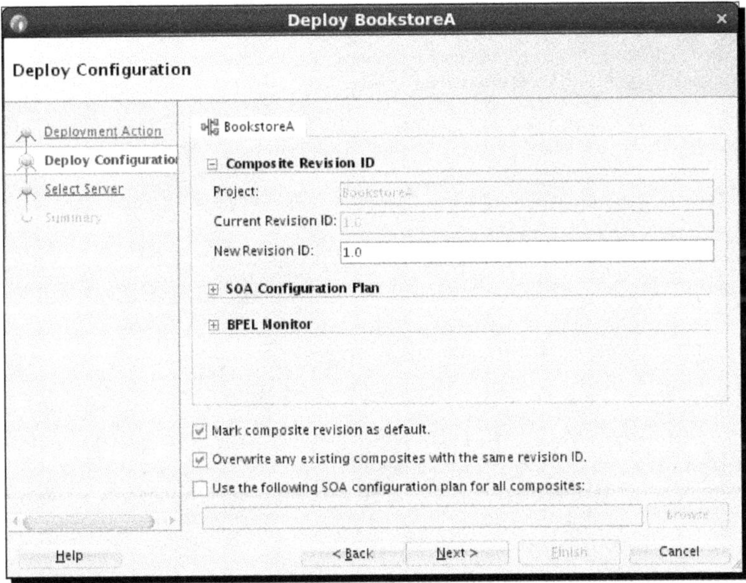

4. Click on the **IntegratedWebLogicServer** server for the deployment and click on **Next**:

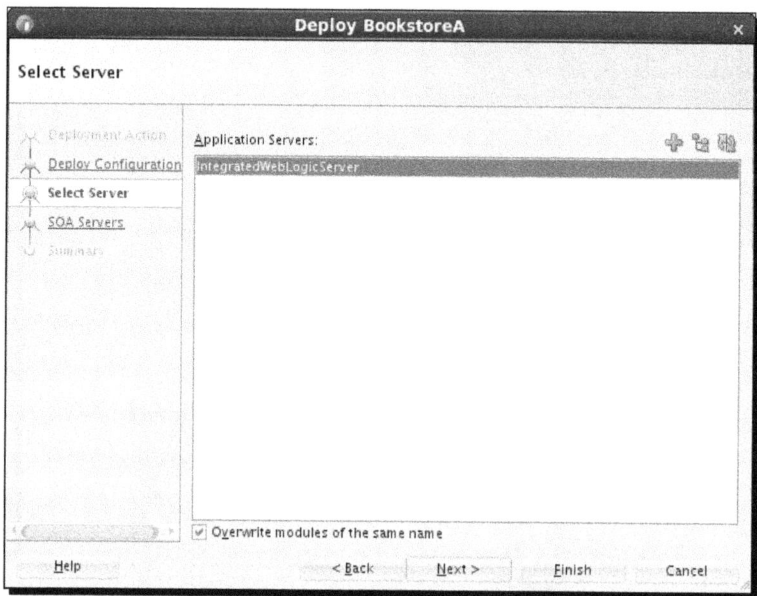

5. We will see the status of the SOA server. Click on **Next**:

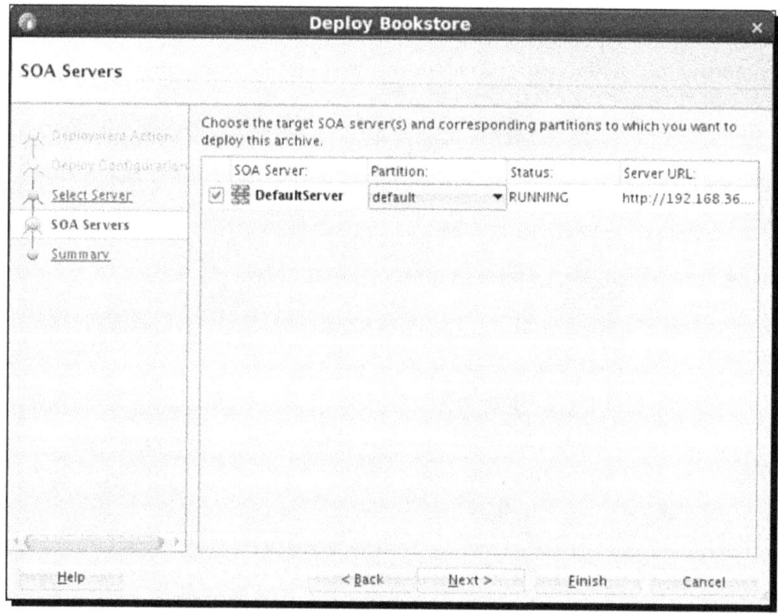

6. Finally, we will see the deployment summary. Click on **Finish**:

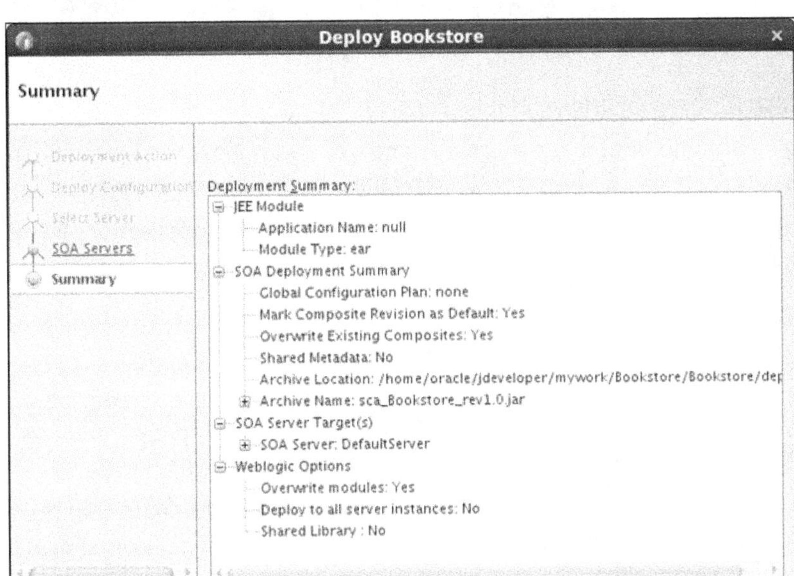

7. Monitor the deployment log windows at the bottom of the screen and look for the **Deployment finished.** message. This means that the BPEL process has been successfully deployed:

```
Deployment - Log
[01:09:29 AM] Adding sar file - /home/oracle/jdeveloper/mywork/Bookstore/Bookstore/deploy/sca_Bookstore_rev1.0.jar
[01:09:29 AM] Preparing to send HTTP request for deployment
[01:09:29 AM] Creating HTTP connection to host:192.168.36.100, port:7101
[01:09:29 AM] Sending internal deployment descriptor
[01:09:29 AM] Sending archive - sca_Bookstore_rev1.0.jar
[01:09:31 AM] Received HTTP response from the server, response code=200
[01:09:31 AM] Successfully deployed archive sca_Bookstore_rev1.0.jar with 0 warning/severe messages to partition "default" on se
[01:09:31 AM] Elapsed time for deployment:  10 seconds
[01:09:31 AM] ----  Deployment finished.  ----
Messages  Extensions  Running: IntegratedWebLogicServer  BPEL  SOA  Deployment
```

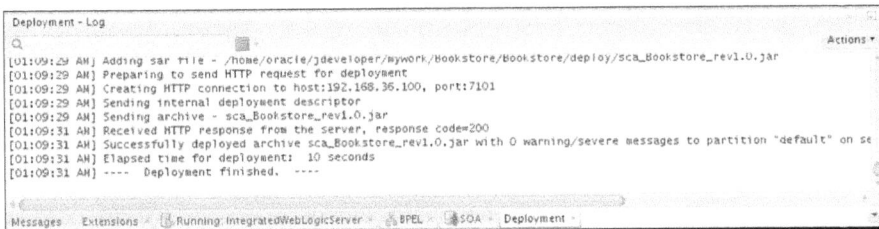

What just happened?

We successfully deployed our BPEL process. More precisely, we deployed the whole composite application, which contains the BPEL process and are now ready to test it.

Testing our first BPEL process

After the successful deployment, we are ready to test the process. We will use the Enterprise Manager Console to invoke the BPEL process and monitor to check whether it has executed.

Time for action – testing the BPEL process

To test our BPEL process, let's perform the following steps:

1. Switch to the Web browser and navigate to `http://localhost:7101/em/`.
2. Log in with the `weblogic` username and `welcome1` password (or a different password, which you have specified by the creation of the domain).
3. At the bottom of the screen, you will see the **Bookstore** application. If you cannot see it, use the scroll bar to find it.
4. After clicking on it, a new screen will be displayed.
5. To test the BPEL process, click on the **Test** button.
6. We will see a quite complex screen. In the lower part of the screen, we will see the payload with the four parameters, which we defined as input parameters for the BPEL process: **BookISSN**, **Title**, **Edition**, and **PublishingYear**.
7. Fill the book ISSN, title, edition, and publishing year. Please note that the publishing year is a `date` type; therefore, it requires `2014-09-01` syntax, as shown in the following screenshot:

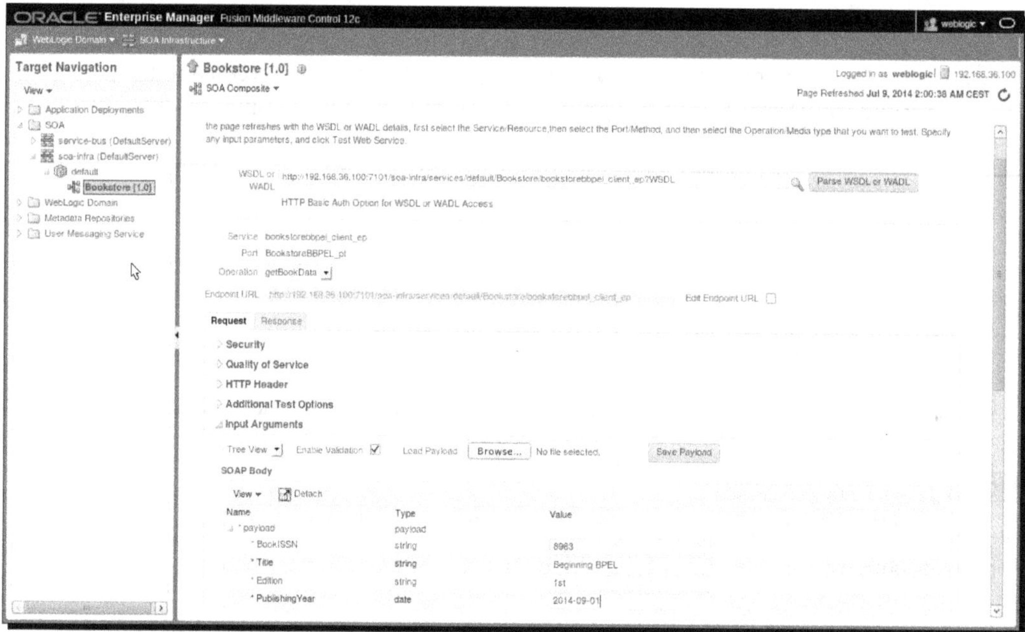

8. Alternatively, we can switch from **Tree View** to **XML View** to get a better understanding that we will send the XML that we defined previously in the XML Schema section. The complete SOAP message is shown in the following screenshot:

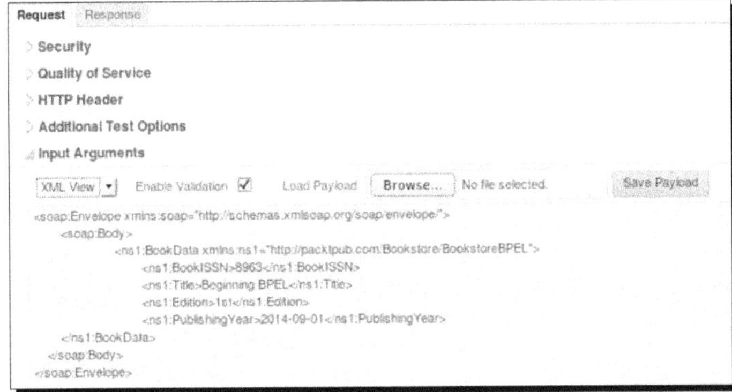

9. Click on the **Test Web Service** button in the upper-right corner of the screen to invoke our BPEL process.

What just happened?

We invoked our BPEL process. Once the process executes, the view switches to the **Response** tab where the response of the BPEL process is displayed. If the invocation has been successful, we will see the quantity of `5`. Indeed, we can see that the process will return the quantity `5` for a selected book. Again, we can switch between **Tree View** and **XML View**:

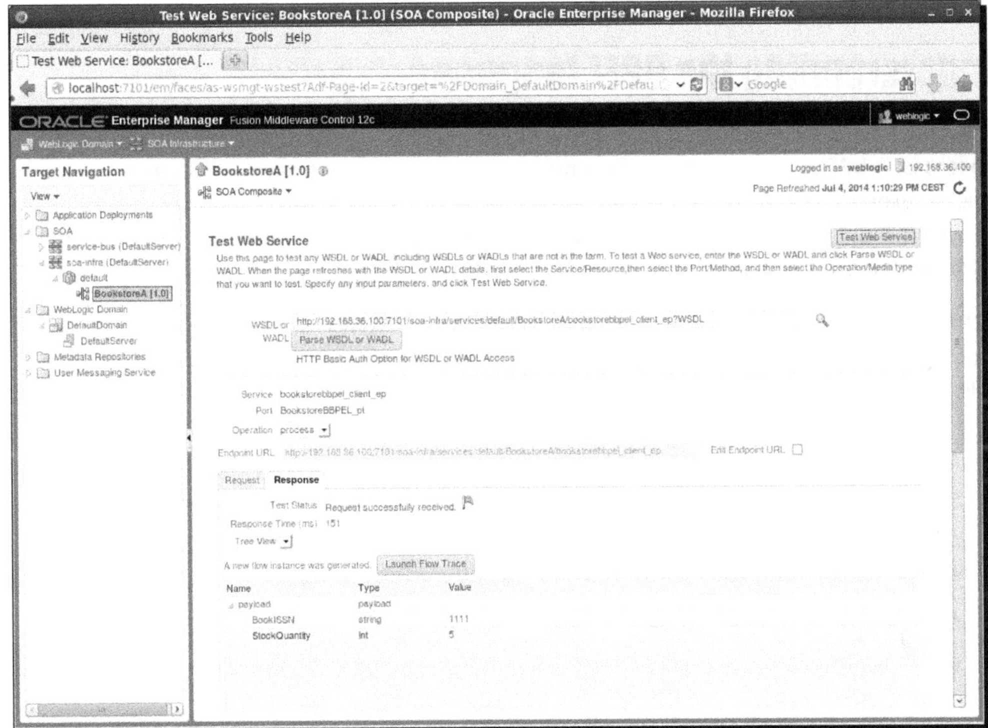

To see the XML representation, the SOAP response message directly, we can switch to **XML View** and we will see the following screenshot:

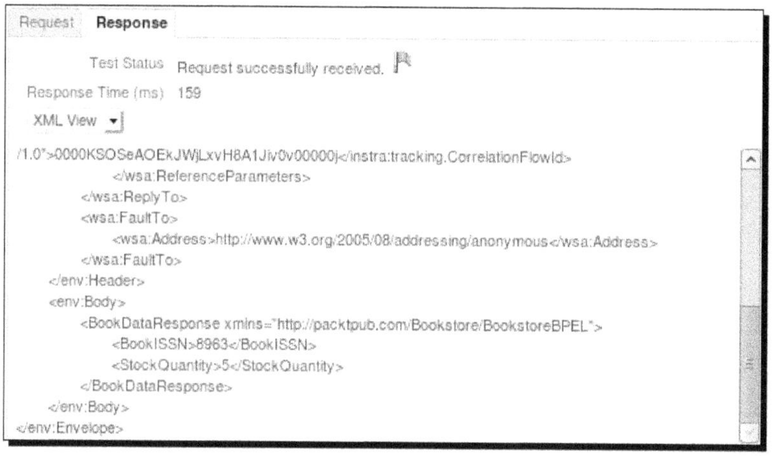

Request Response

Test Status Request successfully received.

Response Time (ms) 159

XML View


```
/1.0">0000KSOSeAOEkJWjLxvH8A1JivOv00000j</instra:tracking.CorrelationFlowId>
            </wsa:ReferenceParameters>
        </wsa:ReplyTo>
        <wsa:FaultTo>
            <wsa:Address>http://www.w3.org/2005/08/addressing/anonymous</wsa:Address>
        </wsa:FaultTo>
    </env:Header>
    <env:Body>
        <BookDataResponse xmlns="http://packtpub.com/Bookstore/BookstoreBPEL">
            <BookISSN>8963</BookISSN>
            <StockQuantity>5</StockQuantity>
        </BookDataResponse>
    </env:Body>
</env:Envelope>
```


With this, we have successfully tested our first BPEL process. It was an oversimplified BPEL process, which took four parameters as an input (book ISSN, title, edition, and publishing year) and returned the quantity of the book together with the ISSN. Moreover, we hardcoded the quantity to 5 units for simplicity purposes.

Understanding the BPEL language

Let's now have a more detailed look into what we did and try to understand what a BPEL process is. A BPEL process is basically a piece of source code with the `.bpel` extension, which is executed on a process server. BPEL uses the XML vocabulary to write the code. So far, we have used the visual editor to compose the BPEL process. However, we can switch to the source code view.

A BPEL process consists of steps. Each step is called an **activity**. BPEL supports basic and structured activities. Basic activities represent basic constructs and are used for common tasks listed, as follows:

- Invoking other web services using `<invoke>`
- Waiting for the client to invoke the business process through sending a message using `<receive>` (receiving a request)
- Generating a response for synchronous operations using `<reply>`
- Manipulating data variables using `<assign>`
- Indicating faults and exceptions using `<throw>` and `<rethrow>`

- Waiting for some time using <wait>
- Terminating the entire process using <exit>

We can then combine these and other basic activities and define complex flows that specify exactly the steps of a business process. To combine basic activities, BPEL supports several structured activities. The most important are as follows:

- Sequence (<sequence>) for defining a set of activities that will be invoked in an ordered sequence
- Flow (<flow>) for defining a set of activities that will be invoked in parallel
- Conditional construct (<if>) for implementing branches
- While, repeat, and for each (<while>, <repeatUntil>, <forEach>) for defining loops
- The ability to select one of the number of alternative paths using <pick>

Each BPEL process will also define partner links using <partnerLinks>. Partner links are other services that use the BPEL process or are used by the BPEL process. A BPEL process also declares variables using <variables>.

The BPEL structure

A BPEL process definition is written as an XML document using the <process> root element. Within the <process> element, a BPEL process will usually have the top-level <sequence> or <flow> element. Within the sequence, the process will first wait for the incoming message to start the process. This wait is modeled with the <receive> construct. Then, the process will perform some activities and return a response. This is shown in the following code excerpt:

```
<process ...>
   ...
  <sequence>

    <!-- Wait for the incoming request to start the process -->
    <receive ... />

    <!-- Perform some activities -->
    ...

    <!-- Return the response -->
    <reply ... />
  </sequence>
</process>
```

To provide an idea of a BPEL process structure, let's look more closely at the `BookstoreABPEL` process. We can see the `<process>` activity, which represents the root element. Within the `<process>` activity, several XML namespaces are defined. The process will also import WSDL. We have already mentioned that each BPEL process requires the interface definition, which is specified in WSDL:

```
<?xml version = "1.0" encoding = "UTF-8" ?>
<!--///////// ... //////-->
<process name="BookstoreABPEL"
               targetNamespace="http://packtpub.com/Bookstore/BookstoreABPEL"
               xmlns="http://docs.oasis-open.org/wsbpel/2.0/process/executable"
               xmlns:client="http://packtpub.com/Bookstore/BookstoreABPEL"
               xmlns:ora="http://schemas.oracle.com/xpath/extension"
               xmlns:ui="http://xmlns.oracle.com/soa/designer"
               xmlns:bpelx="http://schemas.oracle.com/bpel/extension"
         xmlns:bpel="http://docs.oasis-open.org/wsbpel/2.0/process/executable"
         xmlns:ns1="http://packtpub.com/Bookstore/BookstoreBPEL"
         xmlns:xp20="http://www.oracle.com/XSL/Transform/java/oracle.tip.pc.services.functions.Xpath20"
         xmlns:bpws="http://schemas.xmlsoap.org/ws/2003/03/business-process/"
         xmlns:oraext="http://www.oracle.com/XSL/Transform/java/oracle.tip.pc.services.functions.ExtFunc"
         xmlns:dvm="http://www.oracle.com/XSL/Transform/java/oracle.tip.dvm.LookupValue"
         xmlns:hwf="http://xmlns.oracle.com/bpel/workflow/xpath"
         xmlns:ids="http://xmlns.oracle.com/bpel/services/IdentityService/xpath"
         xmlns:bpm="http://xmlns.oracle.com/bpmn20/extensions" xmlns:ess="http://xmlns.oracle.com/scheduler"
         xmlns:xdk="http://schemas.oracle.com/bpel/extension/xpath/function/xdk"
         xmlns:xref="http://www.oracle.com/XSL/Transform/java/oracle.tip.xref.xpath.XRefXPathFunctions"
         xmlns:ldap="http://schemas.oracle.com/xpath/extension/ldap">

    <import ui:processWSDL="true" namespace="http://packtpub.com/Bookstore/BookstoreABPEL"
    location="../WSDLs/BookstoreABPEL.wsdl" importType="http://schemas.xmlsoap.org/wsdl/"/>
```

Partner links

Next, `<partnerLinks>` are declared. Partner links define which services our process is communicating with. The client, which calls the BPEL process, is one of the partners. In our process, it is the only partner, as our `BookstoreA` process does not call any other services or processes.

```
  <!--
    ////////////////////////////////////////////////////////////////////////////////////////////////////
      PARTNERLINKS
      List of services participating in this BPEL process
    ////////////////////////////////////////////////////////////////////////////////////////////////////
  -->
<partnerLinks>
  <!--
    The 'client' role represents the requester of this service. It is
    used for callback. The location and correlation information associated
    with the client role are automatically set using WS-Addressing.
  -->
  <partnerLink name="bookstoreabpel_client" partnerLinkType="client:BookstoreABPEL" myRole="BookstoreABPELProvider"/>
</partnerLinks>
```

Variables

Next, variables are declared. BPEL uses variables much like any other programming language, except that these variables hold the XML elements or primitive types. Two variables are declared by default. The `inputVariable` holds the input payload (input parameters). In our case, these are the four parameters, including ISSN, title, edition, and publishing year. The `outputVariable` activity holds the output, which is returned to the client (the one who has invoked the BPEL process), as shown in the following screenshot:

```
<!--
  //////////////////////////////////////////////////////////////////////////////////
    VARIABLES
    List of messages and XML documents used within this BPEL process
  //////////////////////////////////////////////////////////////////////////////////
-->
<variables>
  <!-- Reference to the message passed as input during initiation -->
  <variable name="inputVariable" messageType="client:BookstoreABPELRequestMessage"/>

  <!-- Reference to the message that will be returned to the requester-->
  <variable name="outputVariable" messageType="client:BookstoreABPELResponseMessage"/>
</variables>
```

The process logic

Next, we specify the process steps. These are gathered within the top-level `<sequence>` activity, which contains all the process flow. Each BPEL process first waits for the initial request message from the client (`<receive>`). Usually, a BPEL process also returns some response to the client. This is true for the synchronous BPEL processes. In this case, the BPEL process will end with a `<reply>` activity through which it will return the response to the client.

In between `<receive>` and `<reply>`, we specify all the required activities for the actual process flow. In our case, this is only an `<assign>` activity, which has been used to manipulate variables and to assign the quantity of `5` to the one of the elements of the `outputVariable`. With more complex processes, we would have several activities listed here. The BPEL source code of our first process looks like the following screenshot:

```
  <sequence name="main">

    <!-- Receive input from requestor. (Note: This maps to operation defined in BookstoreABPEL.wsdl) -
    <receive name="receiveInput" partnerLink="bookstoreabpel_client" portType="client:BookstoreABPEL"
    operation="getBookData" variable="inputVariable" createInstance="yes"/>
    <assign name="DetermineStockQuantity">
      <copy>
        <from>$inputVariable.payload/ns1:BookISSN</from>
        <to>$outputVariable.payload/ns1:BookISSN</to>
      </copy>
      <copy>
        <from>number(5)</from>
        <to>$outputVariable.payload/ns1:StockQuantity</to>
      </copy>
    </assign>
    <!-- Generate reply to synchronous request -->
    <reply name="replyOutput" partnerLink="bookstoreabpel_client" portType="client:BookstoreABPEL"
    operation="getBookData" variable="outputVariable"/>
  </sequence>
</process>
```

This corresponds to the following graphical presentation in the design view:

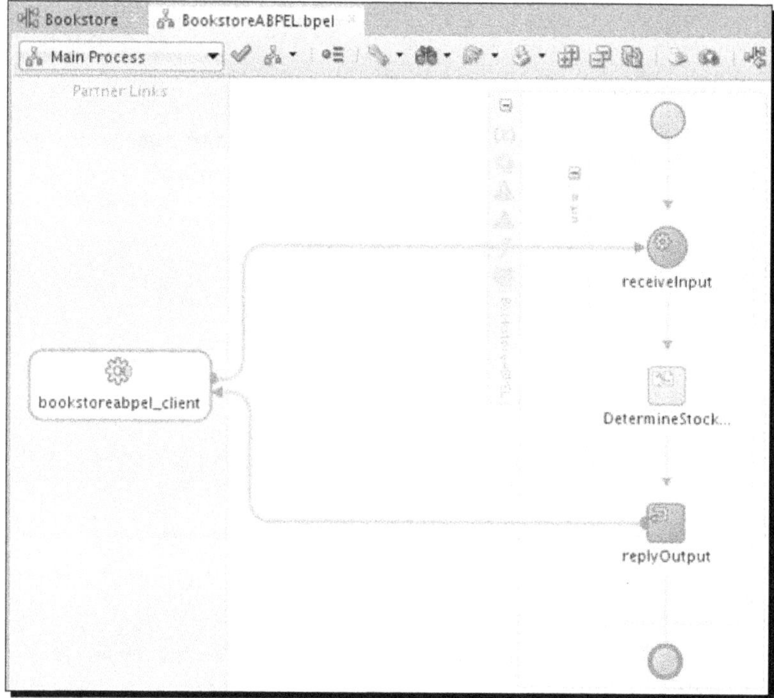

A detailed look at the BPEL activities

In this section, we will have a more detailed look at different BPEL activities. This gives us more information on the syntax of the activities and helps us to understand the BPEL language better.

<process>

Let's focus more closely on the `<process>` tag. This delimits the root element of the BPEL document. The `<process>` tag requires that we specify certain attributes. We have to specify at least the following attributes:

- `name`: This attribute specifies the name of the BPEL business process
- `targetNamespace`: This attribute specifies the target namespace for the business process definition
- `xmlns`: This namespace used by BPEL is available at `http://docs.oasis-open.org/wsbpel/2.0/process/executable`.

Usually, we also specify one or more additional namespaces to reference other involved namespaces (for example, those used by services). If you look at the preceding screenshot, you will see that there are quite a few namespace declarations, such as `xmlns:client`, which has the namespace of the imported WSDL and any reference to elements within WSDL will go through this namespace.

We can also specify additional attributes for the `<process>` tag as follows:

- `queryLanguage`: This attribute specifies which query language is used for node selection in assignments, properties, and other uses. The default (and part of the BPEL standard) is XPath 1.0 (`urn:oasis:names:tc:wsbpel:2.0:sublang:xpath1.0`). However, another language can be specified, such as XPath 2.0 or XQuery. The available options are determined by what is supported by a given BPEL engine.
- `expressionLanguage`: This attribute specifies which expression language is used in the process. The default is again XPath 1.0 (`urn:oasis:names:tc:wsbpel:2.0:sublang:xpath1.0`).
- `suppressJoinFailure`: This attribute determines whether to suppress join failures (`yes` or `no`). Default is `no`. This is used in flow activities with links, which is an advanced scenario of using BPEL.
- `exitOnStandardFault`: This attribute defines how the process should behave when a standard fault occurs. We can specify `yes` if we want the process to exit on a standard fault (other than `bpel:joinFailure`), or `no` if we want to handle the fault using a fault handler. Default is `no`.

<receive> and <reply>

With `<receive>`, the process waits for incoming messages (that is, operation invocations). Usually, it waits for the initial message to start the process. Another typical use of `<receive>` is to wait for callbacks (we'll discuss this in *Chapter 5, Interaction Patterns in BPEL*).

With `<reply>`, a BPEL process can send a response. Usually, it is used in the synchronous BPEL processes. However, in general, it can be used with any open request or response operation. Both activities use the same basic attributes as follows:

- `partnerLink`: This attribute specifies which partner link will be used
- `portType`: This attribute specifies the used port type
- `operation`: This attribute specifies the name of the operation to wait for being invoked (`<receive>`), or the name of the operation that has been invoked but is synchronous and requires a reply (`<reply>`)
- `variable`: This attribute specifies the name of the BPEL variable used to store the incoming message (`<receive>`) or send the outgoing message (`<reply>`)

For each BPEL activity, we can also specify a `name` attribute. We use the `name` attribute to provide names for activities. In most BPEL activities, the name attribute is optional, but we can add it to improve the readability of the code.

<receive>

Let's now take a closer look at the `<receive>` activity. We said that `<receive>` waits for the incoming message (operation invocation), either for the initial to start the BPEL process, or for a callback function. Usually, the business process needs to store the incoming message and it can use the `variable` attribute to specify a suitable variable.

Another attribute for the `<receive>` activity is the `createInstance` attribute, which is related to the business process life cycle and instructs the BPEL engine to create a new instance of the process. Usually, we specify the `createInstance="yes"` attribute with the initial `<receive>` activity of the process to create a new process instance for each client. We will discuss this attribute in more detail in the next chapter.

The following example shows a `<receive>` activity that waits for the `getBookData` operation on the port type `client:BookstoreBBPEL` using the `bookstoreBbpel_client` partner link. As this is the initial `<receive>` activity, the `createInstance` attribute is used. The client request is stored in the `inputVariable` variable:

```
<!-- Receive input from requestor. (Note: This maps to operation
     defined in BookstoreBBPEL.wsdl) -->
<receive name="receiveInput"
         partnerLink="bookstoreBbpel_client"
         portType="client:BookstoreBBPEL"
         operation="getBookData"
         variable="inputVariable"
         createInstance="yes"/>
```

<reply>

The `<reply>` activity is used to return the response for the synchronous BPEL operation. It is always related to the initial `<receive>` through which the BPEL process started. Using `<reply>`, we can return the response, which is the normal usage, or we can return a fault message. Returning a fault message using `<reply>` is discussed in *Chapter 6, Fault Handling and Signaling*.

When we use <reply> to return a response for a synchronous operation, we have to define only one additional attribute—the name of the variable where the response is stored. The following example shows a reply on an initial receive operation. It uses the `bookstoreBbpel_client` partner link and provides a response for the `getBookData` operation on `client:BookstoreBBPEL` port type. The return result is stored in the `outputVariable` variable. Please note that the same `partnerLink`, `portType`, and `operation` name have been used in the initial <receive>:

```
<!-- Generate reply to synchronous request -->
<reply name="replyOutput"
       partnerLink="bookstoreBbpel_client"
       portType="client:BookstoreBBPEL"
       operation="getBookData"
       variable="outputVariable"/>
```

With this, we have concluded our discussion on the fundamental BPEL syntax. We will look more closely into the syntax on other activities in subsequent chapters of this book.

Bookstore BPEL process with branches

To conclude this chapter, we will develop another bookstore BPEL process. This time, this will be the `BookstoreBBPEL` process. Compared to the first version, we will use a more sophisticated data manipulation. Instead of returning a constant stock quantity for each book, we will return a different stock quantity for several different book ISSNs. We will hardcode the results but will get familiar with branches, with the `XPath` expressions, and will use the assigns to manipulate variables.

Time for action – more sophisticated BPEL process

To develop the second BPEL process, we will follow similar steps as in the previous section, where we developed the first BPEL process. This process will be oversimplified too, but this and the previous process will present a solid basis for an even more sophisticated BPEL process, which we will create in *Chapter 2, Service Invocation*.

1. To start, double-click on the **Bookstore** composite in our existing project tree. This will open the SOA composite view, which shows the main building blocks (service components) of our application. So far, we have a BPEL process named `BookstoreABPEL`, which is exposed as SOAP web service through a WSDL interface.

2. Add a second BPEL process named `BookstoreBBPEL`. To achieve this, drag-and-drop the **BPEL Process** component from the right-hand side toolbar to the **Components** space of the SOA composite:

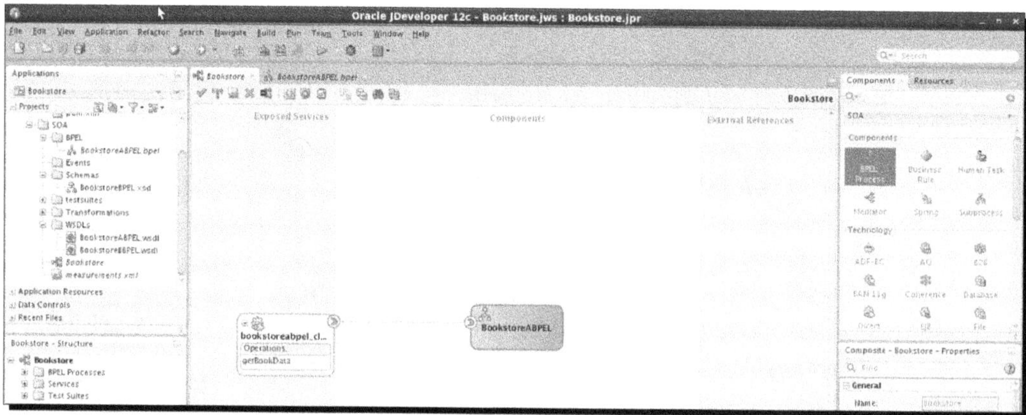

3. Doing this will add the BPEL process component and immediately open the dialog box, where we need to specify the BPEL process name and other details, such as the BPEL version, XML namespace, select the process template, and define the service name. Again, use the BPEL 2.0 specification, name the process `BookstoreBBPEL`, select the namespace from the `packtpub.com` domain, and select the **Synchronous BPEL Process** template, as shown on the following screenshot:

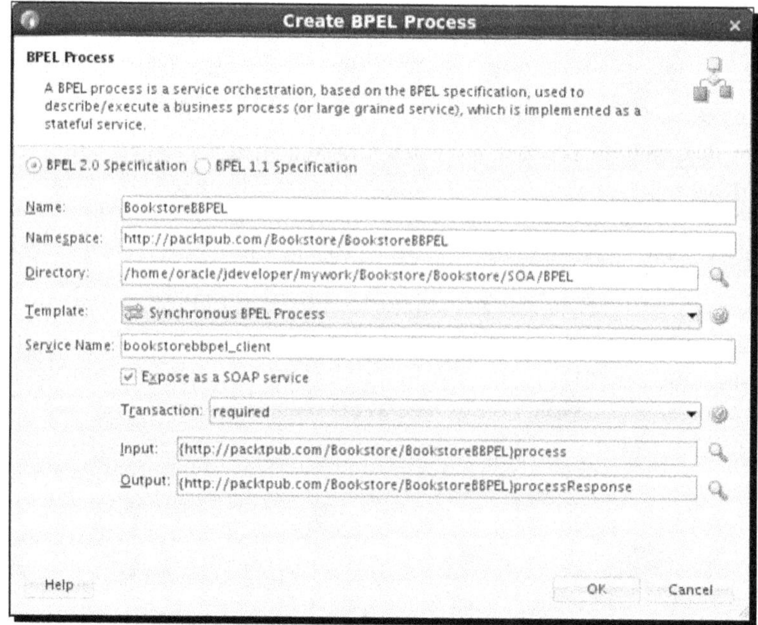

4. After clicking on **OK**, we will see the composite with the added BPEL process. On the left-hand side in the project tree, we can see that several artifacts have been generated, including the WSDL interface and the corresponding XSD (XML Schema).

5. We are now ready to implement the process. To do so, double-click on the `BookstoreBBPEL` component represented by the blue rectangle. This will open the BPEL design perspective.

6. Use the same schemas as in the `BookstoreABPEL` process. To achieve this, we can edit the WSDL file of the `BookstoreBBPEL` process named `BookstoreB.wsdl`. Let's double-click on the file, click on the source tab, and modify the import of the schema. Instead of using the `BookstoreBBPEL.xsd` file, use the `BookstoreBPEL.xsd`. We also need to modify the XML namespace under the client namespace alias:

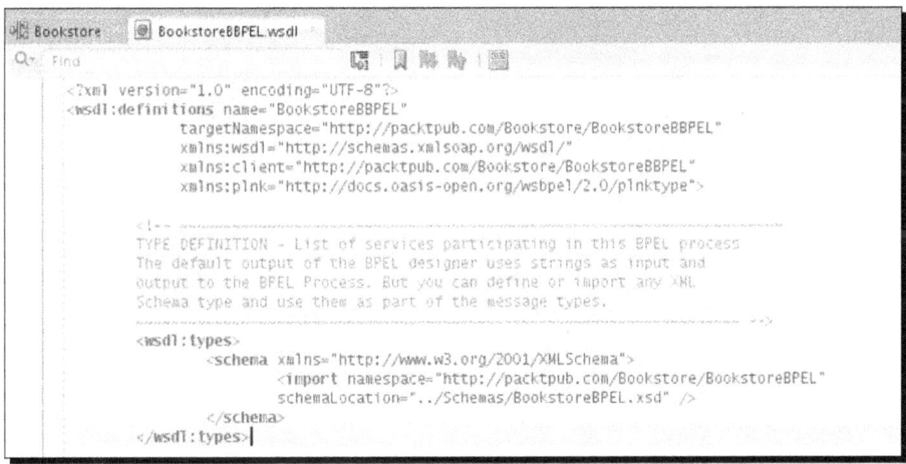

7. We also need to modify WSDL a little bit. We basically need to do the same changes as we did earlier in this chapter for the `BookstoreABPEL` process. To summarize, rename the operation name from `process` to `getBookData`. Modify both message elements to `BookData` and `BookDataResponse` respectively, and modify the schema location to use the `BookstoreBPEL.xsd` file:

8. Let's now go back to the `BookstoreBBPEL` process design window tab. In contrast to the first example, we will hardcode the response for a few predefined book ISSNs for which the BPEL process will return different stock quantities. For the **1111-1111** ISSN, it will return 10 books; for the **2222-2222** ISSN, it will return 20 books; for the **3333-3333** ISSN, it will return 30 books. For all other ISSNs, we will return five books.
9. First, add the `<if>` activity to the BPEL process by dragging-and-dropping the **If** icon from the lower-right side of the toolbar (look under **Structured Activities**). Drop the `<if>` activity between the **receiveInput** and **replyOutput** activities.
10. As we have four choices that we need to cover, first add the two **Else If** branches. Click on the `<if>` activity so that a big green plus sign will appear. Clicking on it will reveal **Else If**:

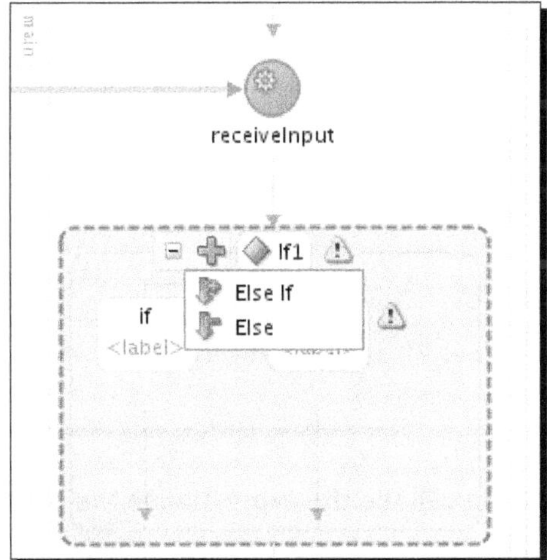

11. Let's now click on the **Else If** branch twice. Next, we need to add expressions, which will serve as the conditions for the **if** and **elseif** branches. Let's click on the first label. Name it `ISSN1`.
12. Next, right-click on the first **if** and select **Edit**. We could enter the condition directly, but will use the **Expression Builder** instead. Let's click on the **Fx** icon, to start **Expression Builder**.

13. In **Expression Builder**, use the **equals** operator to compare strings. Compare the ISSN within the `inputVariable` payload and compare it with the `'1111-1111'` string:

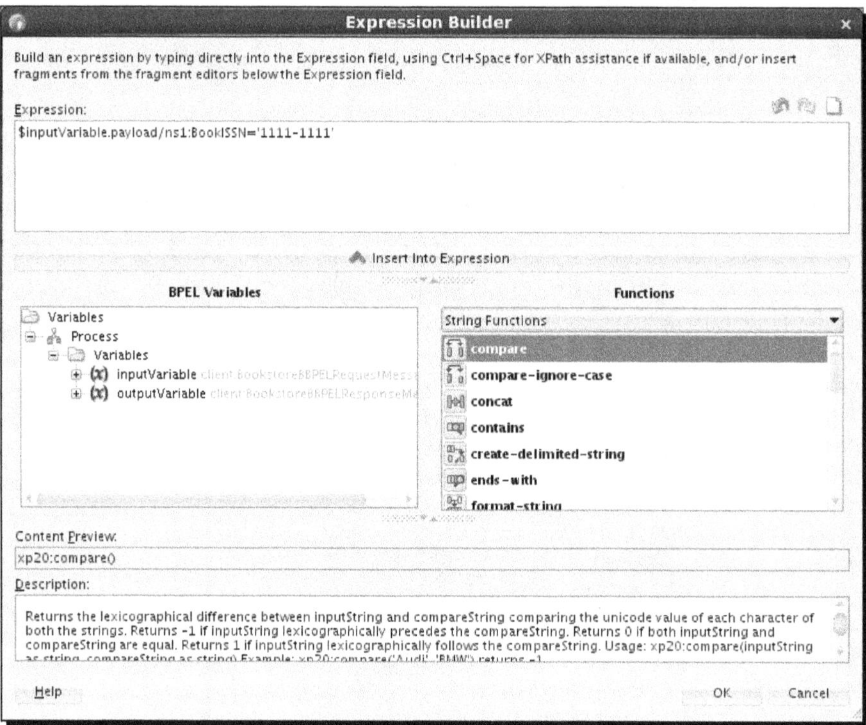

14. After clicking on **OK**, we will see the expression in the initial **Edit If** dialog box:

15. Enter other two conditions in the same way, first for the **2222-2222** ISSN, and **3333-3333** ISSN.

16. For each `<if>` branch, we now have to add the corresponding `<assign>` activity, which will set the stock quantity output variable. We already know how to use the `<assign>` activity, as we have used it in the previous example. However, this time, set the stock quantity within the `<if>` activity only. Set the other parameter, the `BookISSN` in the output variable after the `<if>` activity, as it is the same for all `if` branches.

17. First, let's add the `<assign>` by dragging-and-dropping the activity from the right-hand toolbar. It will appear as **Assign1**. Let's double-click on the **Assign1** activity and create a copy rule, where we will copy the number 10 to the stock quantity:

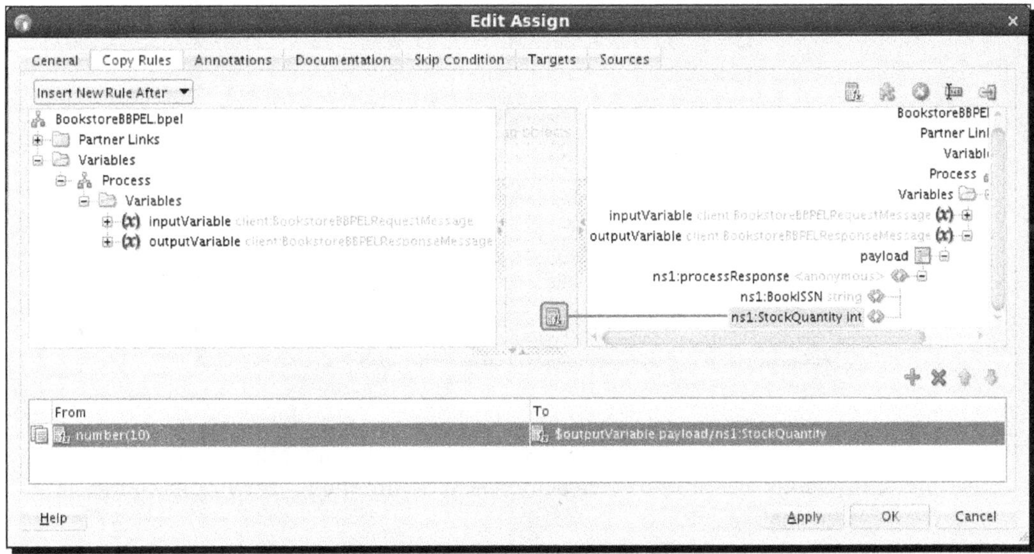

18. Let's now rename the **Assign1** activity to a more meaningful name. We can do this under the **General** tab, as shown in the following screenshot:

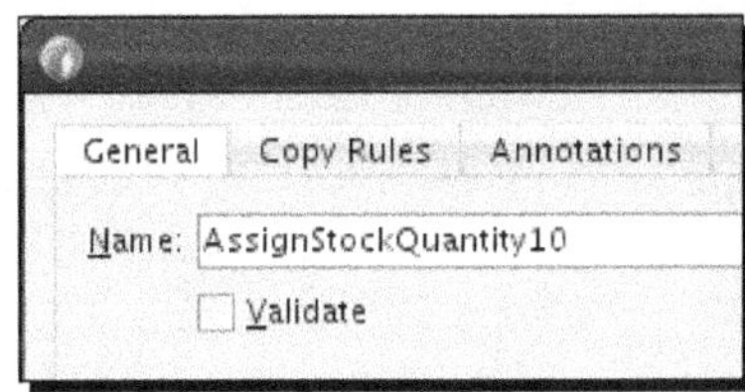

19. Add the other three `<assign>` activities to the BPEL process the same way. The first activity will assign the quantity of `20`, the second `30`, and the last (under the `else` branch) the quantity of `5`.

20. Let's now add the final assign that will copy the `BookISSN` from the input variable to the output variable. Add the assign after the `<if>` activity and before the `replyOutput` activity:

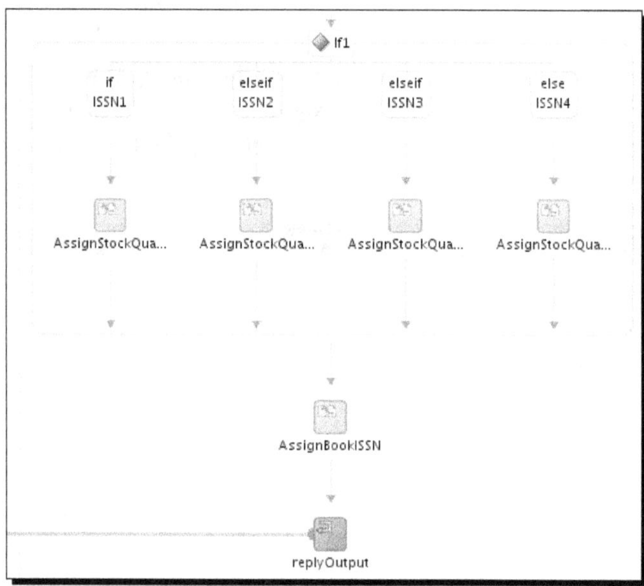

21. The assign will copy `BookISSN` from `inputVariable` to `BookISSN` of `outputVariable`. Please note that it would be the same if this assign activity would be added after the receive activity and before the `if` activity, as shown in the following screenshot:

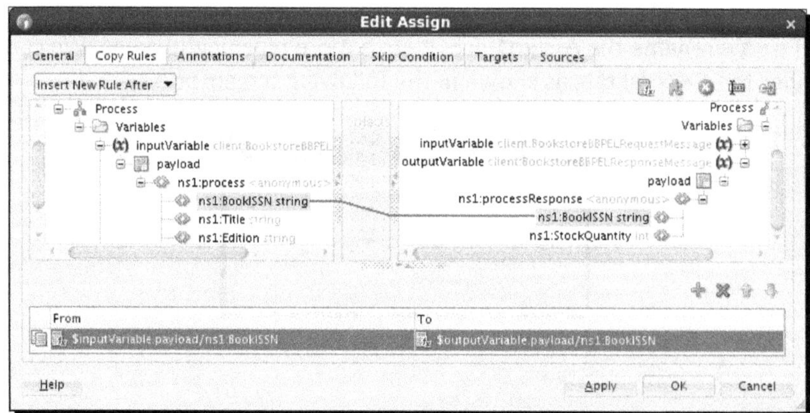

What just happened?

In the second BPEL example, we used the `<if>` activity, which is similar to the syntax of the `if` clause in other programming languages. Using the `<if>` activity, we can create branches in the BPEL process. In each branch, we used the corresponding `<assign>` activity to set the appropriate stock quantity.

We will say more about the `<if>` activity in the later chapters of this book. However, let's now look at the BPEL source code to get a feeling of how the source code looks like. As we've seen before, the process starts with a `<receive>` activity, which is responsible for receiving the input request, sent by the process client:

```
<!-- Receive input from requestor. (Note: This maps to operation defined in BookstoreBBPEL.wsdl) -->
<receive name="receiveInput" partnerLink="bookstorebbpel_client"
portType="client:BookstoreBBPEL" operation="getBookData"
variable="inputVariable" createInstance="yes"/>
```

Next, the `<if>` activity starts. Each `if` and `elseIf` branch contains the condition, which is expressed as the XPath expression. Within the `<if>` branch, the `<assign>` activity is nested:

```
<if name="If1">
  <documentation>ISSN1</documentation>
  <condition>$inputVariable.payload/ns1:BookISSN='1111-1111'</condition>
  <assign name="AssignStockQuantity10">
    <copy>
      <from>number(10)</from>
      <to>$outputVariable.payload/ns1:StockQuantity</to>
    </copy>
  </assign>
  <elseif>
    <documentation>ISSN2</documentation>
    <condition>$inputVariable.payload/ns1:BookISSN='2222-2222'</condition>
    <assign name="AssignQuantity20">
      <copy>
        <from>number(20)</from>
        <to>$outputVariable.payload/ns1:StockQuantity</to>
      </copy>
    </assign>
  </elseif>
  <elseif>
    <documentation>ISSN3</documentation>
    <condition>$inputVariable.payload/ns1:BookISSN='3333-3333'</condition>
    <assign name="AssignQuantity30">
      <copy>
        <from>number(30)</from>
        <to>$outputVariable.payload/ns1:StockQuantity</to>
      </copy>
    </assign>
  </elseif>
  <else>
    <assign name="AssignQuantity5">
      <copy>
        <from>number(5)</from>
        <to>$outputVariable.payload/ns1:StockQuantity</to>
      </copy>
    </assign>
  </else>
</if>
```

Please remember that we can always edit (or even write) the source code, which will reflect in the modified graphical representation and vice versa. We are not ready to write the BPEL code yet, but it is important to understand that the source code is the basis for the execution and that the graphical representation is created from the source code.

After the `<if>` activity, another `<assign>` is located. This assigns copies the `BookISSN` activity from the input to the output variable:

```
<assign name="AssignBookISSN">
  <copy>
    <from>$inputVariable.payload/ns1:BookISSN</from>
    <to>$outputVariable.payload/ns1:BookISSN</to>
  </copy>
</assign>
```

Finally, the process finishes with the `<reply>` activity. In this activity, the process returns the results to the client, which has invoked it. Remember that we selected a synchronous BPEL process, which always returns a reply. Later in this book, we will become familiar with asynchronous processes as well, which might not return responses:

```
    <!-- Generate reply to synchronous request -->
    <reply name="replyOutput" partnerLink="bookstorebbpel_client"
    portType="client:BookstoreBBPEL" operation="getBookData" variable="outputVariable"/>
  </sequence>
</process>
```

We are now ready to deploy and test this BPEL process, which we will do in the next section.

Deploy and test the second BPEL process

We are now ready to deploy and test our second BPEL process. To deploy the process to the SOA Suite server and test it, we will follow the same steps as in the previous example.

Time for action – deploying and testing the second BPEL process

To deploy and test our second BPEL process, we will redeploy the whole SOA composite, which now includes both BPEL processes. Let's perform the following steps:

1. Right-click on the project in the project tree and select the **Deploy** submenu.
2. Then, select **Deploy to Application Server**.
3. We will use the default deployment configuration, but make sure that we check the **Overwrite any existing composites with the same revision ID** option.
4. Choose the **IntegratedWebLogicServer** server for the deployment and click on **Finish**.

After the successful deployment, we are ready to test the process. We will use **Enterprise Manager Console**. As we created the new BPEL process within the same application, we deployed it inside the **Bookstore** composite application. After clicking on the application, click on the **Test** button, which will now have two options, **BookstoreA** and **BookstoreB**.

1. Test the `BookstoreBBPEL` process by clicking on it.
2. Let's do the test for the **1111-1111** ISSN. To perform the test, first select the **XML View**.
3. This time we will enter the request message in plain XML. For this, simply enter the required data in the following predefined XML form:

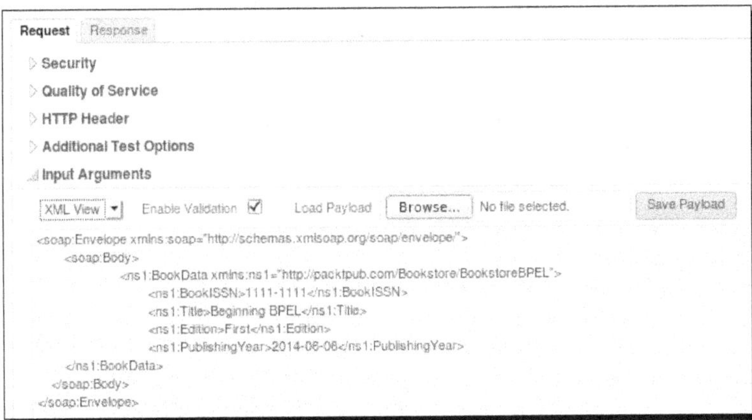

Request
Response
Security
Quality of Service
HTTP Header
Additional Test Options
Input Arguments
XML View
Enable Validation
Load Payload
Browse...
No file selected.
Save Payload
<soap:Envelope xmlns:soap="http://schemas.xmlsoap.org/soap/envelope/">
<soap:Body>
<ns1:BookData xmlns:ns1="http://packtpub.com/Bookstore/BookstoreBPEL">
<ns1:BookISSN>1111-1111</ns1:BookISSN>
<ns1:Title>Beginning BPEL</ns1:Title>
<ns1:Edition>First</ns1:Edition>
<ns1:PublishingYear>2014-06-06</ns1:PublishingYear>
</ns1:BookData>
</soap:Body>
</soap:Envelope>

4. After clicking on the **Test Web Service** button, we will see the screen with the response of `10`:

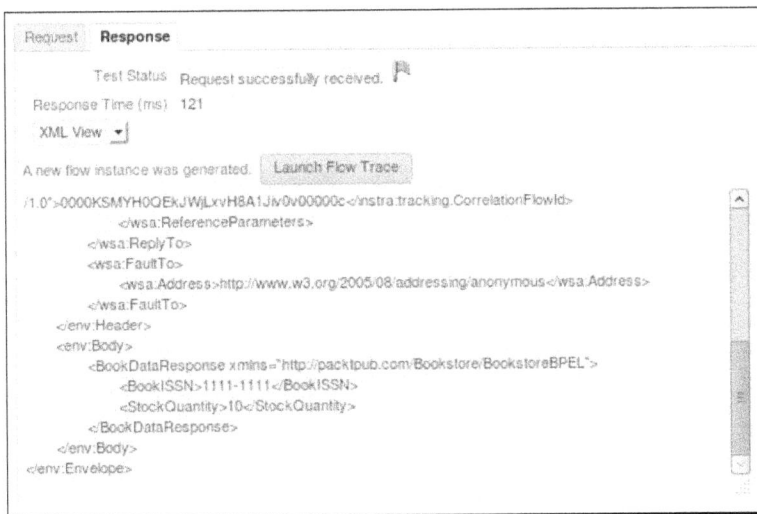

Request | **Response**

Test Status Request successfully received.

Response Time (ms) 121

XML View

A new flow instance was generated. Launch Flow Trace

```
/1.0">0000KSMYHOQEkJWjLxvH8A1Jiv0v00000c</instra:tracking.CorrelationFlowId>
        </wsa:ReferenceParameters>
      </wsa:ReplyTo>
      <wsa:FaultTo>
        <wsa:Address>http://www.w3.org/2005/08/addressing/anonymous</wsa:Address>
      </wsa:FaultTo>
    </env:Header>
    <env:Body>
      <BookDataResponse xmlns="http://packtpub.com/Bookstore/BookstoreBPEL">
        <BookISSN>1111-1111</BookISSN>
        <StockQuantity>10</StockQuantity>
      </BookDataResponse>
    </env:Body>
</env:Envelope>
```

What just happened?

We successfully tested our second BPEL process. First, we redeployed the whole SOA composite application, which now consists of the two BPEL processes. Then, we invoked the `BookstoreBBPEL` process and monitored the response for different ISSNs.

There are other ways to test the BPEL process than using the Enterprise Manager. The SOA Suite test framework can be used directly from JDeveloper to test and debug SOA composites. A popular option is using the SoapUI tool, which can generate the requests and show the responses in a similar way, as we did with the Enterprise Manager. For more information on SoapUI, visit `http://www.soapui.org/`.

To get more insight into the BPEL execution, a nice option is to click on the **Launch Flow Trace** button. This opens a new window, which shows the execution flow trace. Our BPEL process is relatively simple; therefore, we see only one component. If we click on the `BookstoreBBPEL` instance, we will see another view named **Audit Trail**:

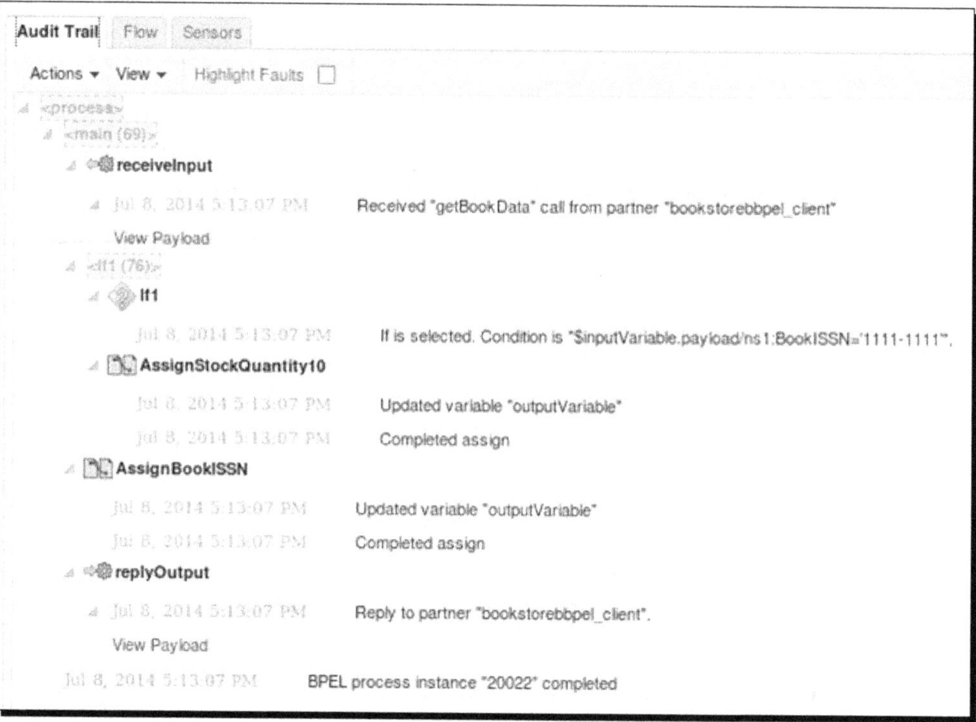

An even more interesting view is the **Flow** view, which can be activated on the **Flow** tab. It shows the visual execution flow. For our process, it will look like the following screenshot:

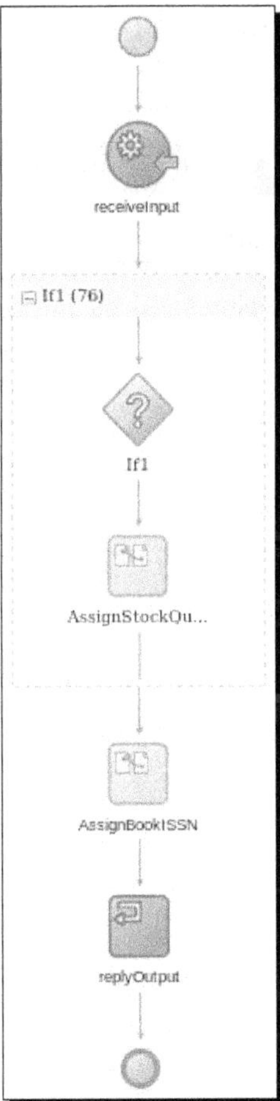

Clicking on any activity on the visual flow allows us to inspect the variables, which is very useful for debugging.

With this, we have concluded our discussion. You have successfully developed, deployed, and tested your second BPEL process, which is already a bit more complex than the first one. Still, it was an oversimplified BPEL process, which took four parameters as an input (the book ISSN, title, edition, and publishing year) and returned the quantity of the book together with the ISSN. However, this time different ISSN returned different stock quantities.

In the next chapter, we will use both BPEL processes, `BookstoreABPEL` and `BookstoreBBPEL`, and will orchestrate them into a more complex process.

Have a go hero – test the process

It's your turn now. Test the `BookstoreBBPEL` process for different parameters, including ISSNs 2222-2222, 3333-3333, and others, and verify that the process returns the correct response.

Pop Quiz – BPEL basics

Q1. Try to answer which of the following items are true:

1. BPEL is a language for composing services and orchestrating and coordinating the flow of services.
2. BPEL is a programming-in-the-small language.
3. BPEL is used to implement specific functionalities.
4. BPEL is used to compose (orchestrate) functionalities exposed though services (service interfaces) into composite applications.
5. BPEL is a graphical language.
6. BPEL code uses XML syntax.

Q2. Which is the latest version of the BPEL language?

1. 1.0.
2. 1.1.
3. 2.0.

Q3. BPEL process starts with which root-element activity?

Q4. Does BPEL support variables?

Q5. Which activity is used to manipulate variables?

Q6. What is the correct syntax of the `<if>` activity?

1. `<if><then><else>`.
2. `<if><then><endif>`.
3. `<if><then><else><endif>`.
4. `<if><elseif><endif>`.
5. `<if><elseif><else>`.

Q7. What is the default expression and query language in BPEL?

1. XQuery.
2. XPath.

Q8. What is the purpose of the <receive> activity?

1. To send response to the client.
2. To wait for incoming messages.
3. To receive e-mail messages.

Downloading the example code

You can download the example code files for all Packt books you have purchased from your account at http://www.packtpub.com. If you purchased this book elsewhere, you can visit http://www.packtpub.com/support and register to have the files e-mailed directly to you.

Summary

In this chapter, we gained the basic understanding of BPEL. We have seen that BPEL is an important orchestration language for SOA. It uses XML syntax. Usually, it is represented graphically for easier development.

In this chapter, we learned how to install Oracle JDeveloper and SOA Suite, how to create a domain on the SOA Suite server, and how to use JDeveloper to develop BPEL.

We developed two simple BPEL processes. The first one was a very simple process returning the stock quantity of a book as a hardcoded constant. The second BPEL process was a little more sophisticated and returned the quantity depending on the ISSN number. In addition to becoming an overview understanding of the BPEL source code, we gained a deeper understanding of the <assign> and <if> activities.

We also learned how to deploy a BPEL processes to the SOA Suite server and how to use the Enterprise Manage console to test the BPEL processes. We have done so for both BPEL processes, which we developed.

In the next chapter, we will develop a more sophisticated BPEL process which will orchestrate the two simple BPEL processes developed in this chapter. We will learn how to invoke services and processes sequentially and in parallel. We will also get a deeper understanding on process WSDL interfaces and partner links.

2
Service Invocation

Services are self-contained units of functionality. BPEL processes specify the exact order in which participating services should be invoked—this is called orchestration. We can do this sequentially or in parallel. With BPEL, we can also express conditional behavior; for example, a service invocation can depend on the return value of a previous invocation. We will see that BPEL processes are essentially graphs of activities.

In this chapter, we will learn how to use BPEL for service invocations using sequential flows. We will develop a BPEL process, which will invoke other services and orchestrate them. This way, the BPEL process will consume services, thus building a composite application.

In traditional programming languages, we used to invoke operations sequentially, one by one. In business processes, however, we often need to execute activities in parallel. We will see that BPEL provides a relatively easy way to invoke services and execute other activities in parallel.

In this chapter, we will extend our example process from the previous chapter and learn how to invoke and compose services in a sequential and parallel manner. In this chapter, we shall:

- Understand service invocation and orchestration of services
- Develop a book warehousing process that will invoke and orchestrate services
- Understand sequential invocation and partner links
- Understand parallel invocation, parallel flows, and develop a process using parallel invocation

So let's get started.

Service invocation and orchestration

In the previous chapter, we learned the basics of BPEL. We learned that BPEL processes can be synchronous or asynchronous. BPEL processes consist of activities. A process usually begins with a `<receive>` activity, which is responsible for receiving the request from the process client. Then, the BPEL process executes some logic. So far, we have become familiar with the `<assign>` activity for manipulating variables and with the `<if>` activity for conditions.

We have also learned that BPEL is a **programming-in-the-large** language, meaning that we do not program distinct functionalities in BPEL. Rather, we use BPEL to orchestrate services—in other words, it invokes several services in a specific order to perform a certain business process.

In a typical scenario, the BPEL business process receives a request. To fulfill it, the process then invokes the involved services and finally responds to the original caller. Every BPEL process specifies the exact order in which the participating services should be invoked. This can be done sequentially or in parallel. With BPEL, we can express conditional behavior; for example, a service invocation can depend on the value of a previous invocation. We can also construct loops, declare variables, copy and assign values, define fault handlers, and so on. By combining all these constructs, we can define complex business processes in an algorithmic manner. We can describe deterministic as well as nondeterministic flows.

To demonstrate how to use BPEL to invoke services and orchestrate them into business processes, we will define a simple business process for book warehousing. Let's consider a big bookstore, which has two bookstores located at different locations in the city. It also has a central office location where all the new books are delivered. When a new book is delivered to the central office, we have to check the stock quantity for this book in each bookstore. Based on this information, we decide how many books we will send to each bookstore. This simplified process flow is shown in the following screenshot:

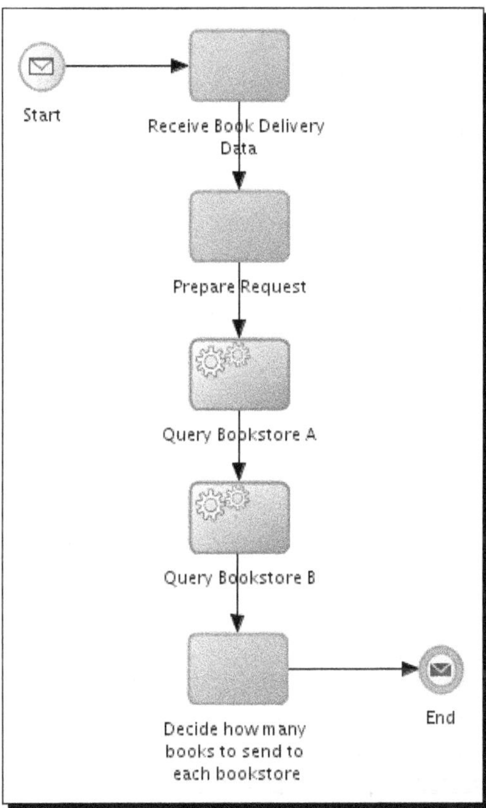

To query the book quantity in **Bookstore A** and **Bookstore B**, we will use both BPEL processes, the `BookstoreA` and `BookstoreB` BPEL processes, which we developed in the previous chapter. These processes return the stock quantity information, which is exactly what we need.

To orchestrate both BPEL processes, we will invoke their operations through the WSDL interface that both processes expose. We have mentioned that each BPEL process is exposed through a WSDL interface, meaning that to the outside world, it looks like a web service.

Although in our example, we invoke BPEL processes for Bookstore A and Bookstore B from the book warehousing process, please remember that with BPEL, we can orchestrate any kind of services, no matter how they are implemented (BPEL, Java, C#, C++, Python, or any other language), or even exposed for an existing application. Therefore, we will refer to them as **services**.

The following figure shows schematically what we are about to do:

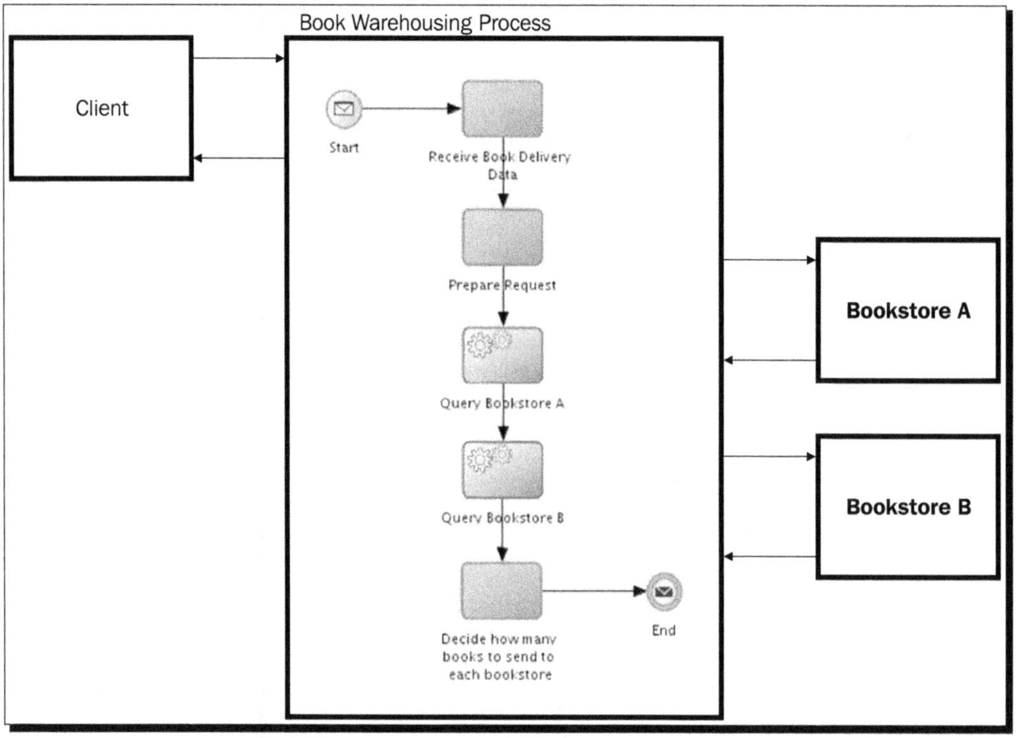

To be able to invoke services, we need to be familiar with their interfaces. For example, the book warehousing process will need to know exactly how to call the `BookstoreA` and `BookstoreB` services (please note that we refer to them as services, when they are called from outside, although they are implemented as BPEL processes). To do this, we need to look into WSDL interfaces. In our example, both bookstore services have the same interface. Actually, we can see the operation name on the SCA composite diagram already. We will have a detailed look into the WSDL interfaces later, when we will explain the notion of partner links. Now, however, let's develop the book warehousing process in BPEL.

Developing the book warehousing process

To develop the book warehousing process, we will start with the JDeveloper project from the previous chapter. In this project, we already have two BPEL processes that return the stock quantity for Bookstore A and Bookstore B.

We will create a new BPEL process, called `BookWarehousingBPEL`, simply by dragging-and-dropping the process to the SOA composite. As the `BookWarehousingBPEL` process will invoke the `BookstoreA` and `BookstoreB` BPEL processes, we will need to connect the `BookWarehousingBPEL` process with the other two processes. This way, we will create a partner link between them and will enable the service invocation. Connecting BPEL processes in JDeveloper is very easy as we only need to draw a wire between them.

In this example, we will use a synchronous BPEL, which we have become familiar with in *Chapter 1, Hello BPEL*. The synchronous request/response operation semantics is appropriate for this example. We will learn about asynchronous BPEL processes in *Chapter 5, Interaction Patterns in BPEL*. Next, we will implement the `BookWarehousingBPEL` process.

Time for action – creating the book warehousing process

Let's create the `BookWarehousingBPEL` BPEL process:

1. We will open the SOA composite by double-clicking on the **Bookstore** in the process tree. In the composite, we can see both Bookstore BPEL processes and their WSDL interfaces.
2. We will add a new BPEL process by dragging-and-dropping the **BPEL Process** service component from the right-hand side toolbar.
3. An already-familiar dialog window will open, where we will specify the BPEL 2.0 version, enter the process name as `BookWarehousingBPEL`, modify the namespace to `http://packtpub.com/Bookstore/BookWarehousingBPEL`, and select **Synchronous BPEL Process**. We will leave all other fields to their default values:

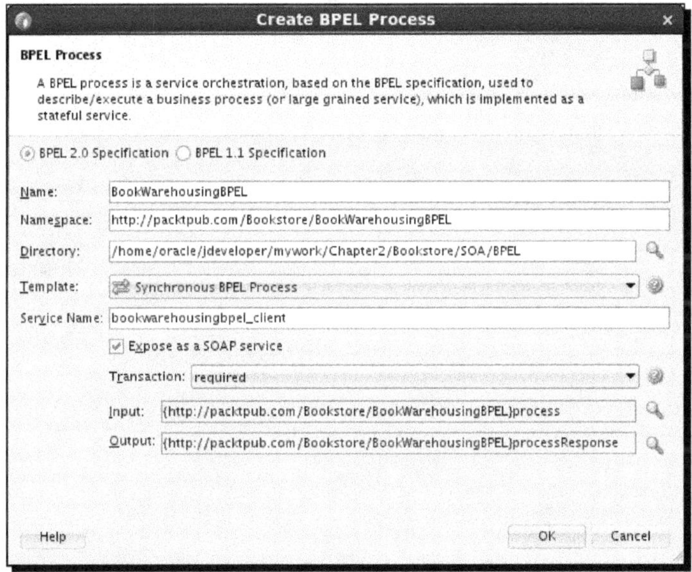

4. Next, we will wire the `BookWarehousingBPEL` component with the `BookstoreABPEL` and `BookstoreBBPEL` components. This way, we will establish a partner link between them. First, we will create the wire to the `BookstoreBBPEL` component (although the order doesn't matter). To do this, you have to click on the bottom-right side of the component. Once you place the mouse pointer above the component, circles on the edges will appear. You need to start with the circle labelled **Drag to add a new Reference** and connect it with the service interface circle, as shown in the following screenshot:

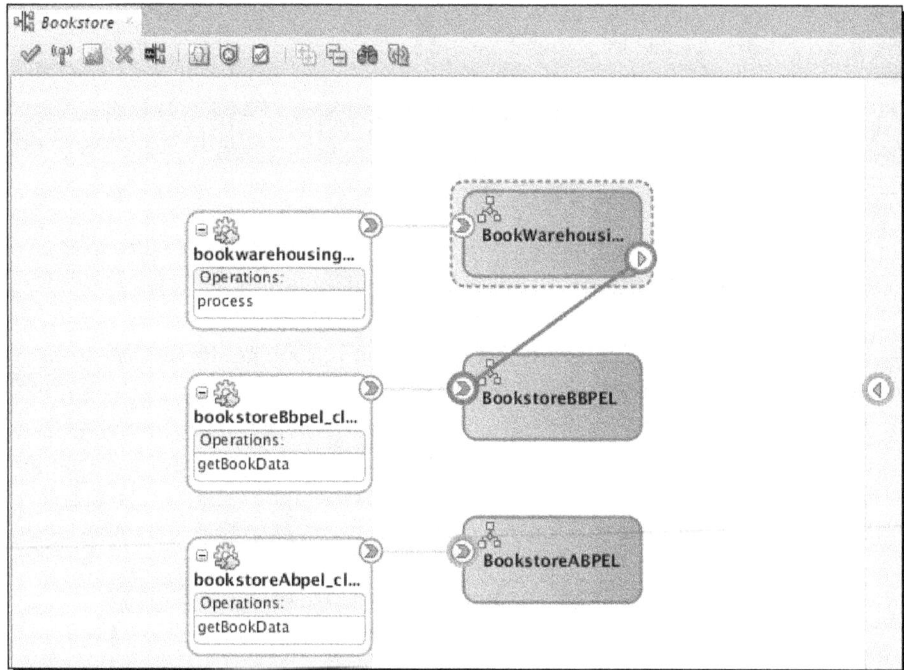

5. You do the same to wire the `BookWarehousingBPEL` component with the `BookstoreABPEL` component:

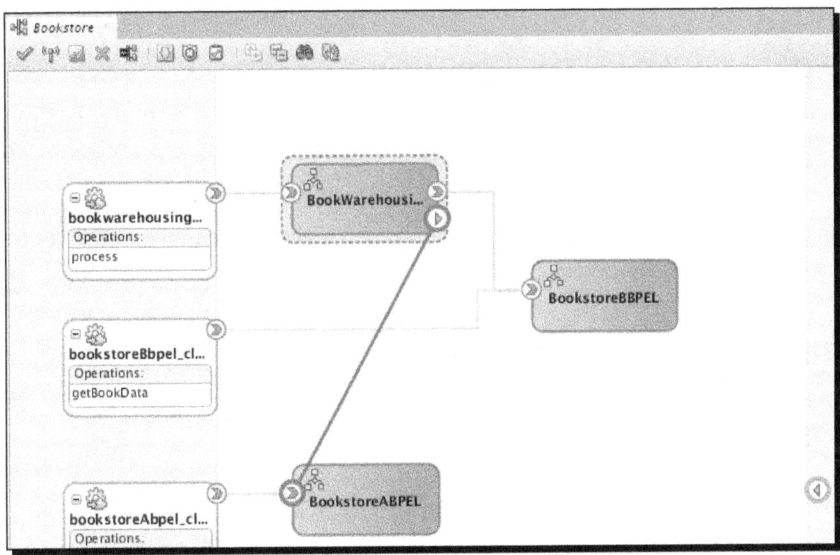

6. We should see the following screenshot. Please notice that the `BookWarehousingBPEL` component is wired to the `BookstoreABPEL` and `BookstoreBBPEL` components:

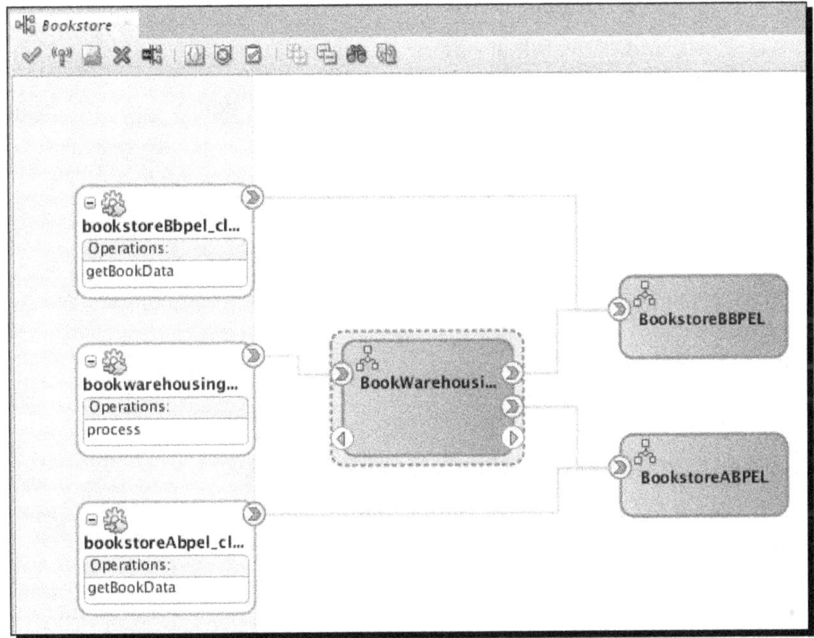

What just happened?

We have added the BookWarehousingBPEL component to our SOA composite and wired it to the BookstoreABPEL and BookstoreBBPEL components. Creating the wires between components means that references have been created and relations between components have been established. In other words, we have expressed that the BookWarehousingBPEL component will be able to invoke the BookstoreABPEL and BookstoreBBPEL components. This is exactly what we want to achieve with our BookWarehousingBPEL process, which will orchestrate both bookstore BPELs.

Once we have created the components and wired them accordingly, we are ready to implement the BookWarehousingBPEL process.

Implementing the book warehousing BPEL

To implement the book warehousing BPEL process, we need to follow a few steps. As already mentioned, we have created a synchronous BPEL process.

> Every synchronous BPEL process starts with a <receive> activity and ends with a <reply> activity. In *Chapter 5, Interaction Patterns in BPEL*, we will learn about asynchronous BPEL processes. These do not need to return a response. If they want to return it, they can use a callback using the <invoke> activity.

First, we have to define the **XSD** schema that will be used for the request and response messages. Let's suppose that the client will send the following data within the request message (the one received in the initial <receive> activity):

- Data about the book, including the book's ISBN, title, edition, and publishing year
- Purchased quantity

The response of the book warehousing BPEL process will be relatively simple and will only include string with the selected bookstore location.

Then, we will follow the process flow, which we defined earlier in this chapter. We will basically need to do the following:

- From the <receive> activity, we will prepare a request for both bookstore BPEL processes. We will use <assign> for this.
- We will invoke both bookstore BPEL processes (services) using <invoke>.
- We will compare the response from both bookstore BPELs using <if> and create a reply.

To hold the request and response messages for `BookstoreA` and `BookstoreB`, we will need four variables: `BookstoreARequest`, `BookstoreAResponse`, `BookstoreBRequest`, and `BookstoreBResponse`. We will create these variables on the fly and discuss variables in more detail in *Chapter 3, Variables, Data Manipulation, and Expressions*.

Time for action – developing the book warehousing process

Let's start with the implementation of the `BookWarehousingBPEL` process. We should follow these steps:

1. We will start with the XML schema definition. To do this, we need to double-click on the `BookWarehousingBPEL.xsd` file (in the `Schemas` folder) and write the following schema, as shown:

```
<?xml version="1.0" encoding="UTF-8"?>
<schema attributeFormDefault="unqualified"
        elementFormDefault="qualified"
        targetNamespace="http://packtpub.com/Chapter2/Bookstore/BookWarehousingBPEL"
        xmlns="http://www.w3.org/2001/XMLSchema">
        <element name="process">
                <complexType>
                        <sequence>
                                <element name="BookData">
                                        <complexType>
                                                <sequence>
                                                        <element name="BookISSN" type="string"/>
                                                        <element name="Title" type="string"/>
                                                        <element name="Edition" type="string"/>
                                                        <element name="PublishingYear" type="date"/>
                                                </sequence>
                                        </complexType>
                                </element>
                                <element name="PurchasedQuantity" type="int"/>
                        </sequence>
                </complexType>
        </element>
        <element name="processResponse">
                <complexType>
                        <sequence>
                                <element name="SelectedBookstoreLocation" type="string"/>
                        </sequence>
                </complexType>
        </element>
</schema>
```

2. Now we can switch back to the BPEL tab (`BookWarehousingBPEL.bpel`). First, we will add an `<assign>` activity to prepare a request for both the bookstore BPEL processes. In `<assign>`, we will copy the whole `BookData` element from `inputVariable` to a new variable, which we will create on the fly. We should do the following:

1. Drag-and-drop `<assign>` to the BPEL process between the `<receive>` and `<reply>` activities.
2. Double-click on the `<assign>` activity to open the dialog window.
3. To hold and store the request for both bookstore BPEL processes, we need a new variable. Therefore, we will right-click on **Variable** and select the **Create Variable** option from the context menu:

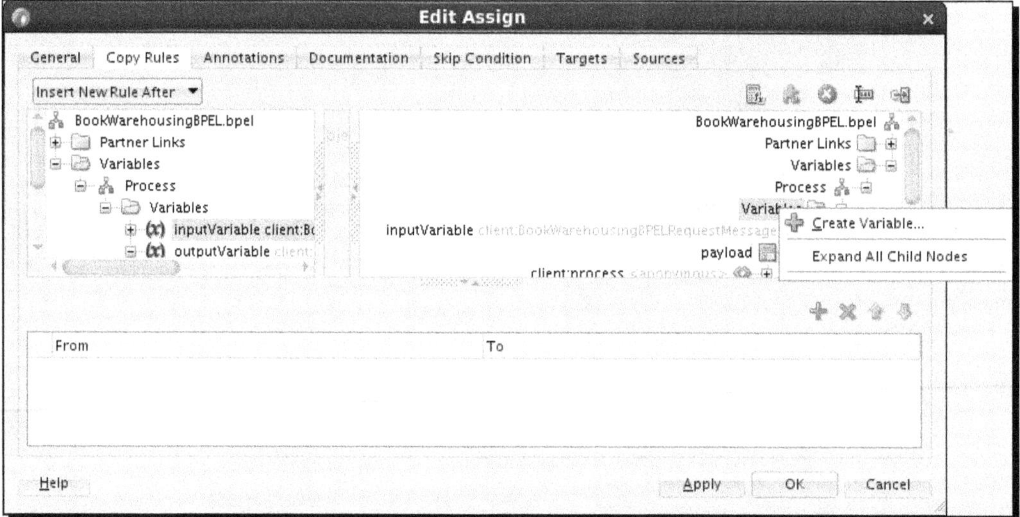

4. A new window will appear where we will name the variable `BookstoreARequest`. As the type, we will choose **Message Type**, as we will prepare the whole message, which will be sent as a request message to `BookstoreABPEL`. We will click on the magnifier icon to browse the message types and select `BookstoreABPELRequestMessage`, as shown:

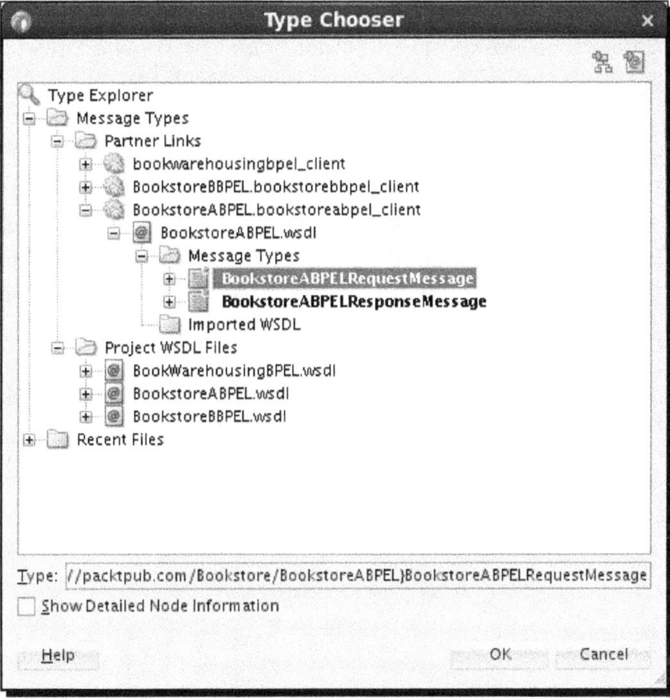

5. We also need a variable, which will hold the response from `BookstoreABPEL`. We will repeat the same steps as before. We will name the variable `BookstoreAResponse`:

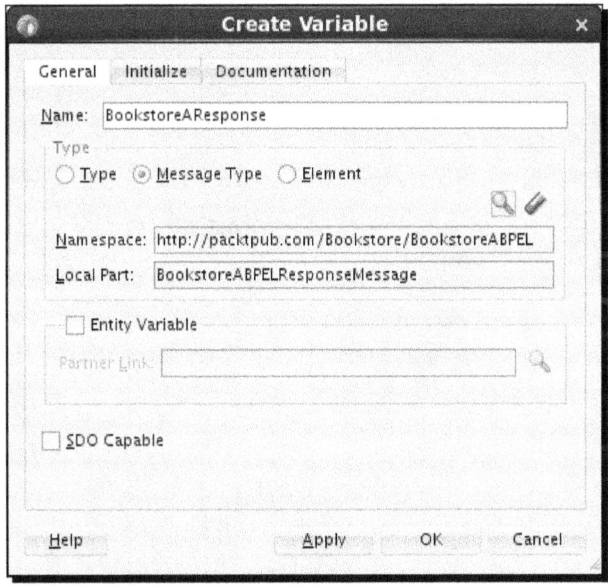

6. We will create two more variables, `BookstoreBRequest` and `BookstoreBResponse`. In order to do this, we will repeat steps 3-5.

7. We are now ready to create a copy of the `BookData` element from `inputVariable` to the `BookData` element of the `BookstoreARequest` variable. We need to do the copy element by element, as `BookData` from `inputVariable` belongs to a different namespace rather than the `BookData` element from the `BookstoreARequest` variable. Therefore, we will need to do four drag-and-drops. In the next chapter, we will explain how we could use the same namespace and simply copy the whole complex element as one, as shown in the following screenshot:

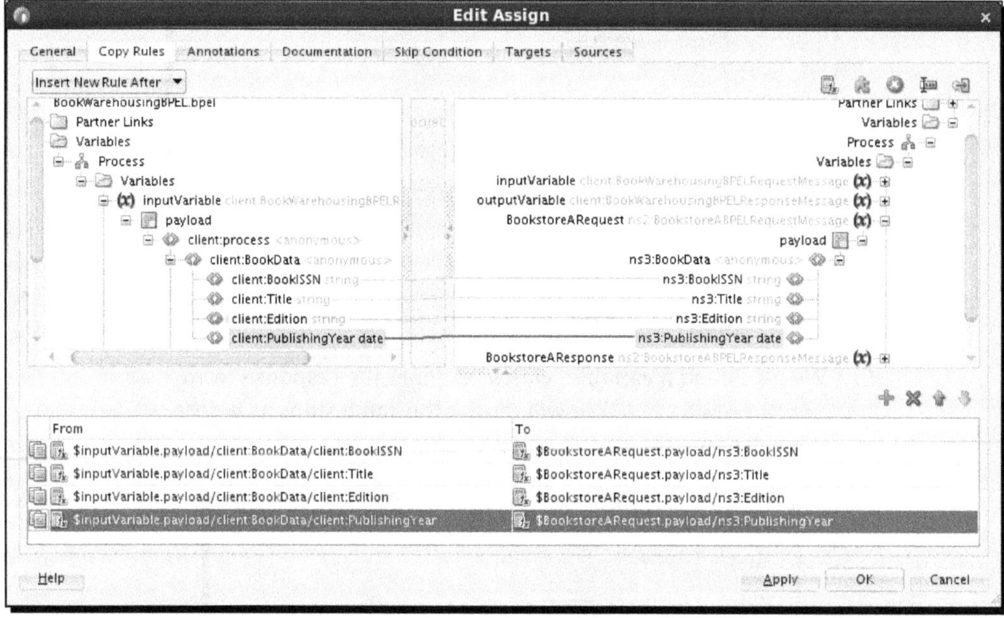

8. We should do exactly the same copy for the `BookstoreBRequest` variable.

9. Finally, let's rename the `<assign>` activity from `Assign1` to `PrepareRequest`.

3. We are now ready to invoke both the bookstore services. First, we will invoke `BookstoreABPEL`. To invoke an external service, we will use the `<invoke>` activity. We will drag the **Invoke** activity from the right-hand side toolbar and drop it on the process flow after `<assign>`, which we've just added.

4. Then, we will connect the `<invoke>` activity with the `BookstoreABPEL` service, listed in the right-hand side of the canvas (under the **Partner Links** section):

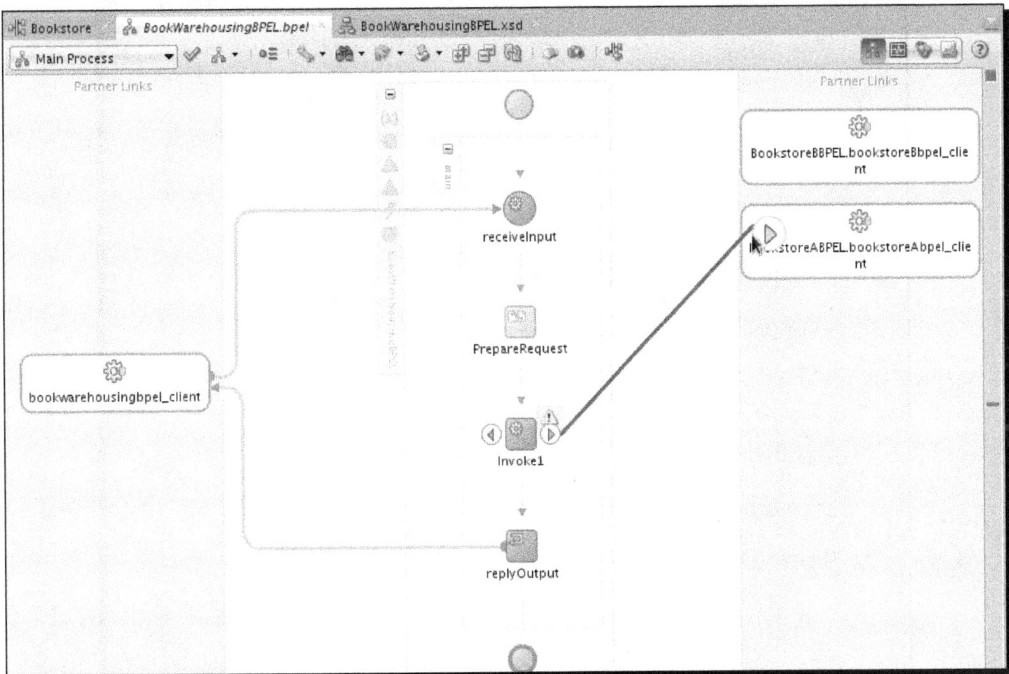

5. A window will open and we will need to specify a few parameters. First, we will name it `BookstoreAInvoke`. The partner link, the port type, and the operation are already selected. We should leave the default values. The operation name is `getBookData`, which is exactly what we are looking for.

6. We will need to specify the input and output variables. The input variable is the variable holding the request message. In our case, this is the `BookstoreARequest` variable. The output variable is the variable that stores the invocation response. This is `BookstoreAResponse`. Let's select both variables, as shown in the following screenshot:

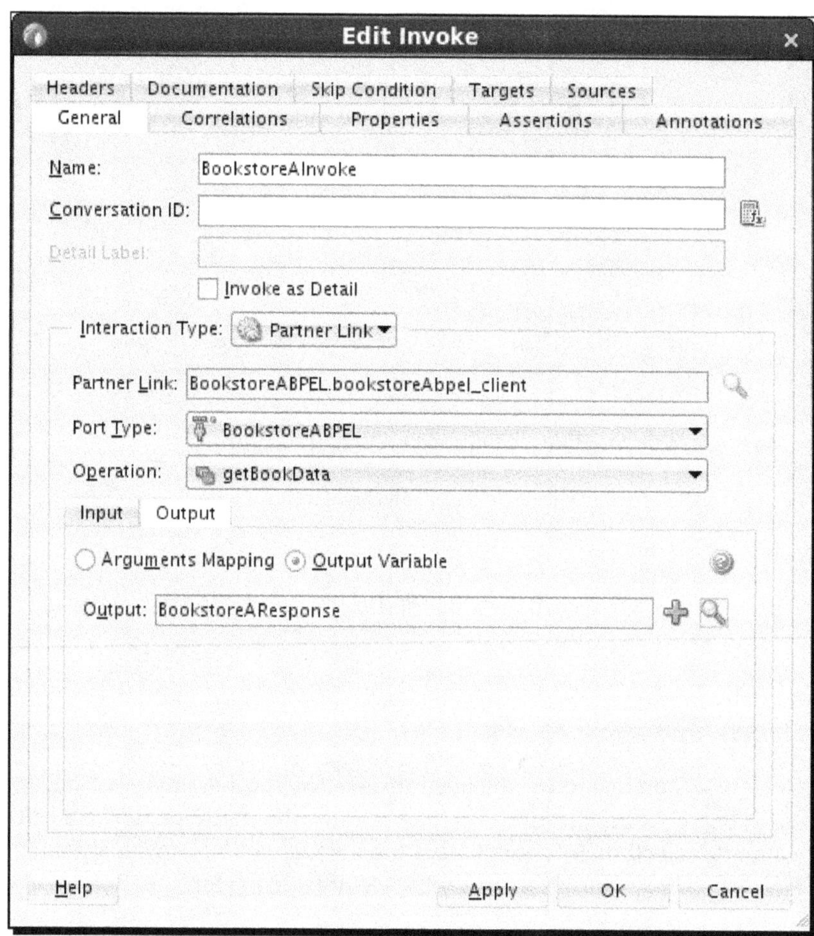

7. We shall do the same for the second invocation. The difference is that this time, we will invoke `BookstoreBBPEL` and use the corresponding `BookstoreB` variables. This should bring us to the following BPEL process flow:

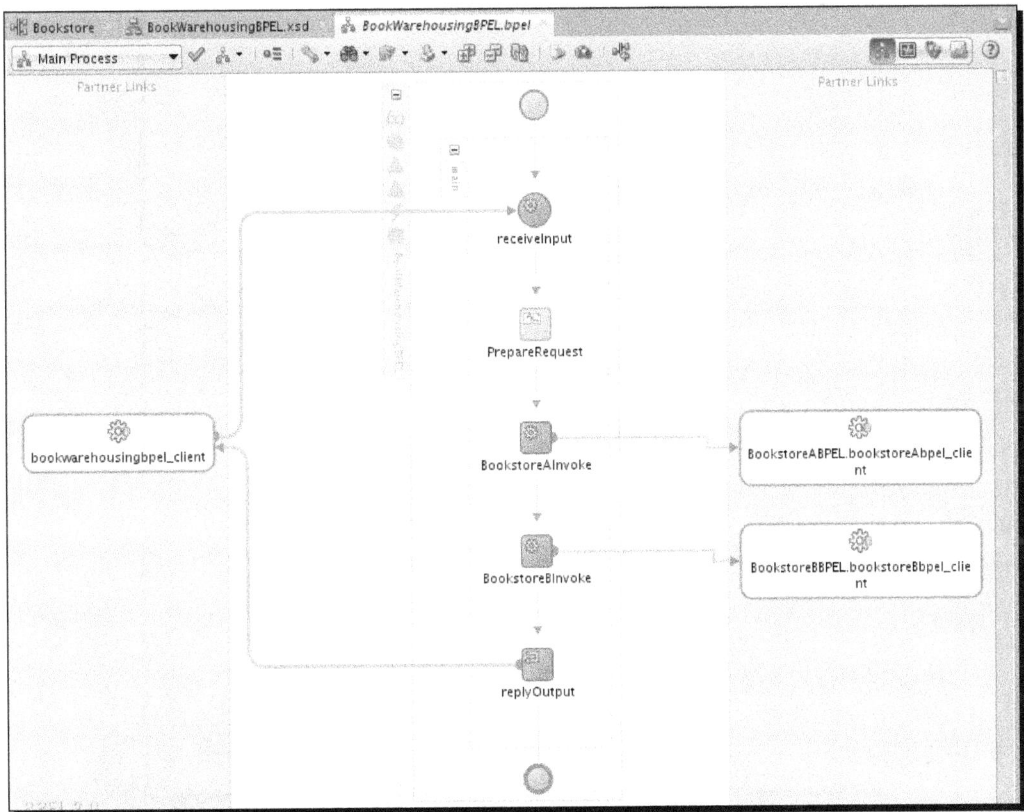

8. The final step is to add the `<if>` activity to compare the response from both the bookstore BPELs and select the bookstore with the lower stock to ship the purchased books.

9. We have already learned how to use the `<if>` activity in the previous chapter. First, we add the `<if>` activity:

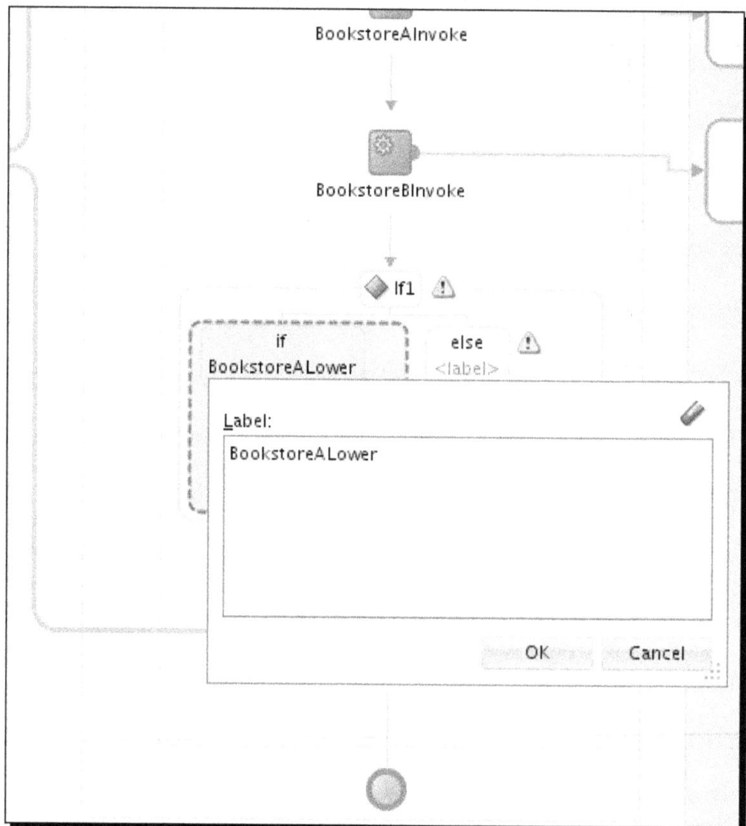

10. Then, we right-click on the new `<if>` activity and select **Edit**, as shown in the following screenshot. In the opened dialog box, we create a condition such that `BookstoreAResponse` stock quantity is lower than the `BookstoreBResponse` stock quantity. In this case, we select Bookstore A:

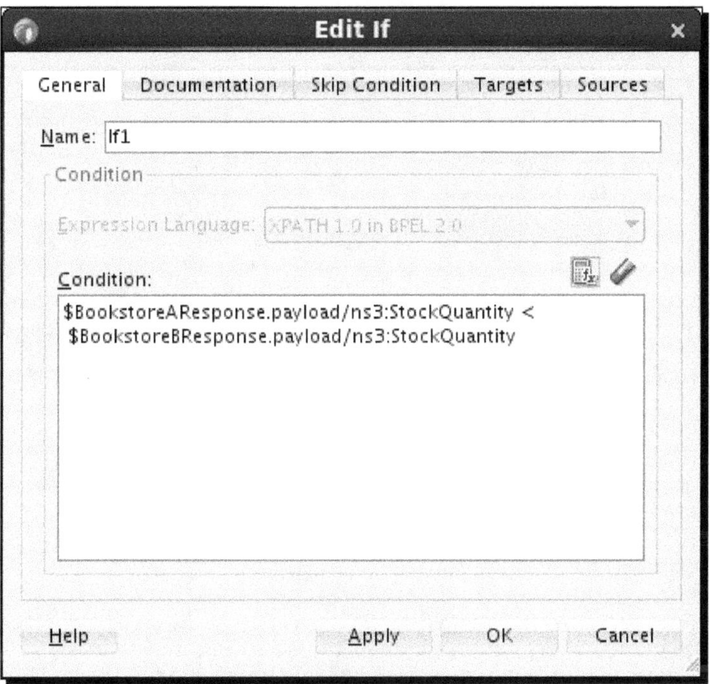

11. Otherwise, we select Bookstore B. In both cases, we add `<assign>` to set the appropriate response for the book warehousing BPEL process:

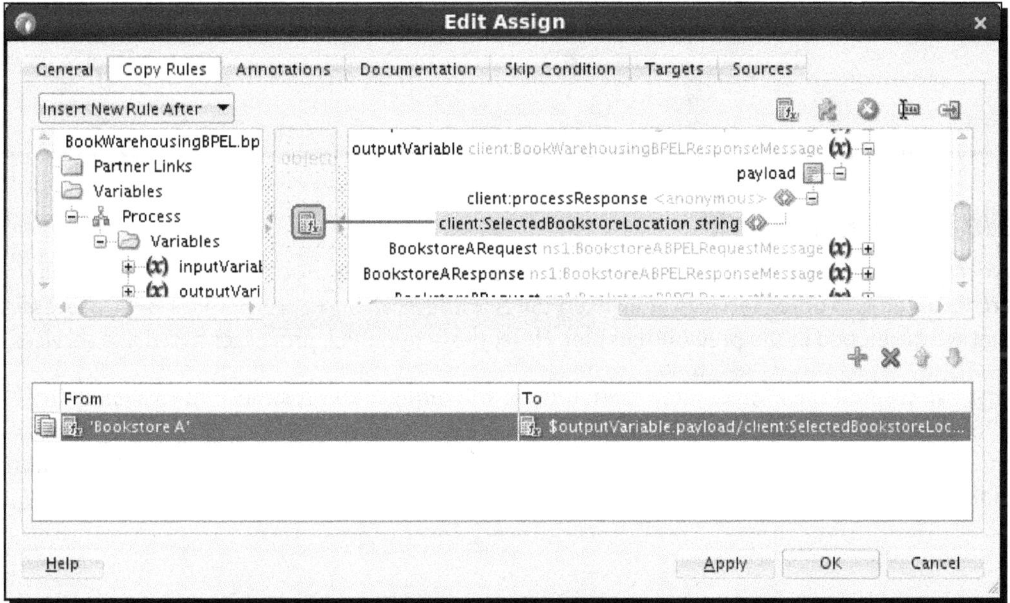

12. The final part of the BPEL process should look like the following screenshot:

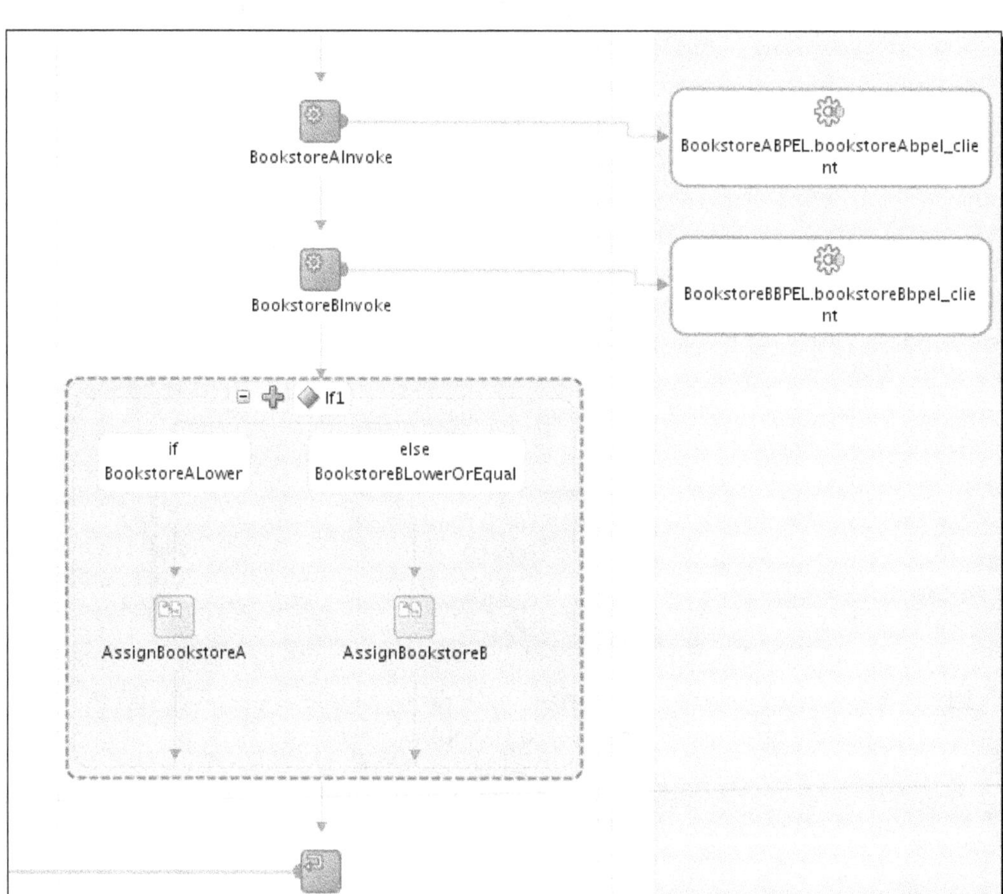

What just happened?

We implemented the process flow logic for the `BookWarehousingBPEL` process. It actually orchestrated two other services. It invoked the `BookstoreA` and `BookstoreB` BPEL processes that we developed in the previous chapter. Here, these two BPEL processes acted like services.

First, we created the XML schema elements for the request and response messages of the BPEL process. We created four variables: `BookstoreARequest`, `BookstoreAResponse`, `BookstoreBRequest`, and `BookstoreBResponse`. The BPEL code for variable declaration looks like the code shown in the following screenshot:

```
<variables>
  <!-- Reference to the message passed as input during initiation -->
  <variable name="inputVariable" messageType="client:BookWarehousingBPELRequestMessage"/>
  <!-- Reference to the message that will be returned to the requester-->
  <variable name="outputVariable" messageType="client:BookWarehousingBPELResponseMessage"/>
  <variable name="BookstoreARequest" messageType="ns2:BookstoreABPELRequestMessage"/>
  <variable name="BookstoreAResponse" messageType="ns2:BookstoreABPELResponseMessage"/>
  <variable name="BookstoreBRequest" messageType="ns1:BookstoreBBPELRequestMessage"/>
  <variable name="BookstoreBResponse" messageType="ns1:BookstoreBBPELResponseMessage"/>
</variables>
```

Then, we added the `<assign>` activity to prepare a request for both the bookstore BPEL processes. Then, we copied the `BookData` element from `inputVariable` to the `BookstoreARequest` and `BookstoreBRequest` variables. The following BPEL code has been generated:

```
<assign name="PrepareRequest">
  <copy>
    <from>$inputVariable.payload/client:BookData/client:BookISSN</from>
    <to>$BookstoreARequest.payload/ns3:BookISSN</to>
  </copy>
  <copy>
    <from>$inputVariable.payload/client:BookData/client:BookISSN</from>
    <to>$BookstoreBRequest.payload/ns3:BookISSN</to>
  </copy>
  <copy>
    <from>$inputVariable.payload/client:BookData/client:Title</from>
    <to>$BookstoreBRequest.payload/ns3:Title</to>
  </copy>
  <copy>
    <from>$inputVariable.payload/client:BookData/client:Edition</from>
    <to>$BookstoreBRequest.payload/ns3:Edition</to>
  </copy>
  <copy>
    <from>$inputVariable.payload/client:BookData/client:PublishingYear</from>
    <to>$BookstoreBRequest.payload/ns3:PublishingYear</to>
  </copy>
  <copy>
    <from>$inputVariable.payload/client:BookData/client:Title</from>
    <to>$BookstoreARequest.payload/ns3:Title</to>
  </copy>
  <copy>
    <from>$inputVariable.payload/client:BookData/client:Edition</from>
    <to>$BookstoreARequest.payload/ns3:Edition</to>
  </copy>
  <copy>
    <from>$inputVariable.payload/client:BookData/client:PublishingYear</from>
    <to>$BookstoreARequest.payload/ns3:PublishingYear</to>
  </copy>
</assign>
```

Next, we invoked both the bookstore BPEL services using the `<invoke>` activity. The BPEL source code reads like the following screenshot:

```
<invoke name="BookstoreAInvoke" bpelx:invokeAsDetail="no" partnerLink="BookstoreABPEL.bookstoreabpel_client"
        portType="ns2:BookstoreABPEL" operation="getBookData" inputVariable="BookstoreARequest"
        outputVariable="BookstoreAResponse"/>
<invoke name="BookstoreBInvoke" bpelx:invokeAsDetail="no" partnerLink="BookstoreBBPEL.bookstorebbpel_client"
        portType="ns1:BookstoreBBPEL" operation="getBookData" inputVariable="BookstoreBRequest"
        outputVariable="BookstoreBResponse"/>
```

Finally, we added the `<if>` activity to select the bookstore with the lowest stock quantity:

```
<if name="If1">
  <documentation>
    <![CDATA[BookstoreALower]]>
  </documentation>
  <condition>$BookstoreAResponse.payload/ns3:StockQuantity &lt;
             $BookstoreBResponse.payload/ns3:StockQuantity</condition>
  <assign name="AssignBookstoreA">
    <copy>
      <from>'Bookstore A'</from>
      <to>$outputVariable.payload/client:SelectedBookstoreLocation</to>
    </copy>
  </assign>
  <else>
    <documentation>
      <![CDATA[BookstoreBLowerOrEqual]]>
    </documentation>
    <assign name="AssignBookstoreB">
      <copy>
        <from>'Bookstore B'</from>
        <to>$outputVariable.payload/client:SelectedBookstoreLocation</to>
      </copy>
    </assign>
  </else>
</if>
```

With this, we have concluded the development of the book warehousing BPEL process and are ready to deploy and test it.

Deploying and testing the book warehousing BPEL process

We will deploy the project to the SOA Suite process server the same way we did in the previous chapter, by right-clicking on the project and selecting **Deploy**. Then, we will navigate through the options. As we redeploy the whole SOA composite, make sure the **Overwrite** option is selected. You should check if the compilation and the deployment have been successful.

Then, we will log in to the Enterprise Manager console, select the project bookstore, and click on the **Test** button. Be sure to select `bookwarehousingbpel_client` for the test. After entering the parameters, as shown in the following screenshot, we can click on the **Test Web Service** button to initiate the BPEL process, and we should receive an answer (Bookstore A or Bookstore B, depending on the data that we have entered).

Remember that our `BookWarehousingBPEL` process actually orchestrated two other services. It invoked the `BookstoreA` and `BookstoreB` BPEL processes. To verify this, we can launch the flow trace (click on the **Launch Flow Trace** button) in the Enterprise Manager console, and we will see that the two bookstore BPEL processes have been invoked, as shown:

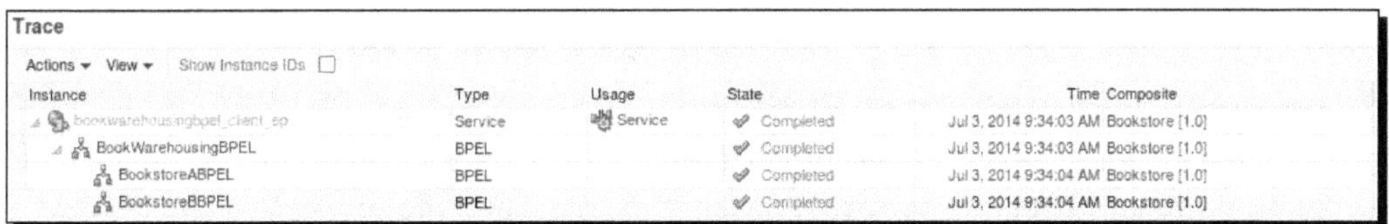

An even more interesting view is the flow view, which also shows that both bookstore services have been invoked. Click on `BookWarehousingBPEL` to open up the audit trail:

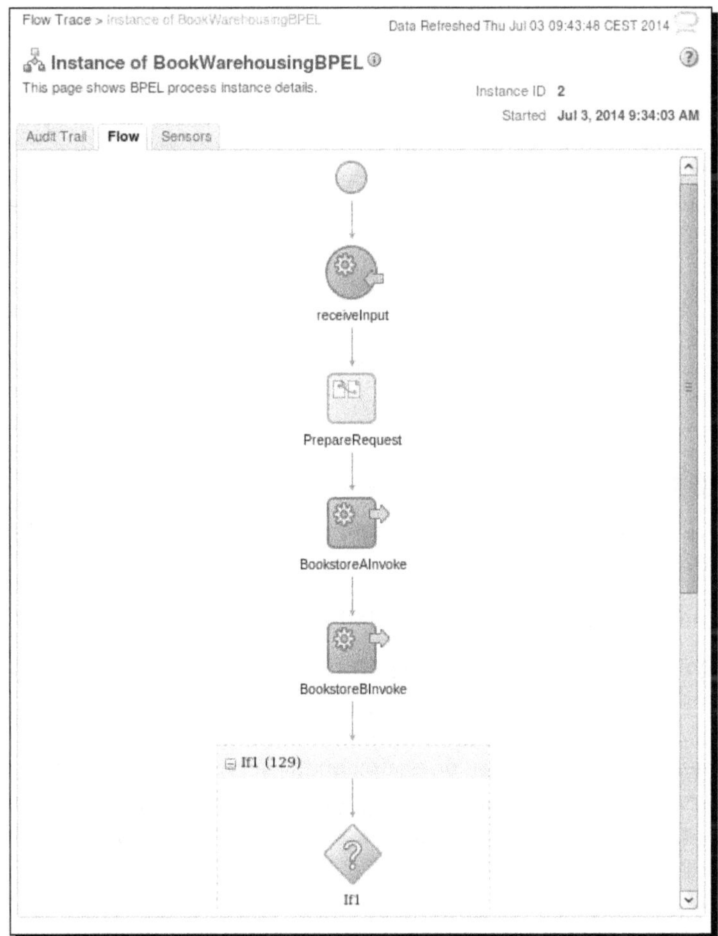

Understanding sequential invocation

Within the `<process>` element, a BPEL process will usually have the top-level `<sequence>` element. Within the sequence, the process will first wait for the incoming message to start the process. This wait is usually modeled with the `<receive>` construct. It could also be modeled with the `<pick>` activity, if we expect more than one incoming message. We will explain the `<pick>` activity in *Chapter 10, Events and Event Handlers*.

Then, the process will invoke the related services using the `<invoke>` construct. Such invocations can be done sequentially or in parallel. If we want to make them sequential, we simply write an `<invoke>` activity for each invocation, and the services will be invoked in that order. Finally, the process will return a response using `<reply>`. This is shown in the following code excerpt:

```
<process ...>
  ...
  <sequence>
    <!-- Wait for the incoming request to start the process -->
    <receive ... />
    <!-- Invoke a set of related services, one by one -->
    <invoke ... />
    <invoke ... />
    <invoke ... />
    ...
    <!-- Return the response -->
    <reply ... />
  </sequence>
</process>
```

A closer look at <invoke>

With `<invoke>`, the BPEL process invokes operations on other services. We have to specify the following attributes:

- `partnerLink`: This specifies which partner link will be used
- `portType`: This specifies the used port type
- `operation`: This specifies the name of the operation to invoke (`<invoke>`)

When the business process invokes an operation on the service, it sends a set of parameters. These parameters are modeled as input messages with services. To specify the input message for the invocation, we use the `inputVariable` attribute and specify a variable of the corresponding type.

If we invoke a synchronous request/response operation, it returns a result. This result is again a message, modeled as an output message. To store it in a variable, `<invoke>` provides another attribute, called `outputVariable`.

We can also specify a `name` attribute. We use the `name` attribute to provide names for activities.

The following code excerpt shows an example of the `<invoke>` activity. We specify that the BPEL process should invoke the synchronous operation `getBookData` on port type `ns2:bookstoreABPEL` using the `BookstoreABPEL` partner link, providing the input from the `BookstoreARequest` variable and storing the output in the `BookstoreAResponse` variable, as shown in the following screenshot:

```
<invoke name="BookstoreAInvoke" bpelx:invokeAsDetail="no"
        partnerLink="BookstoreABPEL.bookstoreabpel_client"
        portType="ns2:BookstoreABPEL" operation="getBookData"
        inputVariable="BookstoreARequest"
        outputVariable="BookstoreAResponse"/>
```

Understanding partner links

When invoking services, we have often mentioned **partner links**. Partner links denote all the interactions that a BPEL process has with the external services. There are two possibilities:

- The BPEL process invokes operations on other services.
- The BPEL process receives invocations from clients. One of the clients is the user of the BPEL process, who makes the initial invocation. Other clients are services, for example, those that have been invoked by the BPEL process, but may return replies.

Links to all the parties that BPEL interacts with are called **partner links**. Partner links can be links to services that are invoked by the BPEL process. These are sometimes called **invoked partner links**. Partner links can also be links to clients, and can invoke the BPEL process. Such partner links are sometimes called **client partner links**. Note that each BPEL process has at least one client partner link, because there has to be a client that first invokes the BPEL process. Usually, a BPEL process will also have several invoked partner links because it will most likely invoke several services.

In our case, the `BookWarehousingBPEL` process has one client partner link and two invoked partner links, `BookstoreABPEL` and `BookstoreBBPEL`. You can observe this on the SOA composite design view and on the BPEL process itself, where the client partner links are located on the left-hand side, while the invoked partner links are located on the right-hand side of the design view.

Partner link types

Describing situations where the service is invoked by the process and vice versa requires selecting a certain perspective. We can select the process perspective and describe the process as requiring `portTypeA` on the service and providing `portTypeB` to the service. Alternatively, we select the service perspective and describe the service as offering `portTypeA` to the BPEL process and requiring `portTypeB` from the process.

Partner link types allow us to model such relationships as a third party. We are not required to take a certain perspective; we just define roles. A partner link type must have at least one role and can have at most two roles. The latter is the usual case. For each role, we must specify a `portType` that is used for interaction.

Partner link types are defined in the WSDLs. If we take a closer look at the `BookWarehousingBPEL.wsdl` file, we can see the following partner link type definition:

```
<!-- ~~~~~~~~~~~~~~~~~~~~~~~~~~~~~~~~~~~~~~~~~~~~~~~~~~~~~~~~~~~~~~~~~~
PARTNER LINK TYPE DEFINITION
~~~~~~~~~~~~~~~~~~~~~~~~~~~~~~~~~~~~~~~~~~~~~~~~~~~~~~~~~~~~~~~~~~~~~~
<plnk:partnerLinkType name="BookWarehousingBPEL">
        <plnk:role name="BookWarehousingBPELProvider"
                   portType="client:BookWarehousingBPEL"/>
</plnk:partnerLinkType>
```

If we specify only one role, we express the willingness to interact with the service, but do not place any additional requirements on the service. Sometimes, existing services will not define a partner link type. Then, we can wrap the WSDL of the service and define partner link types ourselves.

Now that we have become familiar with the partner link types and know that they belong to WSDL, it is time to go back to the BPEL process definition, more specifically to the partner links.

Defining partner links

Partner links are concrete references to services that a BPEL business process interacts with. They are specified near the beginning of the BPEL process definition document, just after the `<process>` tag. Several `<partnerLink>` definitions are nested within the `<partnerLinks>` element:

```
<process ...>
  <partnerLinks>
    <partnerLink ... />
```

```
    <partnerLink ... />
    ...
  </partnerLinks>
  <sequence>
    ...
  </sequence>
</process>
```

For each partner link, we have to specify the following:

- `name`: This serves as a reference for interactions via that partner link.
- `partnerLinkType`: This defines the type of the partner link.
- `myRole`: This indicates the role of the BPEL process itself.
- `partnerRole`: This indicates the role of the partner.
- `initializePartnerRole`: This indicates whether or not the BPEL engine should initialize the partner link's partner role value. This is an optional attribute and should only be used with partner links that specify the partner role.

We define both roles (`myRole` and `partnerRole`) only if the `partnerLinkType` specifies two roles. If the `partnerLinkType` specifies only one role, the `partnerLink` also has to specify only one role—we omit the one that is not needed.

Let's go back to our example, where we have defined the `BookstoreABPEL` partner link type. To define a partner link, we need to specify the partner roles, because it is a synchronous relation. The definition is shown in the following code excerpt:

```
<partnerLinks>
  ...

  <partnerLink name="BookstoreABPEL.bookstoreAbpel_client"
               partnerLinkType="ns1:BookstoreABPEL"
               partnerRole="BookstoreABPELProvider"/>
</partnerLinks>
```

With this, we have concluded the discussion on partner links and partner link types. We will continue with the parallel service invocation.

Parallel service invocation

BPEL also supports parallel service invocation. In our example, we have invoked Bookstore A and Bookstore B sequentially. This way, we need to wait for the response from the first service and then for the response from the second service. If these services take longer to execute, the response times will be added together. If we invoke both services in parallel, we only need to wait for the duration of the longer-lasting call, as shown in the following screenshot:

BPEL has several possibilities for parallel flows, which will be described in detail in *Chapter 8, Dynamic Parallel Invocations*. Here, we present the basic parallel service invocation using the `<flow>` activity.

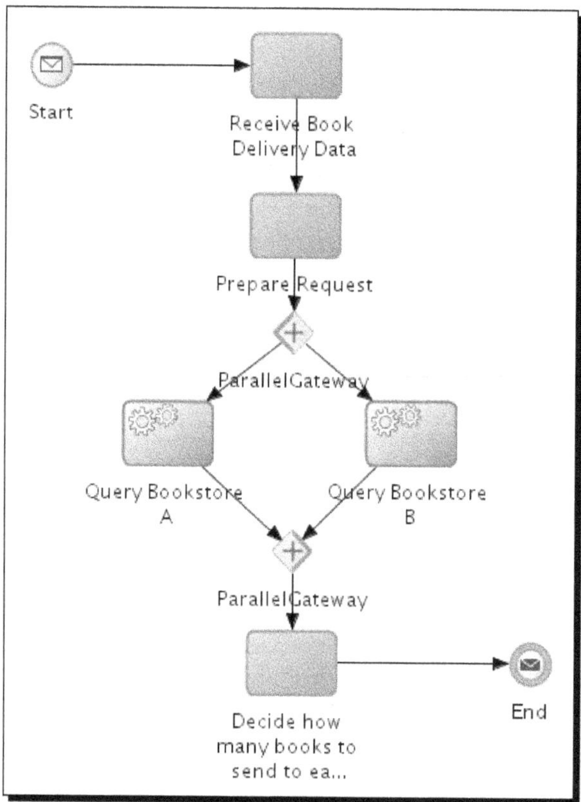

To invoke services in parallel, or to perform any other activities in parallel, we can use the `<flow>` activity. Within the `<flow>` activity, we can nest an arbitrary number of flows, and all will execute in parallel. Let's try and modify our example so that Bookstore A and B will be invoked in parallel.

Time for action – developing parallel flows

Let's now modify the `BookWarehousingBPEL` process so that the `BookstoreA` and `BookstoreB` services will be invoked in parallel. We should do the following:

1. To invoke `BookstoreA` and `BookstoreB` services in parallel, we need to add the **Flow** structured activity to the process flow just before the first invocation, as shown in the following screenshot:

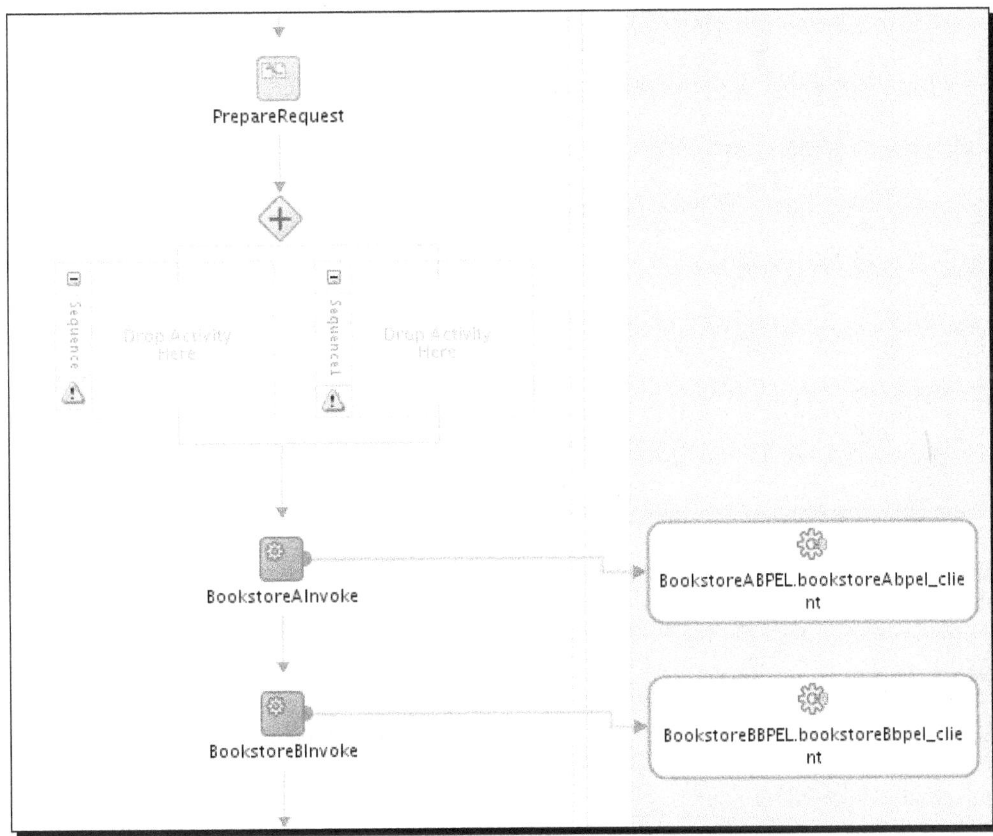

2. We can see that two parallel branches have been created. We simply drag-and-drop both the invoke activities into the parallel branches:

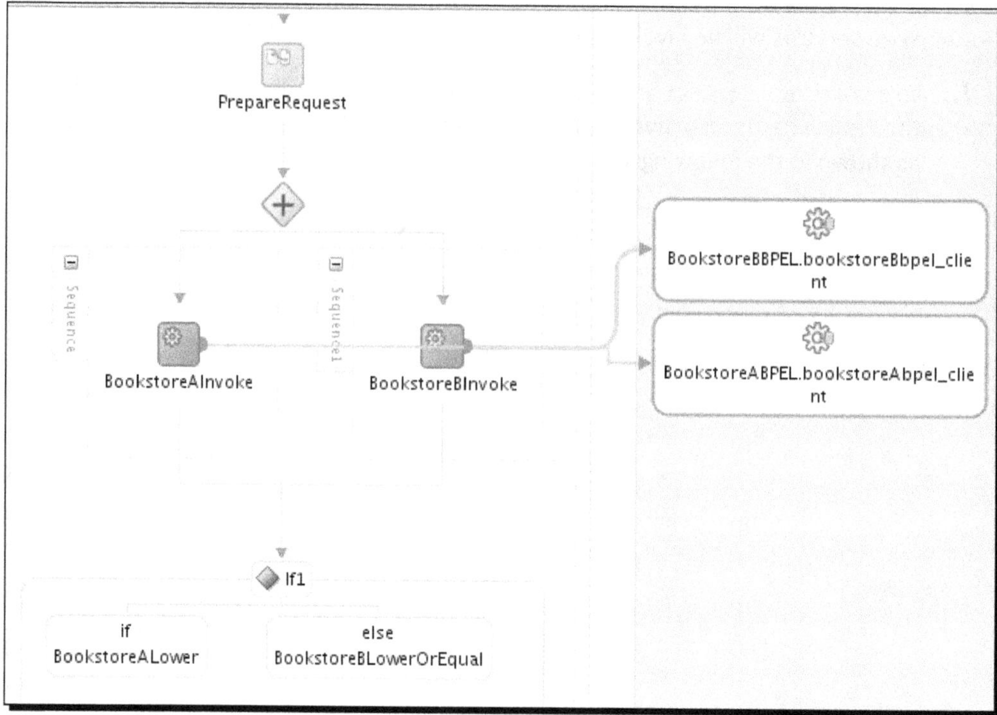

That's all! We can create more parallel branches if we need to by clicking on the **Add Sequence** icon.

What just happened?

We have modified the `BookWarehousingBPEL` process so that the `BookstoreA` and `BookstoreB` `<invoke>` activities are executed in parallel. A corresponding `<flow>`activity has been created in the BPEL source code. Within the `<flow>` activity, both `<invoke>` activities are nested. Please notice that each `<invoke>` activity is placed within its own `<sequence>` activity. This would make sense if we would require more than one activity in each parallel branch. The BPEL source code looks like the one shown in the following screenshot:

```
<flow name="Flow1">
  <sequence name="Sequence">
    <invoke name="BookstoreAInvoke" bpelx:invokeAsDetail="no" partnerLink="BookstoreABPEL.bookstoreabpel_client"
            portType="ns2:BookstoreABPEL" operation="getBookData" inputVariable="BookstoreARequest"
            outputVariable="BookstoreAResponse"/>
  </sequence>
  <sequence name="Sequence1">
    <invoke name="BookstoreBInvoke" bpelx:invokeAsDetail="no" partnerLink="BookstoreBBPEL.bookstorebbpel_client"
            portType="ns1:BookstoreBBPEL" operation="getBookData" inputVariable="BookstoreBRequest"
            outputVariable="BookstoreBResponse"/>
  </sequence>
</flow>
```

Deploying and testing the parallel invocation

We will deploy the project to the SOA Suite process server the same way we did in the previous sample. Then, we will log in to the Enterprise Manager console, select the project **Bookstore**, and click on the **Test Web Service** button.

To observe that the services have been invoked in parallel, we can launch the flow trace (click on the **Launch Flow Trace** button) in the Enterprise Manager console, click on the book warehousing BPEL processes and activate the flow view, which shows that both bookstore services have been invoked in parallel.

Understanding a parallel flow

To invoke services concurrently, we can use the `<flow>` construct. In the following example, the three `<invoke>` operations will perform concurrently:

```
<process ...>
  ...
  <sequence>
    <!-- Wait for the incoming request to start the process -->
    <receive ... />

    <!-- Invoke a set of related services, concurrently -->
    <flow>
      <invoke ... />
      <invoke ... />
      <invoke ... />
    </flow>
    ...
    <!-- Return the response -->
    <reply ... />
  </sequence>
</process>
```

We can also combine and nest the <sequence> and <flow> constructs that allow us to define several sequences that execute concurrently. In the following example, we have defined two sequences, one that consists of three invocations, and one with two invocations. Both sequences will execute concurrently:

```
<process ...>
  ...
  <sequence>
    <!-- Wait for the incoming request to start the process -->
    <receive ... />

    <!-- Invoke two sequences concurrently -->
    <flow>
      <!-- The three invokes below execute sequentially -->
      <sequence>
        <invoke ... />
        <invoke ... />
        <invoke ... />
      </sequence>
      <!-- The two invokes below execute sequentially -->
      <sequence>
        <invoke ... />
        <invoke ... />
      </sequence>
    </flow>
    ...
    <!-- Return the response -->
    <reply ... />
  </sequence>
</process>
```

We can use other activities as well within the <flow> activity to achieve parallel execution. With this, we have concluded our discussion on the parallel invocation.

Pop quiz – service invocation

Q1. Which activity is used to invoke services from BPEL processes?

1. <receive>
2. <invoke>
3. <sequence>

4. `<flow>`
5. `<process>`
6. `<reply>`

Q2. Which parameters do we need to specify for the `<invoke>` activity?

1. `endpointURL`
2. `partnerLink`
3. `operationName`
4. `operation`
5. `portType`
6. `portTypeLink`

Q3. In which file do we declare partner link types?

Q4. Which activity is used to execute service invocation and other BPEL activities in parallel?

1. `<receive>`
2. `<invoke>`
3. `<sequence>`
4. `<flow>`
5. `<process>`
6. `<reply>`

Summary

In this chapter, we learned how to invoke services and orchestrate services. We explained the primary mission of BPEL—service orchestration. It follows the concept of programming-in-the-large. We have developed a BPEL process that has invoked two services and orchestrated them. We have become familiar with the `<invoke>` activity and understood the service invocation's background, particularly partner links and partner link types.

We also learned that from BPEL, it is very easy to invoke services in parallel. To achieve this, we use the `<flow>` activity. Within `<flow>`, we cannot only nest several `<invoke>` activities but also other BPEL activities.

Now, we are ready to learn about variables and data manipulation, which we will do in the next chapter.

3

Variables, Data Manipulation, and Expressions

A very important part of each BPEL process is the orchestration of services (partner links) through the operation invocations. With each operation invocation, messages are exchanged. When a BPEL process invokes an operation on the external service and when it receives the result, we often want to store the messages temporarily, while the BPEL process is executing. The same holds true for other data that is related to the process state. This is where we need to use variables.

BPEL supports variables like any other programming language. It allows data manipulation in different ways, as we will see in this chapter. In contrast to many other programming languages, variables in BPEL are stored in XML. This means that manipulating variables in BPEL requires us to be familiar with XML and XML schemas.

In this chapter, we will learn how to declare and use variables, how to store, assign, copy, and manipulate data within variables, which variable types are supported, and other interesting aspects about variables. We will also learn that variable declaration and manipulation in BPEL is closely related to XML schema and WSDL.

In this chapter, we will take a closer look at the variable declarations, **Web Services Description Language** (**WSDL**), assign activity, and other means for variable data manipulation. In this chapter, we shall:

- Understand BPEL variables
- Know how to declare variables and be familiar with variable types

- Be familiar with data manipulation and the `<assign>` activity
- Understand different possibilities with `<assign>`
- Understand the XPath expressions and know how to access variables from expressions
- Know how to validate variables
- Understand how and when to use XSLT transformations

So, let's get started...

Variables in BPEL

Variables are an essential part of each and every programming language. In BPEL, variables are used to store the data that the process wishes to retain during the execution of each process instance. For example, when a BPEL process invokes an operation on an external service (partner link), this operation may require input parameters. An operation might also return a result as an output parameter. We will use variables to store the result and to prepare the input parameters for the operation. We can also use variables to store other data, required for the process instance execution, even if it is never sent to a service.

Often, a service will require a different schema (structure) of the data to the one used in our BPEL process. Therefore, we will need to map the data to a schema expected by the service. The same holds true for the result. We will use XSLT transformations to achieve this.

As BPEL and web services are based on XML, variables in BPEL are also designed to store XML directly. This means dealing with XML, therefore a good understanding of XML and XML Schema is a prerequisite for successful BPEL development. We will not go into the details of XML and XML Schema in this book; to find out more about these, please refer to the related literature, such as `http://www.w3.org/XML/` and `http://www.w3schools.com/xml/` for XML, and `http://www.w3.org/XML/Schema` and `http://www.w3schools.com/schema/` for XML Schema.

Declaring variables

In BPEL, we have to declare each variable before we use it. We can declare variables globally at the beginning of a BPEL process declaration document. We can also declare local (scoped) variables within scopes. We will discuss scopes in *Chapter 7, Working with Scopes*. In this chapter, we will focus only on globally declared variables.

We declare variables within the `<variables>` activity, which is placed after the `<partnerLinks>` declarations. Within `<variables>`, we declare each variable using the `<variable>` declaration. The following example shows the structure of a BPEL process that uses variables:

```
<process ...>

  <partnerLinks>
  ...
  </partnerLinks>

  <variables>
  <variable ... />
  <variable ... />
    ...
  </variables>

  <sequence>
    ...
  </sequence>
</process>
```

Variable types

We already know that variables store XML data. To achieve type safety, in other words, to be sure that we store the correct structure in each variable, variables in BPEL are typed. When we declare a variable, we have to provide a type.

Variables can store XML Schema simple types, XML Schema elements, or WSDL messages. To declare a variable, we must specify the variable name and type. To specify the type, we have the following three options:

- `type`: This is a variable that stores an XML Schema simple type
- `element`: This is a variable that stores an XML Schema element
- `messageType`: This is a variable that stores a WSDL message

To declare variables of simple types, we use XML Schema simple types. We can use the built-in simple types or declare our own. XML Schema provides a wide selection of well-known simple types, such as `boolean`, `string`, `byte`, `decimal`, `double`, `float`, `int`, `integer`, `long`, `short`, `date`, `dateTime`, `duration`, `time`; and some less common ones, such as `negativeInteger`, `nonNegativeInteger`, `nonPositiveInteger`, `positiveInteger`, `unsignedShort`, `unsignedLong`, `unsignedInt`, `normalizedString`, `anyUR`, `token`, and so on. For a complete list of XML Schema data types, please refer to the specification: `http://www.w3.org/TR/xmlschema11-2/`.

To declare variables that store complex XML structures, we can use any XML element from the XML Schema. This is useful to store XML documents or their fragments.

To store the request for service invocations and responses from services, we will use variables that can store the whole messages accepted or returned from services. For this, we will declare the `messageType` variables. The type of these variables is specified by the WSDL messages.

Variables in BookWarehousingBPEL

We have used variables in the previous chapters. These variables have been created on-the-fly, as we could not invoke services without them. Therefore, we will have a quick look at the existing variables in the `BookWarehousingBPEL` process.

Time for action – review of existing variables

To view existing variables in `BookWarehousingBPEL`, we will do the following:

1. We will open the BPEL process and click on the **(x)** icon:

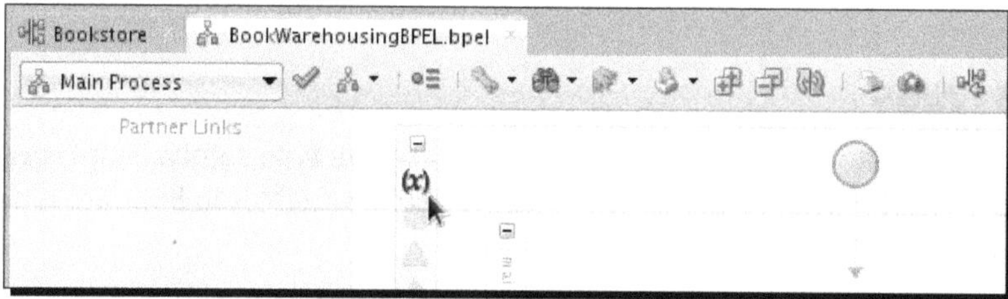

2. This will open a dialog, where we can see that we have six variables, all of them as `MessageType`:

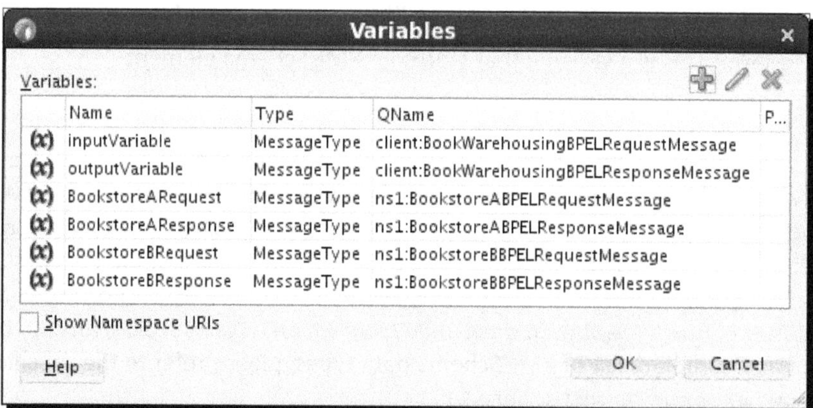

Variables
Variables:
Name
Type
QName
P...
inputVariable MessageType client:BookWarehousingBPELRequestMessage
outputVariable MessageType client:BookWarehousingBPELResponseMessage
BookstoreARequest MessageType ns1:BookstoreABPELRequestMessage
BookstoreAResponse MessageType ns1:BookstoreABPELResponseMessage
BookstoreBRequest MessageType ns1:BookstoreBBPELRequestMessage
BookstoreBResponse MessageType ns1:BookstoreBBPELResponseMessage
Show Namespace URIs
Help
OK
Cancel

What just happened?

We have seen that in the `BookWarehousingBPEL` process we already have six variables. All of them are `MessageType`. The `inputVariable` activity holds the message payload required for the process input. The `outputVariable` activity holds the response that the process will return. The `BookstoreARequest` activity holds the request message for the **BookstoreA** partner link, and the `BookstoreAResponse` activity holds the response message for the same partner link. The `BookstoreBRequest` and `BookstoreBResponse` activities hold the messages for the **BookstoreB** partner link, respectively.

Declaring XML type variables

We will first learn how to declare XML type variables. We will declare two new XML type variables in the `BookWarehousingBPEL` process. First, we will declare a `BookstoreLocationWithLowestStockQuantity` variable. This variable will be of the type `string`. We will use this variable to store the name of the bookstore that has the lowest stock quantity of the selected book.

Another simple type variable will be `LowestQuantity`, which will be of the type `int`. We will use this variable to store the lowest book quantity in any of the bookstores.

Time for action – creating XML type variables

Let's now create the described variables:

1. To create a new variable, we will click on the big + icon in the **Variables** dialog window. The **Create Variable** dialog window will open.

   The declaration is rather simple. We have to provide the name and select the variable type. We have three choices: **Type**, **Message Type**, and **Element**. We select **Type** for the simple XML Schema types. We select **Message Type** for the WSDL `MessageTypes`. We select **Element** for XML element variables.

2. Let's declare the `BookstoreLocationWithLowestStockQuantity` variable. This variable will be of the type `string`. We will enter the variable **Name**, select **Type** for the type, and use the magnifier glass icon to select a `string` from **XML Schema Simple Types**:

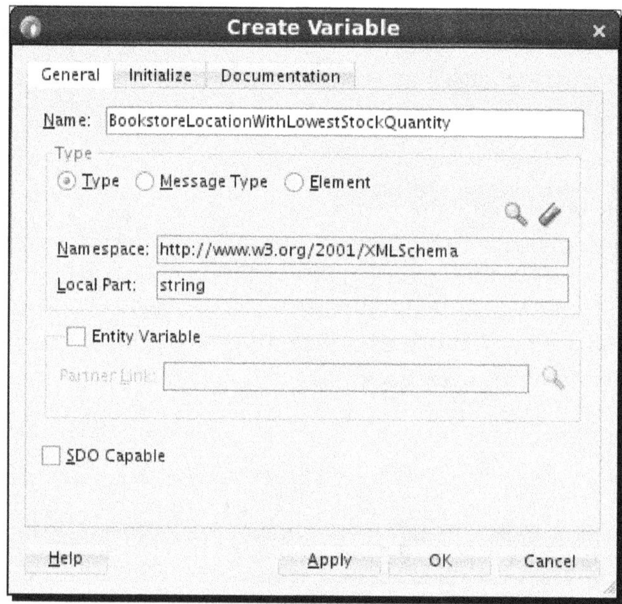

3. We could initialize the variable with the default value. This can be achieved in the **Initialize** tab. We could also enter the detailed description of the variable and its purpose. This can be done in the **Documentation** tab. We will not use these two tabs in this example.

Have a go hero – create the LowestQuantity variable

You can create the `LowestQuantity` variable of the type `int` yourself. We will use this variable to store the lowest book quantity in any of the bookstores. You can proceed the same way as in the previous example.

What just happened?

We have created two new variables, the `BookstoreLocationWithLowestStockQuantity` variable and the `LowestQuantity` variable. Let's look into the source code, where we should see the two new variables created, in addition to the six existing variables. From the source code tab, you can also see the BPEL syntax, if you wish to write the code directly:

```
<variables>
  <!-- Reference to the message passed as input during initiation -->
  <variable name="inputVariable" messageType="client:BookWarehousingBPELRequestMessage"/>

  <!-- Reference to the message that will be returned to the requester-->
  <variable name="outputVariable" messageType="client:BookWarehousingBPELResponseMessage"/>
  <variable name="BookstoreARequest"
           messageType="ns1:BookstoreABPELRequestMessage"/>
  <variable name="BookstoreAResponse"
           messageType="ns1:BookstoreABPELResponseMessage"/>
  <variable name="BookstoreBRequest"
           messageType="ns1:BookstoreBBPELRequestMessage"/>
  <variable name="BookstoreBResponse"
           messageType="ns1:BookstoreBBPELResponseMessage"/>
  <variable name="BookstoreLocationWithLowestStockQuantity"
           type="xsd:string"/>
  <variable name="LowestQuantity" type="xsd:int"/>
</variables>
```

Declaring XML element variables

Let's now declare an XML element variable. We will create a `BookDataVariable` variable. This variable will store the data about the book. It will hold the XML element called `BookData`.

To understand better what we will store in this variable, let's have a look at the corresponding schema, which we have defined in *Chapter 2, Service Invocation*:

```
<?xml version="1.0" encoding="UTF-8"?>
<schema attributeFormDefault="unqualified"
        elementFormDefault="qualified"
        targetNamespace="http://packtpub.com/Bookstore/BookWarehousingBPEL"
        xmlns="http://www.w3.org/2001/XMLSchema">
        <element name="process">
                <complexType>
                        <sequence>
                            <element name="BookData">
                                    <complexType>
                                            <sequence>
                                                    <element name="BookISSN" type="string"/>
                                                    <element name="Title" type="string"/>
                                                    <element name="Edition" type="string"/>
                                                    <element name="PublishingYear" type="date"/>
                                            </sequence>
                                    </complexType>
                            </element>
                            <element name="PurchasedQuantity" type="int"/>
                        </sequence>
                </complexType>
        </element>
        <element name="processResponse">
                <complexType>
                        <sequence>
                                <element name="SelectedBookstoreLocation" type="string"/>
                        </sequence>
                </complexType>
        </element>
</schema>
```

We can see the `BookData` element defined within the `BookWarehousingBPEL.xsd` XML Schema.

Time for action – creating XML element variables

Let's now create the `BookDataVariable` variable:

1. Another way to create a new variable is to open the **Structure** view on the lower left-hand side window and right-click on **Variables**. A menu will appear where we should select **Create Variable**, as shown in the following screenshot:

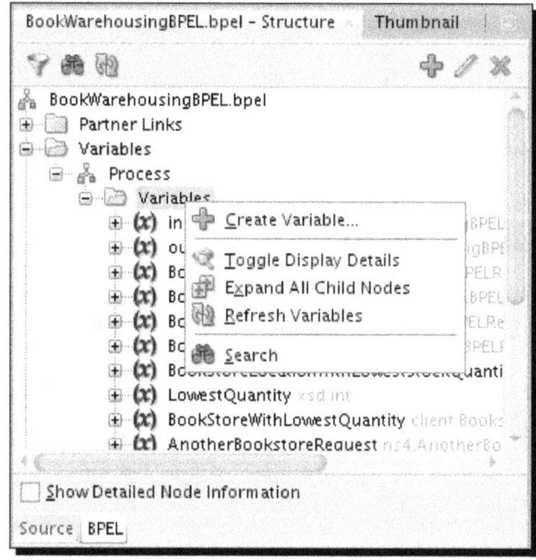

2. The **Create Variable** dialog window will open. We will type `BookDataVariable` as the **Name**. We select **Element** for the XML element variables. Then, we use the magnifier glass icon to select `BookData` from `Project Schema Files/BookstoreBPEL.xsd`:

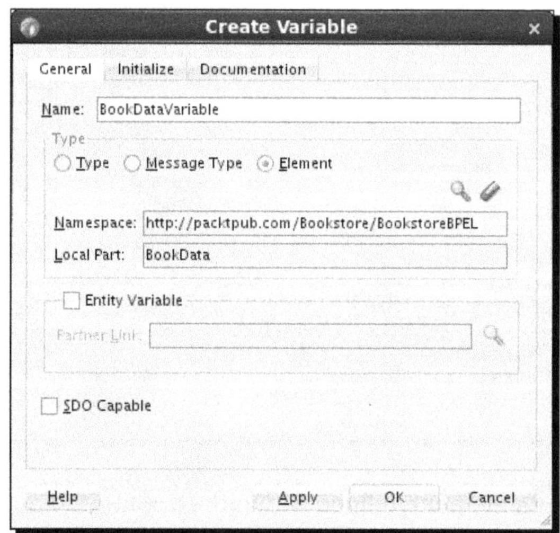

What just happened?

We have created the XML element type variable `BookDataVariable`, which is of the type `BookData`. The BPEL source code looks like the following:

```
<variable name="BookDataVariable" element="ns3:BookData"/>
```

Declaring a WSDL message type variable

Let's now declare a WSDL message type variable. We will create a `BookStoreWithLowestQuantity` variable, where we will store the whole WSDL message response payload. We will need to store the response message from the `BookStoreA` / `BookStoreB` partner link, which holds the data about the stock quantity and book ISSN. We therefore need the message, which will store the `BookDataResponse` from the **BookStoreBPEL.xsd** XML Schema (created in *Chapter 1, Hello BPEL*):

```
<element name="BookDataResponse">
        <complexType>
                <sequence>
                        <element name="BookISSN" type="string"/>
                        <element name="StockQuantity" type="int"/>
                </sequence>
        </complexType>
</element>
```

We can find the message definition in the corresponding `BookstoreABPEL.wsdl` (or in the `BookstoreBBPEL.wsdl`, but we will use `Bookstore A` here):

```
<wsdl:message name="BookstoreABPELResponseMessage">
        <wsdl:part name="payload" element="client:BookDataResponse"/>
</wsdl:message>
```

Time for action – creating a message type variable

Let's now create the `BookStoreWithLowestQuantity` variable:

1. We should open the **Create Variable** dialog window by clicking on the big **+** icon in the **Variables** dialog window or by selecting **Create Variable** from the context menu in the **Structure** window.

2. We should enter the `BookStoreWithLowestQuantity` variable **name** and select a message type. Then, we use the magnifier glass icon to select `BookstoreABPELResponseMessage` from `Message Types/Project WSDL Files/BookstoreABPEL.wsdl`:

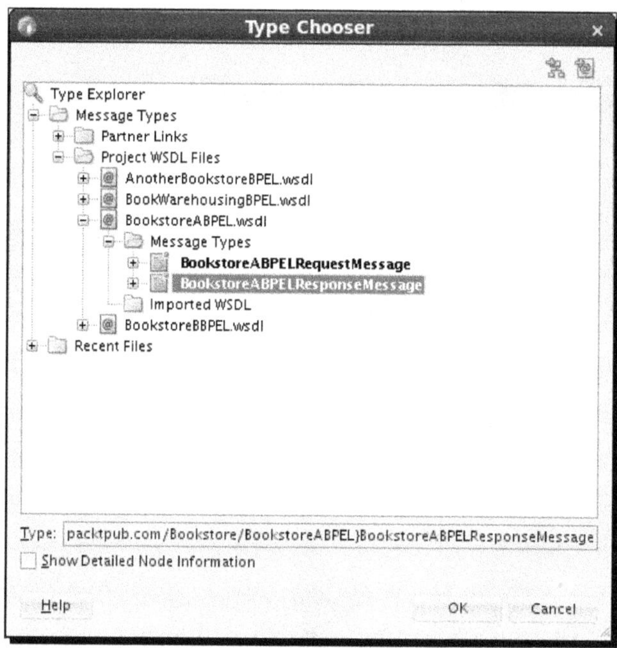

3. After clicking on **OK**, we should see the following window:

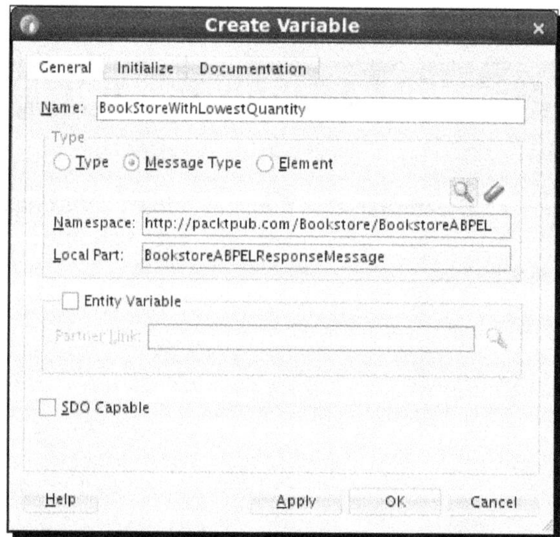

What just happened?

We have successfully created a new variable. Looking into the source code reveals the following code:

```
<variable name="BookStoreWithLowestQuantity"
          messageType="ns2:BookstoreABPELResponseMessage"/>
```

With this, we have concluded our discussion on variable declarations. In the next section, we will become familiar with assignments.

Data manipulation and assignments

In this section, we will get familiar with data manipulation and data copying between variables. To copy data between variables, BPEL provides the <assign> activity. Within it, we can perform one or more <copy> commands. For each <copy> command, we have to specify the source (<from>) and the destination (<to>). The following listing presents the syntax of the <assign> activity:

```
<assign>
  <copy>
    <from ... />
    <to ... />
  </copy>
  <copy>
    <from ... />
    <to ... />
  </copy>
  ...
</assign>
```

There are several choices for the <from> and <to> clauses. To copy values from one variable to the other, we have to specify the variable attribute in the <from> and <to> elements. The following example shows how to copy the BookstoreAResponse variable to the BookStoreWithLowestQuantity variable:

```
<assign>
  <copy>
    <from variable="BookstoreAResponse" />
    <to variable="BookStoreWithLowestQuantity" />
  </copy>
</assign>
```

This copy can be performed only if both variables are of the same type, as in our example. The copy operation can also be performed if the source type is a subtype of the destination type.

Time for action – copying variables

Let's implement the copy between the `BookstoreAResponse` variable and the `BookStoreWithLowestQuantity` variable. To do this, we will do the following:

1. Open the **BookWarehousingBPEL.bpel** window.
2. Scroll to the `<if>` activity and locate the **ifBookstoreALower** branch.
3. Drag-and-drop the **Assign** activity from the right-hand side **BPEL Constructs / Basic Activities** toolbar and place it after the existing `AssignBookstoreA` assignment.
4. Double-click on the assign activity and the **Edit Assign** window will appear. Here you need to connect the `BookstoreAResponse` variable from the left-hand side with the `BookStoreWithLowestQuantity` variable on the right-hand side of the dialog window:

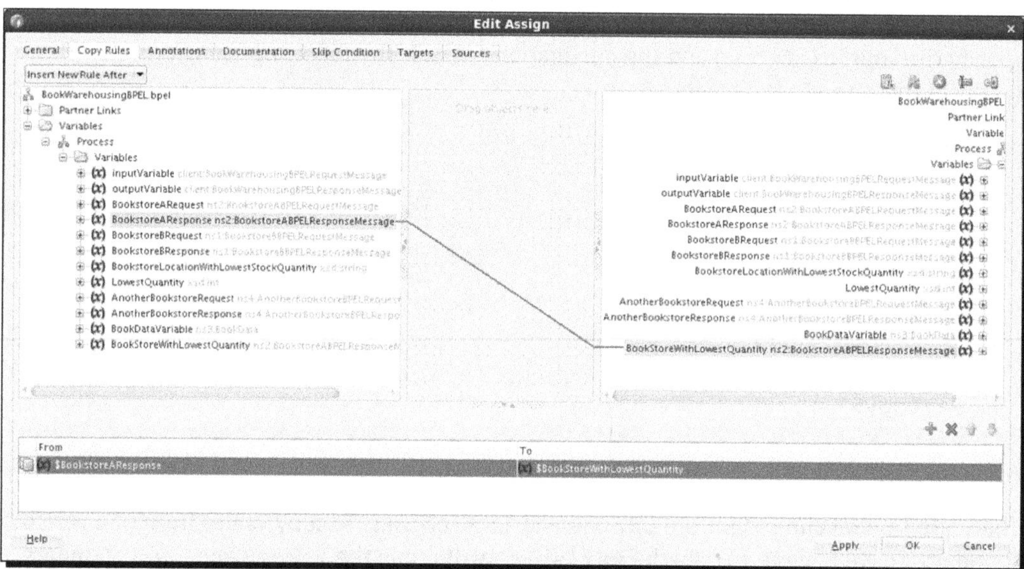

5. Finally, switch to the **General** tab and rename the assign activity name to `AssignBookStoreWithLowestQuantity`.

What just happened?

We have added the assign activity to copy the message type `BookstoreAResponse` variable to the `BookStoreWithLowestQuantity` variable. This is possible because both variables are of the same message type from the same XML namespace.

The following source code has been generated:

```
<assign name="AssignBookStoreWithLowestQuantity">
  <copy>
    <from variable="BookstoreAResponse"/>
    <to variable="BookStoreWithLowestQuantity"/>
  </copy>
</assign>
```

Copying the whole variable is not always necessary. Sometimes, we would prefer to copy just parts of the variable payload. This is where we need **expressions**.

Expressions

Expressions allow us to access parts of the variables. In the `<assign>` activities, we can use expressions to copy parts of variables or specific elements. We specify the expressions within the `<from>` and `<to>` elements. Expressions are written in the selected expression language; the default is XPath 1.0. The XPath language allows us to address XML in a similar way that we address files and folders in the filesystem. For detailed information on XPath, please refer to `http://www.w3.org/TR/xpath/`.

We access BPEL variables in XPath using the `$` operator. This is particularly useful in the `<copy>` assignments, where we would like to access specific nested elements.

To write the copy assignment from the previous example with expression, we can use the `$` operator to access the variable instead of the `variable` attribute. The code would look as follows:

```
<assign>
  <copy>
    <from>$BookstoreAResponse<from/>
    <to>$BookStoreWithLowestQuantity<to/>
  </copy>
</assign>
```

Copying variable parts

To learn how to copy variable parts, we will look at the three types of variables (variables can be of a `messageType`, `element`, or `type`). Let's first look at the `messageType` variables.

We can access variable parts from expressions using XPath in the following way:

```
$variableName.messagePart/ns:node/ns:node...
```

For example, if we would like to access the `Title` from the `BookstoreARequest` variable, we would need to write:

```
$BookstoreARequest.payload/ns2:Title
```

If the variable contains an XML element, then we would navigate through it using the variable name and node steps (without the part, because elements do not contain parts, whereas WSDL messages, on the other hand, do). The same holds true for variables using XML types.

We can access such variables from XPath in the following way:

```
$variableName/ns:node/ns:node...
```

Time for action – copying variable parts

Let's now copy the `BookstoreBResponse` variable to the `BookStoreWithLowestQuantity` variable. Because the `BookstoreBResponse` variable is of a different message type than the `BookStoreWithLowestQuantity` variable, we cannot copy variables directly.

However, both message variables use the same XML element, namely `BookDataResponse` as `payload`. Therefore, we can copy the payloads of both variables:

1. Open the **BookWarehousingBPEL.bpel** window.
2. Scroll to the `<if>` activity and locate the **elseifBookstoreBLowerOrEqual** branch.
3. Drag-and-drop the **Assign** activity from the right-hand side **BPEL Constructs / Basic Activities** toolbar and place it after the existing `AssignBookstoreB` assign.
4. Double-click on the assign activity and the **Edit Assign** window will appear. Here you need to open the `BookstoreBResponse` variable (by clicking on the plus sign in front of it). You also need to open the `BookStoreWithLowestQuantity` variable. Then, you need to connect `payload` from the left-hand side with `payload` on the right-hand side of the dialog window:

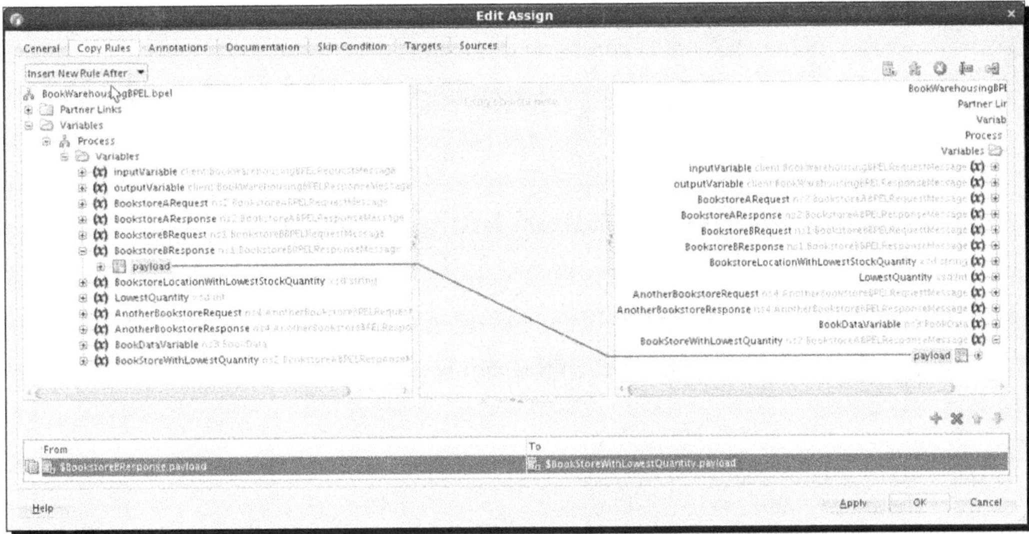

5. Finally, switch to the **General** tab and rename the assign activity name to `AssignBookStoreWithLowestQuantity`.

What just happened?

We have added the assign activity to copy the `payload` part of the `BookstoreBResponse` variable to the `payload` part of the `BookStoreWithLowestQuantity` variable. This is possible because both payloads are of the same XML element from the same XML namespace. The following source code has been generated:

```
<assign name="AssignBookStoreWithLowestQuantity">
  <copy>
    <from>$BookstoreBResponse.payload</from>
    <to>$BookStoreWithLowestQuantity.payload</to>
  </copy>
</assign>
```

Other options for copying data

In addition to copying variable parts, we can also copy constant expressions and literals. The following example shows how to copy a constant string to the `BookstoreLocationWithLowestStockQuantity` variable (which is of the type `string`):

```
<assign>
  <copy>
    <from>string('BookstoreA')</from>
    <to variable="BookstoreLocationWithLowestStockQuantity"/>
  </copy>
</assign>
```

We are not restricted to such simple expressions. We can use any valid XPath 1.0 expressions (or the expressions of the selected expression language).

Another way of expressing the preceding copy would be the following:

```
<assign>
  <copy>
    <from>'BookstoreA'</from>
    <to>$BookstoreLocationWithLowestStockQuantity<to/>
  </copy>
</assign>
```

We can also do a copy to a specific node of the variable, such as:

```
<assign>
  <copy>
    <from>'BookstoreB'</from>
    <to>$outputVariable.payload/
    client:SelectedBookstoreLocation<to/>
  </copy>
</assign>
```

Optional attributes

We can specify two optional attributes for the `<copy>` activity:

- `keepSrcElementName`: This specifies whether the element name of the destination will be replaced by the element name of the source. The default is `No`.
- `ignoreMissingFromData`: This specifies whether the BPEL engine should ignore missing data in the `<from>` part of the copy assignment (and not raise a fault). The default is `No`.

We can also specify an optional attribute for the `<assign>` activity:

- `validate`: If set to yes, the assign activity will validate all variables being modified by the `<assign>` activity. The default is `No`.

Manipulating data for external partner links

To demonstrate how the `<assign>` activity can be used to manipulate larger sets of data, we will create an additional BPEL process, called `AnotherBookstoreBPEL`. This bookstore will return the book stock quantity, similar to the other two bookstores. The only difference will be that it will use a different XML Schema; hence, we will need to map the data elements from one schema to another for the invocation and back (for the response). Using a different schema will demonstrate a scenario that is very common in real-world cases, where services use different schemas; therefore, we need to do mappings and transformations.

For the `AnotherBookstoreBPEL` process, we will use the following schema:

```
<?xml version="1.0" encoding="UTF-8"?>
<schema attributeFormDefault="unqualified"
        elementFormDefault="qualified"
        targetNamespace="http://packtpub.com/Bookstore/AnotherBookstoreBPEL"
        xmlns="http://www.w3.org/2001/XMLSchema">
        <element name="BookData">
            <complexType>
                <sequence>
                    <element name="ISSN" type="string"/>
                    <element name="BookTitle" type="string"/>
                    <element name="PublishingData">
                        <complexType>
                            <sequence>
                                <element name="EditionOrVolume" type="string"/>
                                <element name="YearOfPublishing" type="date"/>
                            </sequence>
                        </complexType>
                    </element>
                </sequence>
            </complexType>
        </element>
        <element name="StockQuantity" type="int"/>
</schema>
```

We can see that the `BookData` element differs considerably from the `BookData` element of the `BookstoreABPEL` and `BookstoreBBPEL` processes. Also, the response from `AnotherBookstoreBPEL` is `StockQuantity` of the type `int`.

Time for action – creating the AnotherBookstoreBPEL process

Let's now develop the `AnotherBookstoreBPEL` process. We have already created BPEL processes in *Chapter 1, Hello BPEL*, and *Chapter 2, Service Invocation*; therefore, we will briefly describe the steps:

1. To create the `AnotherBookstoreBPEL` process, we will add a new BPEL process on the composite. We will enter the XML namespace as shown in the following screenshot and select the **Synchronous BPEL Process** template:

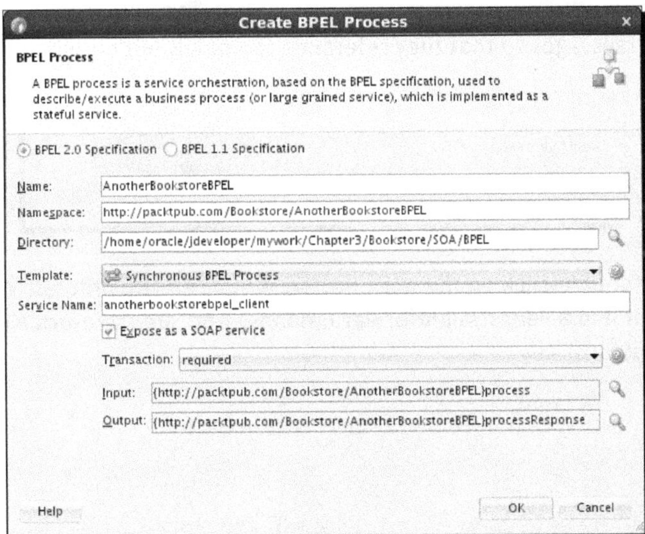

2. Next, we will create a new reference between the `BookWarehousing` process and the `AnotherBookstore` process. To achieve this, we will drag the reference from the `BookWarehousingBPEL` component to the `AnotherBookstoreBPEL` component. You should see the following composite screenshot:

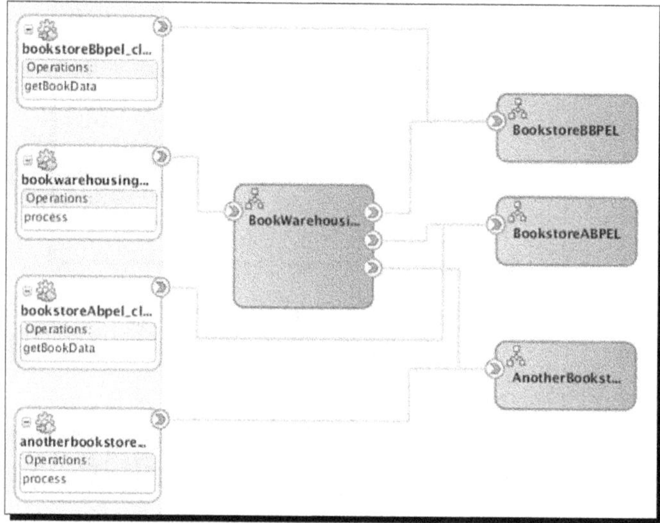

3. We will modify the auto-generated schema for the process. Open the **Schemas** folder in the project tree and double-click on the `AnotherBookstoreBPEL.xsd` schema. Modify the schema content by declaring the `BookData` and `StockQuantity` elements, exactly as shown in the preceding screenshot.
4. Finally, we need to modify the WSDL messages. Open the **WSDLs** folder and double-click on `AnotherBookstoreBPEL.wsdl`. Modify the request and response messages so that they reference the newly added schema elements:

```
<wsdl:message name="AnotherBookstoreBPELRequestMessage">
        <wsdl:part name="payload" element="client:BookData"/>
</wsdl:message>
<wsdl:message name="AnotherBookstoreBPELResponseMessage">
        <wsdl:part name="payload" element="client:StockQuantity"/>
</wsdl:message>
```

5. Let's now double-click on the `AnotherBookstoreBPEL` process. We will implement it in a very straightforward manner and simply return a constant value for `StockQuantity`.

Have a go hero – implementing the AnotherBookstoreBPEL process

It's your turn now. You should implement the `AnotherBookstoreBPEL` process the same way as you did in the previous chapter. The process should return a constant value for `StockQuantity`.

What just happened?

You have developed the `AnotherBookstoreBPEL` process, which should look like the following screenshot:

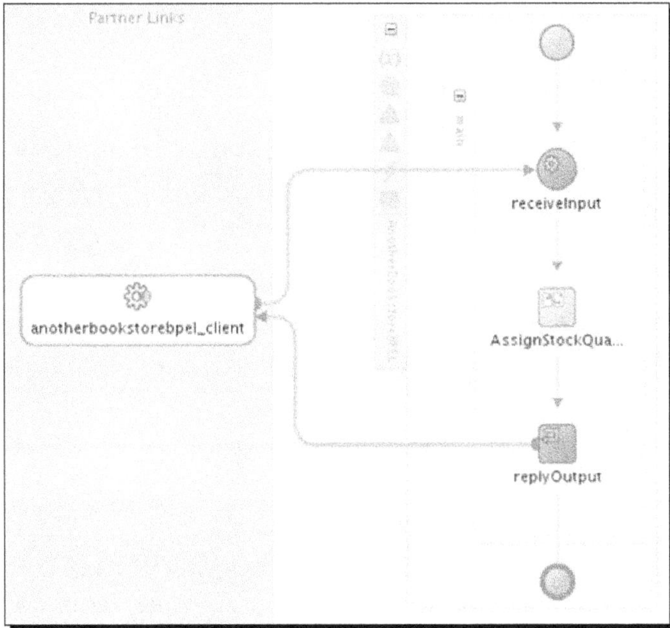

Time for action – extending the BookWarehousing process

We are now prepared to extend the `BookWarehousingBPEL` process. The goal is to invoke the `AnotherBookstoreBPEL` process in addition to the `BookstoreABPEL` and `BookstoreBBPEL` processes. We will do the following:

1. We will add a new `<flow>` branch for the invocation of the `AnotherBookstoreBPEL` process, as shown in the following screenshot:

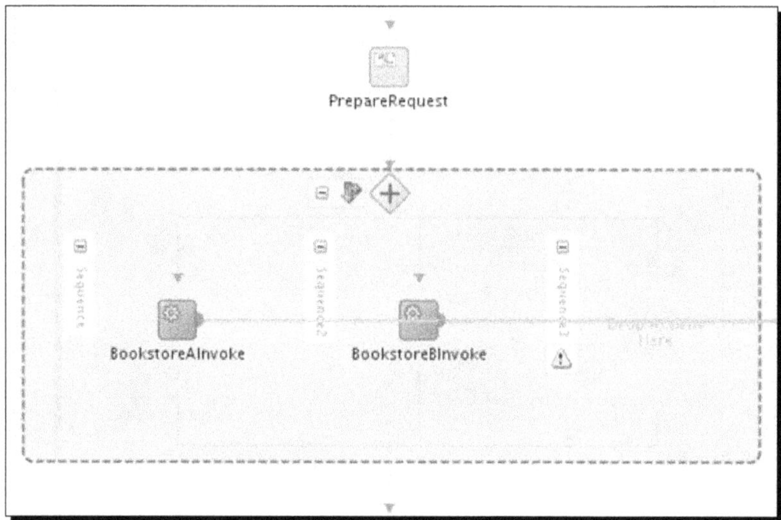

2. Before we can invoke the `AnotherBookstoreBPEL` process, we need to declare two variables, `AnotherBookstoreRequest` and `AnotherBookstoreResponse`. They should be of `AnotherBookstoreRequestMessage` and `AnotherBookstoreResponseMessage` message types, respectively.

3. We will need to assign the values for the `AnotherBookstoreRequest` variable. For this, we will use the `<assign>` activity, which we will drag-and-drop from the **Components** palette to the `<flow>` branch. We will copy field-by-field the book ISSN, title, edition, and publishing year from the `inputVariable` variable to the corresponding elements of the `AnotherBookstoreRequest` variable, as shown in the following screenshot:

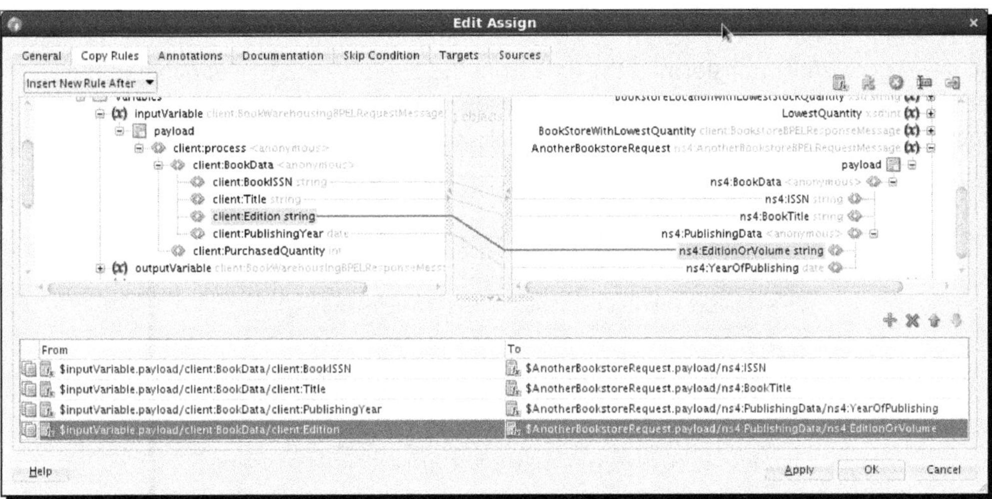

4. Next, we will make the invocation of the `AnotherBookstoreBPEL` process. We will drag-and-drop the `<invoke>` activity to the process, connect it with the `AnotheBookstoreBPEL` process (this way, we will set the partner link), and map the variables. We will use the `AnotherBookstoreRequest` variable for the input and `AnotherBookstoreResponse` variable for the output:

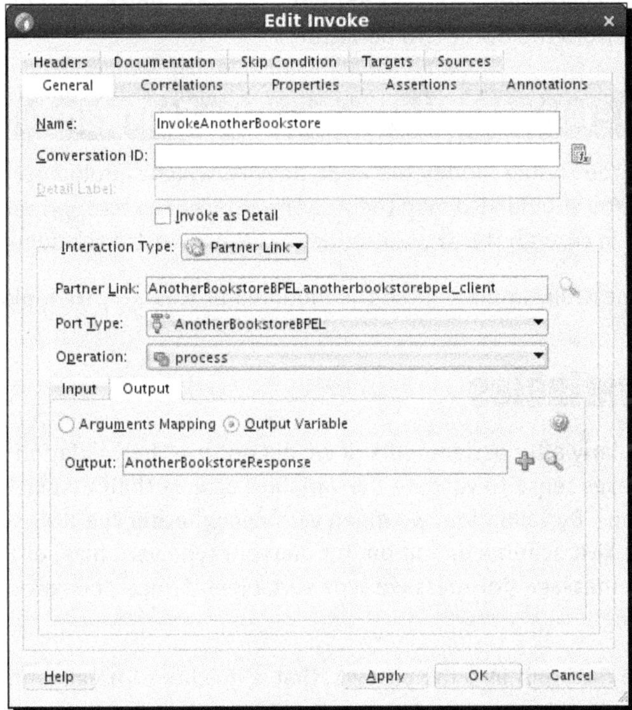

What just happened?

You have successfully transformed the data from the `inputVariable` variable to the `AnotherBookstoreRequest` variable and invoked the `AnotherBookstoreBPEL` process. The source code for this should look like the following:

```
<sequence name="Sequence3">
  <assign name="PrepareInput">
    <copy>
      <from>$inputVariable.payload/client:BookData/client:BookISSN</from>
      <to>$AnotherBookstoreRequest.payload/ns4:ISSN</to>
    </copy>
    <copy>
      <from>$inputVariable.payload/client:BookData/client:Title</from>
      <to>$AnotherBookstoreRequest.payload/ns4:BookTitle</to>
    </copy>
    <copy>
      <from>$inputVariable.payload/client:BookData/client:PublishingYear</from>
      <to>$AnotherBookstoreRequest.payload/ns4:PublishingData/ns4:YearOfPublishing</to>
    </copy>
    <copy>
      <from>$inputVariable.payload/client:BookData/client:Edition</from>
      <to>$AnotherBookstoreRequest.payload/ns4:PublishingData/ns4:EditionOrVolume</to>
    </copy>
  </assign>
  <invoke name="InvokeAnotherBookstore" bpelx:invokeAsDetail="no"
          partnerLink="AnotherBookstoreBPEL.anotherbookstorebpel_client"
          portType="ns4:AnotherBookstoreBPEL"
          operation="process" inputVariable="AnotherBookstoreRequest"
          outputVariable="AnotherBookstoreResponse"/>
</sequence>
```

With this, we have successfully invoked the `AnotherBookstoreBPEL` process. However, we also need to modify the `<if>` activity, which should now select among the three options. We will also need to deal with `AnotherBookstoreResponse`, which has a different structure than the responses from the other two bookstores.

Have a go hero – implementing the rest of the BookWarehousing process

It's your turn now. You should modify the `<if>` activity, which should now select among the three options. You should also map the `AnotherBookstoreResponse` to the `outputVariable` in case `AnotherBookstore` has the lowest stock quantity.

After you have successfully implemented the modified process, try to deploy it and test it.

Validating variables

Sometimes, particularly after assignments (if we did not use the validation in the assignments), it makes sense to validate the variables against their associated XML Schemas and WSDL definitions. By validation, we mean verifying whether the XML stored in a variable corresponds to the XML schema definition (for element type variables) or XML type (for type variables) or WSDL message (for message type variables). Typical scenarios for validation include the following:

- To validate the input into the process, that is, to check for valid input before the process starts working on them

- To validate the input to a service invocation or, even most often, the response from a service, that is, to check for XML conformance before using the variable

We can validate the variables explicitly using the <validate> activity.

It is very simple to validate variables. We just have to list all of the variable names that we would like to validate. We separate the variable names with a space. The syntax is as follows:

```
<validate variables="BPELVariableNames" />
```

For example, if we would like to validate the variables BookstoreAResponse and BookstoreBResponse, we would write the following:

```
<validate variables="BookstoreAResponseBookstoreBResponse" />
```

Time for action – validating variables

Let's now implement the variable validation for the BookstoreAResponse, BookstoreBResponse, and AnotherBookstoreResponse variables. We will add the validation immediately after both invocations. This way, we will validate the response from all three service invocations and make sure that all responses conform to the corresponding XML schema definitions and WSDL message types. This way we can detect (and prevent) when a service returns a misformed XML or an XML that does not conform to the schema. Such misformed responses would most likely cause a fault in our BPEL process if we did not detect them.

To add validation, simply drag-and-drop the **Validate** activity from the right-hand side toolbar to the BPEL process. We should drop it between the <flow> activity and the <if> activity. Next, you should double-click on the **Validate** activity, enter the required name, and add the variables, as shown:

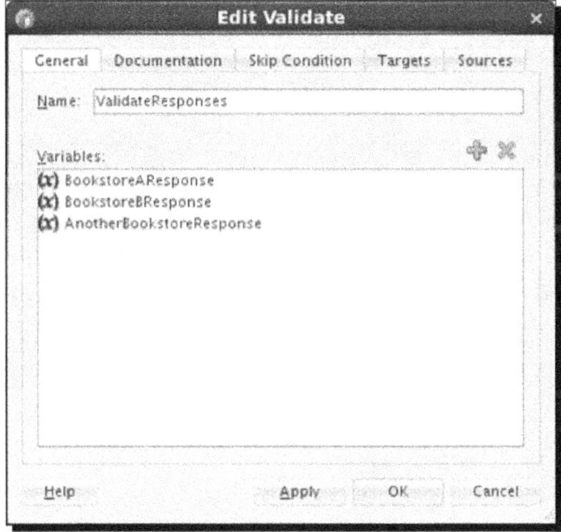

What just happened?

You have added the validate activity. If you switch to the **Source** view, you should see the following:

```
</flow>
<validate name="ValidateResponses" variables="BookstoreAResponse BookstoreBResponse AnotherBookstoreResponse"/>
<if name="If1">
  <documentation>
    <![CDATA[BookstoreALower]]>
  </documentation>
```

The XSLT transformations

Using the assignments to copy data from one variable to another is useful. However, if we deal with complex XML schemas and have to copy several elements (sometimes, tens of elements), using the `<copy>` construct alone would be very time consuming. In such cases, a better approach would be to use XSLT transformations. XSLT transformations also simplify the BPEL code, as the transformation logic is separated in a dedicated XSLT file.

Extensible Stylesheet Language for Transformations (**XSLT**) is not only a well-known language for transforming XML documents into other XML documents, but also to other formats, such as HTML, text or XSL Formatting Objects. XSLT can be used in most modern programming languages. For more information, please refer to `http://www.w3schools.com/xsl/`.

The `<assign>` activity provides support for XSLT transformations. We can invoke an XSLT transformation from an assignment using the `bpel:doXslTransform()` function. The `bpel:doXslTransform()` function is an XPath extension function. The syntax is listed below:

```
bpel:doXslTransform('style-sheet-URI', input,
['xslt-parameter-QName', parameter-value]*)
```

The first parameter is the URI that points to the XSLT style sheet. We have to provide a string literal and cannot use a variable here, because the BPEL process engine has to statically analyze the XSLT style sheet. The second parameter is the node set on which the XSLT transformation should be performed. Here we provide an XPath expression. In most cases, we will provide a variable. Optionally, we can specify XSLT parameters (if our XSLT style sheet requires parameters).

For example, instead of using the `<assign>` activity (as we did in the previous section), we can use an XSLT transformation to transform the data stored in the `inputVariable` variable and copy the result of the transformation to the `AnotherBookstoreInputVariable` variable:

```
<assign>
  <copy>
    <from>
    bpel:doXslTransform("http://packtpub.com/xslt/Bookstore.xsl",
    $inputVariable)
    </from>
    <to>$AnotherBookstoreInputVariable<to/>
  </copy>
</assign>
```

Of course, we also need the XSLT transformation.

Time for action – using XSLT transformations

To demonstrate how we can use the XSLT transformation in our `BookWarehousingBPEL` process, let's add it to the process:

1. Open the **BookWarehousingBPEL.bpel** window.
2. To add a transformation instead of the `<assign>` activity for preparing the `AnotherBookstoreRequest` variable, we will first remove the `<assign>` activity from the third flow branch. It is located just before the `<invoke>` activity for the `AnotherBookstoreBPEL` process.
3. Instead, we will drag-and-drop the **XSLT Transform** activity to the process. We can find the **XSLT Transform** activity under the **Oracle Extensions** part of the toolbar. The **XSLT Transform** activity needs to be dropped just above the invoke activity, that is, the invoke activity that invokes the `AnotherBookstoreBPEL` partner link.

4. After double-clicking on the **XSLT Transform** activity, an **Edit Transform** dialog will appear. The **Source** for the transformation will be `inputVariable`. The **Target Variable** will be `AnotherBookstoreRequest`. In both cases, we will address the **payload** part of the message:

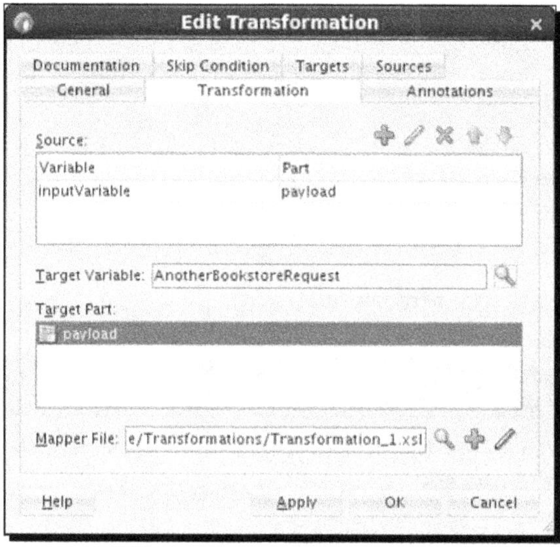

5. To create the XSLT transformation, we will click on the big green + sign, next to **Mapper File**. This will open a new window, where we can graphically (using drag-and-drop) map the various fields.

Please note that, in this simple example, it might not be obvious why XSLT transformations are a better and more efficient way when transforming complex schemas. On a more complex schema, the advantages would become clearer. In addition to mapping, you can also do other data transformations.

6. We will now map the fields. As the schema is simple and the mapping is obvious, this will be straightforward:

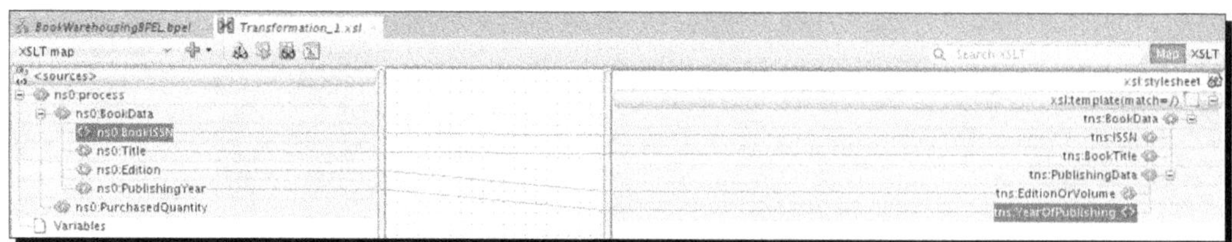

7. After saving both files, we have successfully finished the transformation.

What just happened?

We have created an XSLT transformation and used it in the <assign> activity to transform and map two different variables, each containing data based on its own schema. If we switch to source code, we can see that the following XSLT has been created:

```
<xsl:template match="/">
  <tns:BookData>
    <tns:ISSN>
      <xsl:value-of select="/ns0:process/ns0:BookData/ns0:BookISSN"/>
    </tns:ISSN>
    <tns:BookTitle>
      <xsl:value-of select="/ns0:process/ns0:BookData/ns0:Title"/>
    </tns:BookTitle>
    <tns:PublishingData>
      <tns:EditionOrVolume>
        <xsl:value-of select="/ns0:process/ns0:BookData/ns0:Edition"/>
      </tns:EditionOrVolume>
      <tns:YearOfPublishing>
        <xsl:value-of select="/ns0:process/ns0:BookData/ns0:PublishingYear"/>
      </tns:YearOfPublishing>
    </tns:PublishingData>
  </tns:BookData>
</xsl:template>
</xsl:stylesheet>
```

Also, in the BPEL source code, we can see that the <assign> activity uses the created transformation:

```
<assign name="TransformInput">
  <bpelx:annotation>
    <bpelx:pattern patternName="bpelx:transformation"></bpelx:pattern>
  </bpelx:annotation>
  <copy>
    <from>ora:doXSLTransformForDoc("../Transformations/Transformation_1.xsl", $inputVariable.payload)</from>
    <to variable="AnotherBookstoreRequest" part="payload"/>
  </copy>
</assign>
```

Note that JDeveloper has added the <bpelx:annotation> activity, which could be omitted and is JDeveloper specific. Also note that JDeveloper uses `ora:doXSLTransformationFromDoc()`, which is a JDeveloper-specific function. However, as it follows the same syntax, it could be easily replaced with the BPEL standard `bpel:doXslTransform()` function. To make your code portable on different BPEL run time environments, avoid using vendor-specific syntaxes or functions.

Have a go hero – deploy and test the process

It's your turn now to deploy and test this process and compare the results with the previous implementation. Note that the results should be equal.

With this, we have concluded our discussion on variables and data manipulation.

Pop quiz: variables and data manipulation

Q1. Which activity do you use to declare a variable?

1. `<variables>`
2. `<variable>`

Q2. Which variable types are supported in BPEL?

Q3. Write the declaration of a message type variable named `BookStoreWithLowestQuantity` using the message type `client:BookstoreBPELResponseMessage`.

Q4. Write the code to copy `BookstoreAResponse` variable to the `BookStoreWithLowestQuantity` variable. Assume that both variables are of the same message type. Do not use expressions.

Q5. Which operator is used to access BPEL variables from expressions?

1. /
2. $
3. .
4. :

Q6. Which activity is used to validate variables?

1. `<validate>`
2. `<validateVariable>`
3. `<doValidate>`

Q7. Which function in BPEL specification is used to invoke an XSLT transformation?

1. `ora:doXslTransform()`
2. `bpel:doXslTransform()`
3. `bpel:doXslTransformForDoc()`

Summary

In this chapter, we have learned how to use variables in BPEL and how to manipulate data. We have explained that, in BPEL, all variables store XML. They are not only used to hold the requests and responses for invoked services (partner links), but also to store other data related to the process state. We have seen that we can declare variables of three different types, message types, elements, and simple types.

To manipulate data, we use the <assign> activity. We have become familiar with the <assign> activity and have learned how to use different possibilities when copying data. Probably expressions are used most often. Expressions are written in XPath. We have also learned how to access variables from the expressions, how to validate variables, and how to use XSLT transformation to transform more complex schemas.

In the next chapter, we will learn about loops and conditions.

4

Conditions and Loops

Conditions and loops are important constructs in every programming language. Conditions allow us to implement branches. Loops provide the possibility for the code to execute more than once. In this chapter, we will look at conditions and loops in BPEL. We will look at the `if/elseif/else` activity, which is how conditions are expressed in BPEL. For loops, BPEL has more options. We will become familiar with while, repeat until, and for each loops. We will also explain which to use when. We will look into the detailed syntax of each loop and learn when to use parallel loops.

In this chapter, we will take a closer look at the `if/elseif/else` activity and at the various loop activities provided by BPEL. As we move along the chapter, we will cover the following topics:

- Understanding conditions and learning how to use the `<if>` activity
- Understanding loops
- Getting familiar with the `<while>` loop
- Getting familiar with the `<repeatUntil>` loop
- Getting familiar with the `<forEach>` loop
- Understanding parallel `<forEach>` execution
- Learning about delays, deadlines, and durations
- Understanding how to end a BPEL process

So, let's get started...

Conditions

To make choices based on conditions in BPEL 2.0, we use the `<if>` activity to define the conditional branches, which replaced the `<switch>` activity in BPEL 1.1. The `<if>` activity can have several `<elseif>` branches and one `<else>` branch. The following example shows the structure of the `<if>` activity:

```
<if>
  <condition>boolean-expression</condition>
  <!--activities -->

  <elseif>
    <condition>boolean-expression</condition>
    <!--activities -->
  </elseif>

  <elseif>
    <condition>boolean-expression</condition>
    <!--activities -->
  </elseif>
  ...
  <else>
    <!--activities -->
  </else>
</if>
```

The Boolean expressions for the `<condition>` elements are expressed in the XPath. We can use any valid XPath expression that returns a Boolean value. To use variables in conditions, we can use the `$` operator, the same way as in assignments, which we have covered in *Chapter 3, Variables, Data Manipulation, and Expressions*.

Time for action – selecting the bookstore with the lowest quantity

In the previous chapter, we introduced three bookstores into our composite BPEL application, `BookstoreA`, `BookstoreB`, and `AnotherBookstore`. Let's now modify the conditions in the `<if>` activity, where we select the bookstore with the lowest book quantity. We have to compare three book quantities of stores in the `BookstoreAResponse`, `BookstoreBResponse`, and `AnotherBookstoreResponse` variables. To access the `BookstoreAResponse` quantity, we should use the following XPath expression:

```
$BookstoreAResponse.payload/ns1:StockQuantity
```

Similarly, we would access the `BookstoreB` and `AnotherBookstore` stock quantities.

To select the lowest quantity, we should do the following comparisons:

- Compare the `BookstoreA` stock quantity to `BookstoreB` and `AnotherBookstore`. If the `BookstoreA` stock quantity is lower or equal in both cases, select `BookstoreA`.
- Compare the `BookstoreB` stock quantity to `BookstoreA` and `AnotherBookstore`. If the `BookstoreB` stock quantity is lower or equal in both cases, select `BookstoreB`.
- Compare the `AnotherBookstore` stock quantity to `BookstoreA` and `BookstoreB`. If the `AnotherBookstore` stock quantity is lower or equal in both cases, select `AnotherBookstore`.

Let us now implement this in BPEL:

1. We will need three branches. For the first, we will use `<if>` and for the other two, we will use `<elseif>`. As with the three branches, we have covered all possibilities, and so we will not use the `<else>` activity in this case:

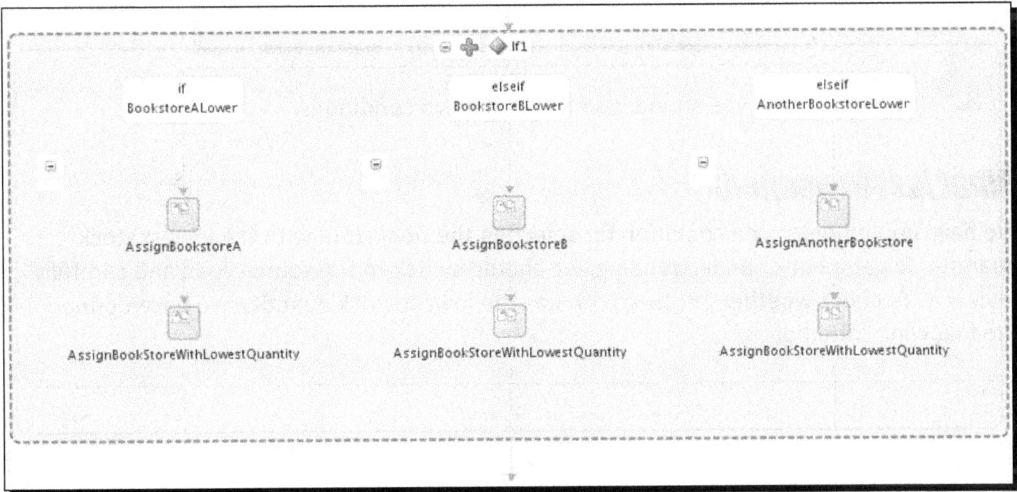

2. Let us now add the conditions. Right-click on the first **if**, select **Edit**, and enter the condition as shown in the following screenshot:

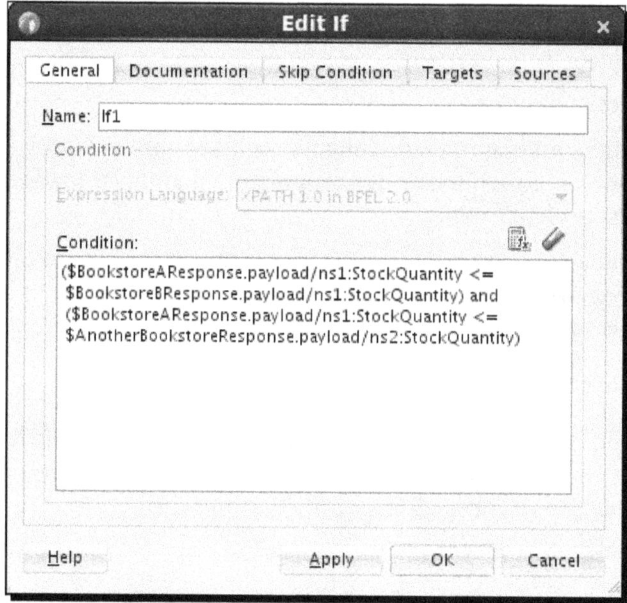

3. In a similar way, you should add the other two conditions.

What just happened?

We have implemented the condition for selecting the bookstore with the lowest stock quantity. To get a better understanding, we should switch to the source code and carefully review it. To check whether `BookstoreA` has the lowest stock quantity, we have defined the following condition:

```
<if name="If1">
  <documentation>
    <![CDATA[BookstoreALower]]>
  </documentation>
  <condition>($BookstoreAResponse.payload/ns3:StockQuantity &lt; $BookstoreBResponse.payload/ns3:StockQuantity)
  and ($BookstoreAResponse.payload/ns3:StockQuantity &lt; $AnotherBookstoreResponse.payload)</condition>
  <sequence name="Sequence1">
    <assign name="AssignBookstoreA">
      <copy>
        <from>'Bookstore A'</from>
        <to>$outputVariable.payload/client:SelectedBookstoreLocation</to>
      </copy>
    </assign>
    <assign name="AssignBookStoreWithLowestQuantity">
      <copy>
        <from variable="BookstoreAResponse"/>
        <to variable="BookStoreWithLowestQuantity"/>
      </copy>
    </assign>
  </sequence>
```

To check whether `BookstoreB` has the lowest stock quantity, we have defined the following condition:

```
<elseif>
  <documentation>
    <![CDATA[BookstoreBLowerOrEqual]]>
  </documentation>
  <condition>($BookstoreBResponse.payload/ns3:StockQuantity &lt;= $BookstoreAResponse.payload/ns3:StockQuantity)
  and ($BookstoreBResponse.payload/ns3:StockQuantity &lt;= $AnotherBookstoreResponse.payload)</condition>
  <sequence>
    <assign name="AssignBookstoreB">
      <copy>
        <from>'Bookstore B'</from>
        <to>$outputVariable.payload/client:SelectedBookstoreLocation</to>
      </copy>
    </assign>
    <assign name="AssignBookStoreWithLowestQuantity">
      <copy>
        <from>$BookstoreBResponse.payload</from>
        <to>$BookStoreWithLowestQuantity.payload</to>
      </copy>
    </assign>
  </sequence>
</elseif>
```

To check whether `AnotherBookstore` has the lowest stock quantity, we have defined the following condition:

```
  <elseif>
    <documentation>
      <![CDATA[AnotherBookstoreLower]]>
    </documentation>
    <condition>( $AnotherBookstoreResponse.payload &lt;= $BookstoreAResponse.payload/ns3:StockQuantity) and
    ($AnotherBookstoreResponse.payload &lt;=$BookstoreBResponse.payload/ns3:StockQuantity)</condition>
    <sequence name="Sequence4">
      <assign name="AssignAnotherBookstore">
        <copy>
          <from>'Another Bookstore'</from>
          <to>$outputVariable.payload/client:SelectedBookstoreLocation</to>
        </copy>
      </assign>
      <assign name="AssignBookStoreWithLowestQuantity">
        <copy>
          <from>$AnotherBookstoreResponse.payload</from>
          <to>$BookStoreWithLowestQuantity.payload/ns3:StockQuantity</to>
        </copy>
      </assign>
    </sequence>
  </elseif>
</if>
```

Please note that in the preceding code, we have used the `<` entity, which is used in XML to represent the < sign, which cannot be used directly. The same holds true for >, which is represented as `>`. For more information on XML and HTML entities, please refer to `http://en.wikipedia.org/wiki/List_of_XML_and_HTML_character_entity_references`.

We have successfully added three complex conditions to our process. To demonstrate the conditions even better, we will introduce a new service called Vintage Bookstore in the next section.

VintageBookstore

Let's extend our example and add `VintageBookstore`. The `VintageBookstore` service will be responsible for selling older books. Older books are the books published before 1970. We will define a conditional branch, based on the publishing year of the book. The BPEL would look like this:

```
<if>
  <condition>
    xp20:year-from-dateTime($inputVariable.payload/client:BookData/
    client:PublishingYear) &lt; 1970
  </condition>
  <!-- perform activities for books older than 1970 -->

  <else>
    <!-- perform activities for books published 1970 or after -->
  </else>
</if>
```

Time for action – implementing VintageBookstore

Let us now implement the Vintage Bookstore. Like before, we will implement Vintage Bookstore as a BPEL process. We will follow these steps:

1. We will extend the assembly diagram and add the `VintageBookstore` BPEL process component, as follows:

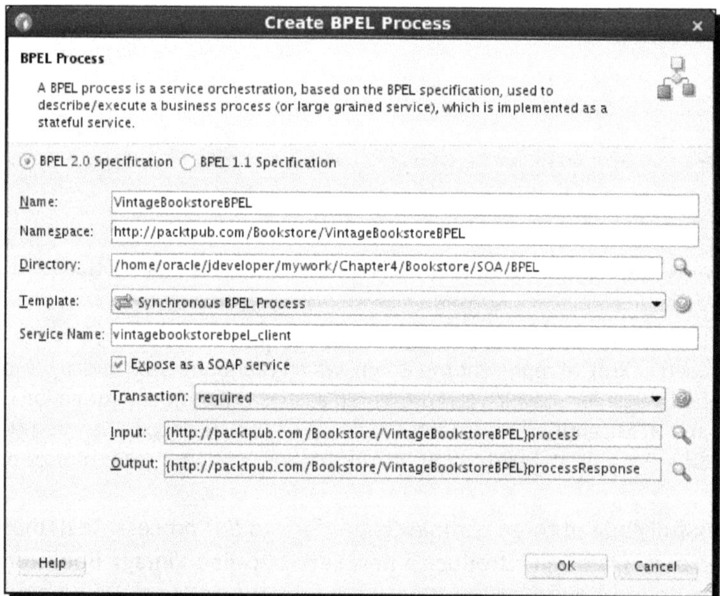

2. We also need to connect the `VintageBookstoreBPEL` process component with the `BookwarehousingBPEL` process:

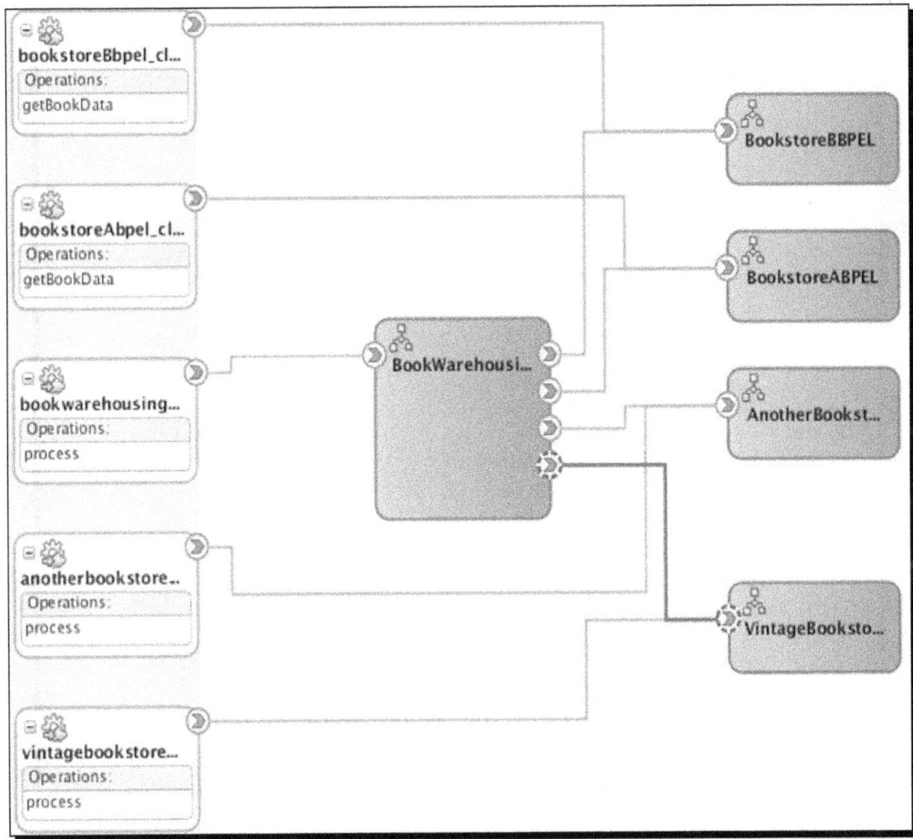

3. We need to implement the `VintageBookstoreBPEL` process.

Have a go hero – implementing VintageBookstoreBPEL process

It's your turn now. You should implement the `VintageBookstoreBPEL` process the same way as we did in the previous chapter. Do not forget to modify the XML Schema for the `VintageBookstoreBPEL` process first (located in the `Schemas` folder with the file name `VintageBookstoreBPEL.xsd`). Also, you might need to modify the WSDL messages to reference the appropriate XSD elements.

What just happened?

You have developed the `VintageBookstoreBPEL` process, which should look something like this:

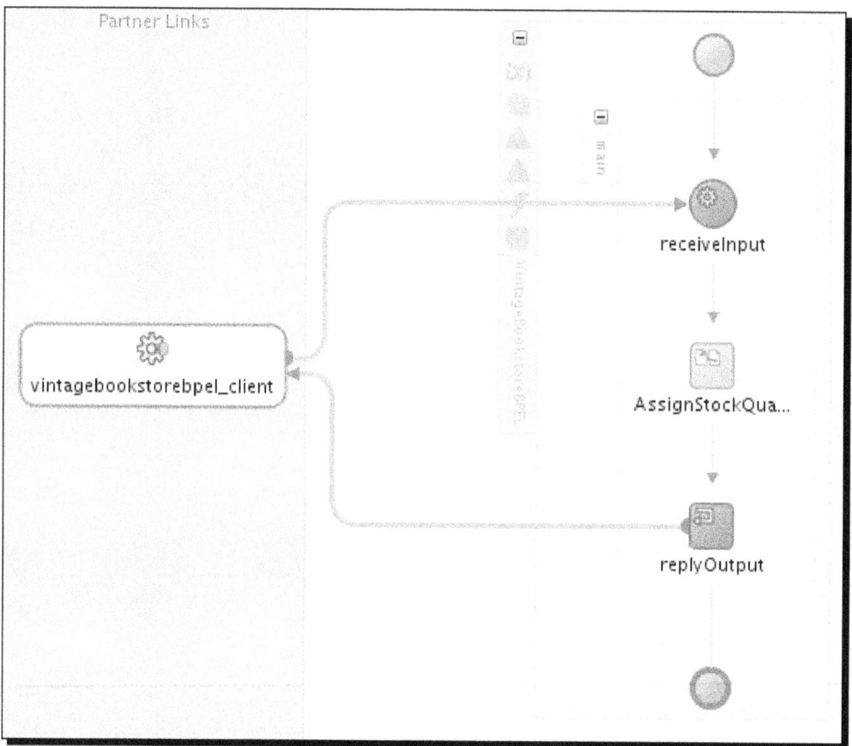

Time for action – selecting VintageBookstore

Let us now implement the condition regarding the publishing year. Each book, published before 1970, should be automatically delivered to `VintageBookstore`. To achieve this, we will perform the following steps:

1. Add a new `<if>` activity to the `BookWarehousingBPEL` process:

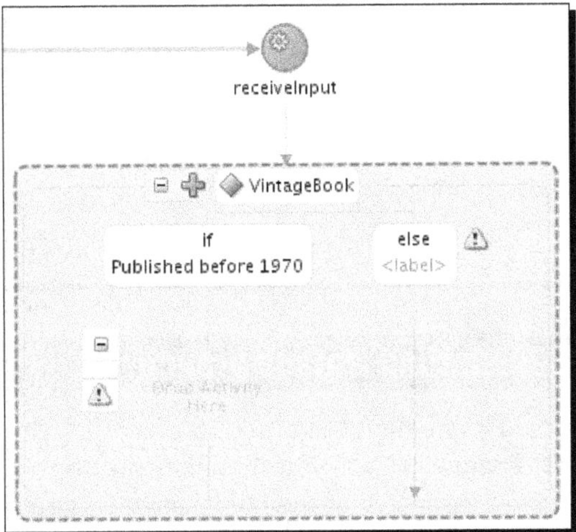

2. We will write the condition using the `year-from-dateTime()` XPath function, which returns the publishing year:

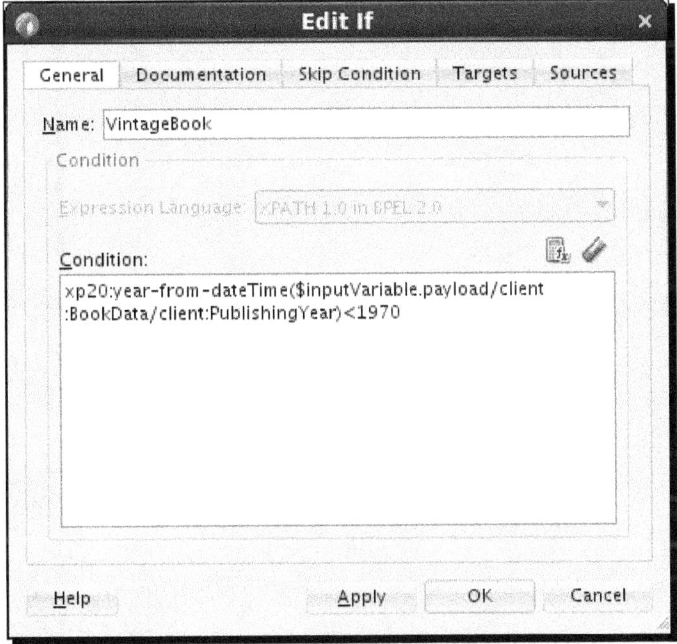

3. If the publishing year is lower than 1970, we should prepare the request and invoke the `VintageBookstoreBPEL` process. Otherwise, we should execute the activities previously defined within the BPEL process.

What just happened?

We have implemented the following BPEL condition:

```
<if name="VintageBook">
  <documentation>
    <![CDATA[if published before 1970]]>
  </documentation>
  <condition>xp20:year-from-dateTime($inputVariable.payload/client:BookData/client:PublishingYear)
  &lt; 1970</condition>
```

Have a go hero – implementing vintage branch

It's your turn now. You should implement the branch for handling the books older than 1970. First, you should prepare the request. Then you should invoke the `VintageBookstoreBPEL` process and finally return the response that the book has been directed to the `VintageBookstore`.

You should develop the `VintageBookstoreBPEL` process, which should look like this:

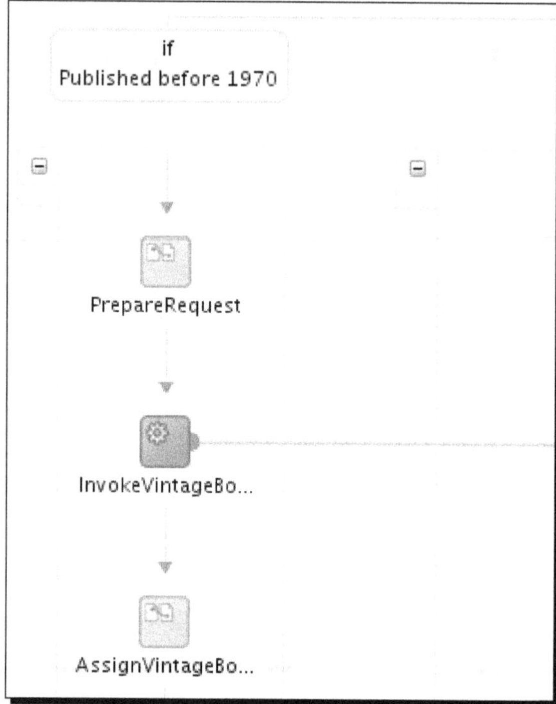

The source code should read like this:

```
<if name="VintageBook">
  <documentation>
    <![CDATA[if published before 1970]]>
  </documentation>
  <condition>xp20:year-from-dateTime($inputVariable.payload/client:BookData/client:PublishingYear)
  &lt; 1970</condition>
  <sequence name="Sequence5">
    <assign name="PrepareRequest">
      <copy>
        <from>$inputVariable.payload/client:BookData/client:BookISSN</from>
        <to>$VintageBookstoreRequest.payload/ns5:ISSN</to>
      </copy>
      <copy>
        <from>$inputVariable.payload/client:BookData/client:Title</from>
        <to>$VintageBookstoreRequest.payload/ns5:BookTitle</to>
      </copy>
      <copy>
        <from>$inputVariable.payload/client:BookData/client:Edition</from>
        <to>$VintageBookstoreRequest.payload/ns5:PublishingData/ns5:EditionOrVolume</to>
      </copy>
      <copy>
        <from>$inputVariable.payload/client:BookData/client:PublishingYear</from>
        <to>$VintageBookstoreRequest.payload/ns5:PublishingData/ns5:YearOfPublishing</to>
      </copy>
    </assign>
    <invoke name="InvokeVintageBookstore" bpelx:invokeAsDetail="no"
            partnerLink="VintageBookstoreBPEL.vintagebookstorebpel_client" portType="ns5:VintageBookstoreBPEL"
            operation="process" inputVariable="VintageBookstoreRequest" outputVariable="VintageBookstoreResponse"/>
    <assign name="AssignVintageBookstore">
      <copy>
        <from>'Vintage Bookstore'</from>
        <to>$outputVariable.payload/client:SelectedBookstoreLocation</to>
      </copy>
    </assign>
  </sequence>
  <else>
```

With this, we have concluded our discussion of conditions. In the next section, we will have a look at loops.

Loops

When defining BPEL processes, some activities often need to execute more than once. For example, let us suppose that we had a business process that needed to warehouse an array of books. Other examples include performing calculations or invoking partner web service operations several times, and so on.

In BPEL, we can choose between three types of loops:

- The `<while>` loops
- The `<repeatUntil>` loops
- The `<forEach>` loops

The `<while>` and `<repeatUntil>` loops are very similar to other programming languages. The `<forEach>` loop can also be found in some programming languages. In BPEL, `<forEach>` also provides the ability to start the loop instances in parallel, which can be very useful.

Let us now look at the `<while>` loop.

While

The `<while>` loop repeats the enclosed activities until the Boolean condition no longer holds true. The Boolean condition is expressed through the `condition` element, using the selected expression language (the default is XPath 1.0). The syntax of the `<while>` activity is shown in the following code excerpt:

```
<while>
  <condition>boolean-expression</condition>

  <!-- Perform an activity or a set of activities enclosed by
  <sequence>, <flow>, or other structured activity -->

</while>
```

Repeat until

The `<repeatUntil>` loop repeats the enclosed activities until the Boolean condition becomes true. The Boolean condition is expressed through the `condition` element, the same way as in the `<while>` loop. The syntax of the `<repeatUntil>` activity is shown in the following code excerpt:

```
<repeatUntil>

  <!-- Perform an activity or a set of activities enclosed by
  <sequence>, <flow>, or other structured activity -->

  <condition>boolean-expression</condition>
</repeatUntil>
```

For each

The `<forEach>` loop is a `for` type loop, with an important distinction. In BPEL, the `<forEach>` loop can execute the loop branches serial or in parallel. The serial `<forEach>` is very similar to the `for` loops from various programming languages, such as Java. The parallel `<forEach>` loop executes the loop branches in parallel, similar to `<flow>`, but unlike a flow activity, the number of parallel branches is not known at design time. Obviously, in parallel `<forEach>`, each branch executes the same set of activities, while in the `<flow>`, each branch can execute different activities. This opens new possibilities in relatively simple parallel execution (for example, invocation of services).

The <forEach> loop requires us to specify the BPEL variable for the counter (counterName), startCounterValue and finalCounterValue . The <forEach> loop will execute (finalCounterValue – startCounterValue + 1) times.

The <forEach> loop requires that we put all activities, which should be executed within the branch, into <scope>. The <scope> loop allows us to group-related activities. We will discuss <scope> in detail later in this book.

The syntax of <forEach> is shown as follows:

```
<forEachcounterName="BPELVariableName" parallel="yes|no">

  <startCounterValue>unsigned-integer-expression</startCounterValue>
  <finalCounterValue>unsigned-integer-expression</finalCounterValue>

  <scope>
    <!-- The activities that are performed within forEach have
    to be nested within a scope. -->
  </scope>

</forEach>
```

Such <forEach> loop will complete when all branches (<scope>) have completed.

Parallel for each

Sometimes, it would be useful if the <forEach> loop would not have to wait for all branches to complete. Rather it would wait for some branches to complete. In <forEach>, we can specify that the loop will complete after at least N branches have completed. We do this using <completionCondition>. We specify the number N of <branches>. The <forEach> loop will complete after at least N branches have completed. We can specify if we would like to count only successful branches or all branches. We do this using the successfulBranchesOnly attribute. If set to yes, only successful branches will count. If set to no (default), successful and failed branches will count. The syntax is shown as follows:

```
<forEachcounterName="BPELVariableName" parallel="yes|no">

  <startCounterValue>unsigned-integer-expression</startCounterValue>
  <finalCounterValue>unsigned-integer-expression</finalCounterValue>

  <completionCondition><!-- Optional -->
    <branches successfulBranchesOnly="yes|no">
      unsigned-integer-expression
    </branches>
  </completionCondition>
```

```
    <scope>
      <!-- The activities that are performed within forEach have
      to be nested within a scope. -->
    </scope>

  </forEach>
```

Arrays

Loops are also very helpful when dealing with arrays. In BPEL, arrays can be simulated using XML complex types where one or more elements can occur more than once (using the `maxOccurs` attribute in the XML schema definition). To iterate through multiple occurrences, we will require loops. We can also use XPath expressions to address multiple occurrences of the same element.

Adding loops to our example

Let us now extend our example to demonstrate how we can use loops. So far, our `BookWarehousing` process has been able to handle one book title only. We will extend this example so that it can handle a list (array) of book titles. The process will iterate through the list and direct each book to the corresponding bookstore.

There are two possibilities to extend our example. The first would be to modify the `BookWarehousingBPEL` process. We would need to modify the corresponding schema for the process to accept a list instead of a single book title. Then, we would need to modify the process flow so that it can handle more than one title.

The other approach that we will use is to add another BPEL process, which we will call `BookOrderManagementBPEL`. The `BookOrderManagementBPEL` process will receive a list of book titles. It will use a loop to iterate through the list. For each book title, it will invoke the `BookWarehousingBPEL` process.

Time for action – adding the BookOrderManagement process

Let us now implement the `BookOrderManagement` process:

1. First, we will add the **BPEL Process** component to the assembly diagram:

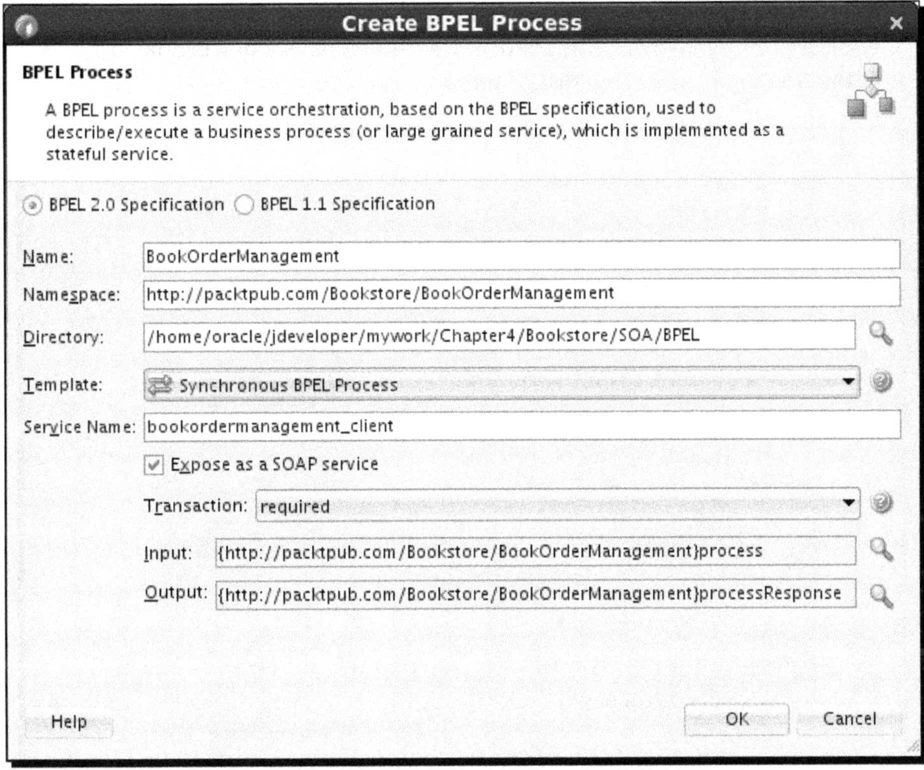

2. Next, we will wire the `BookOrderManagementBPEL` process with the `BookWarehousingBPEL` process:

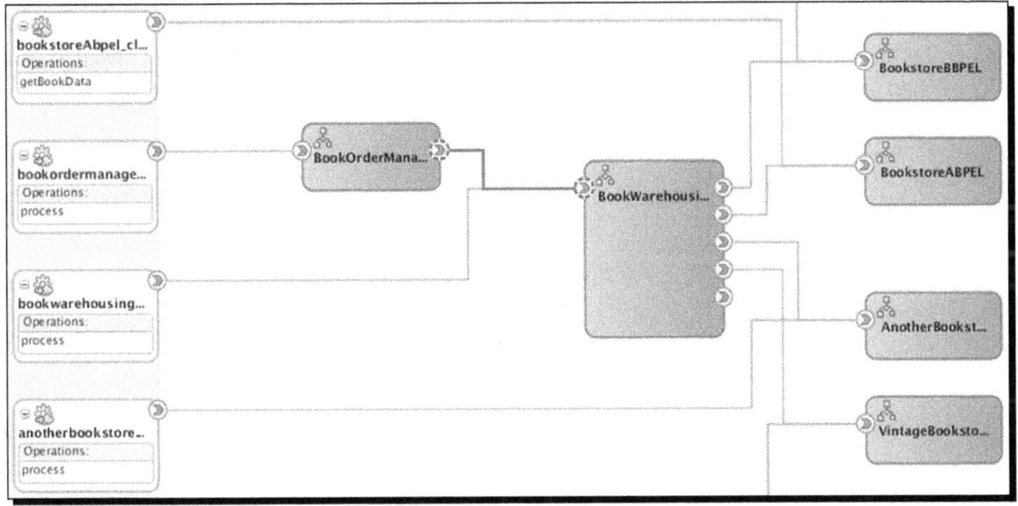

3. Next, we will define the corresponding XML schema for the `BookOrderManagementBPEL` process. Let's first have a quick look at the `BookWarehousing` XML schema:

```
<?xml version="1.0" encoding="UTF-8"?>
<schema attributeFormDefault="unqualified"
        elementFormDefault="qualified"
        targetNamespace="http://packtpub.com/Bookstore/BookWarehousingBPEL"
        xmlns="http://www.w3.org/2001/XMLSchema"
        xmlns:tns="http://packtpub.com/Bookstore/BookWarehousingBPEL">
        <element name="BookData">
                <complexType>
                        <sequence>
                                <element name="BookISSN" type="string"/>
                                <element name="Title" type="string"/>
                                <element name="Edition" type="string"/>
                                <element name="PublishingYear" type="date"/>
                                <element name="PurchasedQuantity" type="int"/>
                        </sequence>
                </complexType>
        </element>
        <element name="process">
                <complexType>
                        <sequence>
                            <element ref="tns:BookData"/>
                        </sequence>
                </complexType>
        </element>
        <element name="processResponse">
                <complexType>
                        <sequence>
                                <element name="SelectedBookstoreLocation" type="string"/>
                        </sequence>
                </complexType>
        </element>
</schema>
```

4. In the `BookOrderManagementBPEL` process, we would like to use a very similar schema. The only difference would be that we would like to accept a list of `BookData` as an input parameter. Therefore, we will import the `BookWarehousing` XML schema and add the `minOccurs` and `maxOccurs` attributes to define the list (array):

```
<?xml version="1.0" encoding="UTF-8"?>
<schema attributeFormDefault="unqualified"
        elementFormDefault="qualified"
        targetNamespace="http://packtpub.com/Bookstore/BookOrderManagementBPEL"
        xmlns="http://www.w3.org/2001/XMLSchema"
        xmlns:bom="http://packtpub.com/Bookstore/BookOrderManagementBPEL"
        xmlns:bwh="http://packtpub.com/Bookstore/BookWarehousingBPEL">

        <import namespace="http://packtpub.com/Bookstore/BookWarehousingBPEL"
                schemaLocation="BookWarehousingBPEL.xsd"/>

        <element name="process">
                <complexType>
                        <sequence>
                                <element ref="bwh:BookData" minOccurs="0" maxOccurs="unbounded"/>
                        </sequence>
                </complexType>
        </element>
        <element name="processResponse">
                <complexType>
                        <sequence>
                                <element name="result" type="string"/>
                        </sequence>
                </complexType>
        </element>
</schema>
```

For the process response, we will use a simple `string`, through which we will communicate the status.

What just happened?

We have created the `BookOrderManagementBPEL` process, wired it with the `BookWarehousingBPEL` process, and created the schema elements for the `BookOrderManagementBPEL` process request and response messages.

The while loop

Now we are ready to implement the `BookOrderManagementBPEL` process. In the BPEL process, we will iterate through the list of `BookData` orders and delegate each `BookData` order to the `BookWarehousingBPEL` process.

In the first attempt, we will implement it using a `<while>` loop. Next, we will use the `<forEach>` loop.

Time for action – adding the <while> loop

Let us start with the `<while>` loop:

1. Before adding the `<while>` loop, construct the BPEL flow. We will add two variables: `NoOrders` and `i`, both of the type `xsd:int`. We can add variables using the big green plus sign in the lower left window:

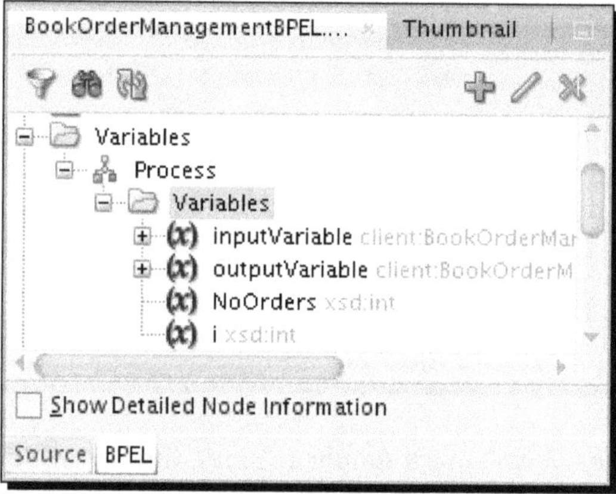

Alternatively, we can write source code directly:

```
<variable name="NoOrders" type="xsd:int"/>
<variable name="i" type="xsd:int"/>
```

2. Then we will need to know how many items we have in our list of book orders. We will use the XPath `count()` function to achieve this. Alternatively, we could use an Oracle extension function `ora:countNodes()`, but this would make our code vendor specific. At the same time, we will initialize the counter variable `i`. We will add an `<assign>` activity to the process flow and make both `<copy>` expressions. You can use the **Edit Assign** dialog windows (as we've shown in *Chapter 3, Variables, Data Manipulation, and Expressions*) or enter the source code directly:

```
<assign name="PrepareLoop">
  <copy>
    <from>count($inputVariable.payload/ns1:BookData)</from>
    <to>$NoOrders</to>
  </copy>
  <copy>
    <from>number(1)</from>
    <to>$i</to>
  </copy>
</assign>
```

3. Now we are ready to add the `<while>` loop construct to the BPEL flow. You should drag-and-drop the **While** activity from the **Components** palette on the right-hand side. You will find **While** under **Structured Activities**:

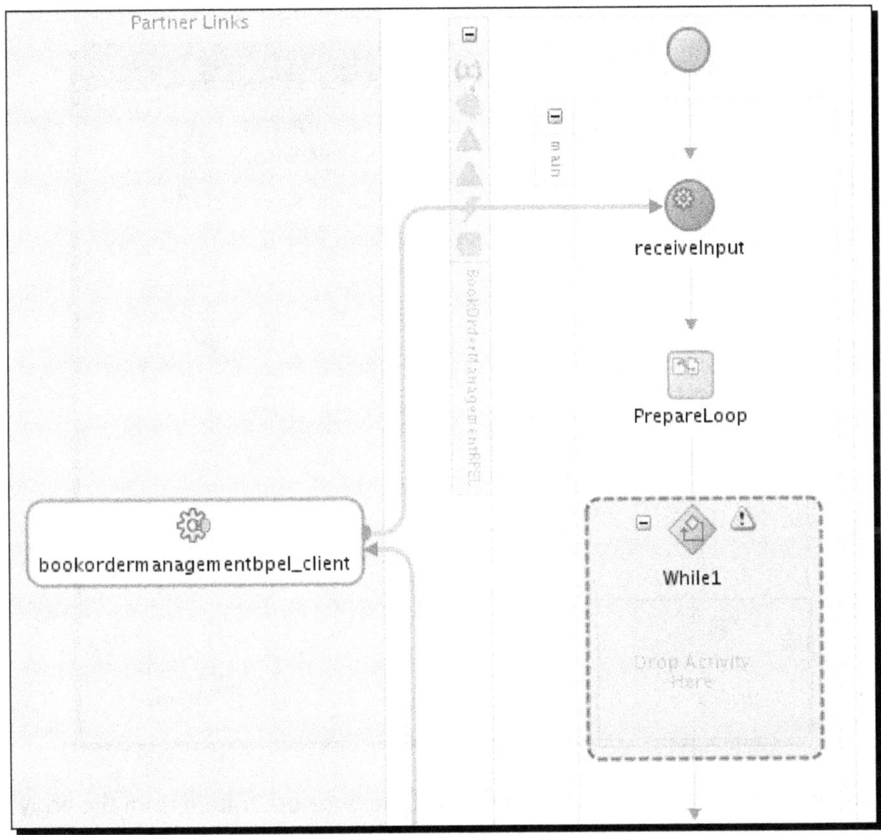

4. We need to set the condition as long as the <while> loop will execute. In our example, the loop will execute while i<= NoOrders. Double-click on the <while> activity to open the **Edit While** dialog and enter the **Condition** and the condition **Name**:

5. Within the <while> loop, we will extract the book order item from the array and prepare the request for the BookWarehousingBPEL process and invoke it. Finally, we will increase the counter i by one.

6. Let's first add the `<invoke>` activity to the process within the `<while>` loop (again, drag-and-drop it from the **Components** palette). We will name the activity `InvokeBookWarehousing`. We will also create two global variables on the fly, `BookWarehousingRequest` and `BookWarehousingResponse`:

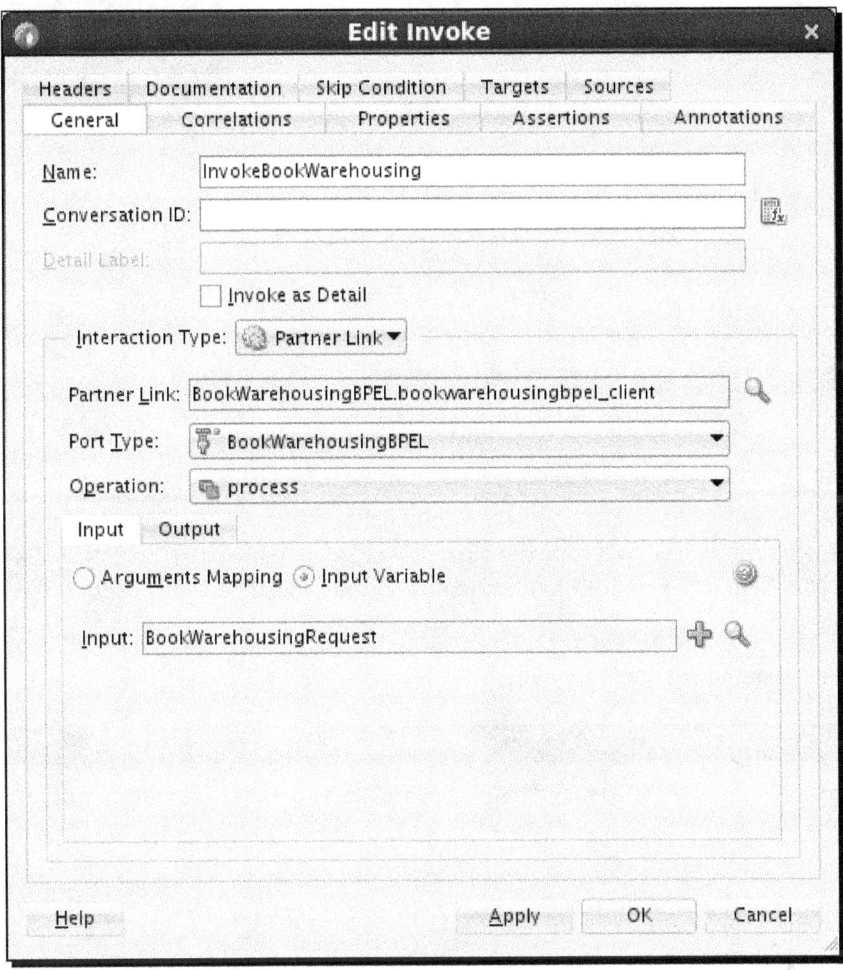

7. Next, we will add the `<assign>` activity to prepare the request. We will add the `<assign>` activity before the `<invoke>` activity and set the following copy expression:

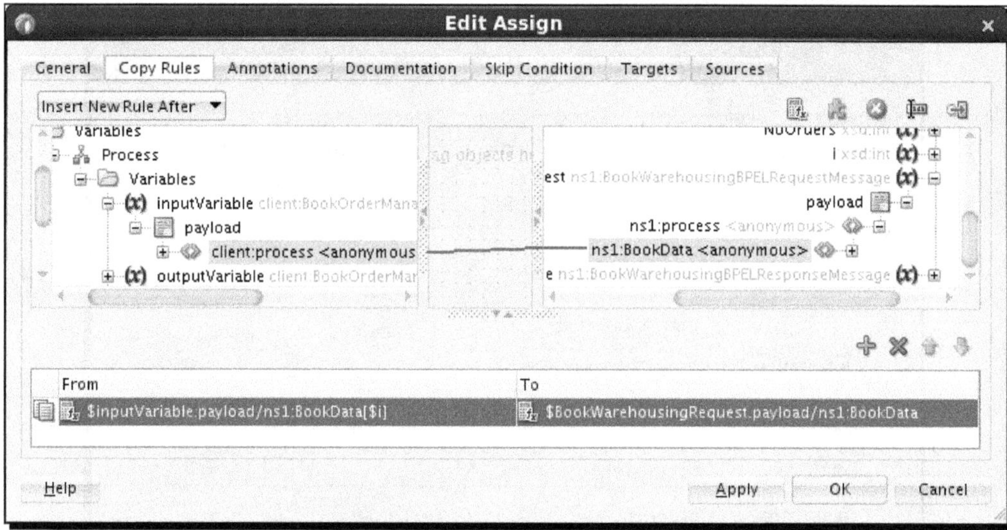

As you can see, we will copy the `$inputVariable.payload/ns1:BookData[$i]` order item to the `$BookWarehousingRequest.payload/ns1:BookData` element.

8. Finally, we need to add another `<assign>` activity after the `<invoke>` activity and increase the counter `i` by one:

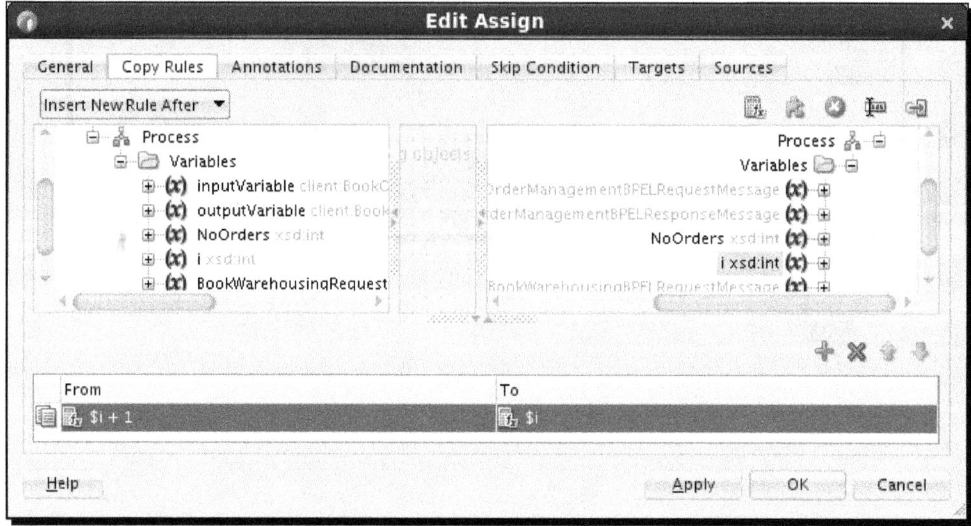

What just happened?

We have successfully developed the `BookOrderManagementBPEL` process, which iterates through book data items using a `<while>` loop. The process flow should look like this:

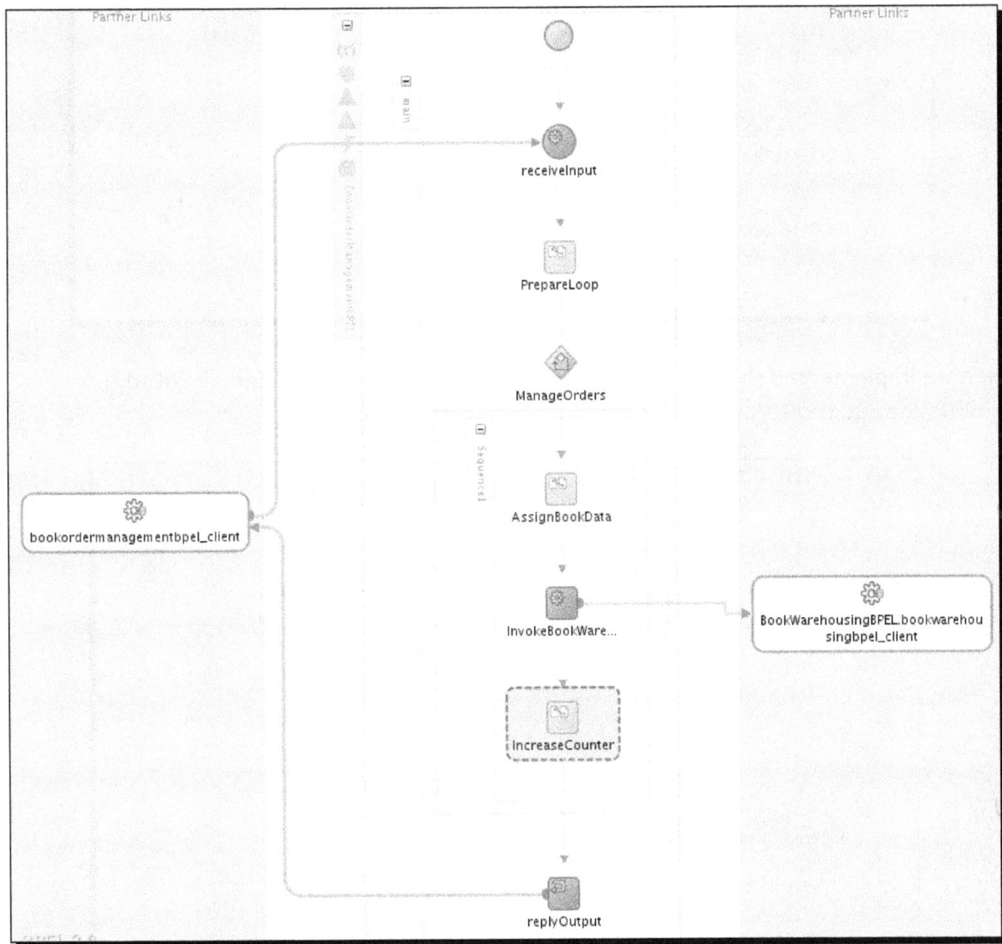

The source code should read as follows. We started with the variable initialization:

```
<sequence name="main">

  <!-- Receive input from requestor. (Note: This maps to operation defined in
  <receive name="receiveInput" partnerLink="bookordermanagementbpel_client"
      portType="client:BookOrderManagementBPEL" operation="process"
      variable="inputVariable" createInstance="yes"/>
  <assign name="PrepareLoop">
    <copy>
      <from>count($inputVariable.payload/ns1:BookData)</from>
      <to>$NoOrders</to>
    </copy>
    <copy>
      <from>number(1)</from>
      <to>$i</to>
    </copy>
  </assign>
```

Then we implemented the loop, where we extracted the book data item, invoked the `BookWarehousingBPEL` process, and increased the counter:

```
<while name="ManageOrders">
  <condition>$i &lt;= $NoOrders</condition>
  <sequence name="Sequence1">
    <assign name="AssignBookData">
      <copy>
        <from>$inputVariable.payload/ns1:BookData[$i]</from>
        <to>$BookWarehousingRequest.payload/ns1:BookData</to>
      </copy>
    </assign>
    <invoke name="InvokeBookWarehousing"
            partnerLink="BookWarehousingBPEL.bookwarehousingbpel_client"
            portType="ns1:BookWarehousingBPEL" operation="process"
            inputVariable="BookWarehousingRequest"
            outputVariable="BookWarehousingResponse"
            bpelx:invokeAsDetail="no"/>
    <assign name="IncreaseCounter">
      <copy>
        <from>$i + 1</from>
        <to>$i</to>
      </copy>
    </assign>
  </sequence>
</while>
```

With this, we have concluded the implementation of our first loop—the `<while>` loop.

Have a go hero – testing the process

It's your turn now. You should deploy and test the `BookOrderManagementBPEL` process. Be sure to select an array of the `BookOrder` items and to check whether they get propagated to the `BookWarehousingBPEL` process and to the individual bookstores.

The repeat until loop

The `<repeatUntil>` loop is very similar to the `<while>` loop. We have explained the syntax at the beginning of this section. The only difference to the `<while>` loop is that the condition is evaluated at the end of the `<repeatUntil>` loop (in `<while>` loop, it is evaluated in the beginning of the loop).

Because of the similarity, we will not show the example here, but instead we will ask you to implement it yourself.

Have a go hero – using <repeatUntil> instead of <while>

To practice loops, you should try to modify the preceding example and use the `<repeatUntil>` loop instead of the `<while>` loop. Please notice when the condition is evaluated in the `<repeatUntil>` loop.

The forEach loop

The `<forEach>` loop is a `for` loop, which can execute the loop branches serial (sequential) or in parallel. We have explained the syntax at the beginning of this section. Now, we will implement our scenario using the `<forEach>` loop (this is the same scenario that we have implemented with the `<while>` loop earlier).

Time for action – the <forEach> loop

Let us now implement the same scenario using the `<forEach>` loop:

1. We don't want to overwrite the `<while>` loop example; therefore, we will add another BPEL process component to the composite diagram. We will call it `BookOrderForEachBPEL`:

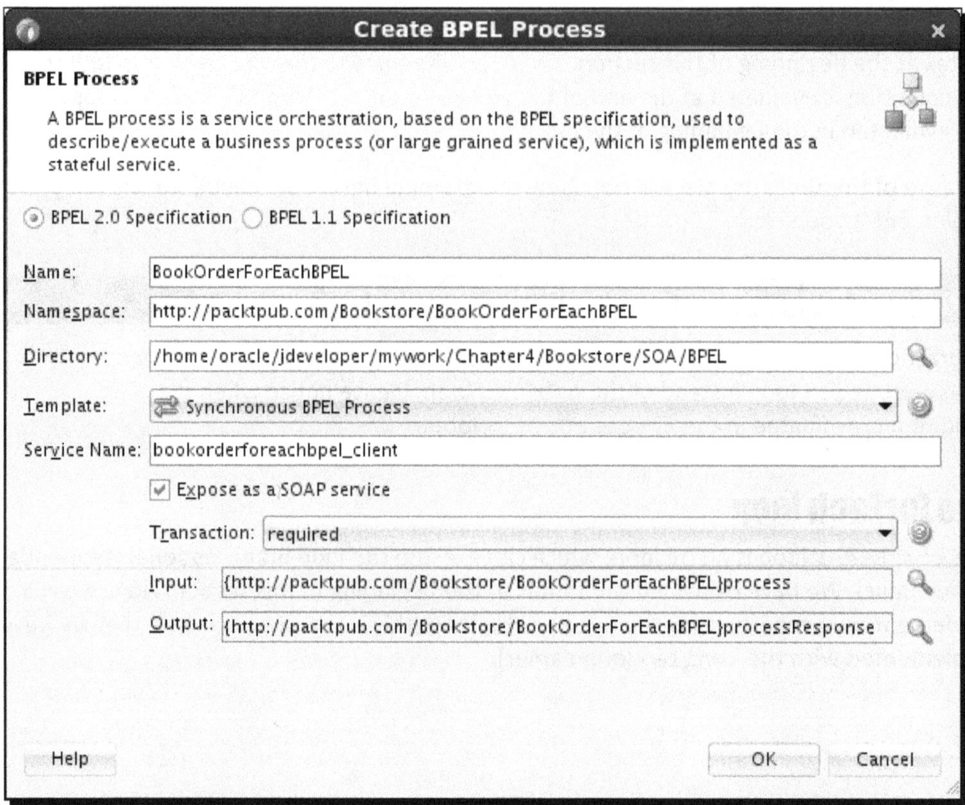

2. We will also wire it with `BookWarehousingBPEL`:

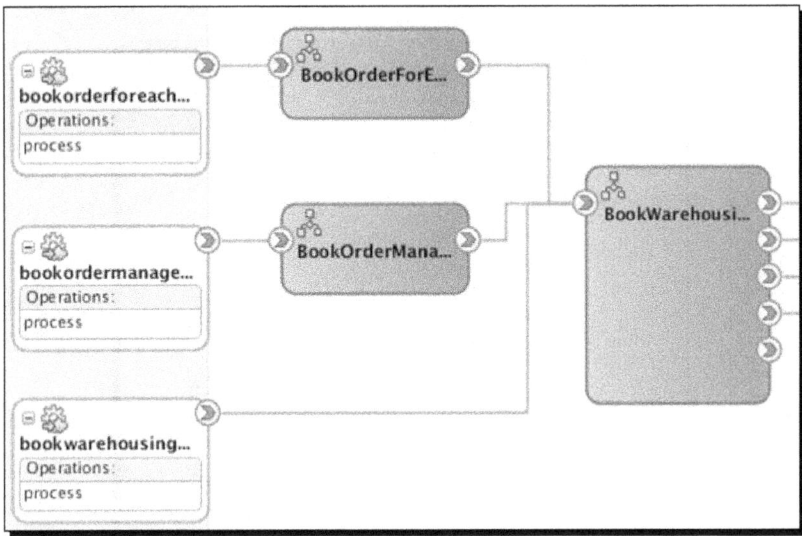

3. We will use exactly the same schema as in the previous example. To implement the BPEL process, we will first add the `<forEach>` activity to the process flow by dragging-and-dropping **For Each** from the **Components** palette (you will find it under **Structured Activities**):

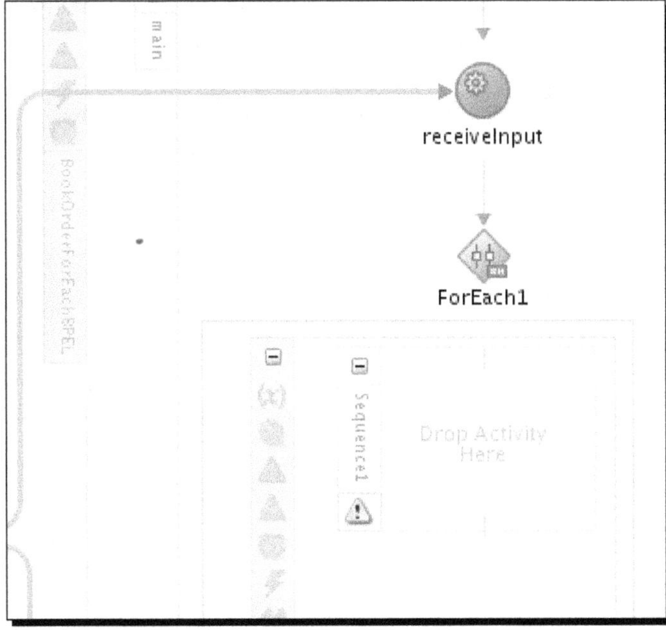

4. We will double-click the `ForEach1` activity and set **Name** as `ManageOrders` and name of the counter variable (**Counter name**) as `OrderCounter`:

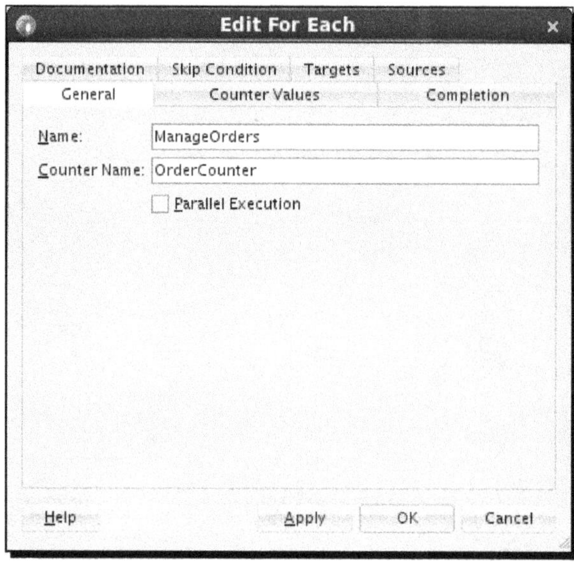

5. In the **Counter Values** tab, we will set the start and the end value for the counter. The start value is `1` and the end value is the `count($inputVariable.payload/ns1:BookData)` expression. With this expression, we will count the number of books in the array. This is exactly the number of times we wish the `<forEach>` loop to repeat:

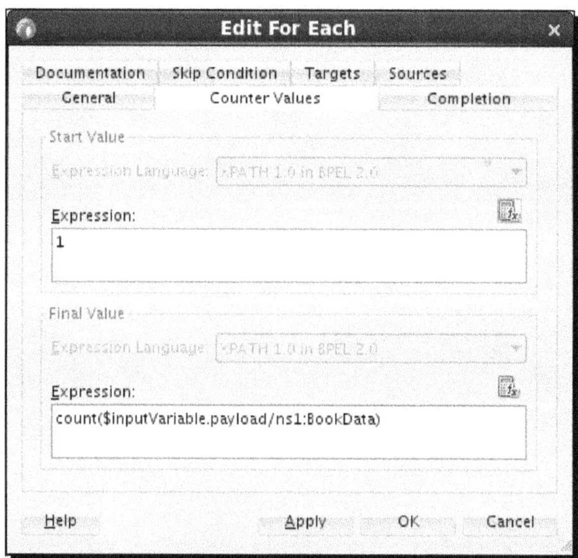

6. You can now click the **OK** button. As in the previous example, within the `<forEach>` loop, we will extract the book order item from the array, and prepare the request for the `BookWarehousingBPEL` process and invoke it. We do not need to manually increase the counter however.

7. Let us first add the `<invoke>` activity. We will name the activity `InvokeBookWarehousing`. We will also create two global variables on the fly, `BookWarehousingRequest` and `BookWarehousingResponse`:

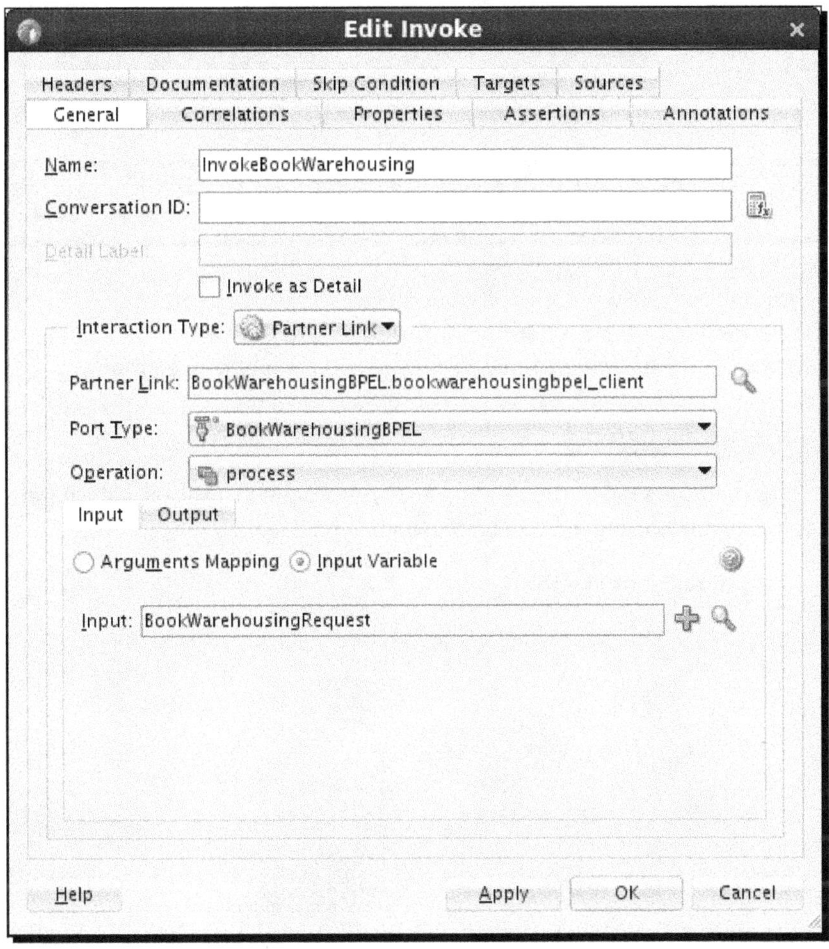

8. Next, we will add the `<assign>` activity to prepare the request. We will add the `<assign>` activity before the `<invoke>` activity and set the following copy expression:

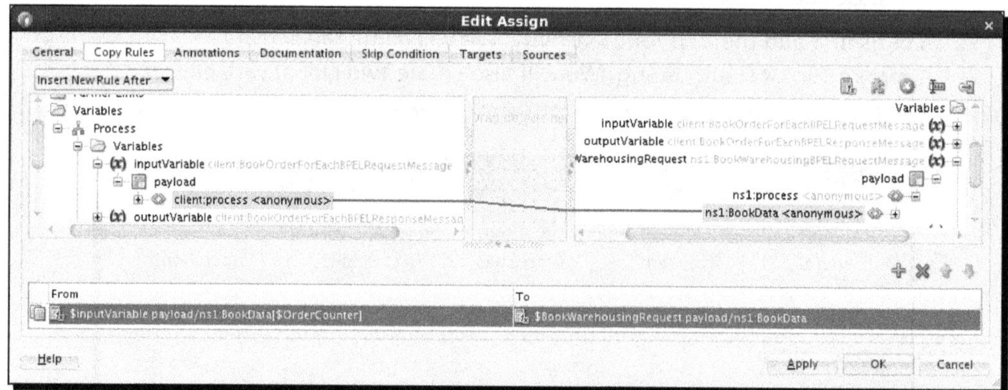

As you can see, we will copy the `$inputVariable.payload/ns1:BookData[$OrderCounter]` order item to the `$BookWarehousingRequest.payload/ns1:BookData` element.

What just happened?

We have successfully developed the `BookOrderForEach` BPEL process, which iterates through book data items using a `<forEach>` loop.

The process flow should look like this:

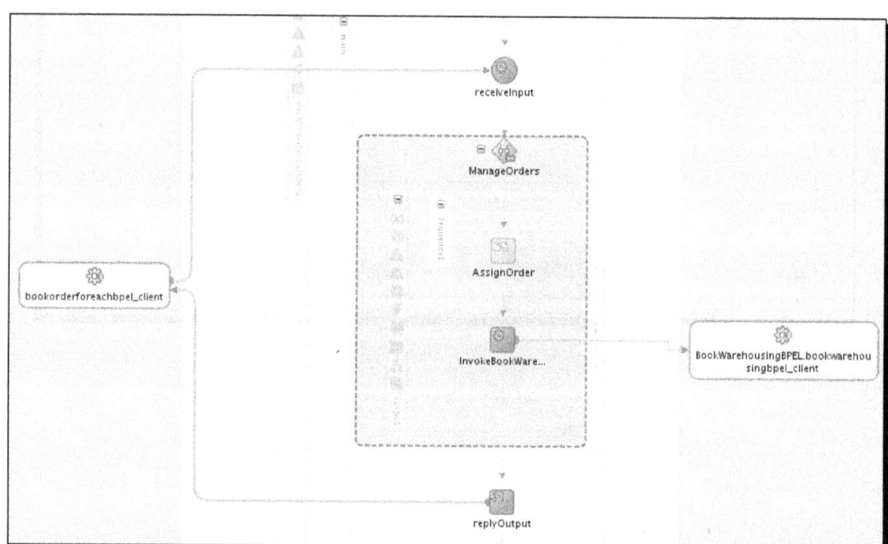

We can see that the `<forEach>` loop is a little simpler, as we do not have to take care of the counter variable manually.

The source code should read as follows:

```
<sequence name="main">

  <!-- Receive input from requestor. (Note: This maps to operation defined in BookOrderForEachBPEL.wsdl) -->
  <receive name="receiveInput" partnerLink="bookorderforeachbpel_client"
        portType="client:BookOrderForEachBPEL" operation="process"
        variable="inputVariable" createInstance="yes"/>
  <forEach parallel="yes" counterName="OrderCounter" name="ManageOrders">
    <startCounterValue>1</startCounterValue>
    <finalCounterValue>count($inputVariable.payload/ns1:BookData)</finalCounterValue>
    <scope name="Scope1">
      <sequence name="Sequence1">
        <assign name="AssignOrder">
          <copy>
            <from>$inputVariable.payload/ns1:BookData[$OrderCounter]</from>
            <to>$BookWarehousingRequest.payload/ns1:BookData</to>
          </copy>
        </assign>
        <invoke name="InvokeBookWarehousing" bpelx:invokeAsDetail="no"
                partnerLink="BookWarehousingBPEL.bookwarehousingbpel_client"
                portType="ns1:BookWarehousingBPEL"
                operation="process"
                inputVariable="BookWarehousingRequest"
                outputVariable="BookWarehousingResponse"/>
      </sequence>
    </scope>
  </forEach>
  <!-- Generate reply to synchronous request -->
  <reply name="replyOutput" partnerLink="bookorderforeachbpel_client"
        portType="client:BookOrderForEachBPEL" operation="process"
        variable="outputVariable"/>
</sequence>
```

Have a go hero – test the process

It's your turn now. You should deploy and test the `BookOrderForEachBPEL` process.

Executing <forEach> in parallel

For now, our `<forEach>` loop has been sequential. We have, however, mentioned that the `<forEach>` loop can also execute in parallel. To achieve this, we simply need to specify the corresponding attribute.

Time for action – executing <forEach> in parallel

To change our example to execute the `<forEach>` loop in parallel, we need to do the following:

1. Double-click the `<forEach>` activity in the `BookOrderForEach` BPEL process. The **Edit For Each** dialog window will appear.
2. Check the **Parallel Execution** checkbox:

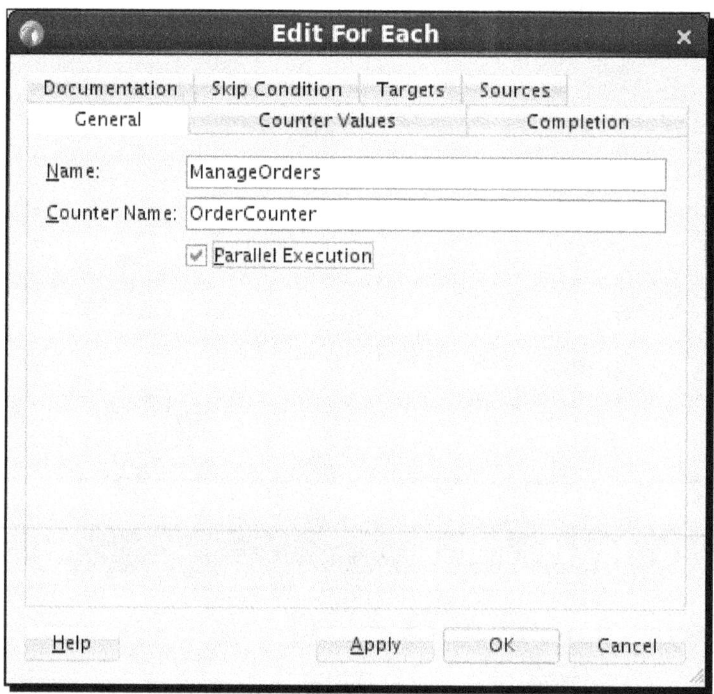

What just happened?

We have modified our `BookOrderForEach` BPEL process to execute the `<forEach>` loop in parallel. This results in the following declaration in the source code:

```
<forEach parallel="yes" counterName="OrderCounter" name="ManageOrders">
```

The `<forEach>` loop will now execute in parallel. You can observe this in the audit trail on the process server.

Delays

Sometimes in loops, but also on other occasions, we may want to program delays into BPEL processes. To do this we can specify durations or deadlines. Typically, we could specify delays to invoke an operation at a specific time, or wait for some time and then invoke an operation. For example, we could choose to wait a few seconds before invoking the `BookWarehousing` process, or before we pool the results of a previously initiated operation, or to wait between other iterations of a loop.

The simplest way to specify the delays is to use the `<wait>` activity. The `<wait>` activity can be:

- `for`: Using this, we can specify duration; we specify a period of time. Consider the following code snippet:

  ```
  <wait>
    <for> duration-expression </for>
  </wait>
  ```

- `until`: Using this, we can specify a deadline; we specify a certain date and time.

  ```
  <wait>
    <until> deadline-expression </until>
  </wait>
  ```

Deadline and duration expressions

To specify deadline and duration expressions, BPEL uses lexical representations of corresponding XML Schema data types. For deadlines, these data types are either `dateTime` or `date`. For duration, we use the `duration` data type. The lexical representation of expressions should conform to the XPath 1.0 expressions. The evaluation of such expressions should result in values that are of corresponding XML Schema types: `dateTime` and `date` for deadline and `duration` for duration expressions.

All three data types use lexical representation inspired by the ISO 8601 standard, which can be obtained from the ISO web page `http://www.iso.ch`. ISO 8601 lexical format uses characters within the date and time information. Characters are appended to the numbers and have the following meaning:

- `C` represents centuries.
- `Y` represents years.
- `M` represents months.
- `D` represents days.
- `h` represents hours.

- m represents minutes.
- s represents seconds. Seconds can be represented in the format ss.sss to increase precision.
- Z is used to designate **Coordinated Universal Time** (**UTC**). It should immediately follow the time of day element.

For the dateTime expressions, there is another designator:

- T is used as time designator to indicate the start of the representation of the time.

Examples of deadline expressions are shown in the following code excerpts:

```
<wait>
  <until>'2014-03-18T21:00:00+01:00'</until>
</wait>
<wait>
  <until>'18:05:30Z'</until>
</wait>
```

For duration expressions, the following characters can also be used:

- P is used as the time duration designator. Duration expressions always start with P.
- Y follows the number of years.
- M follows the number of months or minutes.
- D follows the number of days.
- H follows the number of hours.
- S follows the number of seconds.

To specify a duration of 4 hours and 10 minutes, we use the following expression:

```
<wait>
  <for>'PT4H10M'</for>
</wait>
```

To specify a duration of 1 month, 3 days, 4 hours, and 10 minutes, we need to use the following expression:

```
<wait>
  <for>'P1M3DT4H10M'</for>
</wait>
```

The following expression specifies the duration of 1 year, 11 months, 14 days, 4 hours, 10 minutes, and 30 seconds:

```
<<wait>
  <for>'P1Y11M14DT4H10M30S'</for>
</wait>
```

Adding delay to our book order management process

In the previous section of this chapter, we implemented the BookOrderManagementBPEL process. In the first example, we used the <while> loop to iterate through the books and invoke the BookWarehousingBPEL process for each book.

If we were expecting a long list of books to be processed, and if we did not want to put too much load on the BookWarehousingBPEL process, we could add a delay in the loop. This way, we will wait for a specific period of time each time we invoke the BookWarehousingBPEL process. Let's assume that we would like to wait for 2 seconds.

Time for action – adding <wait>

To add the <wait> activity to the BookOrderManagementBPEL process, we need to do the following:

1. Open the BookOrderManagementBPEL process by double-clicking it in the process tree.
2. Drag-and-drop the <wait> activity from the **Components** palette to the BPEL process. You will find the <wait> activity under **Basic Activities**. Drop it immediately after the <invoke> activity of **InvokeBookWarehousing** and before the <invoke> activity of **IncreaseCounter**.
3. Double-click the <wait> activity. The **Edit Wait** dialog will open. Set the **For Time** as 2 seconds and rename the activity from **Wait1** to **Wait2sec**:

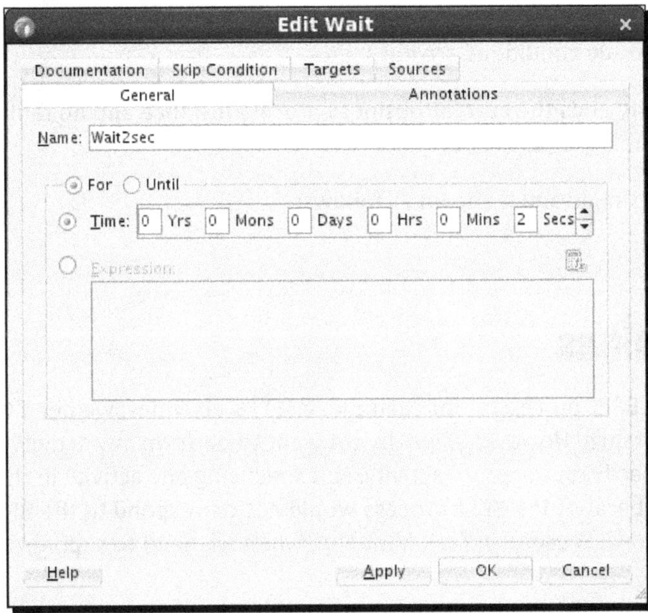

What just happened?

We have modified our `BookOrderManagementBPEL` process to wait for 2 seconds after each invocation of the `BookWarehousingBPEL` process. This has resulted in the following source code:

```
<invoke name="InvokeBookWarehousing" bpelx:invokeAsDetail="no"
        partnerLink="BookWarehousingBPEL.bookwarehousingbpel_client" portType="ns1:BookWarehousingBPEL"
        operation="process" inputVariable="BookWarehousingRequest" outputVariable="BookWarehousingResponse"/>
<wait name="Wait2sec">
  <for>'PT2S'</for>
</wait>
<assign name="IncreaseCounter">
  <copy>
    <from>$i+1</from>
    <to>$i</to>
  </copy>
</assign>
```

Have a go hero – test the process

It's your turn now. You should deploy and test the `BookOrderManagementBPEL` process and observe whether it really waits after each invocation (notice that the total execution time will increase).

Ending a process

Sometimes, in loops, we might want to immediately end a business process before it has finished. BPEL provides the `<exit>` activity to immediately terminate a process instance that is executing. Often, we use `<exit>` in conditional branches, where we need to exit a process when certain conditions are not met.

The `<exit>` activity ends the current business process instance and no fault and compensation handling is performed.

The syntax is very simple and is shown as follows:

```
<exit/>
```

Empty activities

When developing BPEL processes, for example, in `<if>` activities, we need to specify an activity for each branch. However, if we do not want to perform any activity for a particular branch, we can specify an `<empty>` activity. Not specifying any activity in this case would result in an error, because the BPEL process would not correspond to the BPEL schema. Empty activities are also useful in fault handling, when we need to suppress a fault.

The syntax for the `<empty>` element is rather straightforward:

```
<empty/>
```

With this, we have concluded our discussion on loops and conditions.

Pop quiz – conditions and loops

Q1. Which parts of the `<if>` activity is optional?

1. `<if>`
2. `<elseif>`
3. `<else>`

Q2. Which three types of loops are supported in BPEL?

Q3. Which loop evaluates the condition at the end?

Q4. Which loop supports parallel execution?

Q5. Which types of delays are supported in the `<wait>` activity?

Q6. How would you immediately end a BPEL process instance?

1. `<terminate>`
2. `<exit>`
3. `<stop>`

Q7. How would you declare lists (array) in the XML schema?

1. `minOccurs='0'`
2. `minOccurs='1'`
3. `maxOccurs='unbounded'`

Summary

In this chapter, we have learned about conditions in BPEL processes. We explained the syntax of the `<if>`, `<elseif>`, and `<else>` activities and we have shown an example of how to implement conditions.

We have also taken a close look at the loops. We have learned that BPEL provides three types of loops: `<while>`, `<repeatUntil>`, and `<forEach>`. The `<forEach>` loop also provides the ability to execute the loop instances in parallel. We have implemented the `<while>` and `<forEach>` loops, the latter in sequential and parallel ways.

We have also become familiar with delays, which can be useful in loops. With delays, we can specify a certain deadline or duration. We have learned how to specify both. Finally, we have seen how to end a BPEL process with the `<exit>` activity and learned why and when to use `<empty>` activities.

Now that we are familiar with loops and conditions in BPEL, we will move on to asynchronous invocations, which is the topic of the next chapter.

5
Interaction Patterns in BPEL

In the previous chapters, most of the basic concepts required to implement a very simple BPEL process were explained. We learned how to set up communication channels from BPEL process to external web services (Chapter 1, Hello BPEL). Then, we used those communication channels to invoke those external web services (Chapter 2, Service Invocation). Also we learned how to manipulate data within the BPEL process (Chapter 3, Variables, Data Manipulation, and Expressions).

But the mechanism that we learned to communicate with external web services fails at some point where the external web service takes a nondeterministic time to respond back to the BPEL process. In such scenarios, we can use asynchronous communication channels to invoke external web services.

In this chapter, we will cover the following topics:

- Introduction to asynchronous invocations
- Implementing an asynchronous invocation
- Understanding asynchronous invocations
- Callbacks and message correlations
- Understanding asynchronous business processes
- Implementing an asynchronous business process

Understanding asynchronous invocations

There are two general strategies to interact with web services, known as synchronous and asynchronous interactions. In synchronous interactions, both parties communicate in real time (for example, face-to-face conversations, telephone calls, and so on). Both parties maintain the connection intact until the communication is over. In contrast, in asynchronous interactions, both parties communicate outside of real time (for example, e-mails and postal mails). The client establishes a connection with the server, sends the request message, and closes the connection. Then the server of the request message processes the incoming message, generates a response message, establishes a connection with the requesting-party, and sends the response message.

In this section, we realize a common use case where asynchronous invocations play a vital role to achieve the business goal. Let's try to understand the following sample BPEL process and then we will move into the details of implementing such a business process.

The book warehousing process

Imagine a bookstore which has multiple branches spread across a city. At some instance, the bookshelves are required to be updated based on customer requirements. Some of the books that are not high in customer demand have to be stored at a warehouse and we have to bring new books to the shelves. For this, we'll query each of those bookstores and get a list of books that have not sold for the last six months and decide which books need to be warehoused.

The following screenshot shows the book warehousing process:

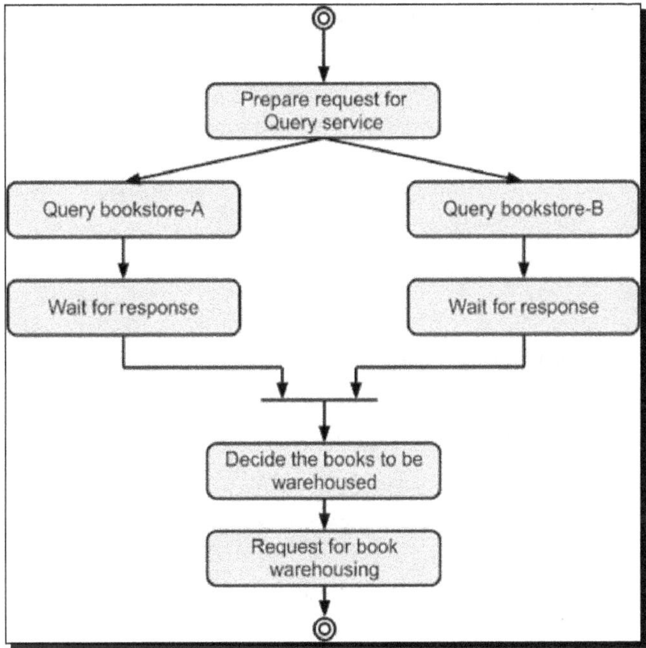

Workflow of the book warehousing process

We need to follow the ensuing set of steps when implementing this sample BPEL process:

1. Prepare requests that are to be sent to the query service on Bookstore A and the query service on Bookstore B.
2. Invoke query service in parallel (query service on Bookstore A and query service on Bookstore B).
3. Wait and retrieve the results from two service invocations.
4. Send those results to the service that determines which books are to be warehoused.
5. Invoke the book warehousing service with the input of books to be warehoused.

Rather than implementing the whole workflow, we will only focus on implementing the external service invocation to the search service on a bookstore in this exercise. The complete BPEL process is available at the sample repository.

Time for action – implementing an asynchronous invocation

Let's take a look at how to implement an asynchronous service invocation where the asynchronous web service is represented by the following WSDL: `http://svn.wso2.org/repos/wso2/carbon/platform/trunk/products/bps/modules/samples/product/src/main/resources/bpel/2.0/SampleAsynchronousProcess/Async-Server/ServerArtifacts.wsdl`.

Download this external service WSDL representation.

Creating an empty WS BPEL 2.0 process

Here, we will create an empty WS BPEL 2.0 process with the **Synchronous BPEL Process** template, as shown in the following screenshot:

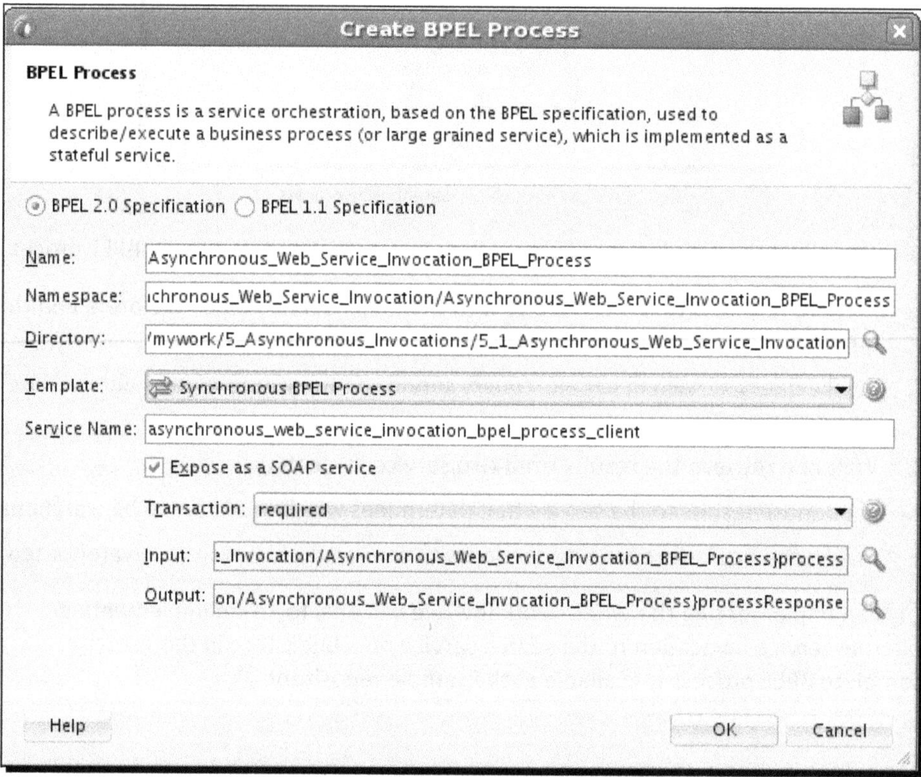

Click on **OK** once you provide the other necessary details such as name, namespace, and directory. Then the initial BPEL process appears in the development environment. In the next step, we will create two partner links required for an asynchronous communication.

Defining the partner link with myRole and partnerRole

Here we are going to define the partner link which represents the asynchronous communication between the BPEL process and the external web service. First drag-and-drop a partner link to the **Partner Links** area of the canvas. Then, a form pops up. This form is used to configure the partner link. Perform the following steps to configure the partner link that was created:

1. Name the partner link `AsynchPartnerLink`.
2. Use the **SOA Resource Browser** icon shown in the following screenshot to locate the WSDL which represents the external web service:

   Once this is done, the WSDL will automatically get copied to the project as well.
3. Now for an asynchronous web service invocation, this partner link should have two channels which are represented by roles in the BPEL world. Choose the partner link type which has two roles. In our case, there is a partner link type called **Server** which has two roles called **ServerProvider** and **ServerRequester**.
4. Now, we have to determine which roles represent the outbound (request) communication and inbound (response) communication:
    1. Select **ServerProvider** as the **Partner Role**. This is because **ServerProvider** represents a port type which in turn represents the operation that is exposed by the external web service.

2. Select **ServerRequester** as **My Role**, as shown in the following screenshot. **ServerRequester** represents a port type which in turn represents the operation that is invoked by the external web service to send back the result. In the BPEL world, we call it the **callback** and that is discussed in the later sections in this chapter.

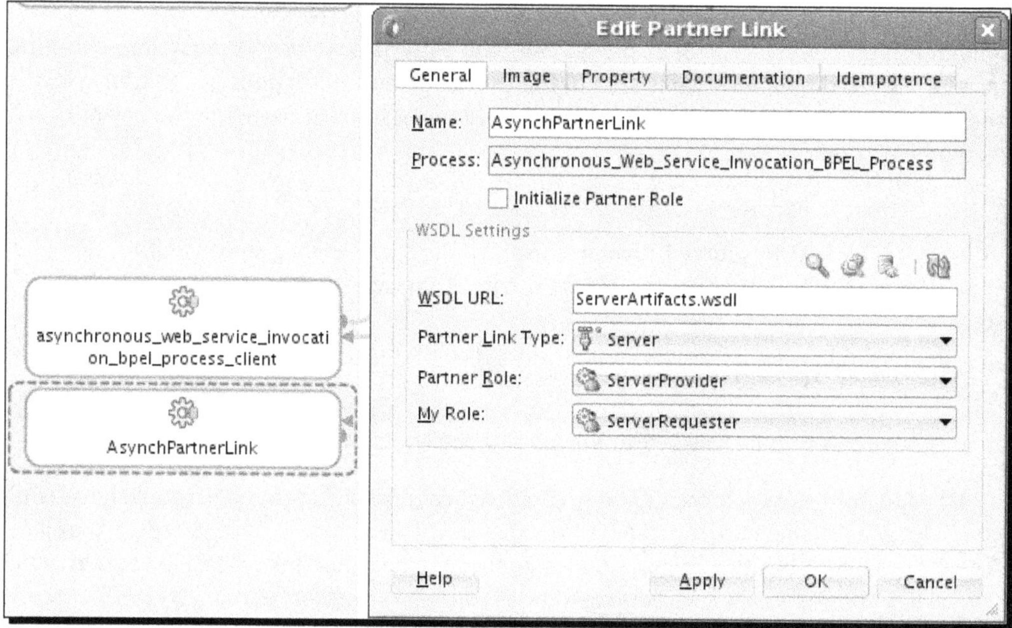

3. Click on **Apply** and then on **OK**.

Defining the invoke activity

In the previous steps, we showed how to add and configure the partner link properly. Now we can add the invoke activity that is used to invoke the external web service asynchronously via the previously defined partner link:

1. Drag-and-drop the invoke activity from the activity palette to the design area:

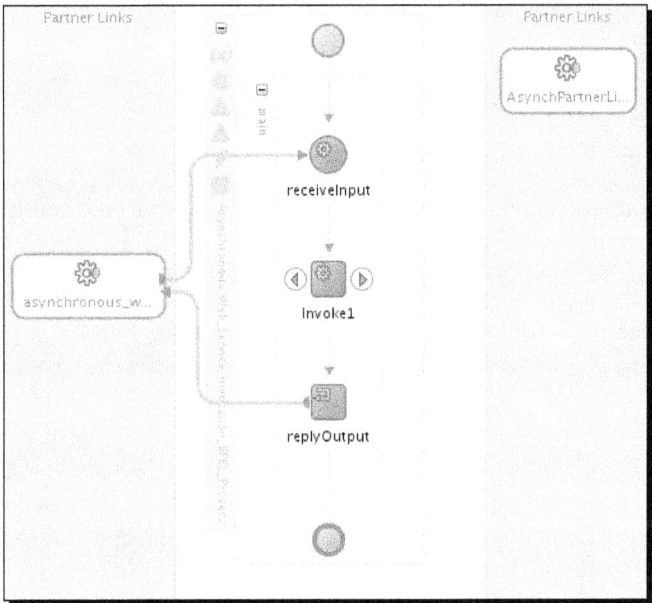

2. Double-click on the invoke activity and a form pops up to configure the invoke activity parameters:

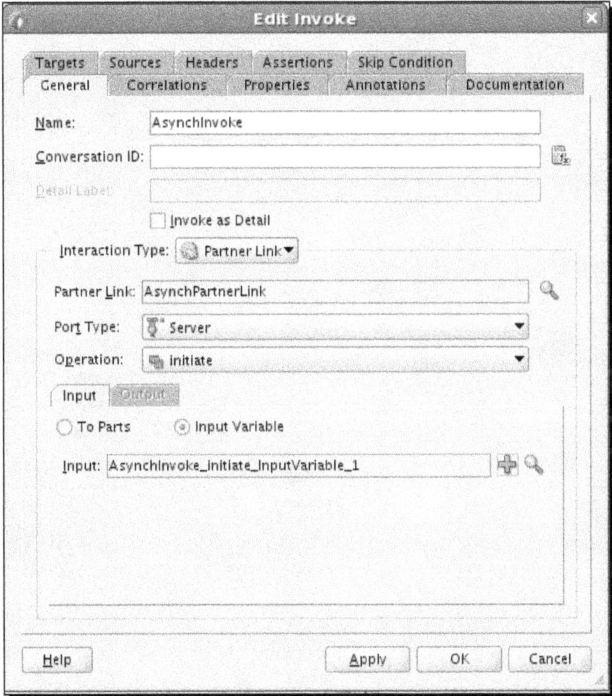

Here you can configure **Partner Link**, **Port Type**, and **Operation** as follows:

- **Partner Link** to `AsynchPartnerLink`
- **Port Type** to **Server**
- **Operation** to **initiate**

These parameters point to the operation at the external web service which accepts the request message.

3. Then, set the input variable, which represents the request message to the external web service. The input variable name is **AsynchInvoke_initiate_InputVariable**. Then click on **Apply** and then on **OK**.

Defining the receive activity

Now we need to configure the activity that accepts the response message from the external web service. This can be done by the `<receive>` activity. The `<pick>` activity can also be used to receive an asynchronous response even though it's not discussed at this point. Follow these steps to define a `receive` activity:

1. Drag a receive activity from the palette to the design area. Make sure to add the receive activity after the invoke activity we added in the previous step, as shown:

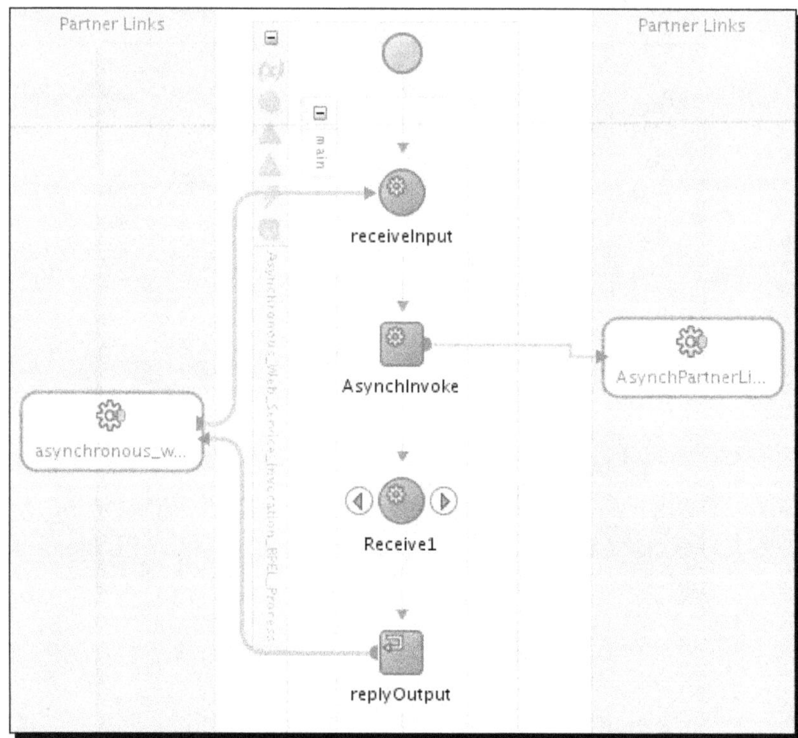

2. Then double-click on the receive activity to configure the parameters:

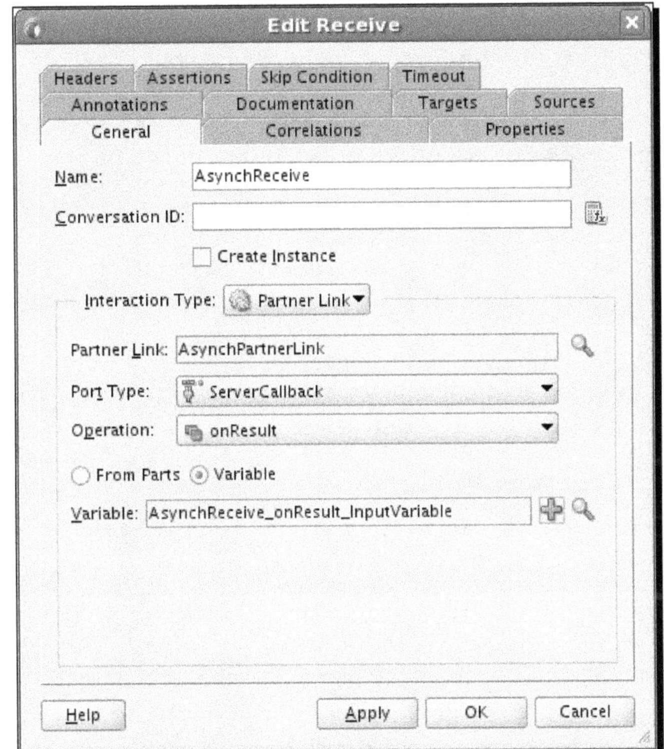

3. Here you can configure **Partner Link**, **Port Type**, and **Operation** as follows:
    - **Partner Link** to `AsynchPartnerLink`
    - **Port Type** to **ServerCallback**
    - **Operation** to **onResult**

   These parameters point to the operation that is exposed by the BPEL service to accept the response message that is sent by the external web service.

4. Then set the variable that represents the response message from the external web service. You can create a new variable to handle this response message. Let's add a new variable named **AsynchReceive_onResult_InputVariable**.

5. Once the preceding steps are completed, the design will look like the following screenshot:

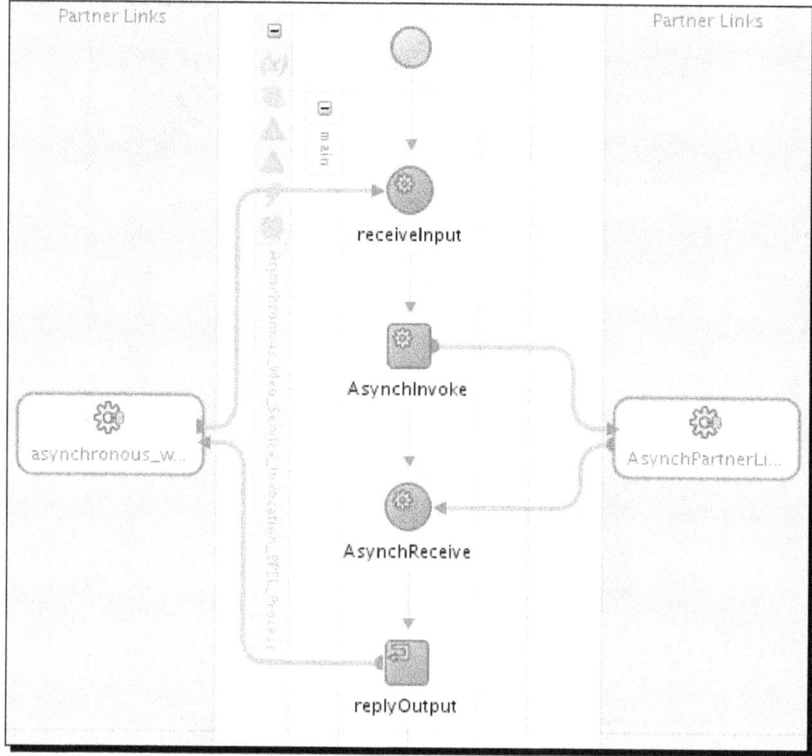

6. At this point, both the `<invoke>` and `<receive>` activities are fully configured for an asynchronous invocation.

Now what is remaining is to set up the WSDL that represents the created BPEL process and to deploy the BPEL process.

What just happened?

In the previous section, we implemented an asynchronous invocation. In this section, we explain the concepts behind an asynchronous invocation and compared it with a synchronous invocation.

First we'll discuss how an asynchronous invocation happens and why it needs a callback. Then we'll explain the concept of correlation, which maps a request for a given response in an asynchronous invocation.

Based on the knowledge of the previous chapters, we can easily implement the sample BPEL process using synchronous invocations as well, but let's explore a little bit more on practical limitations of the implementation of this BPEL process. Let's specifically focus on the external service invocations as shown in the following screenshot:

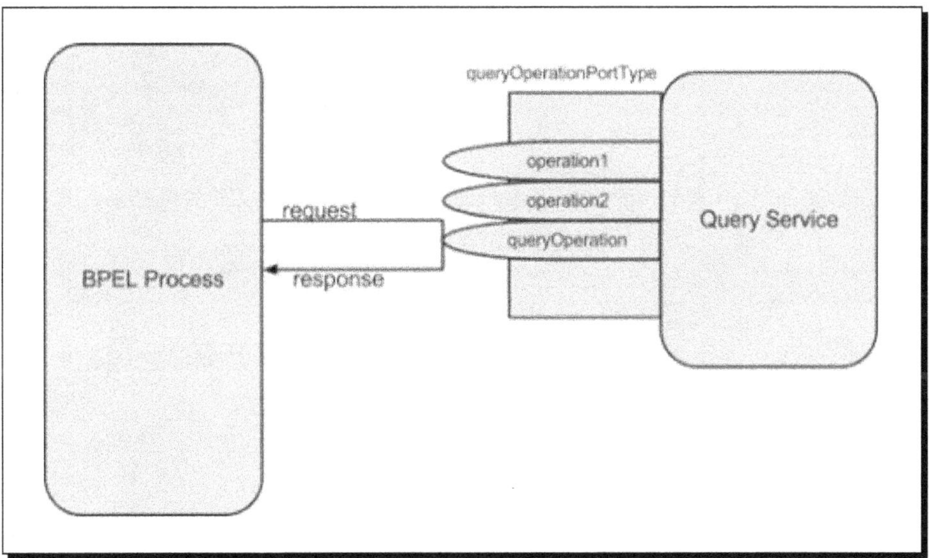

The Request-Response interaction during a synchronous invocation

During each invocation, the BPEL runtime acts as a client for the particular invocation and this client expects to retrieve the response of the service invocations within a predefined time. If the response is not returned within that time period, BPEL runtime declare it to be an error due to service invocation and takes the necessary actions. But in the real world, we don't know when the external services will return their output back to the BPEL process. So this scenario leads to potential service timeouts and consequently it leads the BPEL process to an erroneous state as the expected data from external services is not available. So the big question is, how we can avoid such nondeterministic service timeouts?

This problem can be easily solved by a modification to the service invocations that are implemented in the BPEL process. The modification is to redefine the external service invocation using two communication channels to handle request and response separately. Consequently, the BPEL runtime does not expect the response from external service invocations within a predefined time. Ultimately, the BPEL process now handles external service invocations in a more loosely coupled and reliable manner (refer to the following screenshot).

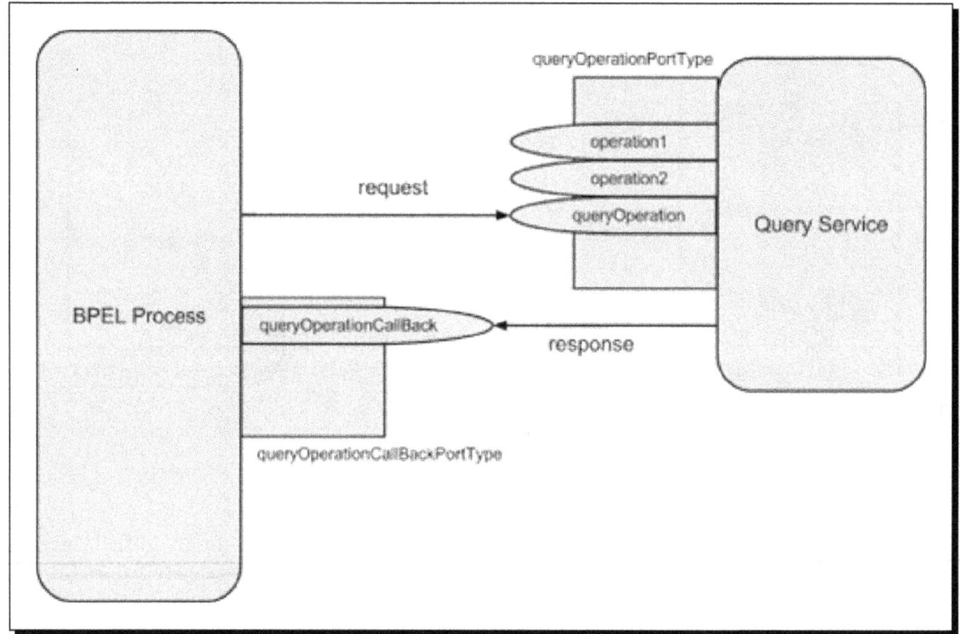

Request-Response interaction during an asynchronous invocation

In a nutshell, asynchronous invocation is useful for external services which takes a long time to process the request and respond back to the BPEL process.

Understanding asynchronous service invocations

Unlike in a synchronous web service invocation, both parties act as client and server during an asynchronous web service invocation. So when sending the request, the BPEL process acts as the client and the external service becomes the server for the particular conversation. Then when the external service sends the response, external service is the client and the BPEL process is the server for that particular conversation.

In contrast with a synchronous web service invocation, those two client-server conversations should be defined separately in an asynchronous web service invocation. Now we will analyze the difference between a synchronous and an asynchronous invocation.

If you consider the implementation of a synchronous process, then you will notice the following facts:

- In the BPEL process, the `<invoke>` activity is used for the whole conversation. So it encapsulates the input and output parameters required for the synchronous communication. Refer to the sample invoke activity included in the next bullet point.
- Within the `<invoke>` construct, the input variables and output variables are used to store request and response from the external web service. Refer to the following sample invoke activity:

```
<invoke name="InvokeCustomerInfo" partnerLink="CustomerInfoPL"
operation="getCustomerSSN" portType="ns1:CustomerInfoPortType" inp
utVariable="customerInfoInput" outputVariable="customerInfoOutput"
/>
```

- During a synchronous service invocation, the complete communication happens within one TCP connection. So the partner link of such an invocation only has one role named `partnerRole`. This `partnerRole` exposes the two-way operation of the external web service, which accepts the request and sends the response back to the BPEL process. Please refer to the following three code snippets:

```
<partnerLinks>
  <partnerLink name="CustomerInfoPL" partnerLinkType="ns1:Customer
Info" partnerRole="CustomerInfoPortTypeRole" />
</partnerLinks>
```

- Because of that, the partner link type also needs to define only one role;

```
<plnk:partnerLinkType name="CustomerInfo">
  <plnk:role name="CustomerInfoPortTypeRole" portType="tns:Custome
rInfoPortType"/>
</plnk:partnerLinkType>
```

- The WSDL of the external web service exposes a request-response-based operation to support synchronous web service invocation. The operation invoked within the `<invoke>` activity is a request-response-based operation. Refer to the sample WSDL port type, which exposes the `getCustomerSSN` operation. This operation is used in the invoke activity that is mentioned in the previous point:

```
<portType name="CustomerInfoPortType">
  <operation name="getCustomerSSN">
```

```
    <input name="input" message="tns:getCustomerSSNRequest" />
    <output name="output" message="tns:getCustomerSSNResponse" />
  </operation>
</portType>
```

However, if you compare the implementation of an asynchronous web service invocation with synchronous invocation, you'll realize the following facts:

- In the BPEL process, `<invoke>` is used to send the outgoing request to the external web service. And `<receive>` is used to retrieve the incoming response from the external web service. Refer to the sample BPEL code snippet in the next point.
- Within the `<invoke>` construct, only the input variable is used and the output variable is not used as output is not handled by `<invoke>`. The output is captured by `<receive>`. So `<receive>` defines a variable to handle the output variable:

```
<invoke name="AsynchInvoke" partnerLink="AsynchPartnerLink"
portType="ns3:Server" inputVariable="AsynchInvoke_initiate_
InputVariable"  operation="initiate" bpelx:invokeAsDetail="no">
...
</invoke>
<receive name="AsynchronousReceive" createInstance="no"
partnerLink="AsynchPartnerLink" portType="ns3:ServerCallback"
variable= Receive1_onResult_InputVariable" operation="onResult">
...
</receive>
```

- During an asynchronous service invocation, the request and response communication happens via separate TCP connections. The partner link of such an invocation needs to have two roles named `myRole` and `partnerRole`. This `partnerRole` role exposes the one-way operation of the external web service which accepts the request from the BPEL process. And `myRole` exposes a one-way operation of the service exposed by BPEL service in order to accept the response from the external web service, as shown in the following code:

```
<partnerLinks>
  <partnerLink name="AsynchPartnerLink"
partnerLinkType="ns3:Server" myRole="ServerRequester" partnerRole=
ServerProvider" />
</partnerLinks>
```

- Because of this, the partner link type also needs to define two roles:

```
<plnk:partnerLinkType name="Server">
  <plnk:role name="ServerProvider" portType="tns:Server" />
  <plnk:role name="ServerRequester" portType="tns:ServerCallback"
/>
</plnk:partnerLinkType>
```

- The WSDL of the external web service exposes a one-way operation which is invoked by the BPEL `<invoke>` construct. This operation defines the schema of the request message for the external web service invocation. The service exposed by the BPEL process defines another one-way operation, which is invoked by the external service. This operation defines the schema of the response message for the external web service invocation, as shown in the following code:

```
<portType name="Server">
  <operation name="initiate">
    <input message="tns:ServerRequestMessage" />
  </operation>
</portType>
<portType name="ServerCallback">
  <operation name="onResult">
    <input message="tns:ServerResponseMessage"
wsaw:Action="http://wso2.org/onResult" />
  </operation>
</portType>
```

The following are the pre-requisites to initiate an asynchronous web service invocation:

- The WSDL interface of the external web service should expose one-way operation to capture the incoming request message from the BPEL process
- The WSDL interface of the BPEL process should expose a one-way operation to capture the outgoing response message from the external web service

The following are the steps to implement an asynchronous web service invocation in a summary:

1. Define the partner link with `myRole` and `partnerRole`.
2. Define the invoke activity with the initialized `inputVariable` that is the outgoing request message from the BPEL process.
3. Define the receive activity to capture the response message correlated with the invoke activity.

Callbacks

In the previous section, we talked about basic building blocks required for an asynchronous web service invocation. We explained why and how a partner link should represent the two communication channels, which manage request and response separately. These two channels are named `partnerRole` and `myRole` in the BPEL world. The `myRole` channel is used to represent the requester of the asynchronous communication. During an asynchronous web service invocation, the requester is the BPEL process. So in the WSDL representation of the BPEL process, `myRole` is pointed to an operation exposed by the BPEL process to accept the response from the external web service. We name this operation a **callback** operation.

A callback operation is used to transfer the response message of an asynchronous web service invocation to the client end from the server end. Here, the client end is the BPEL process and the server end is the external web service. Let's see how to set up the callback to the BPEL process.

Setting up a callback

Setting up a callback happens via the `<receive>` activity. You can configure a `<receive>` activity in a way to accept messages from the external web service. The `partnerLink` and `operation` attributes of the receive activity should point to a one-way operation exposed by the BPEL process such that the external web service can send the callback (response) message back to the BPEL process, as shown in the following code:

```
<invoke name="AsynchInvoke" partnerLink="AsynchPartnerLink"
portType="ns3:Server" inputVariable="AsynchInvoke_initiate_
InputVariable"
operation="initiate" bpelx:invokeAsDetail="no">
...
</invoke>
<receive name="AsynchronousReceive" createInstance="no"
partnerLink="AsynchPartnerLink" portType="ns3:ServerCallback"
variable="Receive1_onResult_InputVariable" operation="onResult">
...
</receive>
```

Mapping response messages from asynchronous invocations

When a message reaches the BPEL server from an asynchronous web service, the BPEL server is responsible to figure out the following details to correlate the `<invoke>` activity which sends the request and the `<receive>` activity that receives the response message. Once the relevant `<receive>` activity is found, the BPEL server routes the particular response message to the correct `<receive>` activity.

- **Correct process**: This is determined by the request URL. The request URL contains the name of the web service that exposes the BPEL process.
- **Correct instance**: The BPEL server determines this by a specification called WS-Addressing. We'll discuss this in the next section.
- **Correct receive/pick-onMessage activity**: This will not be discussed in this book.

> If the asynchronous web service is implemented using Oracle SOA Suite or according to the WS-Addressing specification, Oracle BPEL Server automatically correlates response messages from asynchronous web services. Hence, users do not need to worry about message correlation when they are modeling asynchronous interactions using Oracle SOA Suite. Next, we will discuss about correlation in detail.

Message correlation – why, when, and how is it essential?

In this section, we will discuss an advanced topic that is targeted on readers who are interested in underlying techniques on mapping asynchronous web service responses to the correct BPEL process instance.

In the preceding section, we raised the question of mapping an incoming message to the BPEL server to a particular web service invocation. In an asynchronous web service invocation, there is no relation between the outgoing request message and the incoming response message, but when a message is being received by the BPEL server, the BPEL server should be able to determine which process instance initiated the outgoing asynchronous request. The response message should be routed to that particular process instance.

Let's have a look at the following graph to get a clear idea on this routing task:

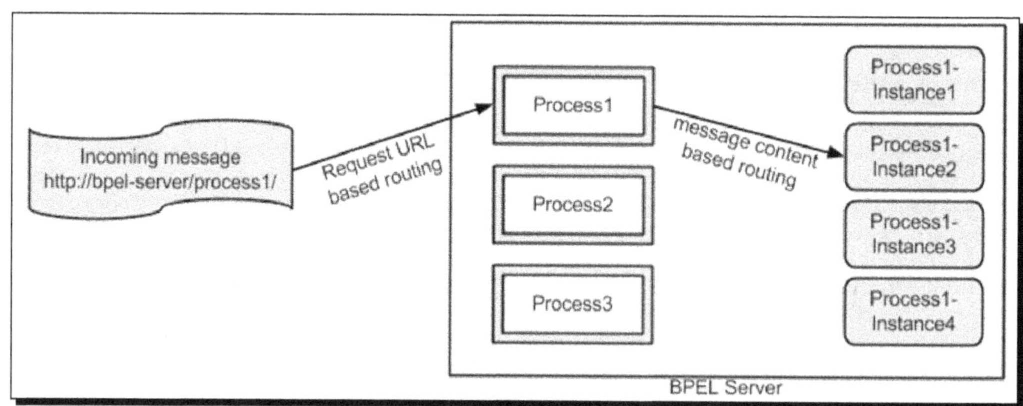

How a request message reaches a process instance

In the preceding figure, you'll realize that there are multiple processes (**Process1**, **Process2**, and **Process3**) and there are multiple instances created from Process1 (that is, Process1-Instance1, Process1-Instance2, and so on). Once an incoming message hits the BPEL server, it can determine the correct process definition by the request URL. Once the process definition is determined, the BPEL server should determine to which instance the message should be routed. This is determined by correlating a specific header element (such as a WS-Addressing header) or a body element (for example, a unique ID included in the message body) of the outgoing and incoming SOAP messages. During an asynchronous invocation, a unique ID is propagated with an outgoing request message and that unique ID is queried in and verified with the incoming response message.

Correlation set is the standard mechanism in WS-BPEL 2.0 that defines the message parts which contain unique IDs that are used to map asynchronous requests and responses. Oracle SOA Suite supports WS-Addressing-based correlation, which doesn't require to specify correlation sets by users. We modeled the asynchronous interactions of the book warehousing process using WS-Addressing. WS-Addressing specification uses a header element in the SOAP message. This WS-Addressing-based header includes a correlation ID (that is a unique ID) and an endpoint location (for example, the URL at which a BPEL process instance is listening for the response message). By processing the WS-Addressing header content, Oracle SOA Suite can automatically route the message to the correct process instance.

In the next sections, we explain how to use correlation sets which are the standard correlation mechanism in WS-BPEL 2.0 for readers who are interested in advanced details.

Setting up a correlation set

Setting up a correlation set is a three-step process:

1. Define the correlation set.
2. Declare the WSDL message property and map it with the correlation set.
3. Define the property aliases for the WSDL message property. These property aliases hold the exact message part which is to be correlated.

Understanding the correlation set

The `<correlationSet/>` construct is defined with a unique correlation set name. This name is referred by the `<invoke>` and `<receive>` constructs to map the outgoing request message with the incoming response message. This `correlationSet` construct has a `properties` attribute. This attribute's value can contain one or more WSDL message property names.

For example, consider the following code:

```
<correlationSets>
  <correlationSet name="AsynchronousServiceInvocationCorrelationSet"
properties="ns4:correlationProperty" />
</correlationSets>
```

WSDL message property

WSDL message properties are defined in the WSDLs and they act as mappings to WSDL message parts. We can define a WSDL message property as the intermediate party which maps a correlation set to the exact message parts of the request and response. The schema of the request and response is different and the values which are used to identify the correlation between request and response can be in different places of the message. The WSDL message property should be able to represent both message parts of the request and response messages. This is achieved by message aliases such as `<vprop:property name="correlationProperty" type="xsd:string"/>`.

Property alias

A message alias represents the exact element of the message which is expected to be used to hold the unique ID for a particular asynchronous web service invocation. It consists of a `<query/>` element which can locate the elements or attributes of the message, such as:

```
<vprop:propertyAlias propertyName="cor:correlationProper
ty" element="ns1:ServerRequest" xmlns:ns1="urn:ode-apache-
org:example:async:server">
  <vprop:query>/ns1:id</vprop:query>
</vprop:propertyAlias>
```

```
<vprop:propertyAlias propertyName="cor:correlationProper
ty" element="ns1:ServerResponse" xmlns:ns1="urn:ode-apache-
org:example:async:server">
  <vprop:query>/ns1:id</vprop:query>
</vprop:propertyAlias>
```

Using a correlation for an asynchronous web service invocation

Now, let's see how to use the correlation defined in the previous section. For an asynchronous web service invocation, the correlation value is initiated when executing the `<invoke>` activity. Then this correlation value is persisted and used when a message is received to the particular BPEL process for routing operations.

A correlation is used when the request message leaves the BPEL server and when the response message reaches the BPEL server. We'll explain these two phases in the next two subsections.

Initializing a correlation at <invoke>

This is where the correlation is initiated for an asynchronous web service, as shown:

```
<invoke name="AsynchInvoke" partnerLink="AsynchPartnerLink"
portType="ns3:Server" inputVariable="AsynchInvoke_initiate_
InputVariable" operation="initiate">
  <correlations>
    <correlation set="AsynchronousServiceInvocationCorrelationSet"
initiate="yes" />
  </correlations>
</invoke>
```

So you have to set `initiate="yes"` within the particular invoke activity.

Referring the initialized correlation at <receive>

This is where the previously initialized correlation is referred to realize whether the incoming message is relevant to the particular process instance, as shown in the following code:

```
<receive name="AsynchronousReceive" createInstance="no"
partnerLink="AsynchPartnerLink" portType="ns3:ServerCallback"
variable= Receive1_onResult_InputVariable" operation="onResult">
  <correlations>
    <correlation set="AsynchronousServiceInvocationCorrelationSet"
initiate="no" />
  </correlations>
</receive>
```

So here the only difference is you don't have to initiate the correlation.

Time for action – creating an asynchronous BPEL process

In the first half of this chapter, we explained how to invoke an asynchronous web service from a BPEL process instance. Hence, the BPEL process instance may remain active for a very long time. For example, a loan approval process may take weeks to be completed. If a BPEL process instance is expected to remain active for an undetermined period of time, the BPEL process itself should be deployed as an asynchronous process because the BPEL process also cannot reply back to its caller within a definite time period due to external asynchronous web service invocations, which happen within the BPEL process. In this section, we will model an asynchronous BPEL process and compare it with a synchronous BPEL process.

Oracle JDeveloper editor supports the creation of an asynchronous BPEL process via a predefined process definition template. You can create an asynchronous BPEL process with following steps:

1. Navigate to **File** | **New** | **From Gallery....** A form up called **New Gallery** pops up.
2. Select **SOA Tier** from the **Categories** list and then select **Service Components**.
3. Now, the **Items** list shows a set of available service component options. Select **BPEL Process** and click on **OK**, as shown:

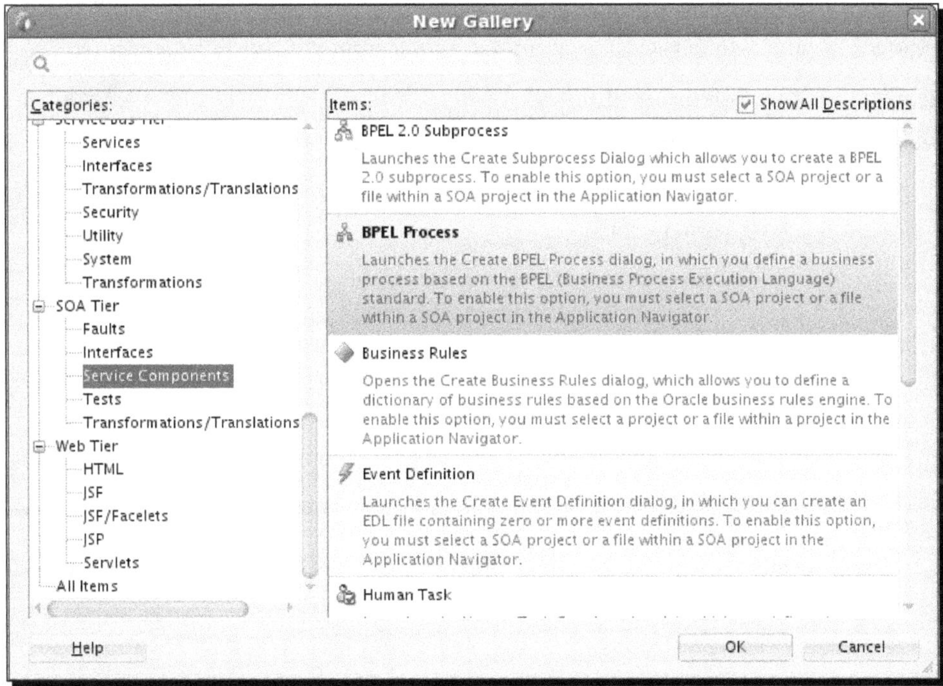

4. Then, a new form named **Create BPEL Process** pops up. This form lets you configure the initial template of the BPEL process. Select the following options:
    - **BPEL 2.0 Specification**
    - **Name** to **Asynch_BPEL_Process**
    - **Template** to **Asynchronous BPEL Process**
    - The other options are set automatically based on the template

    Template is the most important option in order to create an asynchronous BPEL process. The **Create BPEL Process** window is shown in the following screenshot:

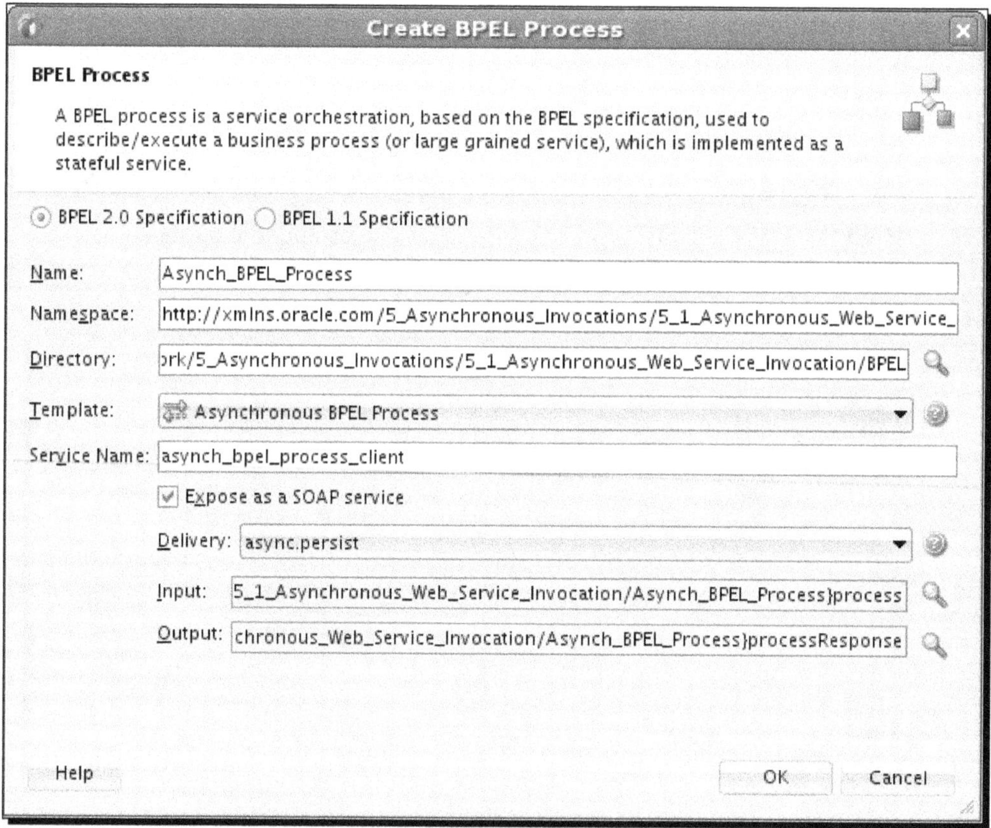

5. Then the initial asynchronous BPEL process is created and you can see the workflow from the design area as follows:

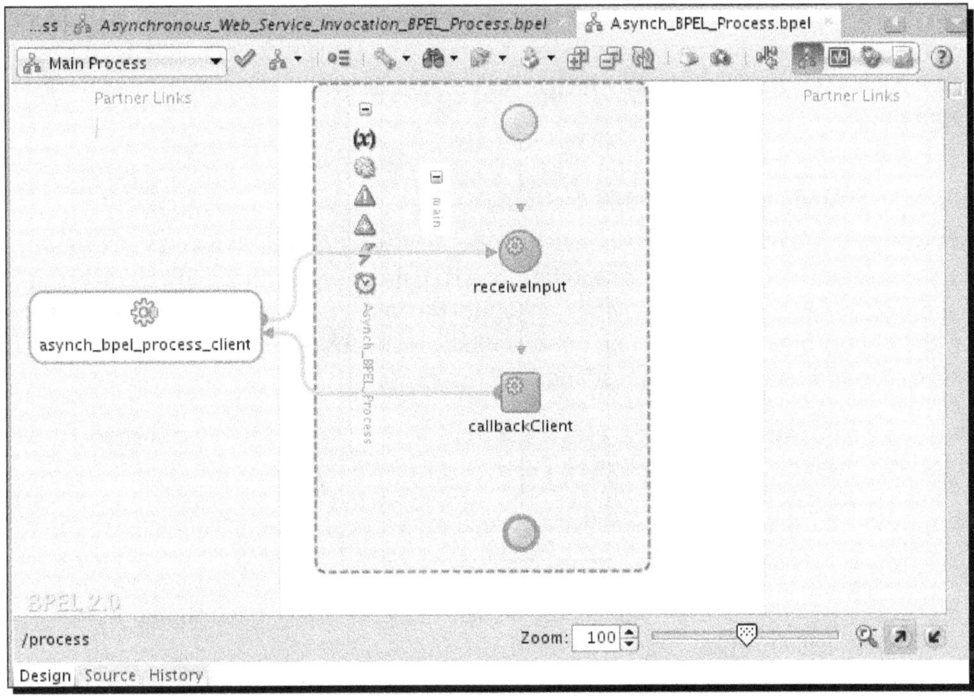

6. Once you initialize the output variable in invoke activity, the BPEL process can be tested for its asynchronous functionality.

What just happened?

A synchronous BPEL process uses the <receive>, <reply> activity pair to receive the request from the caller and to send the response back to the caller, respectively. The <receive> and <reply> activities use a single WSDL two-way operation during a synchronous request response interaction. But for an asynchronous BPEL-process execution, we use a <receive> and <invoke> activity pair, as we have explained in the *Understanding asynchronous service invocations* section. But there are some differences which are as follows:

- An asynchronous web service invocation uses the <invoke> activity to send the request and it uses the <receive> activity to capture the response from the external web service.
- In an asynchronous BPEL process, the <receive> activity is used to capture the request from its caller to start execution within the BPEL process, and it uses the <invoke> activity to send the response back to its caller.

Thus, even though the mechanism of setting up an asynchronous BPEL process and setting up an asynchronous web service invocation is similar, the semantics are a little bit different when it comes to the BPEL activity which is responsible to handle the request and the response of the communication.

Using the <invoke> activity instead of <reply>

If you compare the request and response handling in a synchronous and an asynchronous BPEL process, you will realize the only difference is that the synchronous BPEL process uses the `<receive>` and `<reply>` activities to handle the initial request and final response from the BPEL process and the asynchronous BPEL process uses the `<receive>-<invoke>` activities to handle the initial request and final response.

Thus, the synchronous BPEL process uses a `<reply>` activity to send the response to its caller, and the asynchronous BPEL process uses a `<invoke>` to send the response to its caller.

So why can't we use the `<reply>` activity instead of the `<invoke>` activity in both cases?

This is because, based on the WS-BPEL 2.0 specification, the `<reply>` activity can be used only for synchronous communication. In case of an asynchronous communication, the `<invoke>` activity always has to be used.

Have a go hero – an asynchronous BPEL process with asynchronous service invocations

Improve the sample BPEL process such that it asynchronously invokes the search services to bookstores A and B. Then, improve it such that the BPEL process also can be invoked asynchronously.

Pop quiz

Q1. What are the types of WSDL operations that can be used for an asynchronous communication?

1. Solicit-response
2. One-way
3. Request-response
4. Notification

Q2. Based on what characteristic of the messages, does the BPEL runtime figure out the correlation between the outgoing request message and the incoming response message?

Q3. How many `<receive>` activities can be there with the `createInstance` attribute value set to `yes`, in a working BPEL process?

1. One
2. Two
3. Any number

Q4. Explain why is it not intuitive to invoke an asynchronous web service from a synchronous BPEL process.

Summary

In this chapter, we have learned how to communicate with external web services in an asynchronous manner and also learned how to invoke an asynchronous BPEL process. This chapter is important as the asynchronous communication is essential to be implemented in real-world long-running business processes where the request-response time is undetermined for a particular external web service invocation. Also, there are circumstances where the endpoints defined for the response and for the particular request are exposed by different web services. For an example, a business process can invoke its purchase service. But the confirmation response to that particular request actually comes from the shipping process. In such scenarios, asynchronous communication is inevitable. The concepts we learned in this chapter are useful in real-world business process developments.

In the next chapter, we will learn about fault handling and signaling, which is another interesting and important topic. Fault handling and signaling come into play when the business process needs to handle expected and unexpected behaviors during the business process execution time. Let's discuss this in more detail in the next chapter.

6
Fault Handling and Signaling

So far we have learned how to perform data manipulations, loops, and external service invocations synchronously and asynchronously. Imagine what will happen when the BPEL process invokes an external web service which is not available at the moment. In such a situation, the BPEL process could lead to an erroneous state. How can the BPEL process manage those generated faults and avoid such unexpected states?

WS-BPEL 2.0 provides fault handlers that come to the rescue. It tells the BPEL process how to perform when such an error occurs. In this chapter, we will learn about fault handling capabilities in a WS-BPEL 2.0 process.

In this chapter, we will cover the following topics:

- Introducing faults and fault handlers
- Adding fault handlers to business processes
- Understanding the fault handlers
- Different fault signaling techniques
- Ending and terminating a BPEL process due to a fault

Introducing faults and fault handlers

Business processes are not intended to be a self-contained application. They are intended to cooperate with other existing remote services and to provide a service with much higher business value. So the WS-BPEL 2.0 specification provides constructs to satisfy these semantics.

Thus, a business process written in WS-BPEL 2.0 is capable of external web service invocations and manipulates the data based on the business logic. Speaking of such behavior, during the execution of the business process, it could lead to unexpected behaviors due to errors in the business logic, unexpected inputs, or unexpected behaviors in the environment. For example, an external web service may return a negative value where the client BPEL process expects a positive value. We explain some of those causes more specifically in the next section. Let's first see what sort of potential faults can be generated in a business process execution environment.

Communication issues

When a business process communicates with external web services, this communication happens over a network. This communication is prone to unexpected errors due to unreliability in the transport infrastructure.

The external web service may be unavailable or the web service may be moved to a new location without notifying the business process. So the business process infers it as a service unavailability.

Contract issues

When the external web service changes, the agreed communication contract with the business process can be changed without notification. For example, the security policy or the WSDL representation of the external web service can be changed without any prior notification. This leads to the breaking of the agreed relationship between the business process and the external web service.

Faults thrown from the external web service

The external web service itself can throw errors based on its implementation. And those faults can be propagated back to the business process. We normally call them WSDL faults. We will discuss this type of fault more deeply in an upcoming section.

Faults thrown from the business process

The business process can generate faults due to its business logic. These faults can be twofold:

- **Logical (explicit) errors**: One category of faults is defined by the business process developer. So, for example, if the input variable carries an unexpected value, the business process developer can declare a fault within the business logic. And then the business process should be responsible to take care of that fault. Logical errors are also known as business faults.
- **Execution errors**: The other category of faults is generated by the BPEL runtime. Hence execution errors are also known as runtime faults. Suppose, when a variable is assigned some data, the BPEL runtime generates a fault if the variable is uninitialized. Some of these errors have to be handled at design and development time. The rest of it has to be dealt with at runtime.

Now, we have a high-level view of the possible faults that can be generated during the life cycle of a business process.

Introducing fault handlers

We discussed the potential categories of faults that can be generated in a business process execution environment. In order to deal with them, the WS-BPEL 2.0 specification provides a notion called fault handler, which is used to define the fault handling behavior for a particular fault. In the *Time for action – adding fault handlers*, section we demonstrate how to declare and configure a fault handler. In the next *What just happened?* section, we explain the fault handler in more detail. So let's move on to the sample business process, which declares a fault handler.

Preparing for action

In this exercise, we demonstrate how to declare a fault handler and how it is triggered. We will use the sample BPEL process (book warehousing process) from *Chapter 5, Interaction Patterns in BPEL*. Then, in the next exercise, we extend the book warehousing process to cover more aspects in fault handling and signaling. Thus, we improve the book warehousing process by adding a fault handler to the external web service invocation and signal the fault back to the client of the BPEL process.

Let's remember the example, named book warehousing process, which we introduced in *Chapter 5, Interaction Patterns in BPEL*.

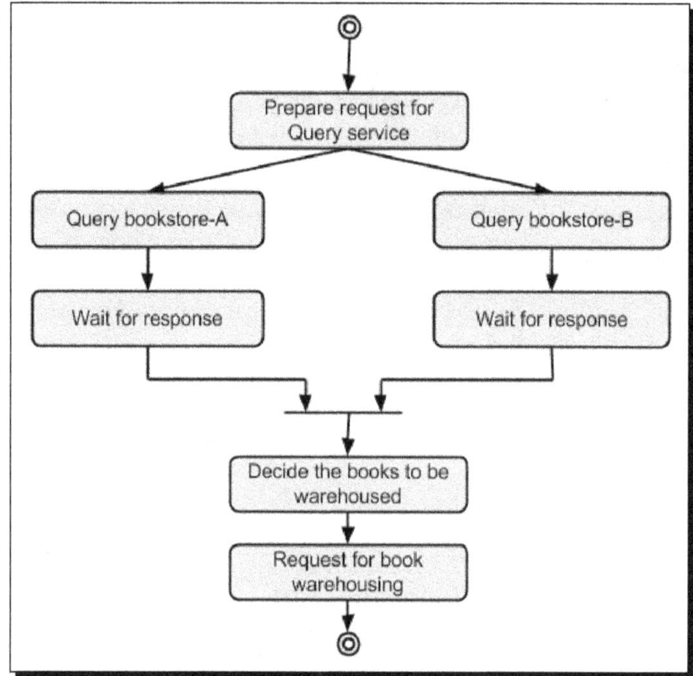

Workflow of the book warehousing process

In this exercise, we will generate a simple fault based on the content of the input. If the value of incoming message of the BPEL process is equal to `error`, then the BPEL process will generate an error.

Time for action – adding fault handlers

The steps for adding fault handlers are as follows:

1. We check the content of the input message before preparing the request to the query services. The `<if>` activity can be used to check the content of input and get an action based on the result. So let's drag-and-drop a new `<if>` activity in between the `<receive>` and `<assign>` activities that prepare the request message to the query service:

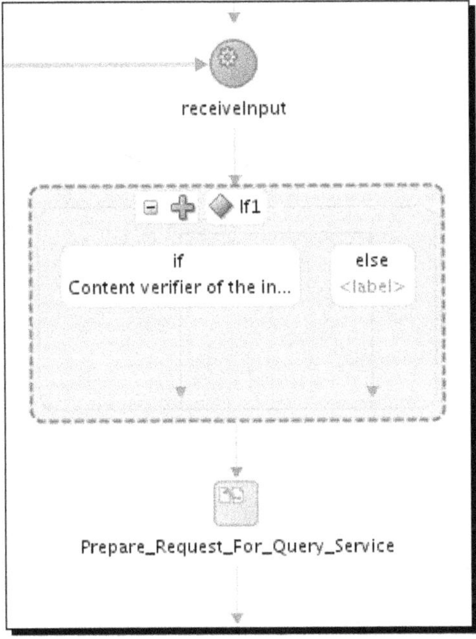

2. Now, let's add the content verification logic as the condition in the `<if>` activity. Click on the `if` case in the `<if>` activity and use **XPath Expression Builder** to generate the expression in the box named **Condition**:

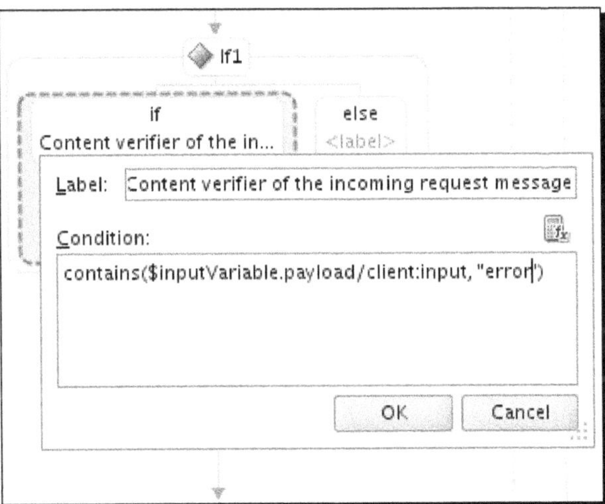

3. Now, if the condition is `true`, the activity defined within the `<if>` case is executed. So let's generate a fault within the `<if>` case. In WS-BPEL 2.0, to generate a fault, the `<throw>` activity is used. Drag-and-drop a `<throw>` activity within the `<if>` case, as follows:

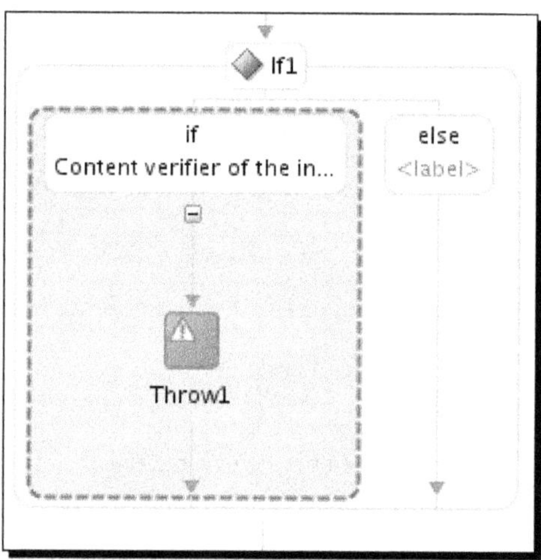

4. The next step is to configure the fault that is generated by the `<throw>` activity. Let's just configure a qualified fault name. Now click on **Apply** and then on **OK**:

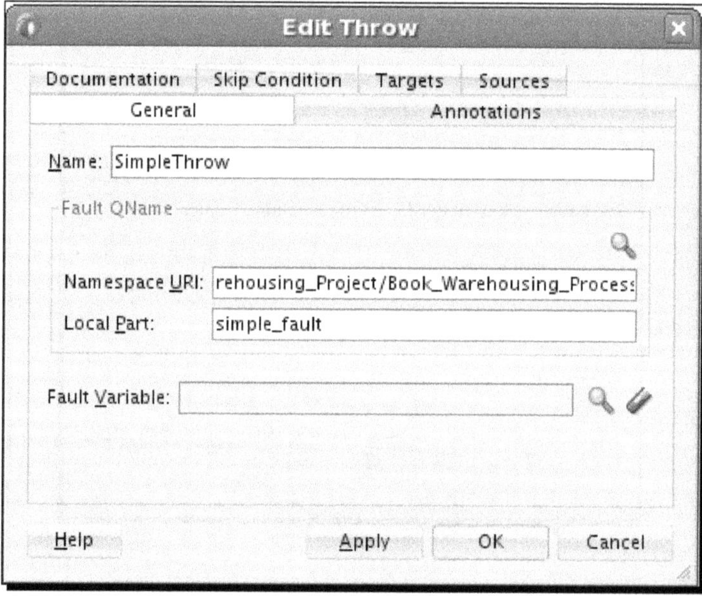

5. Now, similar to traditional programming languages like Java, we need to add a construct that handles the generated fault. In WS-BPEL 2.0, `<faultHandler>` is responsible for this. To add `<faultHandler>` to the process, click on the following icon in the icon pallet of the process definition:

Once you have clicked on that icon, a fault handler is generated with a catch construct:

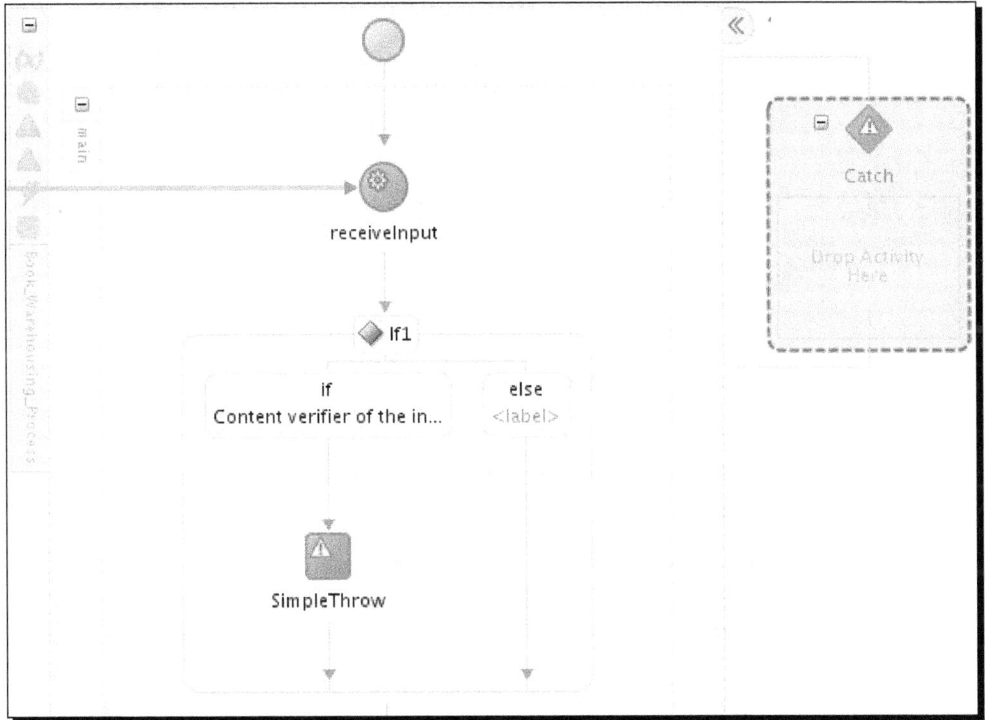

This catch construct can handle a specific type of fault. When we need to generate a fault handler that can handle any type of fault, we can use the `<catchall>` construct which can be generated by clicking on the following icon on the icon palette of the process definition:

6. In step 4, we defined the fault by a qualified name that is generated by a `<throw>` activity. Now in order to handle that particular fault, the catch fault handler should be configured to handle the same qualified name of that fault. So double-click on the catch fault handler and specify the same qualified name as the **Fault Name**:

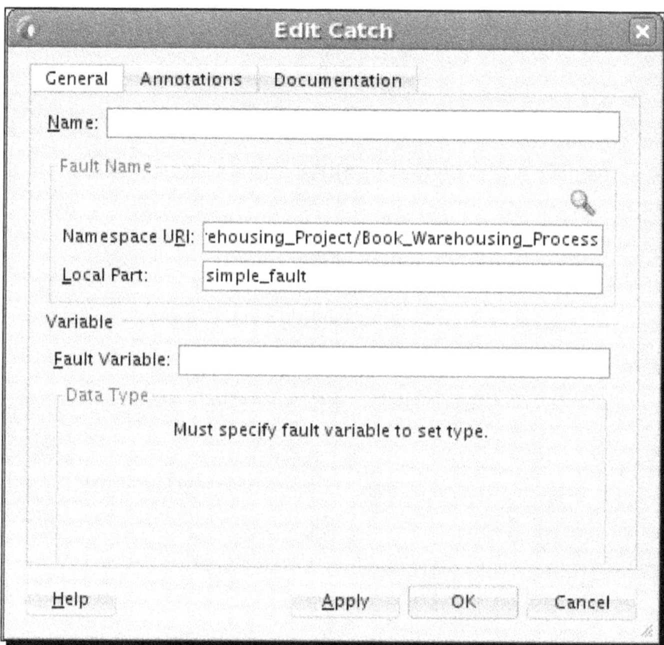

7. As the remaining step of defining a fault handler, what is left is to define a fault handling logic within the fault handler. For the sake of simplicity, we add an `<exit>` activity (as shown in the following screenshot), so the process instance is immediately ended. In the next exercise, we declare a more meaningful fault handling behavior.

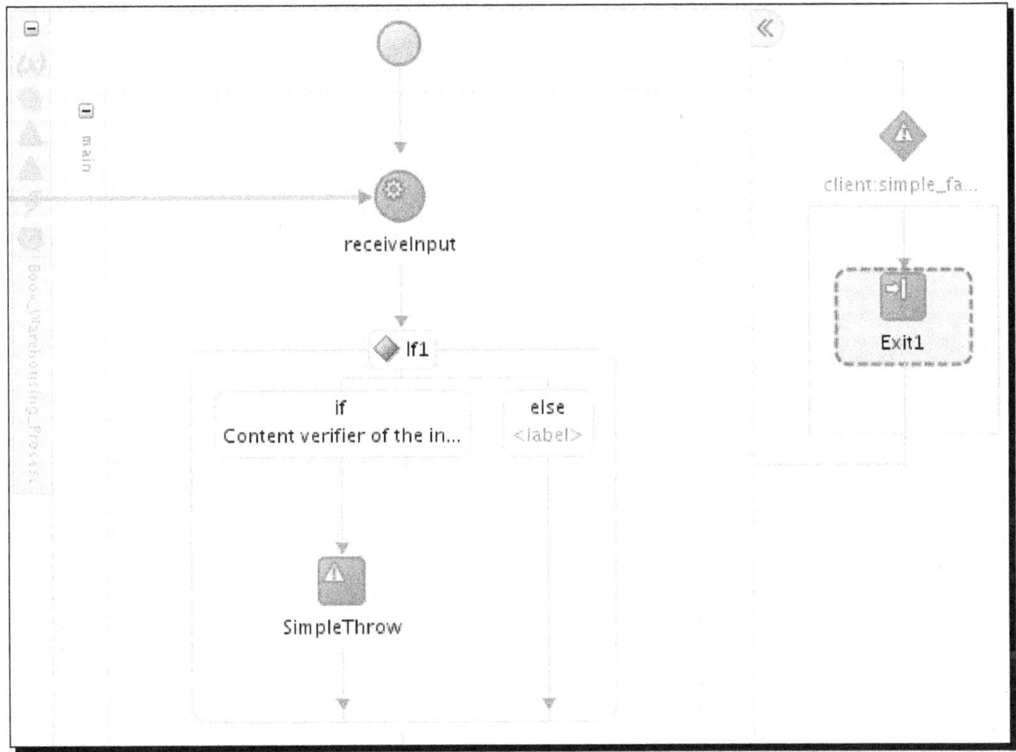

What just happened?

In the previous sections, we introduced a high-level view of the possible faults that can be generated during the life cycle of a business process. They are as follows:

- Communication issues
- Contract issues
- Faults thrown from the external web service
- Faults thrown from the business process itself

Then we demonstrated an example with step-by-step instructions to implement a fault handler for a fault thrown from the business process itself. We generated that fault by checking the content of a variable of the business process. Then a fault handler was added where the fault is handled within the business process. For the sake of simplicity, we used the `<exit>` activity as the fault handling logic. In that example, we introduced a few WS-BPEL 2.0 constructs such as `<throw>`, `<faultHandler>`, and `<catchall>` to signal and handle an error. But we didn't explain their usage in detail. So, in this section, we explain in detail how those constructs model a fault handling behavior within a business process.

We discussed four categories of possible faults that can be generated during the life cycle of a business process in the *Introducing Faults and Fault Handlers* section. The WS-BPEL 2.0 specification models those aforementioned faults based on three different models. They are as follows:

- Modeling execution errors with WS-BPEL 2.0 standard faults
- Modeling logical (explicit) errors with the `<throw>` activity
- Modeling errors propagated from external web services

Modeling execution errors with WS-BPEL 2.0 standard faults

The WS-BPEL 2.0 specification defines a standard set of faults. Each of those faults is defined to represent an erroneous behavior that could occur during a business process execution. Examples of such standard faults include the following:

- `correlationViolation`: It is thrown when the contents of the messages that are processed in `<invoke>`, `<receive>`, `<reply>`, `<onMessage>`, or `<onEvent>` do not match specified correlation information
- `uninitializedVariable`: It shows a fault representing an attempt to refer or access the data in an uninitialized variable
- `uninitializedPartnerRole`: It is thrown when attempting to refer a partner link which has an uninitialized partner role
- `selectionFailure`: It is thrown when a selection operation performed either in a function, such as `bpel:getVariableProperty` or in an assignment, encounters an error

These faults are generated by BPEL at runtime.

Modeling logical (explicit) errors with the <throw> activity

The WS-BPEL 2.0 specification defines the `<throw>` activity, which can be used by the developer to generate faults to handle logical errors. In the *Time for action – adding fault handlers* section, we explain how to use the `<throw>` activity to generate faults and handle them within the `<faultHandler>` construct.

Modeling errors propagated from external web services

In the previous section, we mentioned some examples of possible faults that could be generated from the external web service. We also mentioned that those faults are called WSDL faults. These faults are modeled in WSDL representation of the external web service and we'll explain more about this in the *WSDL faults* subsection.

Previous paragraphs introduced how the problematic behaviors in a business process can be managed in the WS-BPEL 2.0 world based on defined constructs such as `<throw>` and `<faultHandler>`. In the next sections we are going to dig deep into those constructs.

Understanding fault handlers and signaling

Fault handler, as the name suggests, is used in the WS-BPEL 2.0 specification to handle the generated faults. These faults can be logical errors, execution errors, or errors generated due to the external environment of the BPEL process. These faults can be either implicitly generated by the BPEL runtime or explicitly generated using the `<throw>` activity.

The basic `<throw>` activity has the following syntax with an attribute named `faultName`. The value of this attribute can be any qualified name so it can be used to realize the correct fault handler that is responsible for the generated fault. Consider the following code snippet:

```
<throw xmlns:fltns="http://packtpub.com/bpel/faults"
faultName="fltns:faultName" />
```

However, some generated faults can contain data related to the fault. As usual, this data is represented by a BPEL variable and the optional attribute named `faultVariable` is used to refer to the particular variable that contains the data. Consider the following code snippet:

```
<throw xmlns:fltns="http://packtpub.com/bpel/faults"
faultName="fltns:faultName" <!--mandatory attribute-->
faultVariable="variableName" <!--optional attribute--> />
```

Now, let's see the structure of a `<faultHandler>` construct in detail in the upcoming section.

Structure of a fault handler

The following code template depicts the structure of a fault handler:

```
<faultHandlers>
  <catch ... ><!-- First fault handler -->
    <!-- Perform an activity -->
  </catch>
```

```
    <catch ... ><!-- Second fault handler -->
      <!-- Perform an activity -->
    </catch>
    <catchAll>
      <!-- Perform an activity -->
    </catchAll>
  </faultHandlers>
```

So the immediate child elements of a fault handler can be `<catch>` or `<catchAll>`. A `<catch>` element can be used to handle a specific fault and `<catchAll>` is used to handle faults that are not handled by the other `<catch>` elements. Also, the optional `<catchAll>` element should be located as the last element in `<faultHandler>`. We'll get into more detail on the construction of `<catch>` and `<catchAll>` elements in the upcoming sections.

Location of a fault handler

A fault handler cannot be placed in any place in a BPEL process. Basically, it can be placed only at two locations and it can be categorized into two types based on its location as follows.

The global fault handler

The global fault handler is defined for the whole process and it is located as the immediate previous element to the first activity of the BPEL process. It can correspond to faults that occur across the BPEL process. The global fault handler is owned by the process element which houses all other sequences, scopes, and activities.

The local (inline) fault handler

A fault handler can be included within a scope or invoke activity to handle faults generated within the particular `<scope>` or `<invoke>` activity. The `<scope>` activity is a structural activity in the WS-BPEL 2.0 specification and it provides a context boundary to its child constructs. So within a `<scope>` activity, there can be defined variables or partner links which are local to that particular scope. We will discuss scopes more deeply in the next chapter.

Configuring a fault handler

Within `<faultHandler>`, the `<catch>` and `<catchAll>` activities maintain the fault handling logic related to the fault captured by the `<catch>` or `<catchAll>` activity. So the `<catch>` and `<catchAll>` activity should consist of some parameters which precisely define the fault that the particular `<catch>` or `<catchAll>` activity handles. In this section, we discuss how to configure `<catch>` and `<catchAll>` activities such that the generated faults are propagated to the right `<catch>` or `<catchAll>` activity.

Earlier in the chapter, we introduced the structure of <faultHandler>, and how <catch> and <catchAll> are organized within <faultHandler>. We also mentioned that <catch> can be used to handle a specific fault and <catchAll> is used to handle faults that are not handled by the other <catch> elements. Keeping that in mind, let's take a look at the attributes used in <catch> which specifically define the faults that it is supposed to handle. There are few attributes which can be used to realize the faults that a particular <catch> is responsible for. Based on those attributes, the BPEL runtime can realize the faults that a particular <catch> handles. These attributes are as follows:

- `faultName`: This attribute defines the qualified name of the fault. So if a fault is generated with such a qualified name, this <catch> activity becomes a potential candidate to handle it. Consider the following code snippet:

  ```
  <catch faultName="fltns:faultName" >
      ...
  </catch>
  ```

- `faultVariable`: This attribute refers to the variable type used for the fault data. There are two other optional attributes named `faultMessageType` and `faultElement` of which only one can be used with the `faultVariable` attribute at any given point of time. The `faultMessageType` attribute is used to specify the WSDL message type of the `faultVariable` attribute. Alternatively, `faultElement` is used to specify the schema of the `faultVariable` attribute. These attributes help the BPEL runtime to select the most suitable fault handler (<catch> or <catchAll>) for a generated fault. We discuss this selection process in the following section in more detail. The syntax for this attribute is as follows:

  ```
  <catchfaultVariable="fltns:faultVariable" >
      ...
  </catch>
  ```

BPEL runtime fault handler selection

When it comes to programming languages such as Java and C#, they define their own mechanisms to realize that a particular fault handler should be selected based on the generated fault. In WS-BPEL 2.0 too, the specification defines a fault handler selection mechanism based on details embedded in the fault (such as <throw>) and the details embedded in the fault handler (such as <catch>).

We'll see how this works by correlating the attributes defined in the <throw> activity and the attributes defined in the <catch> activity.

Selecting a fault handler when the fault is not associated with data

As mentioned earlier, some faults only consist of a name where some other faults contain some data related to the fault. Some examples are as follows:

- The `<throw>` activity which only has the `faultName` attribute
- A standard fault that is generated from BPEL runtime (`correlationViolation`)

The following mechanism is used to select the correct fault handler for a fault which has no associated data:

1. The `<catch>` element which is configured with the same `faultName` attribute value and that does not specify the `faultVariable` attribute is selected.
2. If there is no such `<catch>` activity, the fault is passed to the `<catchAll>` activity.

Selecting a fault handler when the fault is associated with data

As some generated faults can consist of data, the selection process for such faults becomes quite complicated, rather than selecting a fault handler for a fault that has only a name.

The following mechanism is used to select the correct fault handler for a fault which has associated data:

1. A `<catch>` activity specifying a matching `faultName` value and a `faultVariable` attribute whose type matches the type of the fault data will be selected, if present.
2. Else, a `<catch>` activity with no specified `faultName` and with a matching `faultVariable` attribute will be selected, if present.
3. Else, the default `<catchAll>` handler will be used, if present (`<catchAll>` will execute only if no other `<catch>` activity has been selected).

WSDL faults

In the previous sections, we discussed different types of faults that can be generated. They can be explicitly generated by the BPEL developer or implicitly generated by the BPEL runtime. Also, we mentioned that there can be faults generated due to faults in external web service invocations. And in *Chapter 5, Interaction Patterns in BPEL*, we discussed the synchronous and asynchronous web service invocations. Both of these can generate faults in the BPEL process. But WSDL faults are a special scenario that occurs only due to synchronous web service invocations.

These faults become a special scenario, as the WSDL specification itself defines a WSDL fault for a synchronous web service invocation. So the BPEL runtime implicitly signals faults if it receives something like an incoming fault message rather than defining a `<throw>` activity explicitly to monitor such incoming fault messages and signals.

WSDL fault specification

As we mentioned in the *WSDL faults* section, WSDL faults can be defined in the WSDL itself. So the BPEL process developer does not need to define a schema for the fault on his own, as there is already an existing schema for the fault in the WSDL representation of the web service. Even if the BPEL process is designed to throw faults to its clients who initiate the request to the BPEL process, the BPEL developer needs to define such WSDL faults in the WSDL representation for the BPEL process.

Let's remember the WSDL representation of a synchronous web service invocation without the fault. It is only represented in a two-way operation with an input (request) and an output (response). The message attribute refers to the schema of the request and response message. Consider the following code snippet:

```
<portType name="Warehousing_porttype">
  <operation name="warehousingOperation">
    <input message="tns:inputMessage"/>
    <output message="tns:responseMessage"/>
  </operation>
</portType>
```

Once we add the WSDL fault, it looks like this:

```
<portType name="Warehousing_porttype">
  <operation name="warehousingOperation">
    <input message="tns:inputMessage"/>
    <output message="tns:responseMessage"/>
    <fault message="tns:faultMessage" />
  </operation>
</portType>
```

A WSDL message of the fault message is defined by `tns:faultMessage` and it can be referred to an XML schema as follows:

```
<message name="faultMessage">
  <part name="fault" element="tnst:faultMessageType"/>
</message>
```

Handling faults

Earlier in the chapter, we introduced the fault handlers (<catch> and <catchAll>), where to locate them, and how to configure them. Also, we introduced you to the <throw> activity which signals faults explicitly so that the correct fault handler can trigger its fault handling logic. We also talked about WSDL faults and the fact that the BPEL runtime implicitly signals such faults.

In this section, we discuss how to define the fault handling logic within the fault handler (such as <catch> and <catchAll>).

Defining fault handling logic within <catch> and <catchAll>

The fault handling logic can be defined using any structural activities (such as <sequence>, <flow>, and <scope>) and behavioral activities (such as <invoke>, <assign>, and <reply>) that are defined in the WS-BPEL 2.0 specification. So a <faultHandlers> tag might look like the following code:

```
<faultHandlers>
  <!-- First fault handler -->
  <catch faultName="fltns:incompatibleFormat" >
    <reply ... />
  </catch>

  <!-- Second fault handler -->
  <catch faultName="fltns:faultName" faultVariable="Fault" >
    <sequence>
      <assign ... />
      <invoke ... />
    </sequence>
  </catch>

  <!-- Fourth fault handler -->
  <catchAll>
    <empty/><!--does nothing-->
  </catchAll>

</faultHandlers>
```

Propagating faults to parent scopes

In the *Location of a fault handler* section, we discussed global and inline fault handlers, which handle faults that are generated within that particular scope. But sometimes it's intuitive not to handle the fault at the particular scope and let it be handled by a fault handler defined within the parent scope. In such a scenario, we use the `<rethrow>` activity to trigger a fault handler defined within the immediately enclosed scope. Consider the following code snippet:

```
<faultHandlers>
  <catchAll>
    <!-- Modifying the fault variable -->
    <assign>
      <copy>
        <from>string('Incompatible input')</from>
        <to variable="faultVariable" part="error" />
      </copy>
    </assign>
    <rethrow/>
  </catchAll>
</faultHandlers>
```

In-line fault handling

The WS-BPEL 2.0 specification enables defining fault handlers that are specific to behavioral contexts. In other words, WS-BPEL 2.0 supports defining different fault handlers to different activities from a set of activities. The `<scope>` activity supports the creation of behavioral contexts which can consist of fault handlers, variables, partner links, correlation sets, and so on that are local to that specific `<scope>` activity. We'll talk more about the `<scope>` activity in the next chapter. In this section, we will discuss how to define a fault handler that is specific to a particular activity or a particular set of activities. In the BPEL world, we call them in-line fault handlers.

An in-line fault handler is defined within a `<scope>` activity, so it's only visible to the particular scope and not the whole process definition. Also, a fault handler also can be defined within the `<invoke>` activity in a similar manner. This enables a much shorter way to manage faults that could occur within the execution of the `<invoke>` activity. In the upcoming sections, we discuss those two in-line fault handlers with basic examples which both have similar functionality.

Within a <scope> activity

Once you define a fault handler within a `<scope>` activity, that fault handler can handle only those faults that are generated within that `<scope>` activity. So within the `<faultHandlers>` construct, you can define zero or more `<catch>` activities and can also specify a `<catchAll>` handler. Let's suppose we need to invoke a synchronous web service and handle the faults that could be generated during that web service invocation:

```
<!-- Synchronously invoke the Book Warehousing Web Service -->
<scope name="BookWarehousingInvoke">

  <faultHandlers>
    <catchAll>
      <assign>
        <copy>
          <from expression="false()"/>
          <to variable="WarehousingServicePartnerLink_OutputVariable"
/>"
          part="warehouseSuccessed"/>
        </copy>
      </assign>
    </catchAll>
  </faultHandlers>
  <invoke partnerLink="WarehousingServicePartnerLink"
  portType="ns3:Warehousing_porttype"
  operation="WarehouseOperation"
  inputVariable="WarehousingServicePartnerLink_InputVariable"
  outputVariable="WarehousingServicePartnerLink_OutputVariable" />
</scope>
```

In the previous sample, the faults that occurred during the `<invoke>` activity are handled within the fault handler defined in `<scope>` that encloses that particular `<invoke>` activity. And, if any fault occurs, the `<catchAll>` handler sets the `warehouseSuccessed` part of the output variable in the `<invoke>` activity to `false`.

Within an <invoke> activity

Now, let's see how to achieve the same fault handling functionality using a fault handler within the `<invoke>` activity. Here, the only difference is that there's no need to define fault handlers (`<catch>` and `<catchAll>`) within the `<faultHandlers>` construct, rather you can define them within the `<invoke>` activity. So, within the `<invoke>` activity, you can define zero or more `<catch>` activities and you can also specify a `<catchAll>` handler:

```
<!-- Synchronously invoke the Book Warehousing Web Service -->
<invoke partnerLink="WarehousingServicePartnerLink"
portType="ns3:Warehousing_porttype"
```

```
operation="WarehouseOperation"
inputVariable="WarehousingServicePartnerLink_InputVariable"
outputVariable="WarehousingServicePartnerLink_OutputVariable" />

  <catchAll>
    <assign>
      <copy>
        <from expression="false()"/>
        <to variable="WarehousingServicePartnerLink_OutputVariable"
/>"
        part="warehouseSuccessed"/>
      </copy>
    </assign>
  </catchAll>
</invoke>
```

Time for action – signaling faults

Earlier in the chapter, we categorized the possible types of errors that could be generated. One category of errors can be generated by the BPEL runtime itself. And those errors can be divided again into two subcategories based on whether the faults are signaled implicitly by the BPEL runtime or explicitly by the BPEL process developer. In order to explicitly signal faults by the BPEL process developer, we use the `<throw>` activity. The activity is explained in the *Modeling logical (explicit) errors with <throw> activity* section. But in this section, we demonstrate how to use the `<throw>` activity more thoroughly.

Also, we discussed faults that could be signaled by BPEL runtime implicitly due to the issues in the external environment such as WSDL faults.

These implicitly or explicitly generated faults either should be handled within the BPEL process or they should be propagated to an external party who can manage those faults. In the *Handling faults* section, we learned how to manage the faults within the BPEL process using fault handlers. In this section, we demonstrate how to signal the faults to external parties so they can manage the faults themselves.

So the complete fault handling scenario for this exercise is as follows:

1. The BPEL process instance executes the query service (an external web service)
2. A WSDL fault is generated from the external web service invocation
3. The generated WSDL fault is caught by a `<catch>` fault handler
4. Then, within the fault handler, the fault is modified and propagated to the client of the BPEL process instance.

Let's follow these steps to signal a fault to an external party:

1. Let's reuse the example, named **Book_Warehousing_Process**, which we introduced in *Chapter 5, Interaction Patterns in BPEL*.
2. Add a fault handler with a catch construct to the process:

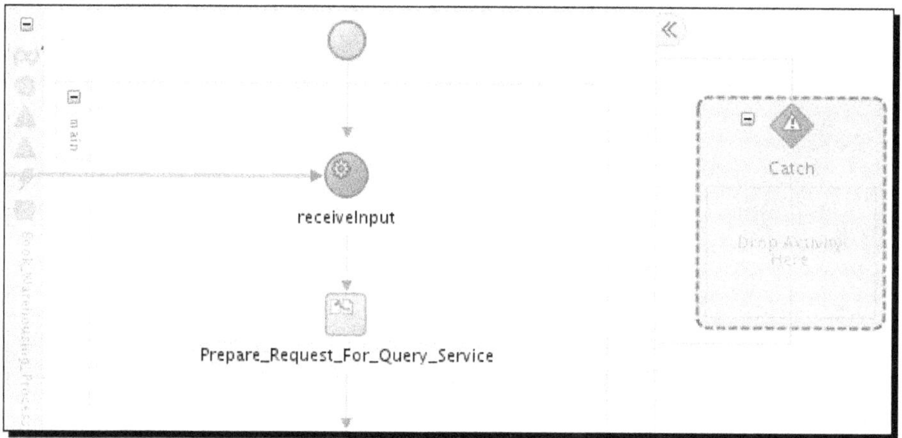

3. Then, go to the configuration window of the catch construct by double-clicking on it.

   In order to catch a WSDL fault, a fault variable should be specified with a message type that is similar to the message type of the WSDL fault. So give a name to the fault variable (**invoke_fault**).

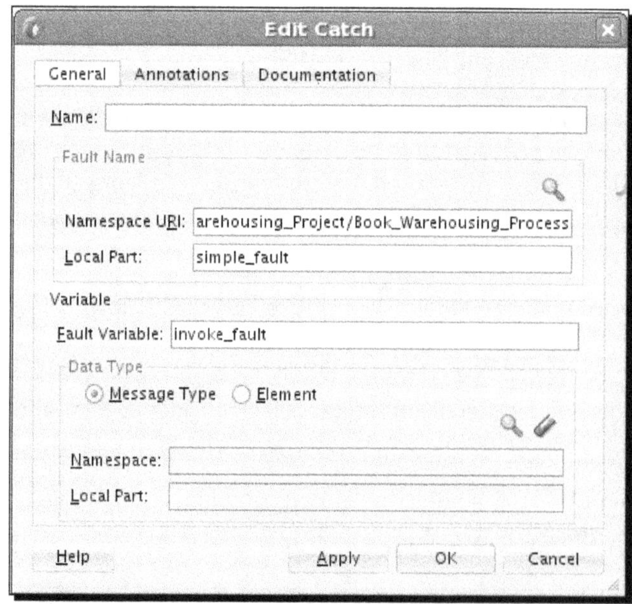

4. Click on the **Message Type** radio button and click on the magnifier icon to search for the correct fault message type.

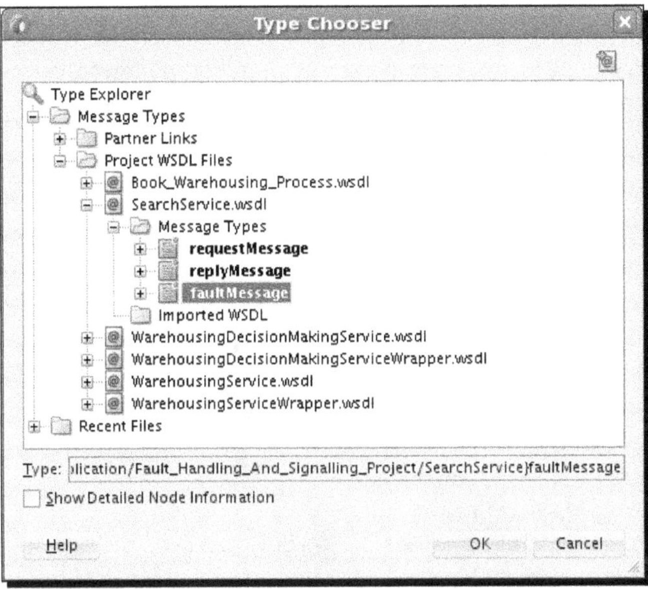

5. Click on the correct fault message type and then click on **OK**. Here we choose the message type names **faultName** from **SearchService.wsdl**. This is because the incoming fault message from the external web service is defined in this WSDL.

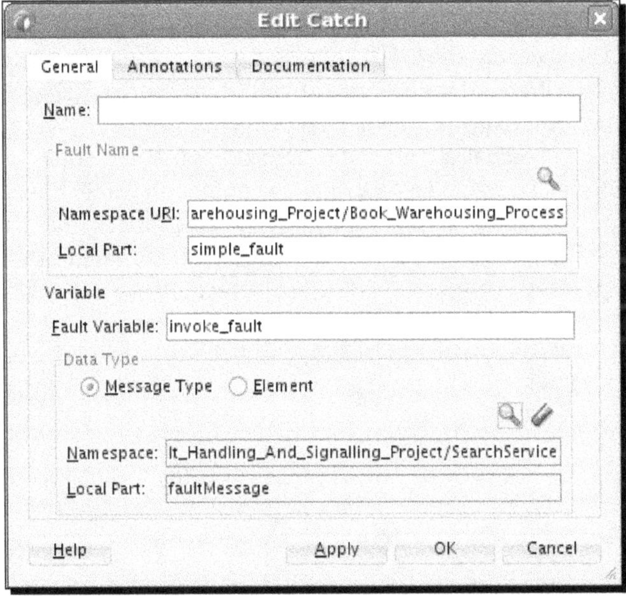

6. After setting the fault message type, save those configurations by clicking on **Apply** and then on **OK**.

   After this step, the added catch construct is ready to handle the WSDL fault generated from the external web service invocation. So the next step is to define the fault handling logic such that the fault handler modifies the fault data and propagates the fault back to the client of the BPEL process instance.

7. In this step, we define the fault handling logic to propagate a fault back to the client of the BPEL process.

   The fault propagation logic can be declared in two ways. It depends on whether the BPEL process is asynchronous or synchronous (that is, the BPEL process uses the same channel to send the response back to its client). If the BPEL process is synchronous, then a `<reply>` activity can be used within the fault handler to send the fault back to its client. So the `reply` activity will look like the following code:

   ```
   <reply partnerLink="partner_link_name"
     portType="port_type_name"
     operation="operation_name"
     faultName="fault_name"
     variable="variable_name" ><!--optional-->
   </reply>
   ```

   But the sample process named **Book_Warehousing_Process** is an asynchronous BPEL process. So we need to define a separate channel to send a fault message as the response back to its client. So we need to modify the WSDL representation of the BPEL process such that it has an additional callback operation that sends the fault message.

   Go to the design view of the WSDL representation of the BPEL process. In our case, the name of the WSDL of the BPEL process is **Book_Warehousing_Process.wsdl**. There are two port types: to invoke the BPEL process (named **Book_Warehousing_Process**) and to handle the callbacks from the BPEL process (named **Book_Warehousing_ProcessCallback**). So we add a new one-way operation within the port type (that is, the port type, named **Book_Warehousing_ProcessCallback**) that handles callbacks. Not only that, we need to add a new message type that defines the structure of the fault message.

8. Create a new message type by clicking on the plus mark in the **Messages** table and specifying a name:

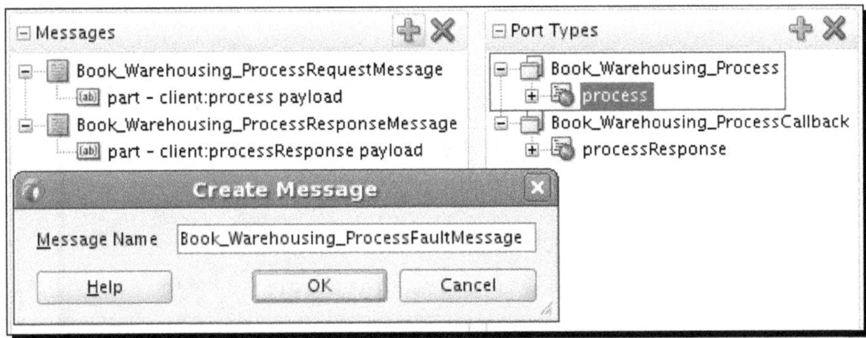

Then add a part within the fault message as well.

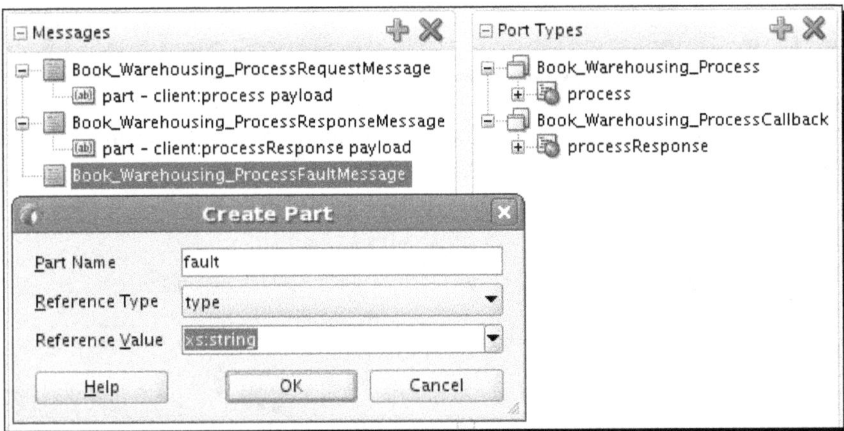

9. The next step is to add the new callback operation, right-click on the port type named **Book_Warehousing_ProcessCallback** and add a new operation within it:

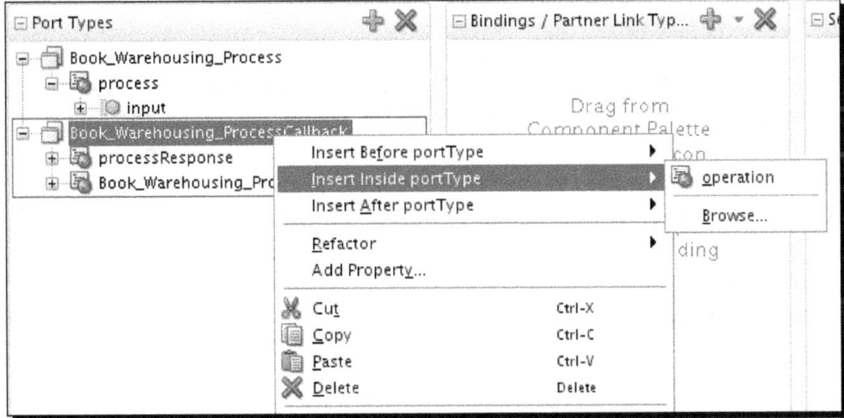

Specify the operation name, type, and the message type as follows:

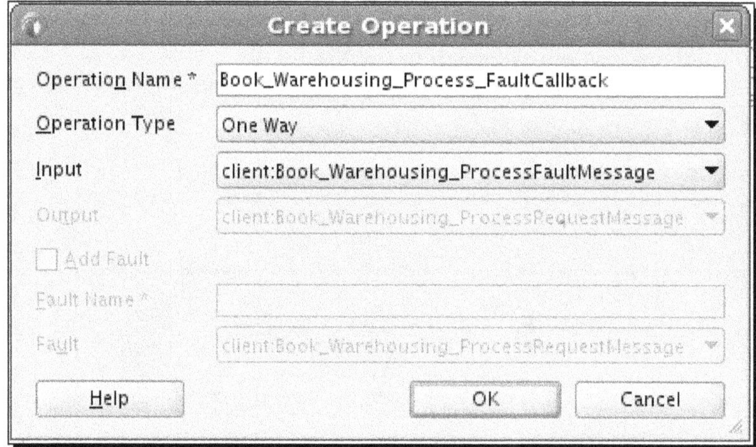

10. Now, the WSDL representation looks similar to the following screenshot with a new fault message type and a new callback operation:

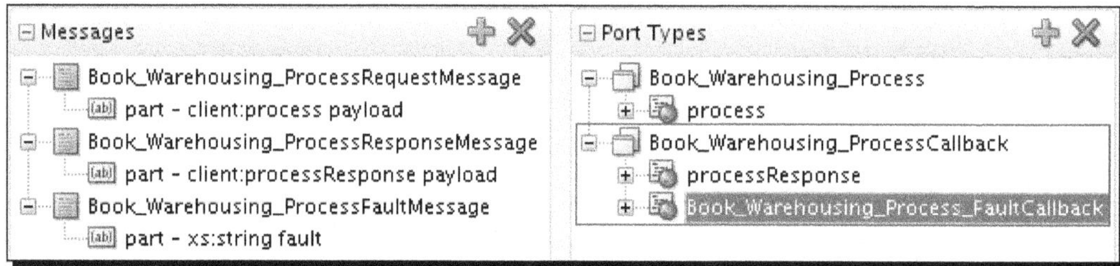

11. Now the WSDL representation of the BPEL process is ready to propagate fault messages back to its client. Thus, using an `<invoke>` activity within the fault handler, we can send the fault details back to the client.

12. Drag-and-drop an `<invoke>` activity and go to the configuration window by double-clicking on it. Select the client partner link (in our case, it is **book_warehousing_process_client**) and select the correct port type and relevant callback operation that sends out the fault message. Then, as the input variable, choose the fault variable we defined to configure the catch fault handler. When constructing the catch fault handler, we specified the fault variable **invoke_fault**. So, let's choose it for the moment. Once the fault handler is triggered, the data stored in the fault variable is directly propagated back to the client of the BPEL process:

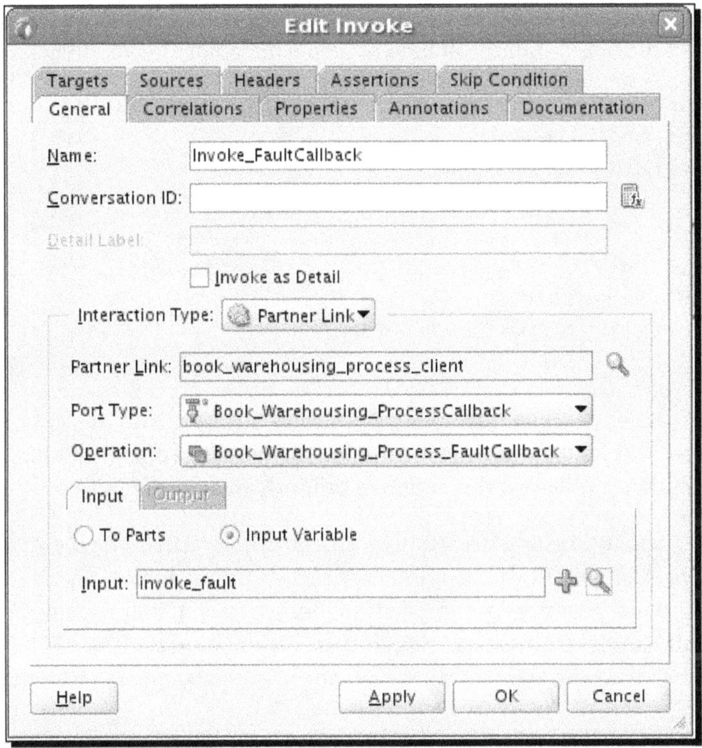

13. Now the process is ready for test and deployment.

What just happened?

Earlier we demonstrated how to declare a fault handler to handle a WSDL fault that is generated from an external web service. Then, in the fault handling logic, we signaled a new fault and propagated the signaled fault back to the client of the business process. In this section, we explained in detail how to signal faults and propagate a fault back to an external party. We also described termination behavior of a business process once a fault is signaled, so the reader gets an insight about what happens behind the scenes when a fault is signaled.

Signaling faults within the BPEL process

For an example, let's consider an external web service invocation. The response message of the web service contains a number which indicates the status of the web service engine. Suppose, based on that number, the BPEL developer needs to signal different faults. In such a situation, the BPEL developer should have the capability to signal faults explicitly, rather than letting the BPEL runtime generate faults, and the BPEL process developer can only define fault handlers to handle the implicitly signaled faults.

This is one example where the explicitly signaled faults become handy as the process of signaling the fault process depends on business-specific data. The WS-BPEL 2.0 specification provides a <throw> activity which can have the following syntaxes:

```
<!--consist only the fault name-->
<throw faultName="QName" >
</throw>

<!--consist only the fault name and fault data-->
<throw faultName="QName"
faultVariable="BPELVariableName" >
</throw>
```

Thus, a <throw> activity should have the faultName attribute and the optional attribute faultVariable. This fault variable can contain data associated with the fault. So, at the fault handler, this data can be used in order to properly handle the fault.

One special thing about the signaled faults by the <throw> activity is that these faults are not required to be defined prior to reference by the <throw> activity. In other words, these fault names are not verified during compile time. So typos of a fault name can prevent the assigned fault handler from being triggered. In such a scenario, the BPEL process will terminate abnormally as the signaled fault was not handled by any fault handler.

Signaling faults to the synchronous clients

The WS-BPEL 2.0 specification provides the <receive> and <reply> activity pair to communicate with a synchronous client. And when it comes to signaling faults to synchronous clients, the <reply> activity is capable of returning a WSDL fault back to its client. This is configured by the faultName attribute, which specifies what the fault to be signaled is, in the <reply> activity. Also, there is an optional attribute named variable which can be used to propagate data associated with the particular fault.

Let's see how <reply> can be configured to signal a WSDL fault and how the WSDL representation of the BPEL should be modified in order to return such a fault:

```
<reply partnerLink="partner_link_name"
  portType="port_type_name"
  operation="operation_name"
  faultName="fault_name"
  variable="variable_name" ><!--optional-->
</reply>
```

The <reply> activity should be as follows in order to signal a WSDL fault. And the particular operation (here operation_name) should be as follows. We have already discussed the WSDL faults in the *WSDL faults* section:

```
<portType name="port_type_name">
  <operation name="operation_name">
    <input message="tns:inputMessage"/>
    <output message="tns:responseMessage"/>
    <fault message="tns:faultMessage" />
  </operation>
</portType>
```

Also note that schema of the variable (here variable_name) should have a message type the same as the fault message type defined in the WSDL operation (here operation_name).

So the variable should be defined as follows:

```
<variable name="variable_name" messageType="tns:faultMessage"/>
```

Signaling faults from the asynchronous process

In the previous section, we explained how to signal a WSDL fault to a synchronous client. In this section, we will discuss signaling a fault to an asynchronous client.

In *Chapter 5, Interaction Patterns in BPEL*, we introduced the asynchronous BPEL processes and saw that the main difference between a synchronous and an asynchronous BPEL process is that a synchronous BPEL process uses the <receive> and <reply> activity pair to communicate with the BPEL client; where as, the asynchronous BPEL process uses the <receive> and <invoke> activity pair. Here, the <invoke> activity is used for the callback operation which is exposed from the client. This callback operation that is defined in WSDL representation can only handle one type of message schema. So in order to handle another type of message schema, another operation should be defined in the WSDL representation. Thus, the WSDL port type which represents the callback operation needs an extra operation to accept the fault message. The WSDL representation that has an extra client callback is as follows:

```
<portType name="ServerCallback">
  <operation name="onResult"><!--normal callback operation-->
    <input message="tns:ServerResponseMessage"
      wsaw:Action="http://wso2.org/onResult" />
  </operation>
  <operation name="onFaultResult"><!--callback operation on fault-->
    <input message="tns:ServerResponseFaultMessage"
      wsaw:Action="http://wso2.org/onFaultResult" />
  </operation>
</portType>
```

Ending and terminating a BPEL process

When a fault occurs within the BPEL process, all the running activities and event handler instances are terminated and a matching fault handler is executed. This behavior is similar when a fault occurs within a scope activity as well. If there is no matching fault handler, the fault is thrown to the immediately enclosing scope, if present. Otherwise, the process will terminate abnormally. The abnormal termination of a process is similar to using the `<exit>` activity. So when an `<exit>` activity executes, all the running activities are terminated immediately and the process instance is marked as unsuccessful.

Another way to end a BPEL process when a standard fault happens is to define the `exitOnStandardFault` attribute with value `yes` in the `<process>` or `<scope>` activity. When this attribute is set to `yes`, when a standard fault occurs, except `bpel:joinFailure`, the BPEL process terminates immediately as if an `<exit>` activity has been reached.

But in some scenarios, we need to define a customized terminating behavior such as sending a notification to its client or garbage cleanup. In such cases, WS-BPEL 2.0 provides the `<terminationHandler>` construct that supports such customized termination behavior. But this can be defined only within a scope and we will discuss some details about this in the next chapter.

Have a go hero – adding fault handlers to BPEL process

In the previous *Time for action – signaling faults* section, we demonstrated how to propagate a signaled fault to a synchronous client using an activity pair of `<receive>` and `<reply>`. And in the *What just happened?* section, we explained how to propagate a signaled fault to an asynchronous client using an activity pair of `<receive>` and `<invoke>`.

So, in this section, write a simple WS-BPEL 2.0 process to propagate an explicitly signaled fault to an asynchronous client.

Pop quiz

Q1. What is the difference between the `<throw>` and `<rethrow>` activities?

Q2. What is the main difference between signaling a fault from a synchronous and an asynchronous process back to its client?

Q3. What are the six possible `<catch>` faultHandler configurations?

Q4. What are the three impossible `<catch>` faultHandler configurations?

Summary

In this chapter, we first had an idea about what faults could be generated within a business process. Then we looked at what a fault handler is. Then we moved on to a sample which covers those aspects and explained how the WS-BPEL 2.0 specification models the aforementioned faults. We categorized those faults into three groups as follows:

- Modeling execution errors with WS-BPEL 2.0 standard faults
- Modeling logical (explicit) errors with the `<throw>` activity
- Modeling errors propagated from external web services

We described how logical (explicit) faults are signaled within the business process definition and then explained how a signaled fault is propagated back to the client of the business process. So, at the end of this chapter, the reader is capable of declaring a fault handling behavior to a business process.

In the next chapter, we are going to discuss the `<scope>` activity which is really useful in organizing a business process into hierarchical parts.

7
Working with Scopes

So far, we learned about data manipulation and fault handling within a BPEL process. We also learned about synchronous and asynchronous web service invocations. One thing that we can observe from any previous chapters is that all the resources such as variables, partner links, and correlations sets which are referred by some activity, are defined in the top level of the BPEL process. Those resources are visible to any activity. However, what if we need to restrict the visibility of such resources to a particular activity or a set of activity? The `<scope>` *activity comes to the rescue. It helps us organize the BPEL process into hierarchical organized parts. Let's see how it works.*

In this chapter, we will cover the following topics:

- Introducing scopes
- Adding scopes to a business process
- Understanding scopes
- Fault and termination handling within scopes
- Introduction to event and compensation handling within scopes
- Isolated scopes

Introducing scopes

As we observed in the previous chapters, when the amount of the <invoke> activities increases, the amount of variables and partner links that requires to handle the runtime status of those <invoke> activities also grows. In synchronous invocations, each <invoke> activity has to have two variables in order to hold input and output of the external web service invocation. Additionally, it may need to keep another variable to maintain fault data. So, it is inevitable that the number of activities in a business process grows when the complexity of business process logic grows. As a consequence, a developer has to spend more time on implementing and verifying the business logic.

Hence, it is advantageous to have some structural activities that encapsulate the blocks keep this complexity to a minimum level. The <scope> activity enables us organize the WS-BPEL 2.0 process into hierarchical organized parts. In other words, a <scope> activity can maintain a set of local data (for example, variables and partner links) and handlers (for example, fault handlers and compensation handles) so that only visible to the activities resides within the scope. We explain how to use the <scope> activity to organize a WS-BPEL 2.0 process.

As with most of the programming languages such as Java and C#, BPEL also has the concept of defining scopes, which defines restrictions to resources, manipulated during the program execution. In Java, we can define a variable with different access levels named as local, instance, and static. A local variable can be only accessible within a Java method block. So, it cannot be accessed outside of the particular method block. In other words, variables defined in a Java method block are not visible to the world outside of that method block. On the other hand, any Java object can access the static variable.

Likewise, WS-BPEL 2.0 provides the <scope> activity, which enables to define different contexts within a BPEL process definition. Within the <scope> activity, you can define variables, partner links, correlation sets, fault handlers, and so on, that are only visible to the activities defined within the particular scope. This means those resources that are local to the <scope> activity affect the behavior of the activities defined within the particular <scope> activity. In more general terms, we can say that the <scope> activity provides behavioral contexts for activities defined within the <scope> activity. In the previous chapter, we talked about inline fault handlers, which is a very useful example of the <scope> activity.

> The <scope> activity not only allows you to define variables, partner links, correlation sets, and fault handlers, but it also allows the user to define compensation handlers, event handlers, termination handlers, and message exchanges, some of which are discussed later in this book.

In this chapter, we refine the main example mentioned in *Chapter 5, Interaction Patterns in BPEL* (asynchronous invocations) such that the partner links, variables, correlation sets, and fault handlers related to each service invocation are encapsulated within child scopes. So, it brings more readability to the process. And in the second phase of the chapter (from the *Time for action – the fault and termination handlers* section), we explain more important use cases such as inline fault handling, termination handling, and so on.

Let's reuse the example, named **Book_Warehousing_Process**, which we introduced in *Chapter 5, Interaction Patterns in BPEL*:

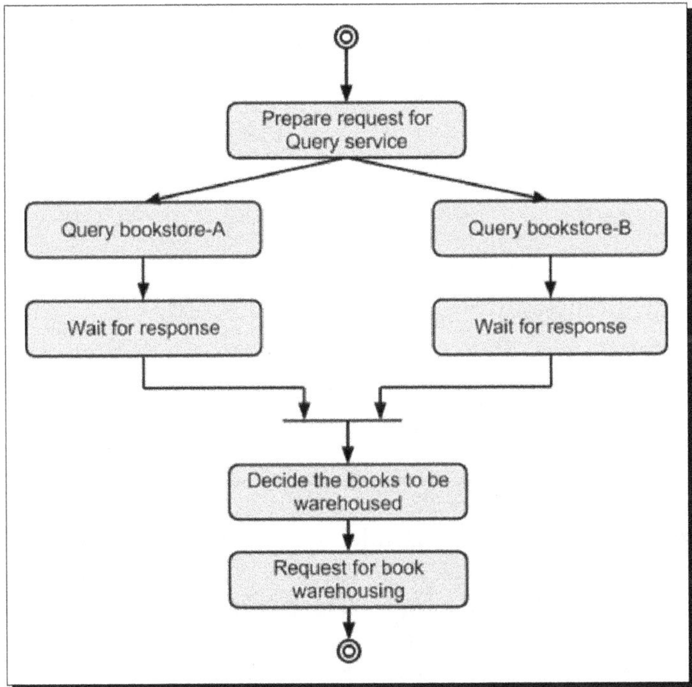

Workflow of the book warehousing process

If you take a look at the BPEL source code, you may realize that all the `<variable>` and `<partnerLink>` activities are defined at the top level of the `<process>` definition. We call this the global level, as once the `<variable>` and `<partnerLink>` activities are defined, they are visible to all the activities defined within the BPEL process. So, they can be referred anywhere. However, at some point we may wish to restrict the scope of access to those resources. As an example, we may need to restrict access of variables on to an `<invoke>` activity, which is the only activity used in the mentioned variables. In such a case, we need to define a `<scope>` activity and enclose that `<invoke>` activity.

Keeping this in mind, if we take a look at the preceding sample workflow, it has several external service invocations. They are listed here:

- **Query bookstore-A**
- **Query bookstore-B**
- **Decide the books to be warehoused**
- **Request for book warehousing**

In this exercise, we only consider the scoping of two `<invoke>` activities. These activities are **Query_BookStore_A** and **Query_BookStore_B** and those are executed within a `<flow>` activity, as shown in the following screenshot:

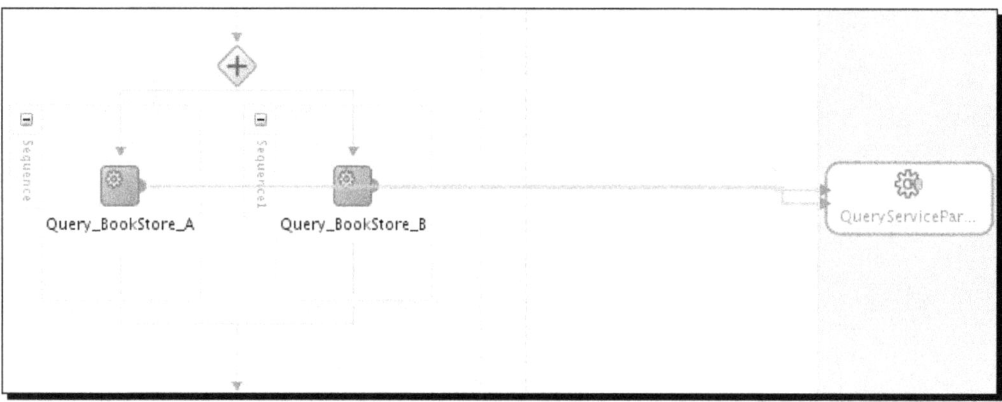

So by examining those two `<invoke>` activities, we can realize that these two `<invoke>` activities share the same partner link (`QueryServicePartnerLink`) and the input variable (`Query_BookStore_serach_InputVariable`), but use different output variables. The `<invoke>` activity named `Query_BookStore_A` uses `Query_BookStore_A_serach_OutputVariable` and the other `<invoke>` activity named `Query_BookStore_B` uses `Query_BookStore_B_serach_OutputVariable`, as shown in the following code:

```
<flow name="Flow1">
    <sequence name="Sequence">
        <invoke name="Query_BookStore_A"
            partnerLink="QueryServicePartnerLink"
            portType="ns1:search_port_type" operation="search"
            inputVariable="Query_BookStore_search_InputVariable"
            outputVariable="Query_BookStore_A_search_OutputVariable"
            bpelx:invokeAsDetail="no"/>
    </sequence>
    <sequence name="Sequence1">
```

```
        <invoke name="Query_BookStore_B"
            partnerLink="QueryServicePartnerLink"
            portType="ns1:search_port_type" operation="search"
            inputVariable="Query_BookStore_search_InputVariable"
            outputVariable="Query_BookStore_B_search_OutputVariable"
            bpelx:invokeAsDetail="no"/>
    </sequence>
</flow>
```

So, what we can do is restrict the access of variables such as `Query_BookStore_A_serach_OutputVariable` and `Query_BookStore_B_serach_OutputVariable` only to the `<invoke>` activity that refers the particular resource. In the same way, we can restrict the access of variable `Query_BookStore_serach_InputVariable` and the partner link `QueryServicePartnerLink` only to the two `<invoke>` activities given the condition that these resources are only utilized within those two `<invoke>` activities.

Time for action – adding scopes

1. Let's create two scopes and add those two `<invoke>` activities into those two scopes separately, so we can define local variables, partner links, and so on, which are only visible within a particular `<scope>` activity. So drag-and-drop the `<scope>` activities inside the sequences where the `<invoke>` activities are, as shown in the following screenshot:

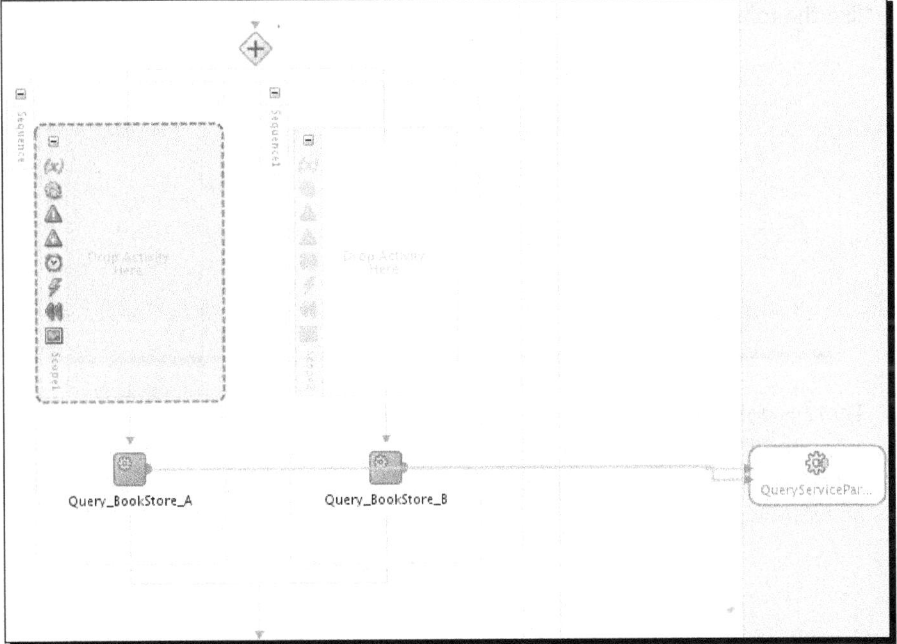

2. Now we can drag the existing <invoke> activities into the newly added <scope> activities:

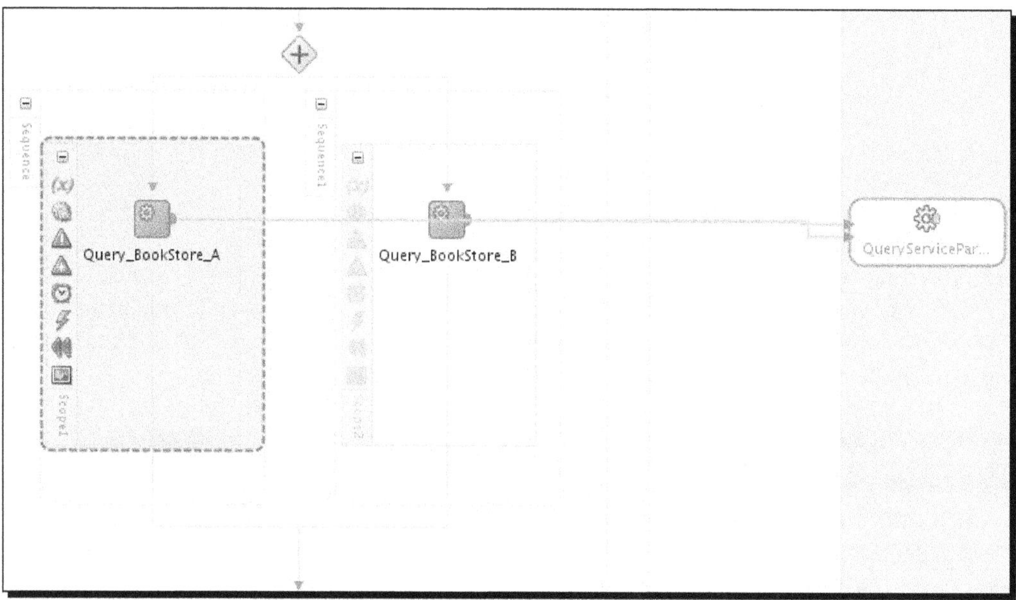

3. Now, the remaining task is to transfer the variables from the global phase to local phase. If you look at the variable hierarchy within the process definition, it looks like the following screenshot:

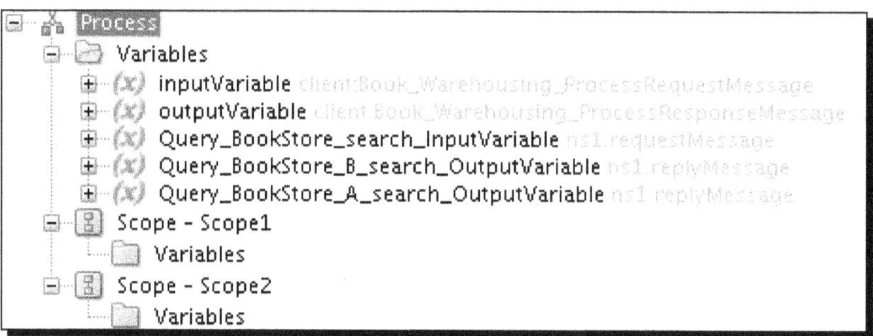

4. There is not a straightforward transfer mechanism. So, to transfer what we can do is to clone the definition on the global variable within the <scope> activity and delete the global variable. So, the final variable hierarchy within the process definition will be as shown:

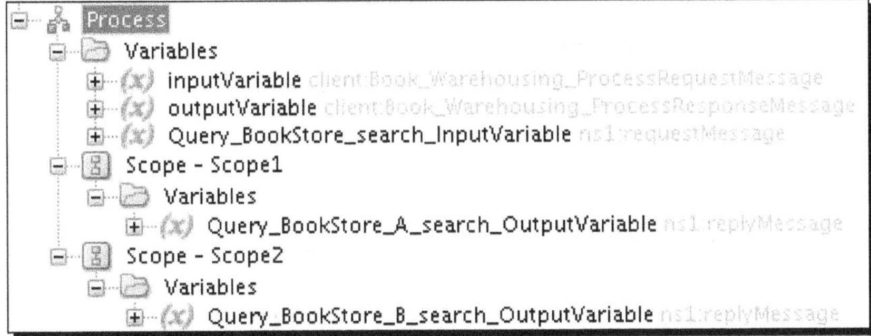

5. Likewise we can further modify the BPEL process, by adding new `<scope>` activities to provide different contexts of resources such as variables, partner links, correlation sets, and so on. Also, the handlers that are fault handlers, termination handlers, event handlers, and compensation handlers also can be defined within the scopes.

What just happened?

In the preceding section, we reused the main example defined in *Chapter 5, Interaction Patterns in BPEL*, and moved global variables, partner links, and invoke activities into scopes. We demonstrated how to encapsulate partner links, variables, correlation sets, and fault handlers related to each service invocation within child scopes. And now we realized that the WS-BPEL 2.0 process can maintain multiple variables with the same name but in different scopes.

How to organize scopes

In the previous section, we gave a general introduction on the `<scope>` activity and the basic use of it. In this section, we discuss the semantics of the `<scope>` activity in detail. So, we explain the difference between a `<scope>` and a `<process>` activity, and why the `<scope>` activity is helpful compared to structured activities such as `<sequence>` or `<flow>`. Then, we explain how to define a scope within a BPEL process definition.

Using <scope> in place of <process>

As we explained the `<scope>` activity in the introduction, a `<scope>` activity is capable of maintaining a set of resources that are local to the particular scope and its enclosed activities. On the other hand, we can define such resources at global level by defining them in the top level `<process>` construct. However, why do we need to define resources within scopes?

To figure out the answer, let's take an example of a BPEL process that has two different web service invocations (for example, the main example defined in *Chapter 5, Interaction Patterns in BPEL*). These two invocations need to declare two separate input variables. So, the two `<invoke>` activities can refer those input variables to send the outgoing request messages to the external web services.

Once we define the two input variables at global level, then both the `<invoke>` activities can see each other's input variables. This is not a good practice of BPEL programming because these variables are either used by only one `<invoke>` activity. However, both `<invoke>` activities can see each other's input variables. Another issue is the global level variables retained in the memory until the BPEL process completes. What if we declare an input variable, relevant partner link, and the associated `<invoke>` activity within a `<scope>` activity? Both the `<invoke>` activities are encapsulated along with the resources that are only associated with the relevant `<invoke>` activities. A performance improvement is BPEL runtime which now only needs to keep the variables in memory until the scope completes. This improves the readability of the BPEL code and makes the BPEL code more simplified. The overall performance of the execution of BPEL processes is also improved. Generally, the resources should not be declared globally unless it is really necessary.

Another reason is that the `<process>` construct does not support compensation handler and termination handler. However, in some cases, we may need to define compensation and termination behavior to activities such as `<invoke>`. In such a scenario, the `<scope>` activity becomes essential as the enclosing activity of such activities. On the contrary, the `<scope>` activity doesn't support the `<import>` and `<extensions>` declarations. So, the `<import>` and `<extensions>` activities should be declared only at the global level.

One other difference is that the `<process>` is not considered as an activity. And it is only used as the top-level element in a BPEL process definition. There's only one `<process>` element in a BPEL process definition. On the other hand, the `<scope>` activity can enclose other child `<scope>` activities and there can be multiple `<scope>` activities that are not related to each other.

Based on those explanations, there are significant differences among a `<scope>` activity and a `<process>` activity, and in a nutshell, declaring resources at the local level is a best practice compared to global level resources.

Using <scope> in place of <sequence> or <flow>

In the previous section, *Using <scope> in place of <process>*, we discussed the differences between `<process>` and the `<scope>`. In this section, we discuss the difference between the `<scope>` activity and a structural activity such as `<sequence>` and `<flow>`.

We already know that the <scope> is capable of defining local resources such as partner links and variables, but the structural activities do not have such support. In order to define local variables such as resources to a structural activity, the particular structural activity should be enclosed within a scope and define such resources within it as follows:

```
<scope name="EnclosingScope">
  <variables>...</variables>
  <faultHandlers>
    <catchAll>...</catchAll>
  </faultHandlers>
  <sequence>
    <!-- Prepare the input for external Web Service invocation -->
    <!-- Synchronously invoke the external Web Service -->
  </sequence>
</scope>
```

What to consider when defining a scope

In the *Using <scope> in place of <process>* and *Using <scope> in place of <sequence> or <flow>* sections, we realized some major differences of the <scope> activity compared to <process> and the structural activities. That discussion helps to realize some of the considerations to keep in mind when defining a <scope> activity. Here are some facts that we need to consider when defining a <scope> and determining enclosed activities of that <scope> activity.

Encapsulating a logical unit of work

A <scope> activity can be used to divide a BPEL process into hierarchically organized parts. These parts should encapsulate one logical thing. As an example, suppose a BPEL process that invokes two external web services. There should be two <assign> activities that manipulate the input variables required for two invocations. The BPEL process can be divided by creating two <scope> activities so that each enclose the <assign> and <invoke> activities, as shown in the following code:

```
<flow>
  <scope name="EnclosingScope1">
    <variables>...</variables>
    <partnerLinks>...</partnerLinks>
    <sequence>
      <!-- Prepare the input for external Web Service 1 invocation --
>
      <!-- Synchronously invoke the external Web Service 1 -->
    </sequence>
  </scope>
```

```
    <scope name="EnclosingScope2">
      <variables>...</variables>
      <partnerLinks>...</partnerLinks>
      <sequence>
        <!-- Prepare the input for external Web Service 2 invocation --
>
        <!-- Synchronously invoke the external Web Service 2 -->
      </sequence>
    </scope>
  <flow>
```

Using two scopes, both the service invocations get better encapsulation as they can contain their own local variables, partner links, fault handlers, and so on. If we defined those two service invocations within one `<scope>` activity, then the variables, partner links, and so on, are visible to both invocations. Also, the fault handling logic has to be defined within a single fault handler.

A unit of work that needs customized compensation or termination

Apart from the better encapsulation, the `<scope>` activity becomes essential when there is an activity or a set of activities that require compensation or termination. This is because the compensation or termination handlers are only supported by the `<scope>` activity.

Fault and termination handling within scopes

Previously, we discussed how to add variables, partner links to a `<scope>` activity. During the remaining part of this chapter, we will discuss about handlers that can be defined within a `<scope>` activity and the isolated scopes. As a concrete example, let's first realize how to define a fault handler within a scope.

In the section entitled *Time for action – adding scopes*, we separately enclosed two selected `<invoke>` activities with two `<scope>` activities. We moved variables, which are referred only by those `<invoke>` activities, into those scopes. In the next exercise, we will improve the same BPEL process.

W are going to add an inline fault handler to the `<scope>` activity that includes an external service invocation. If a fault occurs during the external service execution, the inline fault handler is triggered, as shown in the following screenshot:

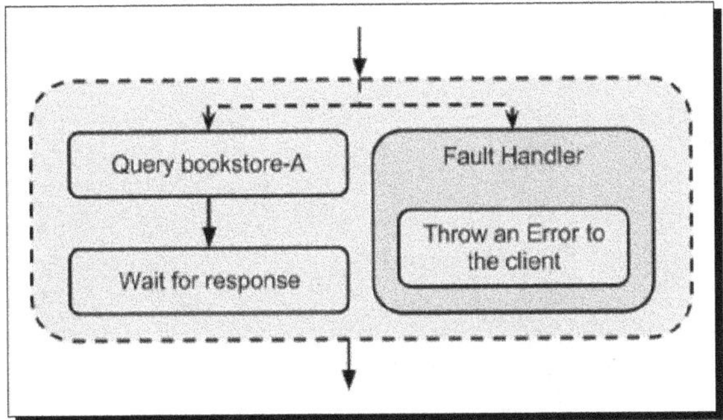

An inline fault handler to signal generated faults to the client

Time for action – the fault and termination handlers

Open the BPEL process that was used in the *Time for action – adding scopes* section and follow the ensuing steps:

1. Initially, the `<invoke>` activity looks like the following screenshot:

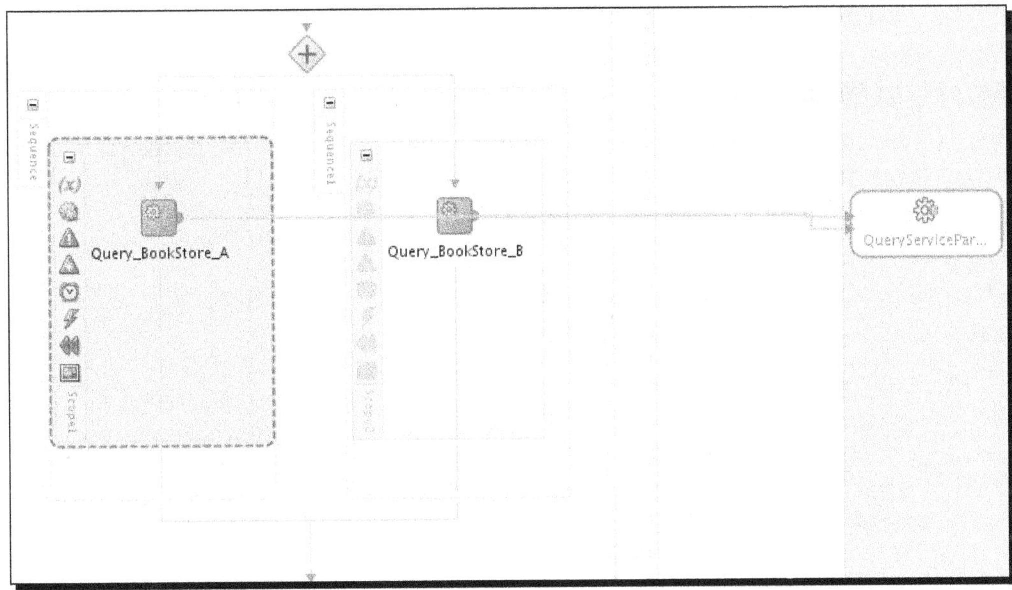

2. Click on the following icon of the `<scope>` activity and create a fault handler with a `<catch>` construct:

3. The <scope> activity looks as follows:

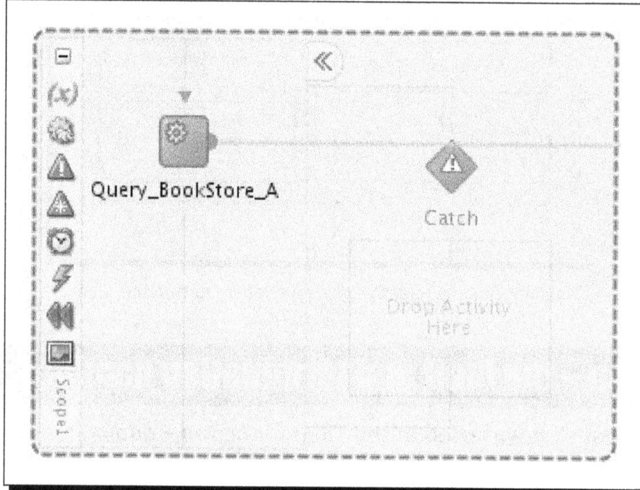

4. The remaining task is to define the error handling logic. It can be any logic as we explained in *Chapter 6, Fault Handling and Signaling*.

What just happened?

In this section, we discuss the inner structure of the <scope> activity. We discuss defining local variables, partner links, handlers, and so on.

We can specify <partnerLinks>, <messageExchanges>, <variables>, <correlationSets>, <faultHandlers>, <compensationHandler>, <terminationHandler>, and <eventHandlers> locally for the scope, as shown in the following code. All are optional.

```
<scope>
    <partnerLinks>
        <!-- Local partner links definition -->
    </partnerLinks>
    <messageExchanges>
        <!-- Local message exchanges -->
    </messageExchanges>
    <variables>
        <!-- Local variables -->
    </variables>
    <correlationSets>
        <!-- Local correlation sets -->
```

```
    </correlationSets>
    <faultHandlers>
        <!-- Fault handlers local to scope. -->
    </faultHandlers>
    <compensationHandler>
        <!-- Local compensation handlers.-->
    </compensationHandler>
    <terminationHandler>
        <!-- Local termination handler. -->
    </terminationHandler>
    <eventHandlers>
        <!-- Local event handlers. -->
    </eventHandlers>

    activity
</scope>
```

Inner structure of a scope is similar to an overall BPEL process definition. However, there are several differences, as follows:

- A `<process>` construct cannot contain `<process>` as it is not an activity. However, the `<scope>` can.
- A compensation handler and a termination handler can only be defined for a `<scope>` construct, not for a `<process>` construct.
- `<scope>` supports concurrent access to its shared resources such as variables and correlation sets. However, the `<process>` construct has no such support. We explain about this in the *Isolated scopes* section.

Based on the defined local variables, partner links, and so on, the behavior of the activities is defined within the scope changes, so we can say a `<scope>` activity provides behavioral contexts for the enclosed activities.

Let's realize what we discussed with an example scope activity with an inline fault handler. This sample was introduced in the *Inline fault handling* section in *Chapter 6, Fault Handling and Signaling*. The primary activity of the scope is `<invoke>` and the faults generated within the `<invoke>` activity are handled by the inline fault handler. The primary activity of a `<scope>` activity can be either a behavioral activity such as `<invoke>` or a structural activity such as `<sequence>`, `<scope>`, and `<flow>`, as shown in the following code:

```
<!-- Synchronously invoke the Book Warehousing Web Service -->
<scope name="BookWarehousingInvoke">

    <faultHandlers>
```

```
            <catchAll>
          <assign>
              <copy>
            <from expression="false()"/>
            <to variable="WarehousingServicePartnerLink_OutputVariable"
/>" part="warehouseSuccessed"/>
        </copy>
          </assign>
      </catchAll>
        </faultHandlers>

        <invoke partnerLink="WarehousingServicePartnerLink"
            portType="ns3:Warehousing_porttype"
      operation="WarehouseOperation"
      inputVariable="WarehousingServicePartnerLink_InputVariable"
      outputVariable="WarehousingServicePartnerLink_OutputVariable" />

    </scope>
```

If the enclosed primary activity of the <scope> activity is a structured activity such as <sequence> or <scope>, it can have many child activities and the depth of the tree is arbitrary.

The variables defined within <scope> are only visible to the enclosed activities. So, there can be multiple variables with the same name but in different scopes that are not enclosed with each other. This rule is applied for any resource such as partner links and correlation sets.

When it comes to handlers, such as fault handler, it handles the faults generated from all the enclosed activities. The faults that are not caught by the inline fault handler are thrown to the enclosing <scope> or <process> activity.

Similar to fault handlers, compensation handlers, event handlers, termination handlers, and so on, can be defined within the <scope> activity. In the next section, we will introduce those handlers. Also the event handling and compensation handling are discussed in detail as separate chapters (*Chapter 10, Events and Event Handlers*, and *Chapter 11, Compensations*).

Handlers

There are four types of handlers that can be installed within a <scope> activity. They are as follows:

- Fault handler
- Event handler
- Compensation handler
- Termination handlers

Out of these four, the fault handler and event handler can be immediately enclosed within a `<process>` activity as well. However, the compensation handler and termination handler is not allowed to be installed within a `<process>` activity.

A fault handler

We discussed the fault handler in *Chapter 6, Fault Handling and Signaling*, in detail. We discussed how to signal faults and handle faults within the `<scope>` activity:

```
<!-- Synchronously invoke the Book Warehousing Web Service -->
<scope name="BookWarehousingInvoke">
  <faultHandlers>
    <catchAll>
  <!—Fault Handling Logic-->
  </catchAll>
  </faultHandlers>
  <invoke … />
</scope>
```

An event handler

As a fault handler is triggered by a signaled fault, an event handler is triggered when the corresponding event occurs. Those events are twofold. An event can be generated due to an incoming message that corresponds to a WSDL operation, or they can be due to a user-defined alarm. An alarm can be configured to fire at a specific point in time or after a specific amount of time period. Also, an alarm can be configured to repeatedly trigger each time the duration period expires, as shown in the following code:

```
<scope name="bookWareHousingProcess" >
   <eventHandlers>
      <!-- Alarm triggers when a message that correspond to a WSDL
operation-->
      <onEvent partnerLink="QueryServiceClientPartnerLink"
         operation="searchOperationStatus" ...>
         <scope>...</scope>
      </onEvent>
      <!-- Alarm triggers after one hour-->
      <onAlarm>
         <for>'P0DT1H'</for>
         <scope>...</scope>
      </onAlarm>
   </eventHandlers>
</scope>
```

We will discuss event handlers in detail in *Chapter 10, Events and Event Handlers*.

A compensation handler

When an error occurs, some of the work already done has to be undone. The compensation handler comes into play in such scenarios. We discuss compensation handlers in detail in *Chapter 11, Compensations*. The following code is an example:

```
<scope>
   <compensationHandler>
      <!--Undo logic-->
      <invoke name="withdrawSubmition" ... />
   </compensationHandler>
   <invoke name="submit" ... />
</scope>
```

A termination handler

A scope can be terminated forcefully when the scope or process enclosing it has faulted or the <forEach> activity, that enclosing a scope, can also forcefully terminate it. In such a scenario, the termination handler supports a customized termination behavior such as sending a notification to its client or garbage cleanup, as follows:

```
<scope>
   <terminationHandler>
      <!-- termination logic -->
   </terminationHandler>
   <sequence>
      <!-- business logic -->
   </sequence>
</scope>
```

Isolated scopes

In the preceding sections, we introduced the functionality of the <scope> activity. We discussed how to define local variables, partner links, handlers, and so on. Also, we mentioned that the activities enclosed within a <scope> activity can access the shared variables, partner links, and so on, which are defined in a parent <scope> activity or in the global level. There can be scenarios that involve several <scope> activities that concurrently access the shared global variables, partner links, and so on. In such situations, there should be some concurrency control to avoid conflicting situations due to concurrent accesses.

WS-BPEL 2.0 defines the concept of isolated scopes, which supports concurrency control over shared global variables, partner links, and dependency links. In this section, we are going to discuss concurrency control feature in the <scope> activity. Isolated scopes ensure that the results of each <scope> activity are equal if the conflicting activities on shared resources are reordered in any possible sequence.

There will be no conflict states in the BPEL process due to concurrent access of shared resources by isolated scopes. The semantics of isolated scopes are similar to the isolation level called serializable, which is the highest isolation level in the concurrency control.

Let's learn how to define an isolated scope. There is only one attribute named `isolated` to configure an isolated scope. Consider the following example, where two `<scope>` activities within a `<flow>` activity access the same global variable called `global`:

```
<process ...>
   <variables>
      <variable name="global" element="..." />
   </variables>
   <flow>
      <scope name="S1" isolated="yes">
         <sequence>
            ...
            <invoke ... outputVariable="global" />
            ...
         </sequence>
      </scope>
      <scope name="S2" isolated="yes">
         <sequence>
            ...
            <assign>
               <copy>
                  <from>...</from>
                  <to variable="global" />
               </copy>
            </assign>
            ...
         </sequence>
      </scope>
   </flow>
</process>
```

Have a go hero – restructuring a BPEL process into scopes

Now, you have an idea on how the `<scope>` activities can be used in BPEL processes and how to use a fault handler and a termination handler within a `<scope>` activity.

In this section, you should restructure the complete book warehousing process and add relevant fault handlers to each external web service invocation taking place.

Pop quiz

Q1. Find the correct sentences regarding the isolated scopes.

1. An isolated scope can enclose isolated scopes.
2. An isolated scope cannot access the resources defined within the global level.
3. Executional semantics of an isolated scope and nonisolated scope become similar if both of them do not access variables, partner links, and dependency links outside of the scope.

Q2. What are the handlers that are only allowed within a `<scope>` activity?

1. `<faultHandler>`
2. `<compensationHandler>`
3. `<eventHandler>`
4. `<terminationHandler>`

Q3. What constructs are not allowed within a `<scope>` activity?

1. `<sequence>`
2. `<import>`
3. `<extensions>`
4. `<variables>`

Q4. Select the possible local variable declarations out of the following:

1. A scope can have a local variable that has a same name and same type as a variable in a parent scope.
2. A scope can have a local variable that has a same name but different type as a variable in a parent scope.
3. A scope can have a local variable that has a different name and same type as a variable in a parent scope.

Summary

In this chapter, we introduced the concept of the `<scope>` activity and described the advantages of it. Then, we realized how to add the `<scope>` activities to hierarchically organize the book warehousing sample. Some of the differences of the `<scope>` activity and other activities such as `<process>`, `<sequence>`, and `<flow>` were explained. Then, we realized how to add a fault handler and a termination handler to a `<scope>` activity. Finally, we introduced the concept of isolated scopes. By the end of this chapter, the reader is capable of declaring a `<scope>` activity to organize a WS-BPEL 2.0 process hierarchically.

In the next chapter, we will learn about activities that facilitate to model parallel and repetitive tasks such as sending an invoice to 100 clients. These activities facilitate users to inherently model parallel tasks without much of a hassle while improving the execution performance of the BPEL runtime.

8

Dynamic Parallel Invocations

Until now we have seen how to do parallel activity execution with a `<flow>` *activity. We also learned about the* `<while>` *and* `<repeatUntil>` *activities, which support for repetitive executions. Suppose the BPEL process needs to read 10 data entries from a database. The BPEL process should execute the same data retrieval command with a different index in each command. This is a repetitive task, so we can use* `<while>` *or* `<repeatUntil>` *to achieve it. However, this can be parallelized as well. Each data retrieval command is executed in a parallel manner than in a sequential repetitive manner. How can a BPEL process execute a set of repetitive tasks in parallel?*

The `<forEach>` *activity comes to the rescue. It lets us define repetitive tasks in sequential or in parallel. Let's see how it works.*

In this chapter, we will cover the following topics:

- Introducing dynamic parallel invocations
- Adding dynamic parallel invocations to a BPEL process
- Configuring the `<invoke>` activity within a `<forEach>` activity
- Initializing the input variable within a `<forEach>` activity
- Initializing a dynamic partner link within a `<forEach>` activity
- Introducing a parallel `<forEach>` activity and its execution semantics

Introducing dynamic parallel invocations

In this section, we introduce a new sample named book querying process that reads a book name as input, searches it across all the bookstores (Bookstore A, Bookstore B, and Bookstore C), and returns the bookstores in which the book is available. The sample is as shown in the following screenshot:

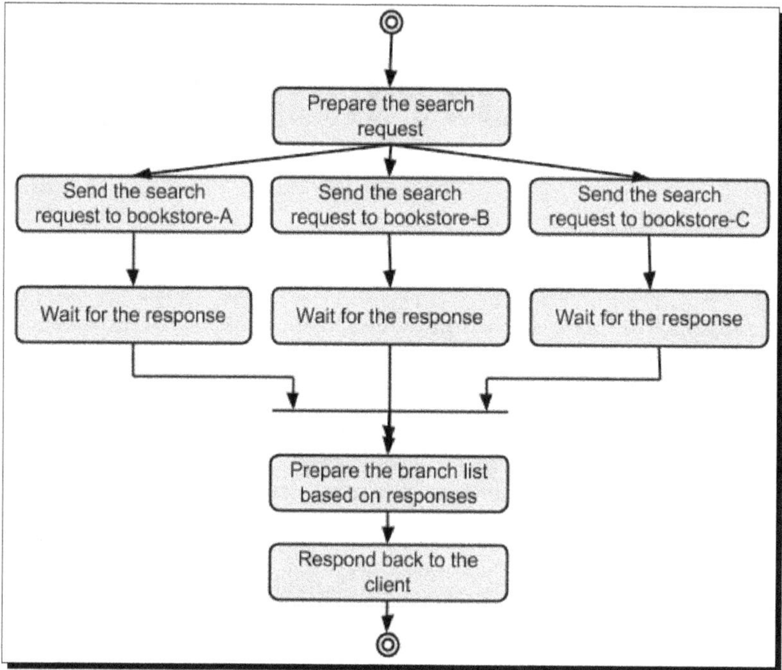

Creating the <forEach> activity

Let's move on to the creation of the `<forEach>` activity creation. Within the `<forEach>` activity, we use the `<invoke>` activity to send search requests. During the `<invoke>` creation process, the input and output variable creation also can be configured. First of all, let's create a new asynchronous BPEL 2.0 process named **Book_Querying_Process**. We illustrated creating an asynchronous BPEL process in *Chapter 5, Interaction Patterns in BPEL*.

Time for action – adding a <forEach> activity

Carry out the following steps:

1. Drag-and-drop a `<forEach>` activity from the BPEL constructs palette in between the `receiveInput` and `callbackClient` activities. Then, the basic configurations of the `<forEach>` activity can be set as follows:

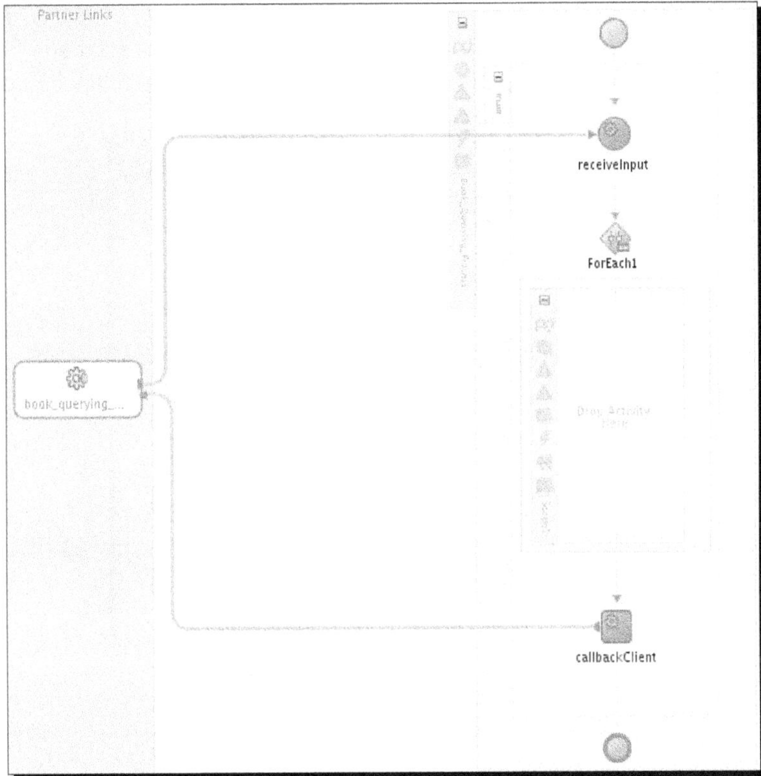

2. To set the **Counter Name**, double-click on the added `<forEach>` activity. On the **General** tab, set **Counter Name** as `foreach_counter`. Subtasks within the `<forEach>` activity can be parallalized by ticking the **Parallel Execution** checkbox, as shown in the following screenshot:

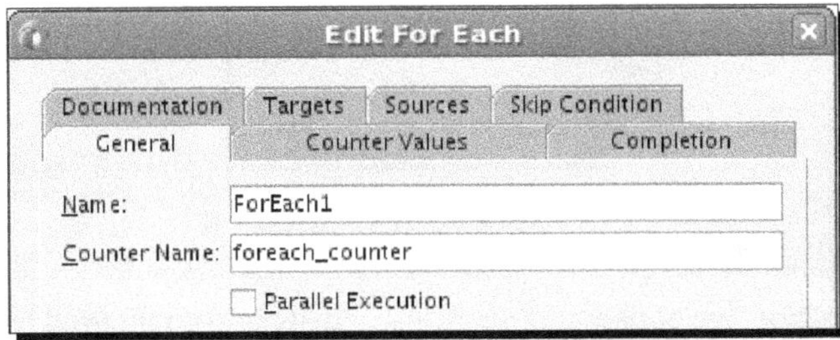

3. To set the `<startCounterValue>` and `<finalCounterValue>`, go to the **Counter Values** tab. Set the unsigned integer expressions for start and final counter values. Then click on **Apply** and then on **OK**, as shown in the following screenshot:

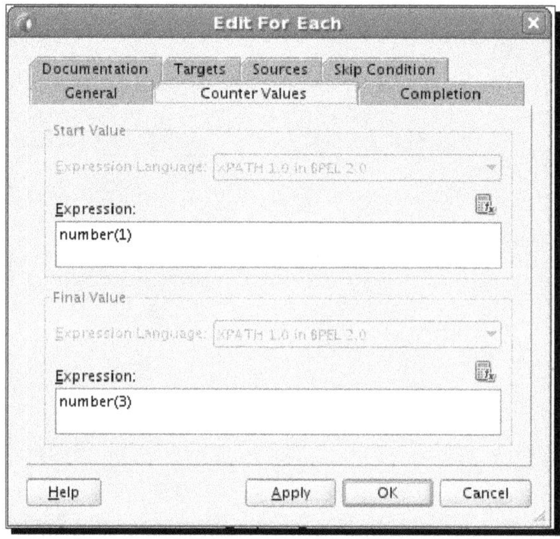

4. Let's create an `<invoke>` activity within the `<forEach>` activity so the `<invoke>` activity can be repeatedly executed:

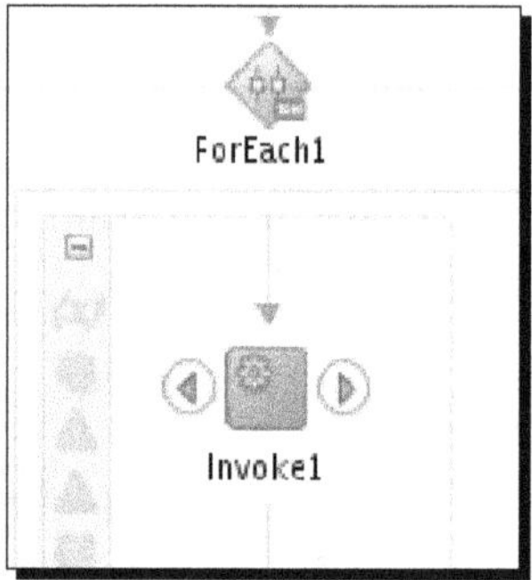

What just happened?

In the preceding section, we added a `<forEach>` activity and configured its essential parameters such as initial counter value and counter value at completion. Finally, we added an uninitialized `<invoke>` activity that will be configured in the next section as the repetitive execution logic. There are other configuration parameters that define the execution behavior of a `<forEach>` activity, which were not covered in the last section. However, they are discussed later.

Time for action – configuring the <invoke> activity within a <forEach> activity

We will now configure the `<invoke>` activity such that it talks to the search service, using the following steps:

1. For creating the partner link, we will create the local partner link within the scope where the previous `<invoke>` activity was created, as shown in the following screenshot:

2. For creating the input and output, we create local variables within the scope where the previous `<invoke>` activity was created, as shown:

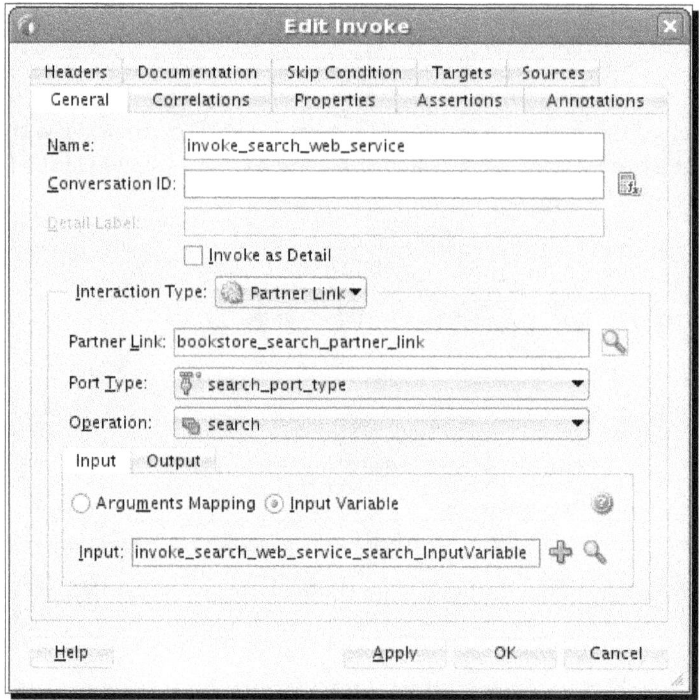

3. Once the `<invoke>` activity is properly configured, click on **Apply** and then on **OK** to close the window.

What just happened?

In the preceding section, we configured the `<invoke>` activity that realizes the repetitive execution logic within the `<forEach>` activity. We configured the `<invoke>` activity to invoke the bookstore search service. In the next section, we focus on how to prepare the request message or the input variable of this `<invoke>` activity.

Initializing the input variable

Now that the input output variables have been already created, we just need to initialize and assign values to the input variables. We assign the string value of the incoming request message (to the BPEL process) to the string value of the outgoing request message (to the bookstore search service).

Time for action – initializing the input variable within a <forEach> activity

Carry out the following steps:

1. Create an `<assign>` activity within the `<forEach>` activity:

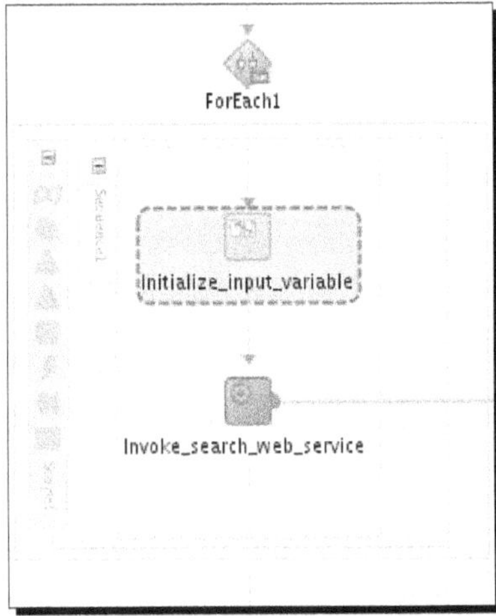

2. Map the string values to initialize the input variable of the `<invoke>` activity:

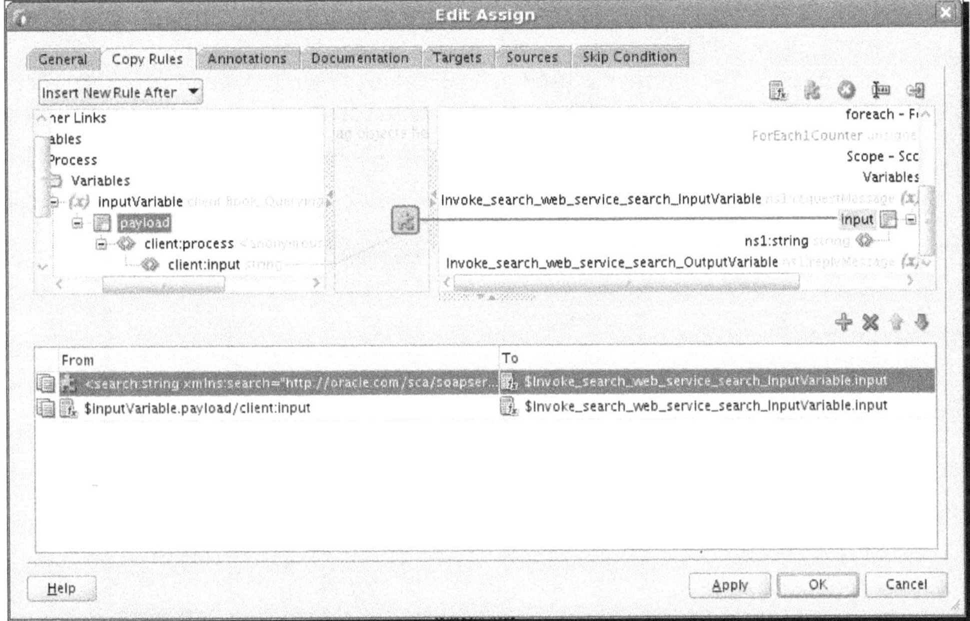

What just happened?

In the preceding section, we focused on preparing the input variable of the <invoke> activity. We first initialized the input variable named `Invoke_search_web_service_search_InputVariable` and assigned the keyword value from the client of the BPEL process. In the next section, we explain how to invoke different service endpoints using the same <invoke> activity.

Initializing a dynamic partner link

In previous exercises, we used static partner links that are defined at the design time, but in a <forEach> activity where the repetitive execution logic is implemented within a <scope> activity. In order to invoke different service endpoints, we need to dynamically change the endpoint data stored in the partner link. In this step, we create a new local variable that can hold partner link data. Then at each iteration, we modify the endpoint data stored in that local variable. Then, we assign the values in that local variable to the local partner link in order to modify the endpoint data of the local partner link within a different <assign> activity named `Initialize_Partner_Reference`.

Time for action – initializing a dynamic partner link

Carry out the following steps:

1. Create a new local variable named `partnerlink_reference`. The schema of this variable is an element called `service-ref`, which is defined in Service Reference Schema for WS-BPEL 2.0 (`http://docs.oasis-open.org/wsbpel/2.0/serviceref`). This element is used as an envelope to wrap the endpoint reference of a partner link. Here, we use WS-Addressing schema (`http://schemas.xmlsoap.org/ws/2004/08/addressing`) to represent an endpoint reference, as shown in the following screenshot:

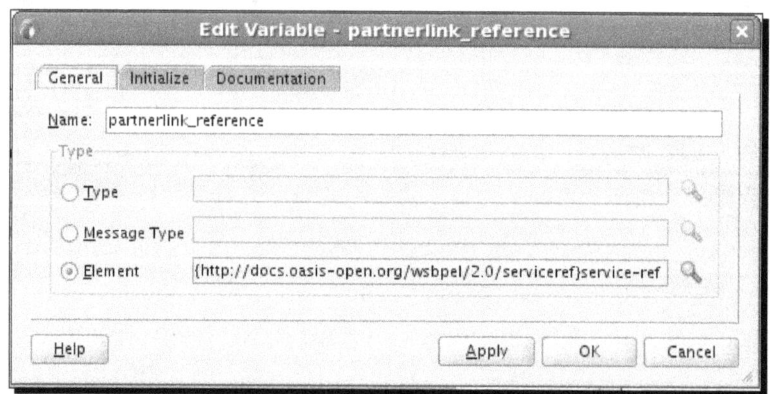

In the sample repository, these schema files (ws_addressing.xsd and ws-bpel_serviceref.xsd) have been already included within the project directory.

2. Drag-and-drop a new assign activity in between the <assign> activity named initialize_input_variable and the <invoke> activity named invoke_search_web_service. This assign activity is used to initialize the variable that holds the endpoint data and then that value is assigned to the partner link, as shown in the following screenshot:

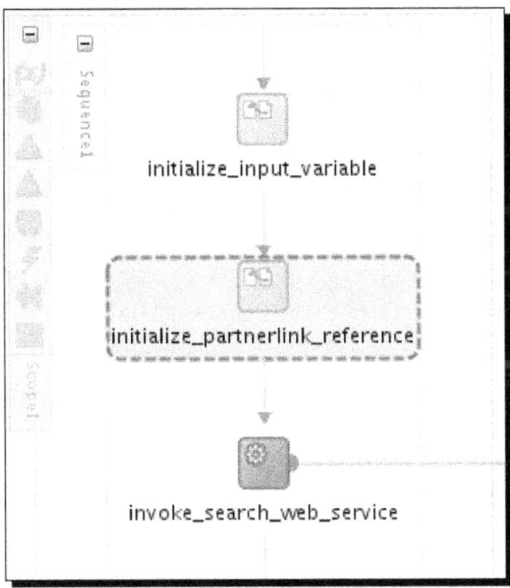

3. Double-click on the newly added <assign> activity and go to the **Copy Rules** tab, which allows you to define data manipulation rules.
4. Initialize the local variable named partnerlink_reference with a literal value as follows:

```
<sref:service-ref xmlns:sref="http://docs.oasis-open.org/
wsbpel/2.0/serviceref">
    <EndpointReference xmlns="http://schemas.xmlsoap.org/
ws/2004/08/addressing" xmlns:ns1="http://oracle. com/sca/
soapservice/Fault_Handling_And
        _Signalling_Application/Fault_Handling_And_Signalling_
Project/SearchService">
        <ServiceName>ns1:search_bookstore</ServiceName>
    </EndpointReference>
</sref:service-ref>
```

5. Append the counter value of the `<forEach>` loop to the child element named `ServiceName` of `partnerlink_reference`, as follows:

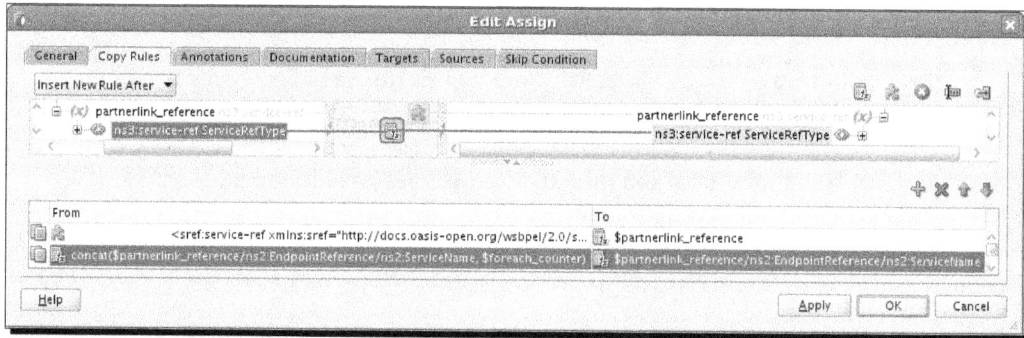

6. We have modified the endpoint values in the `partnerlink_reference` variable and we can assign it to the partner link named `bookstore_search_partner_link`. We can do that by just adding another copy rule to the `<assign>` activity named `initialize_partnerlink_reference`. Add another copy rule by connecting the `partnerlink_reference` variable to the partner link named `bookstore_search_partner_link`, as shown:

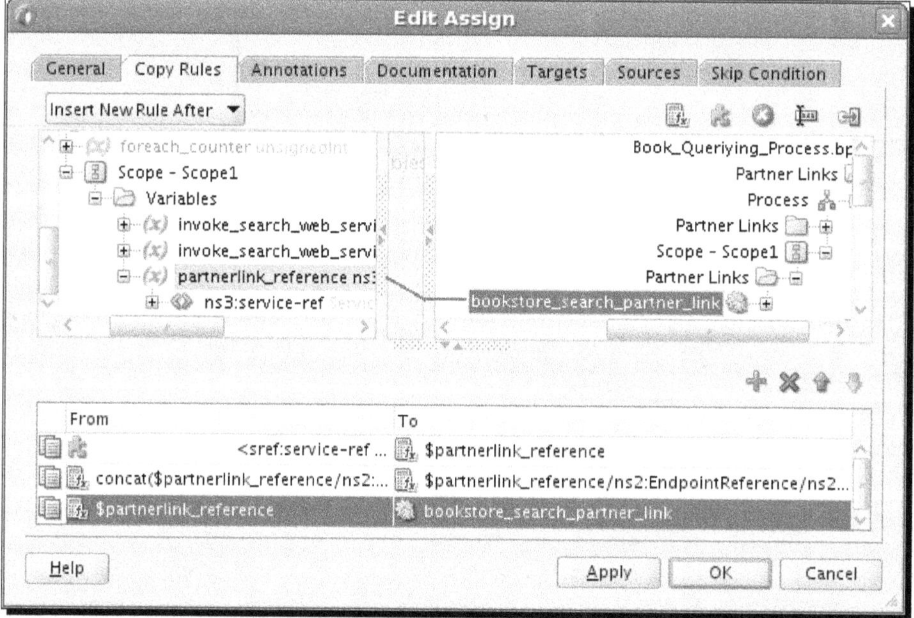

What just happened?

In the preceding section, we focused on using a dynamic partner link to invoke the external web service. First, we create a new local variable named `partnerlink_reference` that can handle partner link data. Then, we create another `<assign>` activity that is used to initialize and assign endpoints to the `partnerlink_reference` variable. Then we initialize that variable and assigned a dynamic endpoint based on the counter value of the `<forEach>` activity. Finally, we assign the value of the `partnerlink_reference` variable to the partner link named `bookstore_search_partner_link`.

Constructing the response variable of the BPEL process

We have implemented the BPEL process up to the external service invocation. The remaining task is to combine all the responses from external web services to the response variable of the BPEL process, so the response message consists of data extracted from each bookstore relevant to the book specified by the request message to the BPEL process. For this task, we use a new `<assign>` activity after the added `<invoke>` activity and simply append the string returned by the `<invoke>` activity to the output variable of the BPEL process.

Time for action – appending multiple values to a variable

Carry out the following steps:

1. Drag-and-drop an `<assign>` activity after the `<invoke>` activity named `invoke_search_web_search`, double-click on it, and go to the **Copy Rules** tab. Create a new copy rule and then choose `$invoke_search_web_service_search_OutputVariable.output` as the **From** expression and `$outputVariable.payload` as the **To** expression. Then right-click on that copy rule and go to **Change rule type** and select **Append**. Then click on **Apply** and then on **OK**, as shown in the following screenshot:

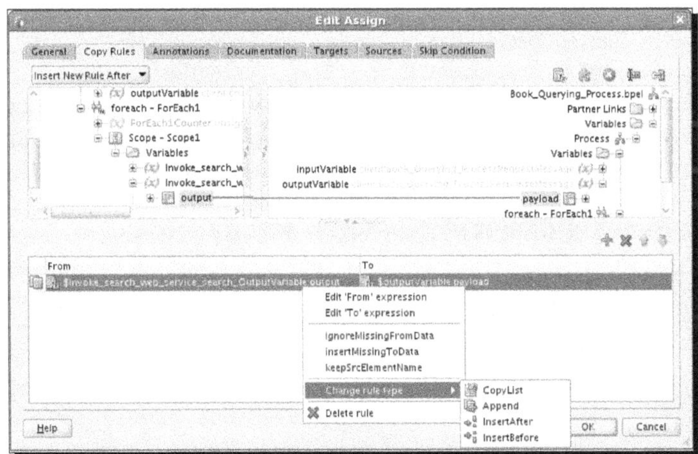

2. The BPEL is ready for testing and deployment:

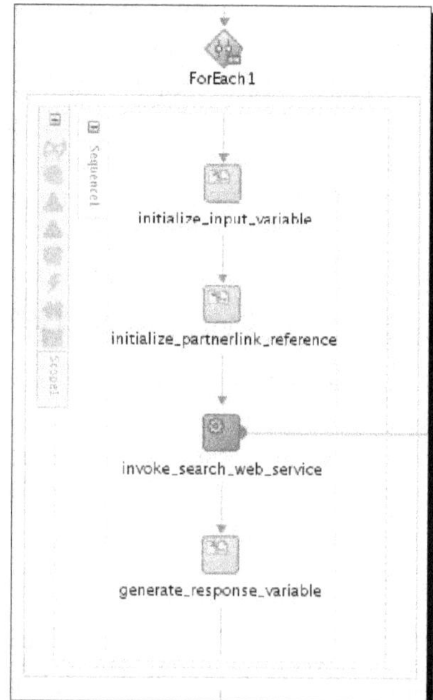

What just happened?

In the preceding section, we collated all the responses from repetitive web service invocations into a single variable called `outputVariable`.

Understanding the <forEach> loop

Frequently in real life, we need to perform some tasks repeatedly. This typical behavior is common for computer programs, as well. Almost all the programming languages define language constructs that support to execute repetitive tasks. Similarly, WS-BPEL 2.0 also provides `<while>`, `<repeatUntil>`, and `<forEach>` activities to support repetitive execution in different ways. In contrast, the `<forEach>` activity supports repetitive execution of the contained activity in a parallel manner for a predefined number of times. Let's discuss the `<forEach>` activity in detail in the coming sections.

Required elements and attributes of a <forEach> activity

As we introduced the `<forEach>` activity in the previous section, in order to determine the number of repetitions, there are two elements named `<startCounterValue>` and `<finalCounterValue>`, as shown:

```
<forEach counterName="BPELVariableName" parallel="yes|no">
  <startCounterValue>
```

```
      unsigned-integer-expression
    </startCounterValue>
    <finalCounterValue>
      unsigned-integer-expression
    </finalCounterValue>
    <scope>
      ...
    </scope>
  </forEach>
```

The contained activity is executed *N + 1* times, where *N* is equal to value of `<finalCounterValue>` minus the value of `<startCounterValue>`.

N = expression value of <finalCounterValue> - expression value of <startCounterValue>

Number of Iterations = N + 1

When the `<forEach>` activity is started, the expression values of `<startCounterValue>` and `<finalCounterValue>` are evaluated and those values remain constant during the lifespan of the activity.

Declaring the invocation logic of a <forEach> activity

One important thing to notice is that the `<forEach>` activity can only contain the `<scope>` activity as the top-level structured activity. All the activities that are supposed to be executed within the `<forEach>` activity should be included within the top-level `<scope>` activity.

Additionally, the `<forEach>` activity has an attribute named `counterName`. The attribute refers to a variable that is implicitly declared in the contained scope of the `<forEach>` activity. The variable has the value of current counter during the repetitive execution. In other words, the contained `<scope>` can refer to the current counter value during each execution by accessing the variable referred by `counterName`. In other words, at each repetition, the contained `<scope>` sees a different value for this variable. During the first iteration, the contained `<scope>` activity sees the value of the variable referred by `counterName`, as the value of the `<startCounterValue>` element. Similarly, during the final iteration, the contained activity sees the value of the variable referred by `counterName`, as the value of `<finalCounterValue>` element.

Configuring a parallel <forEach> activity

The remaining attribute in the `<forEach>` activity is the attribute named `parallel`. This attribute enables to execute the contained `<scope>` activity in parallel or serial. This is very important and one significant difference between other activities such as `<while>` and `<repeatUntil>` that support repetitive executions. If the attribute value is `yes`, then all the repetitive executions start in parallel. Otherwise, the loop branches are executed one after the other. The `<forEach>` activity has one important advantage of simple definition of parallel executions. We discuss more about this parallel `<forEach>` loop in the next section.

Declaring a customized completion condition in a <forEach> activity

We discussed the attributes of the `<forEach>` activity and the top-level child activities such as `<startCounterValue>` and `<finalCounterValue>`. These parameters are required enough to define a simple repetitive behavior that is executed serially or in parallel. There is one optional top-level child element left that can be used to define completion condition for the `<forEach>` activity, which is the `<completionCondition>` element. This element is defined as follows:

```
<forEach counterName="BPELVariableName" parallel="yes|no">
  <startCounterValue>
    unsigned-integer-expression
  </startCounterValue>
  <finalCounterValue>
    unsigned-integer-expression
  </finalCounterValue>
  <completionCondition>
    <branches successfulBranchesOnly="yes|no">
      unsigned-integer-expression
    </branches>
  </completionCondition>
  <scope>
   ...
  </scope>
</forEach>
```

The `<completionCondition>` element enables us to terminate the repetitive execution even before completing all the loop branches. The `<forEach>` activity completes when all the loop branches are completed unless there is a `<completionCondition>` element. If the `<completionCondition>` exists, we can specify that only specific number of loop branches get completed in order to complete the `<forEach>` activity. We can configure this by the value of the `<branches>` element that is defined within the `<completionCondition>` element. The value is an unsigned integer, which can be defined using an XPath expression.

However, what if we only need to complete the <forEach> activity when only a specific number of successful loop branches are completed rather counting both successful and failed loop branches. This can be configured using the attribute named successfulBranchesOnly within the <branches> element. We discussed the configuration parameters of the <completionCondition> element. Now, we discuss how it affects the behavior of the <forEach> activity. At the end of each iteration, the <forEach> activity evaluates the <completionCondition> element and if the completion condition is met, the <forEach> activity does not trigger further iterations.

Let's explore all the discussed parameters with a simple example.

Suppose you needed to collect ten random images from a set of hundred image sources. However, out of those hundred image sources, some of them can be unreliable at some times. The BPEL process should invoke all those image sources and retrieve ten images from images sources that are reliable at that time. This problem can be easily implemented using the <forEach> activity with a completion condition as follows:

```
<forEachcounterName="BPELVariableName" parallel="no">
  <startCounterValue>
    fn:number('1')
  </startCounterValue>
  <finalCounterValue>
    fn:number('100')
</finalCounterValue>
  <completionCondition>
    <branches successfulBranchesOnly="yes">
      fn:number('10')
    </branches>
  </completionCondition>
  <scope>
    <invoke... /><!-- Invoking the image source and retrieve the
image-->
    <sequence... /><!-- Necessary steps to persist the retrieved image
-->
  </scope>
</forEach>
```

Counter for the <forEach> activity starts from 1 and it increments until 100. During the start of each execution, the BPEL runtime evaluates the completion condition. In this example, the BPEL runtime checks whether there is at least ten successful branches completed at the time of evaluation. If so, the execution of the <forEach> activity is marked as completed. In the example, the loop branches are executed in a serial order. In the next section, we discuss the behavior of the <forEach> activity when the loop branches are executed in parallel.

Understanding the parallel <forEach>

In the preceding section, we discussed all the parameters that configure the behavior of the `<forEach>` activity. One parameter that can make a significant impact on the behavior of the `<forEach>` activity is the attribute named `parallel`. This is because if the attribute's value is set to be `true`, the loop branches are executed in parallel. Also, the resultant behavior, when the completion condition meets, also changes.

Also, in some cases, a BPEL developer has to implement the activities within the enclosed scope differently based on the execution manner (that is, serial or parallel). One example would be, if the enclosed scope reads and modifies a global variable, then the scopes should be implemented as isolated scopes (we discussed about isolated scopes in the preceding chapter) to avoid unexpected behavior. In a serial execution, the scope can be either isolated or not. However, we will not go into details on this in this book.

In the upcoming subsections, we discuss the behavior of the parallel `<forEach>` activity.

What happens when starting the <forEach> activity

At the start of a parallel `<forEach>` activity, the expression values of `<startCounterValue>` and `<finalCounterValue>` are evaluated and based on those values, the required number of iterations are determined. Then based on those required number of iterations, the enclosed `<scope>` is executed concurrently. Even though, the behavior of the variable specified by `counterName` is similar to the serial `<forEach>` execution. Each enclosed `<scope>` execution sees a variable specified by the `counterName` attribute with a unique integer value. This unique integer value spans from the expression value of `<startCounterValue>` to the expression value of `<finalCounterValue>`.

What happens when the completion condition is met

The completion condition is evaluated at the end of each iteration. The interesting fact in a parallel `<forEach>` activity is, at the end of an iteration, we do not know whether the other concurrent enclosed scopes are completed or not. However, in a serial `<forEach>` activity, we know that there is no instance of enclosed `<scope>` activities at the end of an iteration. So unlike in a serial `<forEach>`, if the completion condition is met, then all the running enclosed `<scope>` activities should be terminated. Consequently, the termination handler of each enclosed `<scope>` is triggered.

Understanding the difference between <flow> and parallel <forEach>

In the previous section, we discussed the behavior of the parallel `<forEach>` activity. Also, we already discussed about the `<flow>` activity in *Chapter 2, Service Invocation*. Both these constructs support parallel execution of its enclosed activities. The BPEL developer have the option of using the `<flow>` activity or `<forEach>` activity to implement the parallel execution. Let's discuss what is lacking in the `<forEach>` activity compared to the `<flow>` activity in terms of parallel execution.

Lack of synchronization dependencies

When there are concurrent executions happening, sometimes the BPEL developer needs to define some coordination among those executions. The `<flow>` activity utilizes constructs (for example, `<links>`, `<sources>`, `<targets>`, and so on), which support to define synchronization dependencies. However, the parallel `<forEach>` doesn't have such support. Rather, it executes the enclosed `<scope>` activity concurrently without any concern of synchronization among such iterations. The `<flow>` activity should be used when there is a requirement of a coordinated execution.

Repeating the same activity rather than different activities

The parallel `<forEach>` activity is very useful when implementing inherently parallel set of similar tasks. Those tasks have no dependency among themselves. Also, the tasks should be similar, for example, invoking a web service. In such a scenario, using the `<flow>` activity just only incurs an excess amount work.

So based on those reasons, the BPEL developer should choose the better option among the parallel `<forEach>` activity and `<flow>`activity.

Pop quiz

Q1. What are the values that do not change over the time of an execution of a `<forEach>` loop?

1. Counter variable (value of the variable referred by the `counterName` attribute)
2. Start counter value (value evaluated from the expression in `<startCounterValue>`)
3. Final counter value (value evaluated from the expression in `<finalCounterValue>`)
4. Branches value (value evaluated from the expression in `<branches>`)

Q2. What will happen if the `<startCounterValue>` is larger than the `<finalCounterValue>`?

Q3. What will happen if the value of `<branches>` exceeds the possible number of iterations?

Q4. What can be the child activity of a `<forEach>` activity?

1. `<sequence>`
2. `<flow>`
3. `<scope>`
4. `<invoke>`

Summary

In this chapter, we learned the `<forEach>` activity in detail. It lets us define repetitive tasks in a sequential or in a parallel manner. First, we learned a practical use case of the `<forEach>` activity by try outing an example. We then discussed how to configure a `<forEach>` activity systematically. During this exercise, we also learned about dynamic partner links as a requirement to invoke different endpoints within the `<forEach>` activity in parallel. After that exercise, we explained each configuration within the `<forEach>` activity that determines the repetitive and parallel behavior. Therefore, at the end of this chapter, the reader is capable of declaring the `<forEach>` activity to define repetitive tasks in a sequential or in a parallel manner.

In the next chapter, we will introduce the concept of human interactions in WS-BPEL 2.0 processes. We will learn how the BPEL4People extension is based on the WS-HumanTask specification to implement user interactions. You can make use of the concepts, we will learn in the next chapter, in real-world scenarios to model business processes with human interactions.

9
Human Tasks

Human tasks enable human interactions in business processes. Business processes are not generally fully automated and certain activities have to be carried out by humans. Business users whether employees, customers, or suppliers often need to participate in business processes. Examples of human interactions include approval, decision making, error and exception handling and so on. For instance, a human interaction might be necessary for cancelling the order due to product unavailability, increasing the manufacturing of a product due to increase in demand and so on. In a nutshell, human tasks provide a description or speculation of tasks to be performed by humans within business processes.

In this chapter, we will take a closer look at the human tasks and explain the human workflow integration into BPEL processes. In this chapter, we will:

- Understand human tasks
- Get familiar with the Human Task workflow service
- Understand how to design and create human tasks
- Understand how human tasks are executed
- Get familiar with web forms development for human tasks
- Get to know the BPM worklist application

So let's get started...

Understanding human tasks

Human tasks in business processes allow us to include activities that are carried out by humans. So far, we have seen that in BPEL processes we can invoke external services. We call these automated activities. However, often an activity needs to be included that requires human intervention.

Human interactions in business processes can be very simple, such as approval of certain tasks or decisions, or complex, such as delegation, renewal, escalation, nomination, chained execution, and so on. Human interactions can include data entries, process monitoring and management, process initiation, exception handling, and so on.

One of the simplest and probably the most common human interactions is approval. In our book warehousing business process, which we developed in *Chapter 4, Conditions and Loops*, a human task might be required to get an approval of the selected bookstore by a business user, instead of letting the process select the appropriate bookstore (Bookstore A, B, and so on) itself. We can achieve this by adding a human task for approval, before the books are warehoused.

In BPEL, human tasks are implemented similarly as other service invocations. For human interaction, a special service is provided by the process server. In case of Oracle SOA Suite, this service is called human workflow. The human workflow component provides a set of interfaces that allow a BPEL process or other SOA composite component to invoke a human task and assign it to a specific user or a group of users. The human workflow component also provides a set of interfaces that allow querying for all human tasks assigned to a specific person, displaying the human task and fulfilling it.

BPEL does not make a distinction between services provided by applications and other interactions, such as human tasks. Therefore, to implement a human task, our BPEL process will call the special service—the human workflow service. As human tasks usually can take a while to fulfill, the human workflow service will be called asynchronously.

Preparing an asynchronous example

In *Chapter 2, Service Invocation*, *Chapter 3, Variables, Data Manipulation, and Expressions*, and *Chapter 4, Conditions and Loops*, we have implemented the book warehousing process, which selected the most appropriate bookstore in order to warehouse the books. It selected between four bookstores, **BookstoreA**, **BookstoreB**, **AnotherBookstore**, and **VintageBookstore**. The selection criteria included the stock quantity and the publishing date of a book.

In this chapter, we will build upon the example from *Chapter 4, Conditions and Loops*. However, the `BookWarehousingBPEL` process in this chapter will have to be asynchronous. In *Chapter 4, Conditions and Loops*, we were not familiar with asynchronous processes yet. Therefore, we implemented all processes as synchronous. In *Chapter 5, Interaction Patterns in BPEL*, you learned about asynchronous processes and invocation. In contrast to a synchronous process, an asynchronous BPEL process does not require the client (process consumer) to wait for the BPEL process to end. It also does not return a response. Rather, it uses a callback invocation to return a result (if required, some asynchronous processes might not return anything).

Human tasks are asynchronous by nature. As human users need to fulfill the human tasks, it is impossible to foresee how long it will take to get a response from a human task. Therefore, all human interactions are modeled with an asynchronous message exchange pattern. Remember that an asynchronous interaction does not require the client to wait for the human task to complete, which is the only logical choice, given the fact that we cannot foresee when the user will fulfill the human task. This means that BPEL processes which will use human tasks should also be asynchronous.

As human tasks are asynchronous, the BPEL process that will contain the human task should also be asynchronous. Although in theory a synchronous BPEL process could contain the human task, it is not a sound design practice to have a synchronous component containing an asynchronous component. Because a synchronous component would depend on an asynchronous component, we could not guarantee synchronous behavior for the first component. In other words, as human tasks are asynchronous by their nature, it would make no sense calling the asynchronous human task from a synchronous BPEL process. A synchronous BPEL process requires the client (process consumer) to wait for the outcome of the process, which it provides through the `<reply>` activity at the end of the BPEL process that returns the outcome. If we include a human task into a synchronous BPEL process, we have no idea when a human task will be fulfilled. It could take minutes, hours, days, or even weeks, if the user is on vacation. Therefore, making the client wait for the response would be a bad design practice. A much better choice is to make the BPEL process asynchronous as well. This way the client will not wait for the response and will anticipate that it can take a while to get the outcome. Therefore, remember that human tasks should always be invoked from asynchronous processes.

Now, let us convert the `BookWarehousingBPEL` process into an asynchronous process.

Have a go hero – converting BookWarehousingBPEL to an asynchronous process

It is your turn now. Let's convert the `BookWarehousingBPEL` process from a synchronous process to an asynchronous process. You should perform the following steps (and refer to *Chapter 5, Interaction Patterns in BPEL*, for more information):

1. In the WSDL, add the `callback` port type and the `callback` role for `partnerLinkType`.
2. In the BPEL, modify the partner link to include the new role.
3. Also in the BPEL, replace the final `<reply>` with the `<invoke>` callback activity.
4. In the composite diagram, double-click on the exposed service endpoint of the BPEL process and add the callback port type.
5. Modify the way `BookOrderManagementBPEL` and `BookOrderForEachBPEL` invoke `BookWarehousingBPEL`. Instead of using a synchronous `<invoke>`, you should use a pair of `<invoke>` and `<receive>` activities. The `<receive>` activity will wait for the callback.
6. To make the example even better, convert the `BookOrderManagementBPEL` and `BookOrderForEachBPEL` processes to asynchronous processes as well. Use the same steps as described earlier.

Alternatively, you can download the prepared project, where the process has already been changed into an asynchronous process. This way you can progress with the rest of this chapter immediately. The project is called `Chapter9initial` and is part of the code samples for this book.

After you have converted the `BookWarehousingBPEL` process (and the `BookOrderManagementBPEL` and `BookOrderForEachBPEL` processes) from synchronous to asynchronous, the composite diagram for our application should look like this:

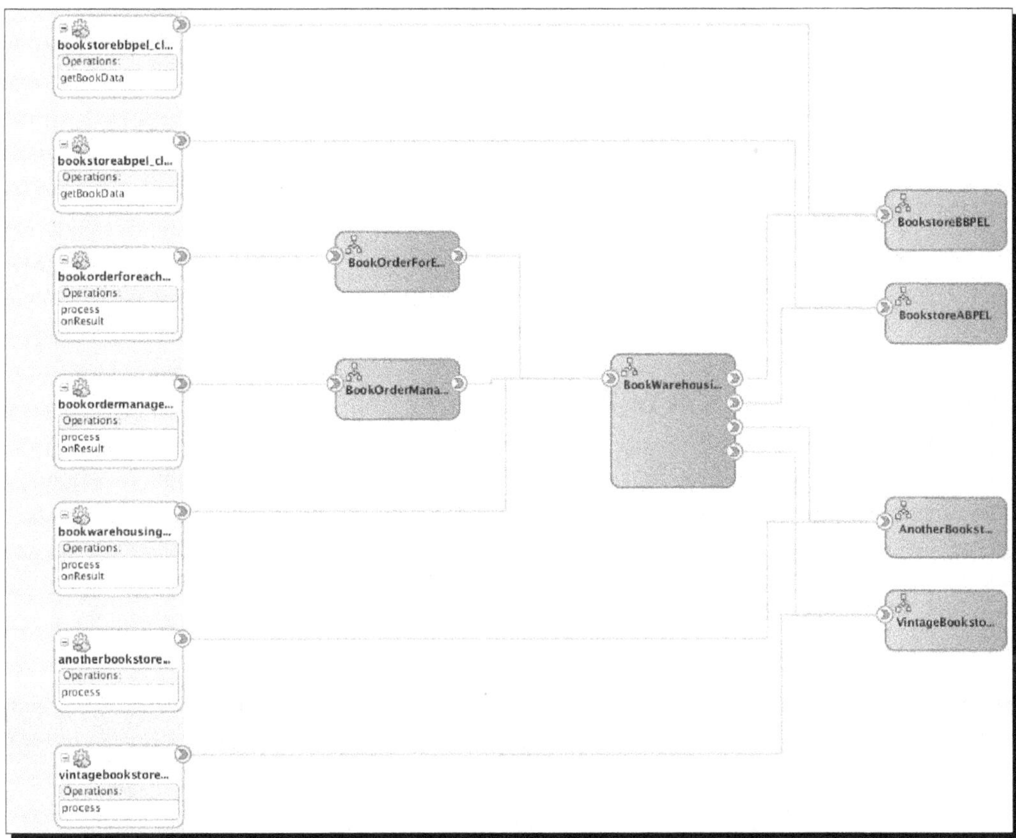

You can also look at the asynchronous `BookWarehousingBPEL` process. Notice the `<invoke>` callback activity at the end of the process, instead of the synchronous `<reply>` activity.

Adding a human task to the BookWarehousingBPEL process

Let us now enhance the `BookWarehousingBPEL` process and include a human task to approve the book store selection. We will place the human task at the end of the BPEL process, after the `<if>` activity and before the callback `<invoke>` activity.

In order to add a human task to the BPEL process, we need to follow the ensuing steps:

1. Create a human task definition.
2. Configure the human task.
3. Add a human task to the BPEL process.
4. Configure human task case branches.
5. Create human task forms.

Let's get started!

Creating a human task definition

A human task definition is a template, which is used to create the actual human task instances. Having a human task definition is useful, as we can use the same definition for other similar human tasks, which is often the case for more complex business processes. A human task definition defines the task title, description, outcomes, payload (the information shown to the user), who the human task is assigned to, who is the owner, what are the deadlines for fulfilling the task, the escalation policy, and some other details, which we will explain in the upcoming sections.

Time for action – creating a human task definition

To create a new human task definition, we will start at the composite diagram. We will drag-and-drop the **Human Task** service component from the **Component Palette** onto the composite application. We will do this the same way as we have done with other components, such as the BPEL process.

We will proceed as follows:

1. Drag-and-drop the **Human Task** service component from the **Component Palette** onto the composite application diagram.
2. The **Create Human Task** window will open. We will set the name of the human task to `BookstoreApproval`. For the namespace, we will use `http://packtpub.com/Bookstore/BookstoreApproval`. If we invoke the human task within the application composite (in our case from the BPEL process), we will leave **Create Composite Service with SOAP Bindings** unchecked. We would check the option if we wanted a separate web service endpoint to be created for the human task. This would enable invoking the human task from external applications via the web service call.

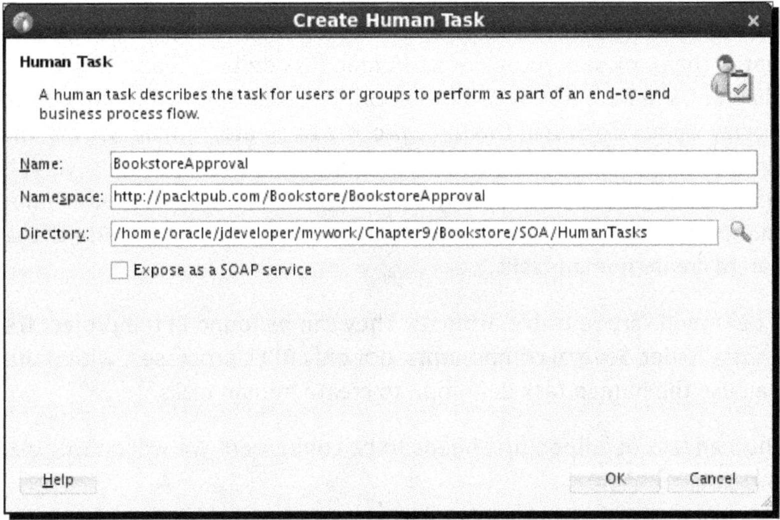

3. Next, we will wire the human task with the `BookWarehousingBPEL` process:

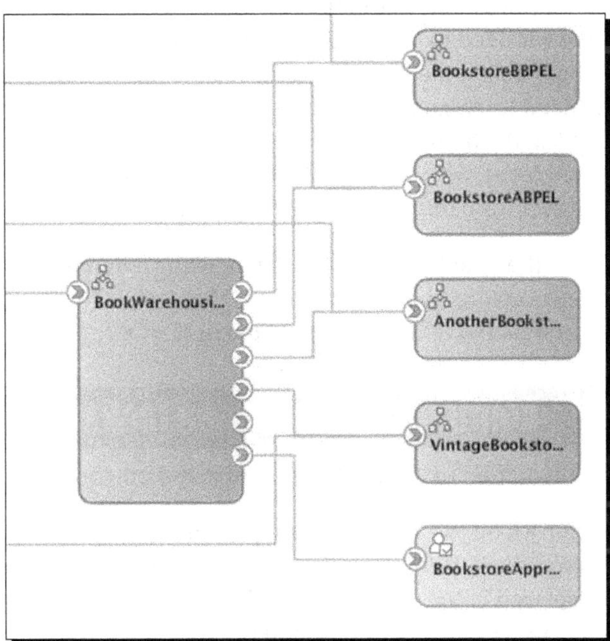

By wiring the human task and the BPEL process, a partner link for the human `TaskService` is automatically created in the `BookWarehousingBPEL` process.

What just happened?

We have created the `BookstoreApproval` human task definition and added it to our composite diagram. We have also wired the `BookstoreApproval` human task to the BPEL process. This way we have enabled the BPEL process to create human task instances based on the human task definition. During runtime, a BPEL process will create several human task instances (we will simply call them human tasks), all based on the same human task definition. In more complex examples, more than one BPEL process can use the same human task definition to create human tasks.

Human task definitions are reusable artifacts. They can be found in the project tree in the `HumanTasks` folder. Several components, not only BPEL processes, within the same composite can use the human task definition to create human tasks.

However, a human task definition first needs to be configured. We will do this in the next section.

Configuring human tasks

After we have created the human task definition for our `BookstoreApproval` human task, we need to configure it. We will need to set up several parameters, such as Human Task title and outcome, payload that will define the data that is sent to the human task and received as an outcome. We will also need to assign the human task to a specific user or group of users, who are responsible for fulfilling the human task. Sometimes we will know exactly which user should fulfill the task. Even more often, we will assign the human task to a group of users, such as an order department. Any user from this group will be able to claim and fulfill the human task.

Furthermore, we will set the deadlines that will define when a human task must be completed. Finally, we will configure the notifications that will define who to notify if the human task is not completed in the specified time or if an error occurs.

Time for action – configuring the human task title

Let's start with the configuration of the human task title and outcome:

1. We will double-click on the `BookstoreApproval` human task to open **Task Definition Editor**. We will enter `Book store Approval` as the task title. The task title will be displayed in the user interface. In our case, this will be the BPM worklist application. We will also add a description of the human task.
2. To define the outcomes, we will need to check those that apply. For our example, the `APPROVE` and `REJECT` outcomes are sufficient. The `APPROVE` and `REJECT` outcomes are the default outcomes. However, we could still click on the magnifier icon next to **Outcomes** and **Outcomes Dialog** would open. In our scenario, we will check the `APPROVE` and `REJECT` outcomes and click on **OK**.

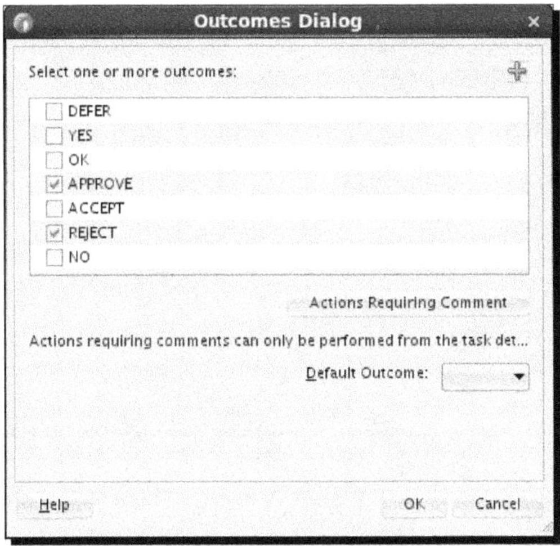

3. We will also select the owner of the human task. The owner has administrative privileges on the task. To select the human task owner, we click on the magnifier icon. The **Identity Lookup** dialog opens. Here we can search for users and select them. In our example, we select the `weblogic` user and click on **OK** to close the dialog. The `weblogic` user is one of the precreated users. We can create additional users and groups within the WebLogic user realm. For more information about adding users and groups refer to `http://docs.oracle.com/cd/E24329_01/web.1211/e24484/realm_chap.htm`.

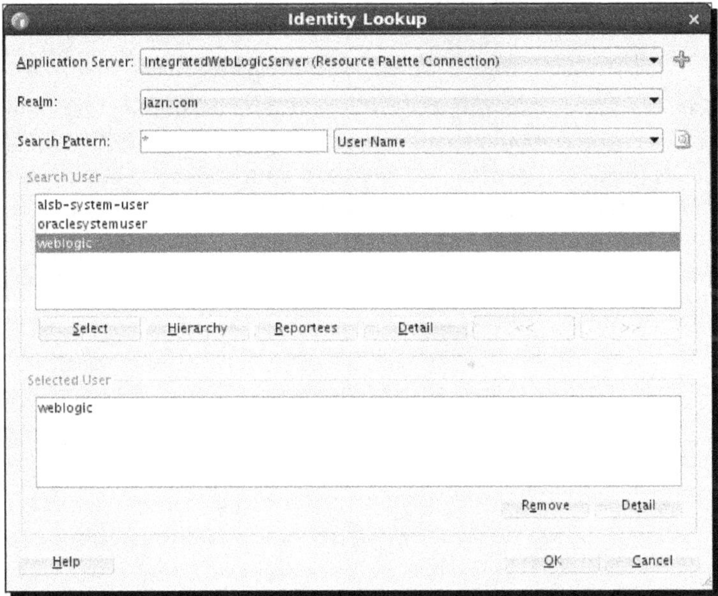

4. We should see the following screen:

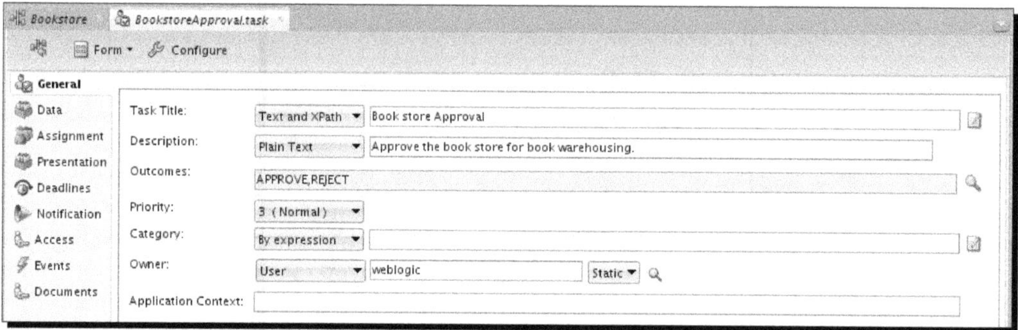

What just happened?

We have configured the general settings of the human task definition, including the task title, human task owner, and the outcomes. Next, we will specify the human task payload.

Time for action – specifying a human task payload

A human task will, through the web user interface that we will discuss later, show specific information to the user. In our case, the human task will show the selected bookstore to the user and require an approval. Therefore, we need to configure the human task payload. The payload specifies the data that is sent to the human task and the outcome from the human task. We need to specify the XML element from the corresponding XML Schema.

We proceed as follows:

1. To specify the payload for our `BookstoreApproval` human task definition, we need to select the **Data** tab to the left of **Task Definition Editor**. We have to set the payload, as the approval manager will need data about the book and the selected bookstore to decide whether to approve the warehousing or not.

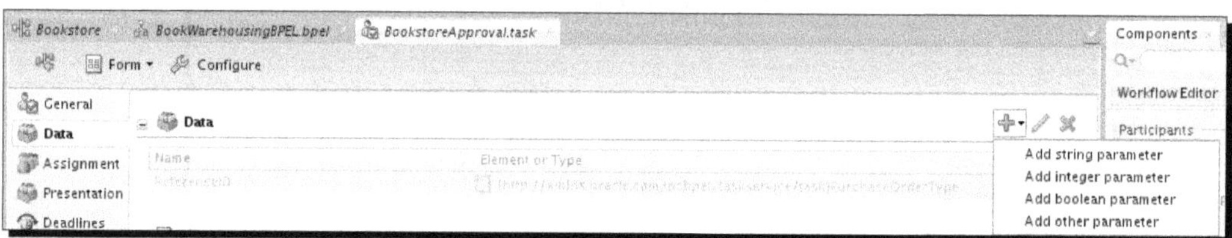

2. Under the **Data** section, we will click on the plus icon and select **Add other parameter**. The **Add/Edit Task Parameter** dialog opens:

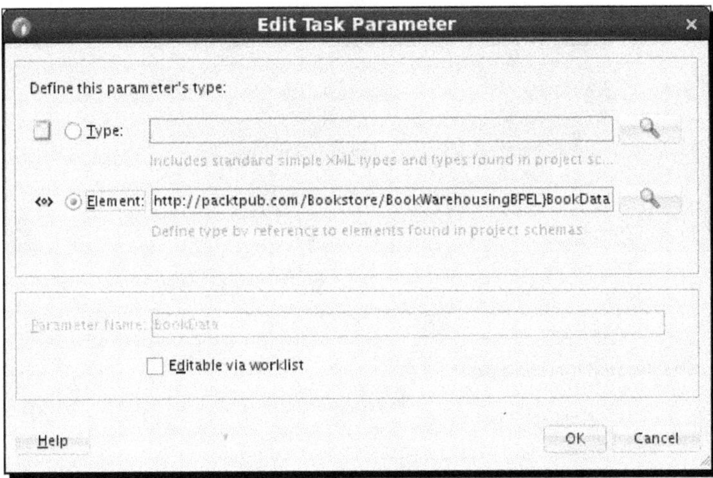

3. First, we will add the book data. To achieve this, we will select **Element** and browse for the `BookData` element which is defined in the `BookwarehousingBPEL.xsd` schema.

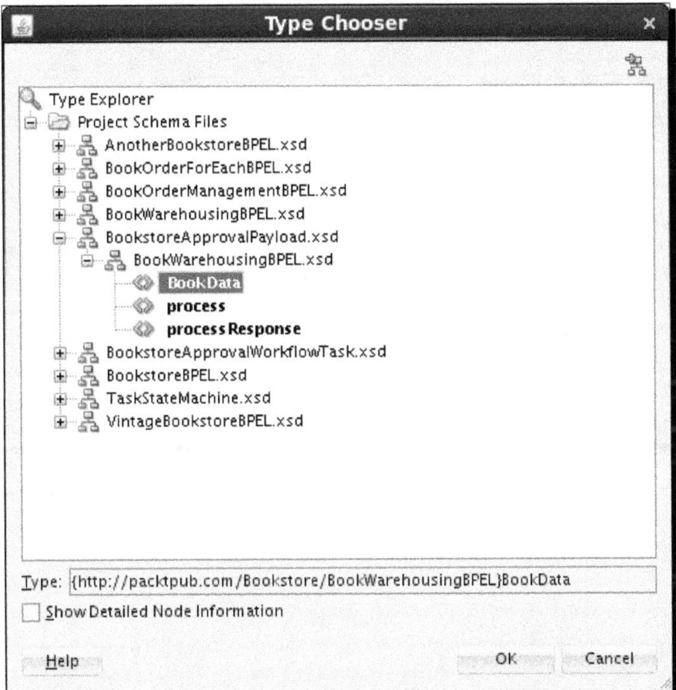

4. Next, we will add the data about the selected bookstore. We have stored this data in a BPEL process variable of type string. Therefore, we need to add a string parameter:

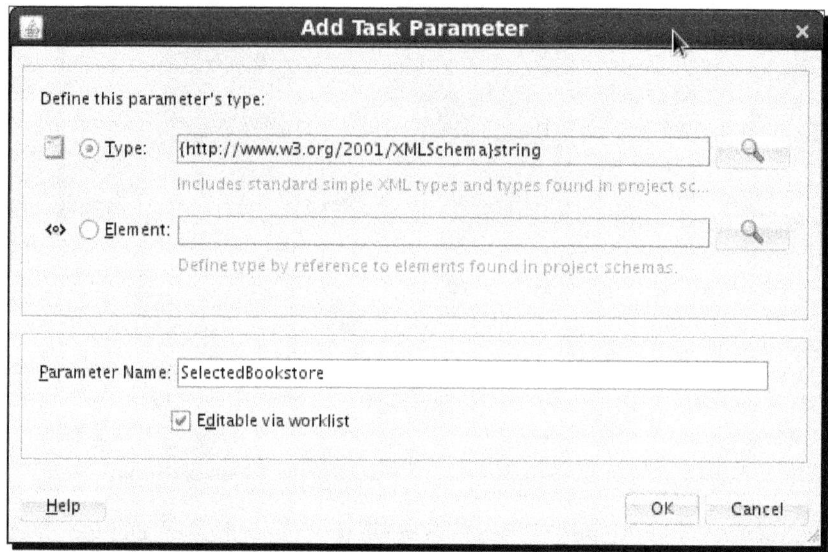

5. We will name the parameter `SelectedBookstore`. We will check **Editable via worklist**, as we will enable that the user modifies the selected bookstore in the human task. The final data payload configuration should look like this:

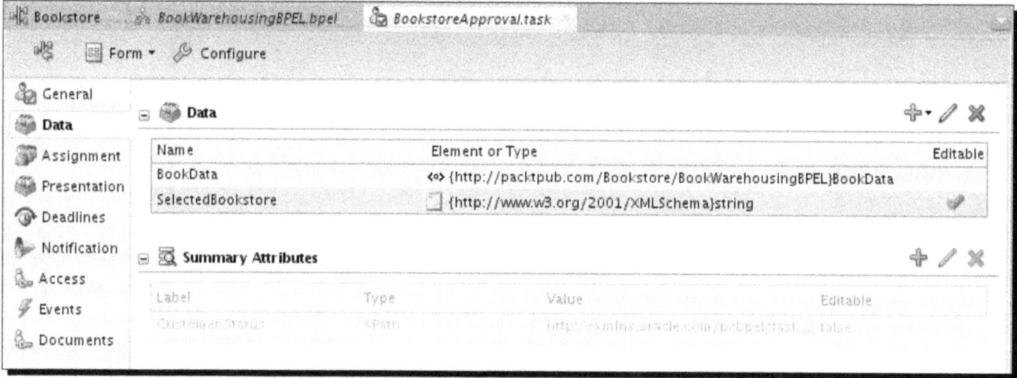

What just happened?

We have configured the human task payload for our human task definition. We have selected two data elements as human task payload: the book data, for which we have used the `BookData` element from the `BookwarehousingBPEL.xsd` schema, and `SelectedBookStore` of simple XML type `string`. Next, we will assign the human task to the user who should fulfill it.

Time for action – assigning a human task

Each human task has to be assigned to a human to fulfill it. Such a human is called a participant. Generally, we can assign a human task to a specific user or group of users. In the latter case, a user has to claim a task before he can start working on it. We assign a human task to a specific user if we know exactly who should fulfill the task. Otherwise, we can assign the task to a group, and a user (for example an employee) from that group can claim the task and fulfill it.

To simplify our example, we will assign the human task to a specific user:

1. To assign the human task, we will switch to the **Assignment** tab, where we can assign the human task to a user, group, or an application role.
2. We will drag-and-drop the **Single Participant** component from the **Components** window to the main assignment window.

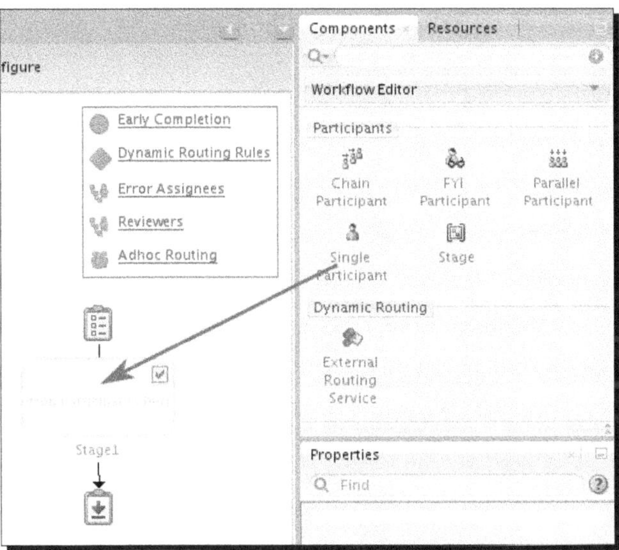

3. We double-click on the added participant. The **Edit Participant Type** dialog opens. We will use the default type (**Single**) and enter the label of the participant (`Approval Manager`). Then we will click on the plus sign to add a participant and select **Add User**. Again, we will assign the task to the `weblogic` user. Similarly, as we did earlier, we will see the list of users and groups, which have been created in the WebLogic user realm. We could create additional users and groups within the WebLogic user realm. For more information about adding users and groups, refer to `http://docs.oracle.com/cd/E24329_01/web.1211/e24484/realm_chap.htm`.

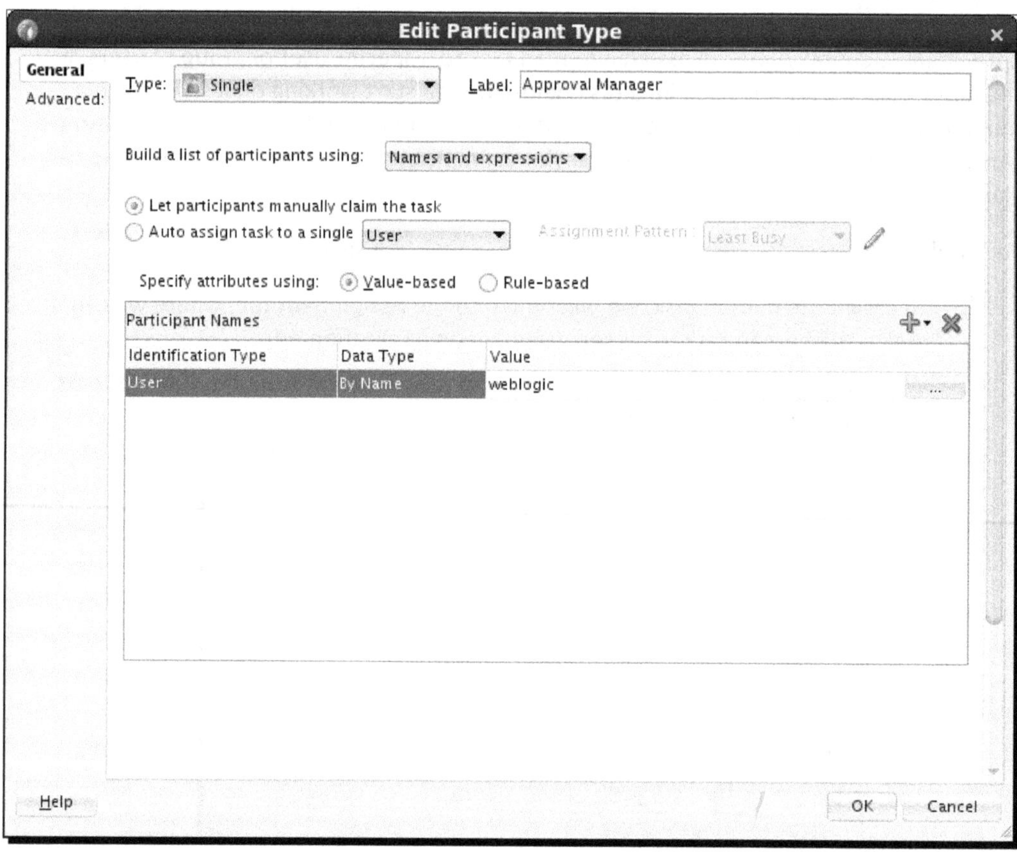

4. Instead of static assignment, the user could also be set dynamically using the value from the task payload. In that case, we would have to change the data type to **By Expression** and use **Expression Editor** to compose the XPath expression. After we have made the assignment, we should see the following:

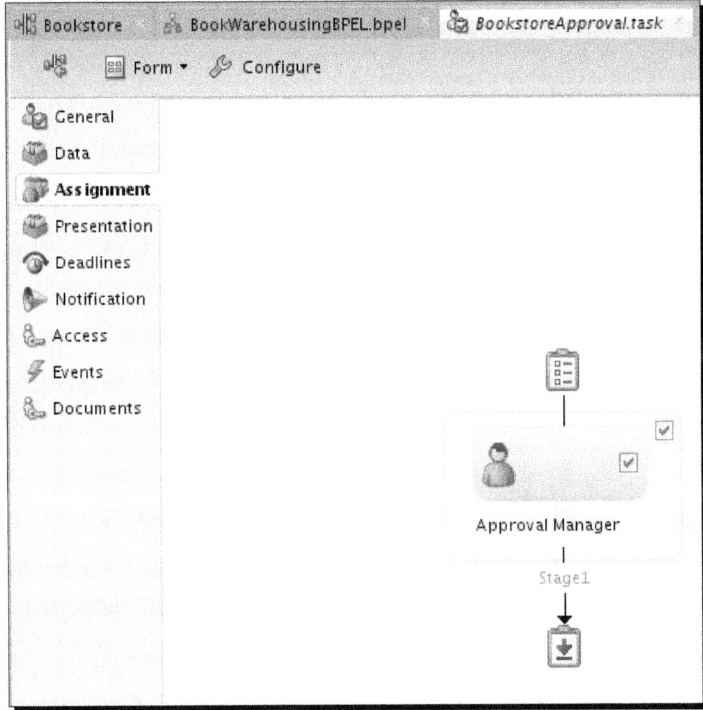

In addition to assigning the user participants that will need to fulfill the human task, we can also assign the user who will be responsible for performing corrective actions in case of errors, and the user who will be able to review the human task.

5. To assign the **Error Assignee**, let's go to **Task Definition Editor** and click on the **Error Assignees** link under the **Assignment** tab. The **Add Error Assignees** dialog will open. Click on the green plus icon and add the `weblogic` user as **Error Assignee**:

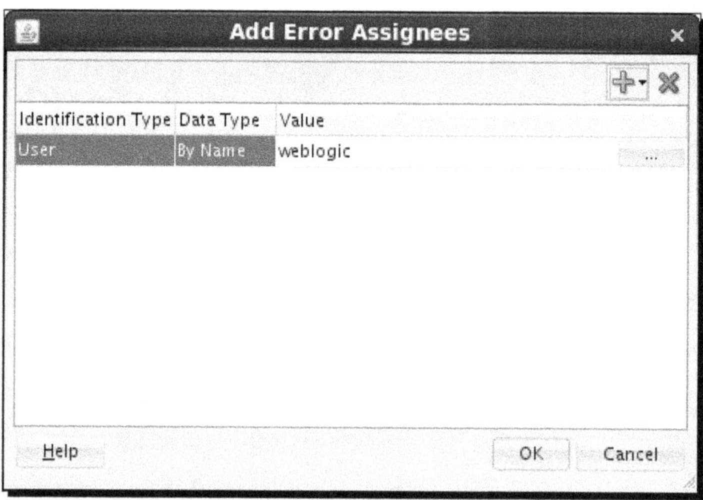

What just happened?

We have assigned the users for the human task, who should fulfill it. We have seen that there are several options for user assignments, from simple assignments to a specific user, over assignments to groups, and complex assignments. In our example, we have assigned the human task to the `weblogic` user. We have also assigned error assignees, who are responsible for handling errors. In our example, we have used the same `weblogic` user. In real-world examples, we would first create additional users and groups in the WebLogic realm and select from them. Creating users and groups is out of the scope of this chapter, as it is specific to the application server that is used. For WebLogic, refer to `http://docs.oracle.com/cd/E24329_01/web.1211/e24484/realm_chap.htm` for more information about adding users and groups.

For more information on human tasks refer to `http://docs.oracle.com/middleware/1213/soasuite/develop-soa/soa-bpm-human-task-design.htm#SOASE87304`.

In the next step, we will continue with the configuration of deadlines.

Time for action – configuring human task deadlines

Next, we will configure the deadlines. It makes sense to define a deadline when a human task has to be fulfilled. This prevents scenarios where a human task is assigned to a certain person or group but gets forgotten. For example, we could define that the human task for approving the book store location should be fulfilled in a certain amount of time.

If the user does not fulfil the human task in the specified time, an action will be taken. This action can be expiration, renewal, or escalation. A human task can expire after a certain time. This means that the human task will expire and the control will be returned to the caller (in our case this is our BPEL process). As the user has not fulfilled the human task, the BPEL process will not get a decision; therefore, it will need to act accordingly. Although human task expiration might not look very useful at the first sight, it prevents a human task from waiting indefinitely for the user to fulfill it and the BPEL process calling the human task from stalling.

The second option is that the human task is renewed after a certain time, which means that the human task will be initiated once again and all the users (participants) will be notified again. This way we can easily make sure that the users are notified after a certain amount of time if a human task is waiting. We can specify how many times we would like to renew the human task.

The third option is that the human task is escalated after a certain period of time. This means that the human task will be assigned to the user or group which is higher in the hierarchy. In other words, the human task will be assigned to the manager of the user who has not fulfilled it. We can configure how many escalation levels should be used for our human task and who is the highest approver title that can get the human task assigned.

For our example, we will define that our human task will renew after 5 minutes. We have selected a short time, as it will be easier to test the human task. To achieve this, we have selected **Renew after** and **Fixed Duration** of **5** minutes, as shown in the following screenshot. We should also set the **Maximum Renewals** count. In our example, we set it to **10**:

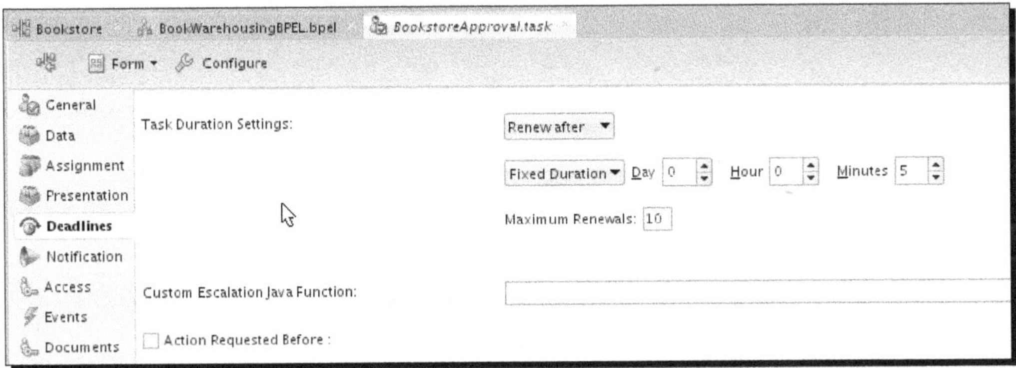

In more complex scenarios, we could define the duration by expression. In this case, we would use an XPath expression and would address a process variable.

What just happened?

We have configured a 5-minute deadline for our human task. After that deadline, it will be renewed. This means that it will be reassigned to the same user. Although 5 minutes is too short for real-world examples, it is appropriate for our example as it will make testing easier. In real-world examples, it is more likely to renew the human task after 24 hours and even to take into consideration the working days of a week.

In the next step, we will continue with the configuration of notifications.

Time for action – configuring human task notifications

Here we can configure various notifications for the human task. We can configure that a specific user is notified when the human task is completed, expired, suspended, withdrawn, updated, and so on. This way we can make sure that we have control over human tasks and can supervise when, how, and by whom the human tasks are fulfilled.

We can choose to notify the human task owner, assignees, initiator, approver, or reviewer. Finally, we can define the notification message, which specifies the content that will be sent as a part of the notification.

In our example, we will configure a notification for the process owner when the human task is assigned. To achieve this, we will follow these steps:

1. To configure a notification to the process owner for the task assignment, we will select **Owner** in the **Assign** row of **Task Status**. In a similar way, we could set the notifications for other task statuses:

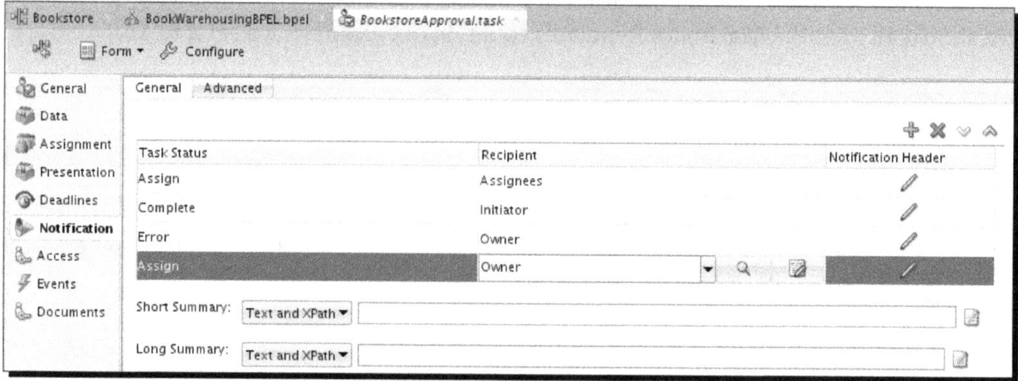

2. We will also set the text for the notification, which we can achieve by clicking on the **Notification Header** icon. The following is the default notification message. We could modify the message by simply editing the default text:

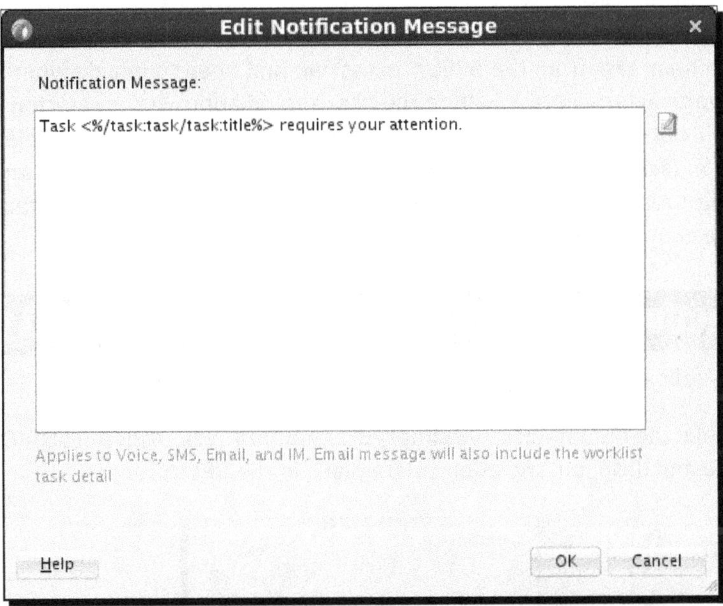
Edit Notification Message
Notification Message:
Task <%/task:task/task:title%> requires your attention.
Applies to Voice, SMS, Email, and IM. Email message will also include the worklist task detail
Help
OK
Cancel

What just happened?

We have configured human task notifications. We have seen that we can configure notifications for events, such as when the human task is completed, expired, suspended, withdrawn, updated, and so on.

To summarize the human task configuration again, we have configured the human task, including the outcome and payload. We have assigned the human task to a specific user or a group of users. We have set the deadlines for human task competition and configured the notifications. It is important to understand that these settings can be used for all instances of a human task.

Invoking a human task from the BPEL process

After we have created and configured the human task definition and added it to the composite, we will need to invoke it from the BPEL process. The BPEL process has to invoke the human task in order to create a human task instance in the Human Workflow component.

To invoke the human task from the BPEL process, we first need to decide where to place it. As this is an approval human task, where the user should approve the selected bookstore location, we will put the human task after the bookstore location has been selected. We will place the human task at the end of the BPEL process, after the `<if>` activity and before the `<reply>` activity. Also, we will need to handle the human task outcomes to take appropriate actions if the user approves or rejects the bookstore location, respectively.

Time for action – invoking a human task from the BPEL process

We proceed as follows to invoke a human task from the BPEL process:

1. To invoke the human task, we simply drag **Human Task** from the **SOA Components** palette and drop it in the appropriate place in the BPEL process.

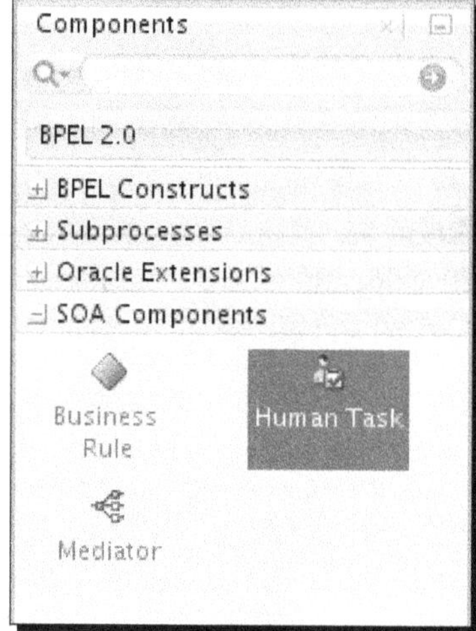

We have decided to place it at the end of the BPEL process, after the `<if>` activity and before the callback `<invoke>` activity:

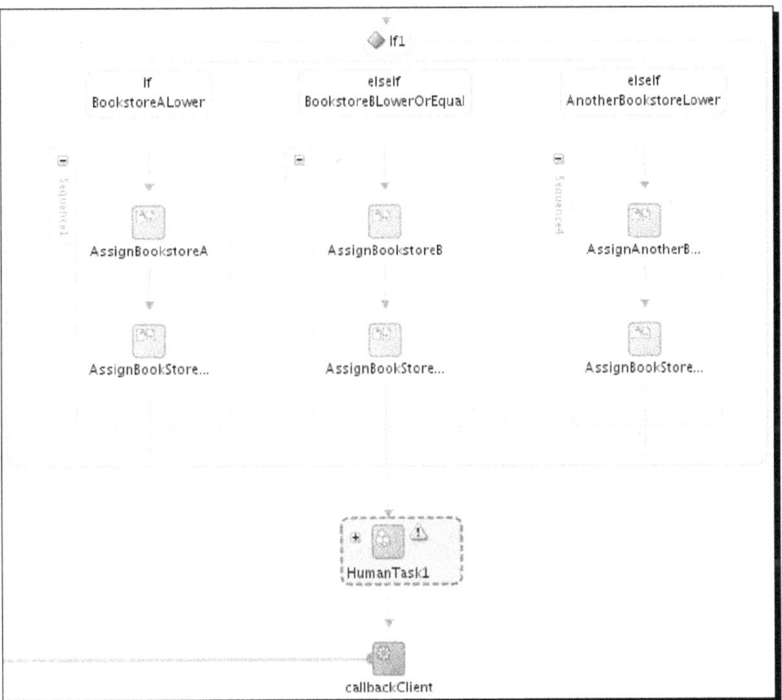

2. Next, we will double-click on the human task and a dialog for human task configuration will open. Here, we will select the **BookstoreApproval** human task definition:

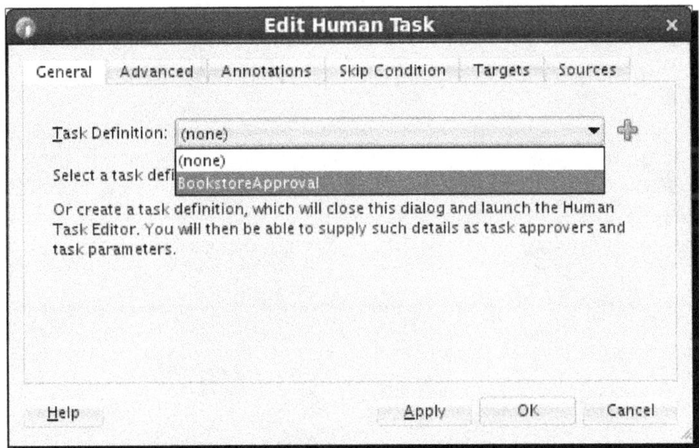

3. We can skip **Task Title** (in which case the default task name will be used) and proceed straight to **Task Parameters**. We need to provide the `BookData` and `SelectedBookstore` parameters. We will use the appropriate variables for both parameters.

4. For **BookData**, we will use the BPEL variable with the same name—`BookData`. As this variable does not exist yet, we need to create it. Refer to *Chapter 3, Variables, Data Manipulation, and Expressions*, for variable creation. The `BookData` variable should use the XML element `BookData` from the `BookWarehousingBPEL.xsd` XML schema. We also need to assign the values to the `BookData` variable, which we should do in the corresponding `<assign>` activities: `AssignBookstoreA`, `AssignBookstoreB`, and `AssignAnotherBookstore` respectively.

5. For **SelectedBookstore**, we will use the `SelectedBookstoreLocation` string from the `output` variable:

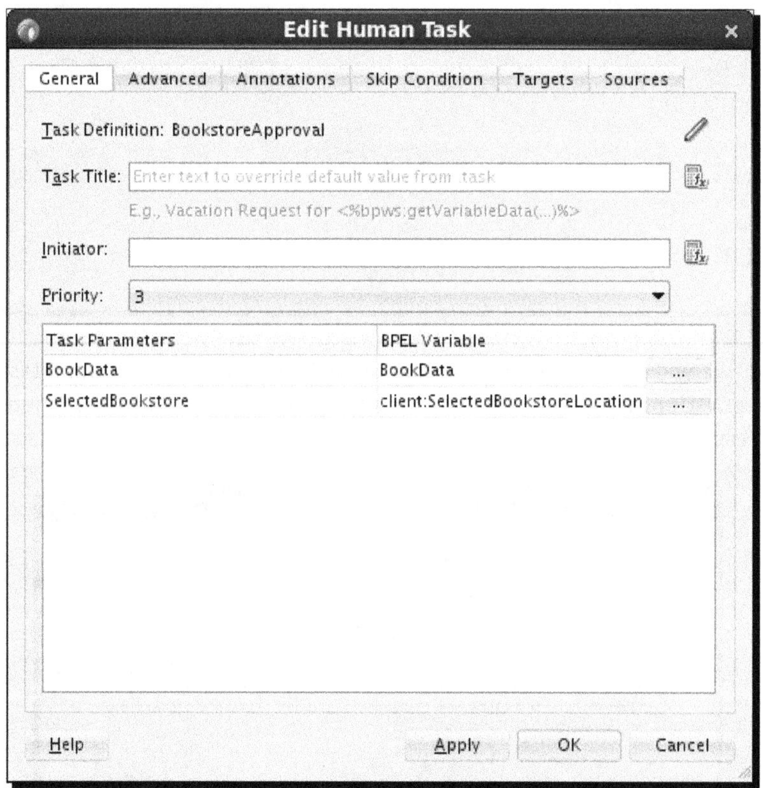

What just happened?

We have successfully invoked the human task from the BPEL process flow. The human task does not differ considerably from a service invocation. Similarly, as for a service invocation, we needed to provide the parameters for the human task. In our case, we have defined two parameters, `BookData` and `SelectedBookstore`. We have obtained the data from the BPEL process variables.

We can look closer into the human task invocation and we will see that it is a structured activity, which asynchronously invokes the `BookstoreApproval` service (the human task service):

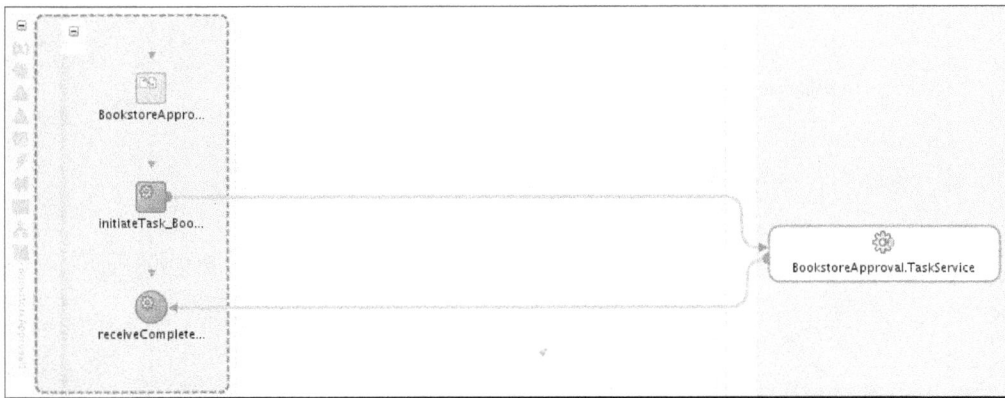

Configuring human task case branches

Next, we need to configure the human task case branches. We remember that we have defined the possible outcomes of the human task. In our case, we have defined the **APPROVE** and **REJECT** outcomes.

Therefore, we need to specify, in the BPEL process, what the process will do if one of the outcomes is selected by the user. Additionally, we also have to specify what happens if the human task outcome is not defined. This could happen if the human task expires, if it is canceled, or if an error occurs.

Time for action – configuring human task case branches

To configure the human task case branches, an `<if>` activity needs to be added to the BPEL process. Fortunately, the JDeveloper has done this for us. If we look at our BPEL code, we will see that the `<if>` activity with the appropriate branches has been added:

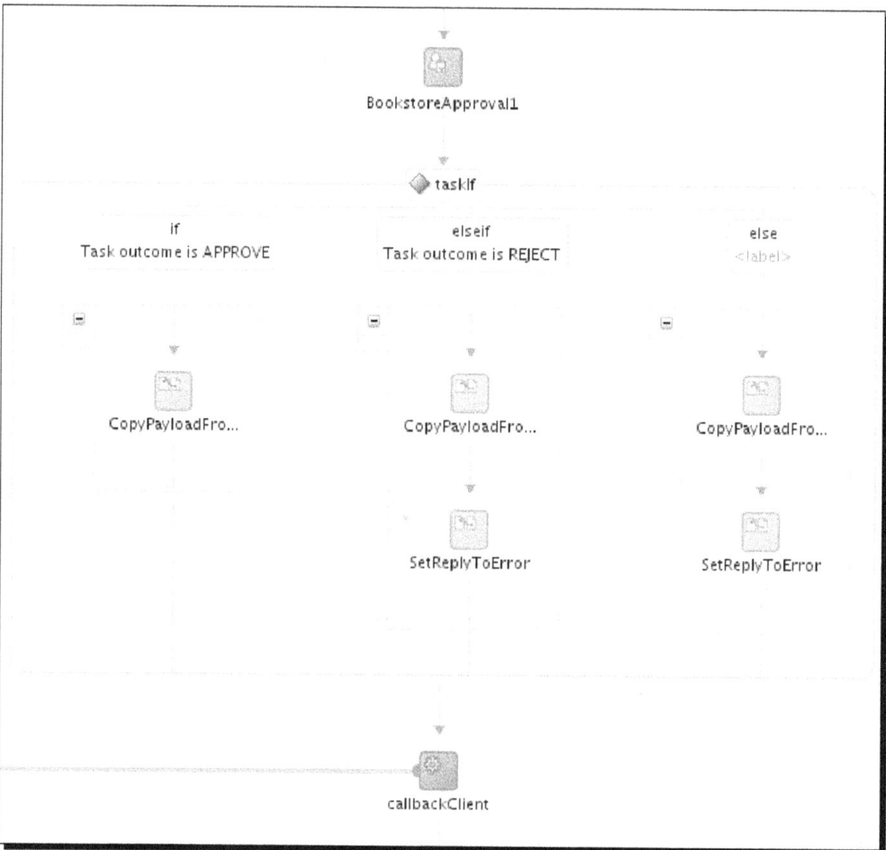

All we need to do is specify the corresponding activities for each branch. We have to specify the activities for the **APPROVE** outcome, the **REJECT** outcome, and for all other situations where the outcome is not selected (for example, if a human task has expired).

In our process, we will do the following:

1. For the **REJECT** outcome and the `for else` branch, we will copy the corresponding text (**Rejected** or **Error**) to `SelectedBookstoreLocation` in the `output` variable.
2. For the **APPROVED** outcome, we will not do anything, as the output is already prepared.

What just happened?

We have added the activities to handle the human task outcomes. In our case, we have added the assign activities to update the process output accordingly. After the added assigns, the process should look like this:

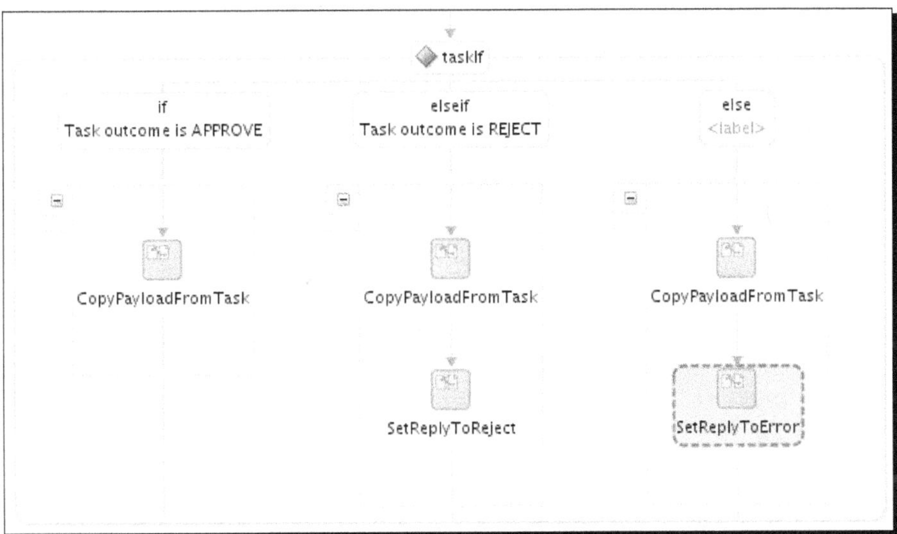

Creating human task forms

The task form is used to display the content of the task to the user. In general, any custom user interface can be used. Oracle SOA Suite also provides a generic worklist application, the Oracle BPM Worklist application. In Oracle SOA Suite 12c, we can create a task form using the **Oracle Application Development Framework** (**Oracle ADF**). When creating the task form, we have two options:

- We can use a wizard to autogenerate the task form.
- We can create a custom ADF task form in a separate application, create a new project and browse for the `.task` file for the human task.

As ADF is out of the scope of this book, we will just show how to autogenerate the task form using a wizard.

Time for action – creating human task forms

To create the human task forms, we will proceed as follows:

1. Open the **BookstoreApproval** human task and select the **Auto-Generate Task Forms** from the upper-left drop-down menu:

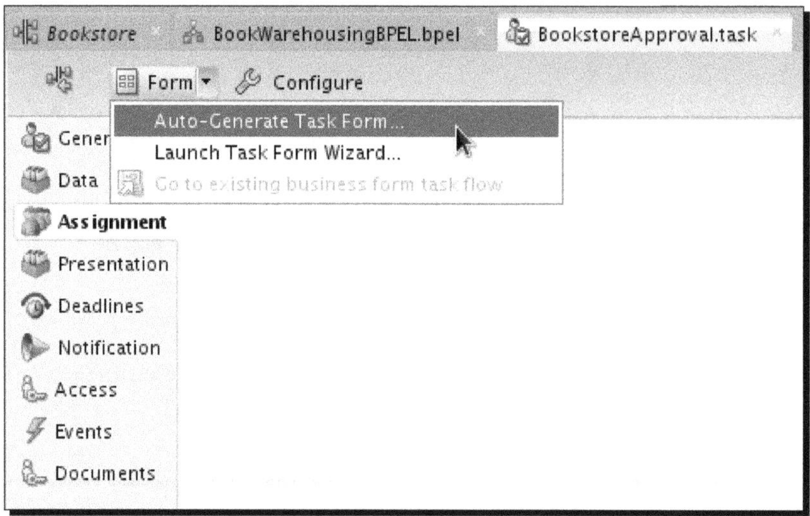

2. The **Create Project** dialog opens. We name the project `FormBookstoreApproval` and click on **OK**:

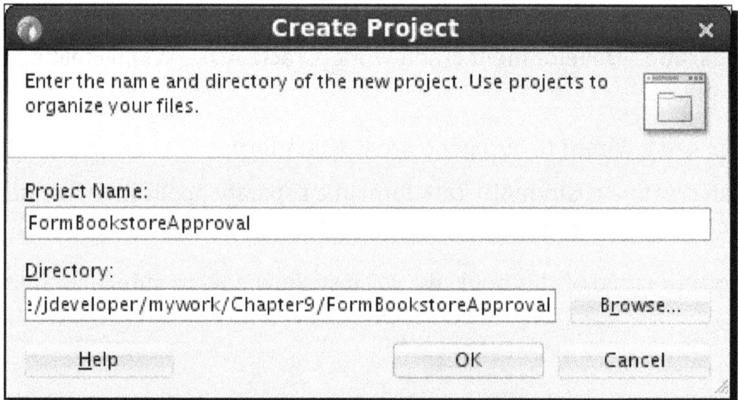

3. After clicking on **OK**, we have to wait for a while, as a new project is being generated in the background, until the `taskDetails1.jspx` page opens:

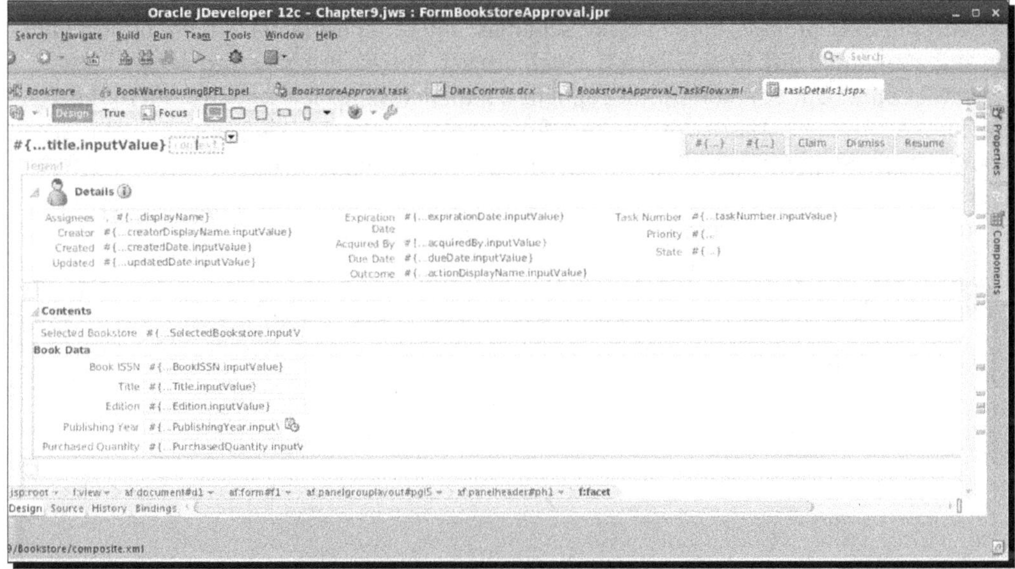

4. We can see that the task form was successfully created and is ready to be deployed. We save the project by clicking on the **Save All** icon in the toolbar and close the task form.

What just happened?

We have autogenerated the task form that is used to show the human task with the corresponding data to the user. The human task form will be used within the worklist application. You can inspect the form and its source code to learn more.

Alternatively, we could custom develop the form. For forms, we can use ADF. We could also implement them in other technologies, but then they could not be used from the worklist application.

Deploying and testing human tasks

We are ready to deploy the modified BPEL process and the corresponding project with the task form.

Time for action – deploying the human task

In order to deploy and test our example, we need to deploy the project with the SOA content (the BPEL process, human tasks, schemas, and other artifacts) and the project with the auto-generated task form, which is a web project. The easiest way is to deploy both projects at once. Our SOA composite contains a human task, which is connected to the task form ADF project. Therefore, the **Task flow deployment** screen will appear within the SOA composite deployment wizard, as shown in the following screenshot. In the **Task flow deployment** screen, we should select the **FormBookstoreApproval** project. This way it will be automatically deployed just after the SOA composite project:

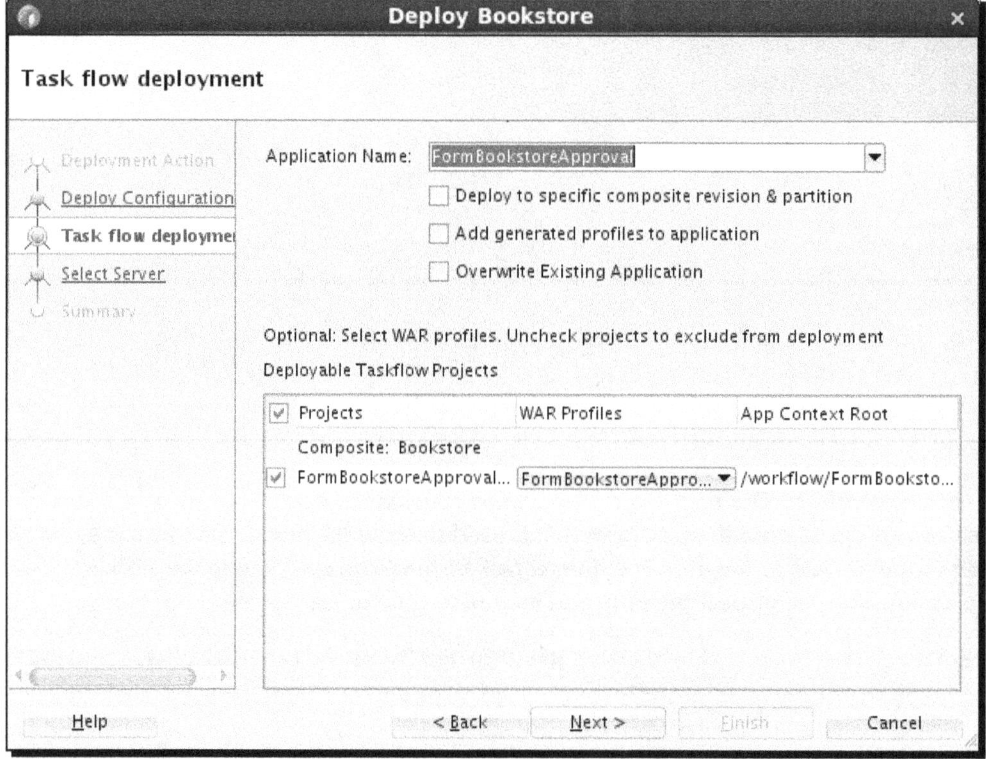

Time for action – testing the human task

To test our BPEL process with the human task, we will first need to start the BPEL process. We do this the same way as we did in the previous chapters. If we look at the trace of the instance, we can see that the instance is still running and is waiting for the `BookstoreApproval` human task to complete.

Worklist application

To complete the human task, we have to log in to the Oracle BPM Worklist application using the URL `http://host_name:port/integration/worklistapp/`, where `host_name` is the name of the host on which the worklist application is installed and `port` is the port number of the SOA managed server (default is `8001`). Oracle BPM Worklist is a very powerful application, not only allowing users to act on tasks, but also providing the following features:

- Customizing the visual appearance and behavior
- Reassigning tasks to other users
- Escalating, renewing, withdrawing, and suspending tasks
- Setting the vacation period to automatically reassign tasks during absence
- Creating reports on task productivity, time distribution, and so on
- Sending notifications and alerts

However, we will not discuss advanced features in this section. Now, we log in to the BPM Worklist application as the user `weblogic`, as the task is assigned to him. The BPM Worklist application opens as shown in the following screenshot:

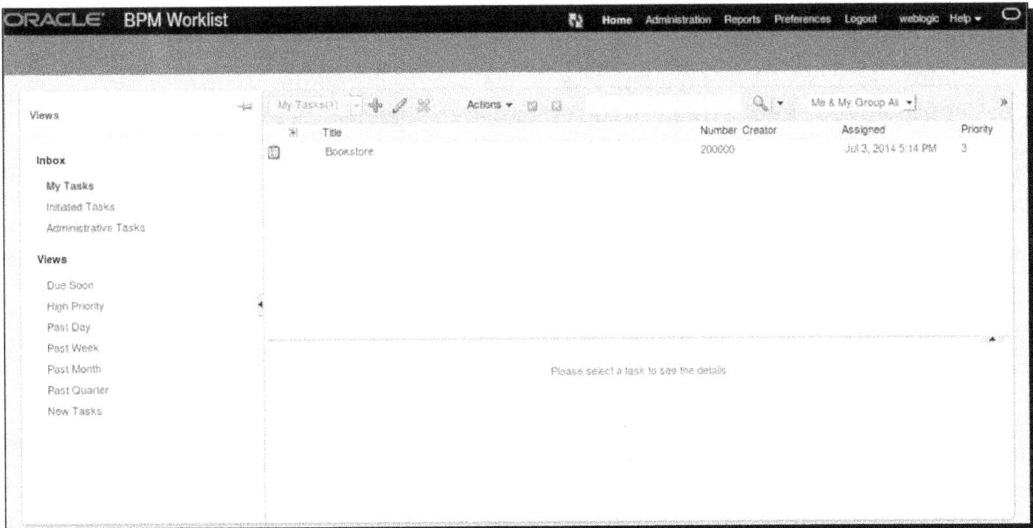

By default, the **Inbox** worklist view is selected and the user can see all tasks assigned to him in the **My Tasks** list. In our case, there is only one active task: bookstore approval. Remember that this is the name of the human task that we set during the creation of the human task definition.

If we want to see the task details, we have to select the task. The generated ADF task form displaying the task details shows at the bottom of the page.

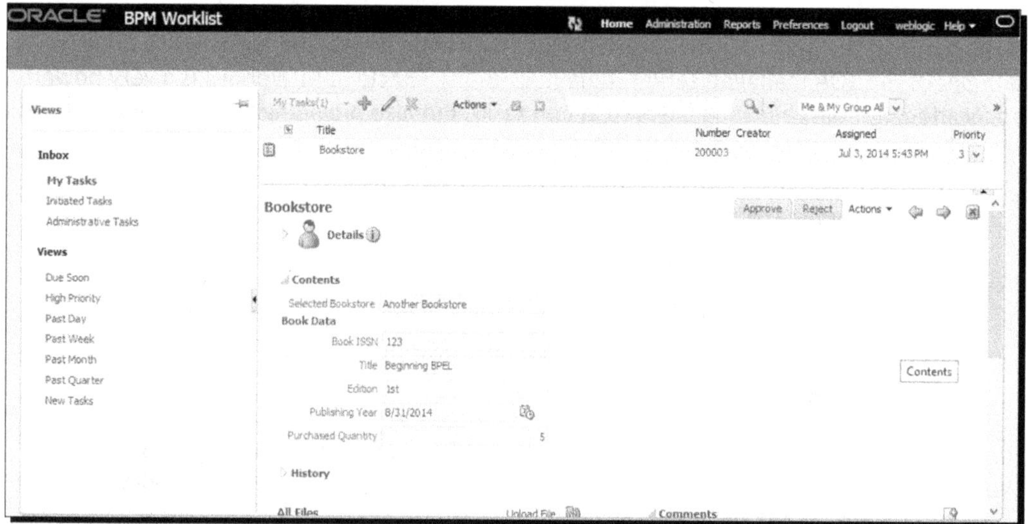

Completing the task

In the upper-left corner, there is a task title. In the upper-right corner, we can see two buttons (**Approve** and **Reject**), which correspond to the defined task outcomes. In order to complete the task, we have to click on one of those two buttons. In the **Contents** section, we can see the payload of the task, displaying information about the selected flight ticket. At the bottom of the task form, we can also see the task history and add comments and attachments.

Now, we will complete the task by clicking on the **Approve** button (we will approve the flight ticket). The task is completed and is removed from the **My Tasks** list.

If we look at the flow trace of the instance, we can see that the instance has successfully completed.

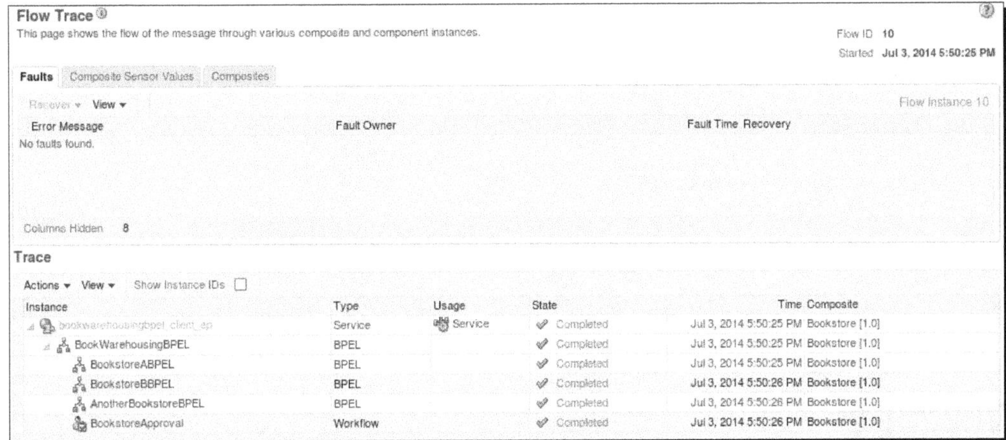

We have successfully added a human task to our BPEL process, deployed the BPEL process and the human task form, executed the BPEL process, and completed the human task.

Pop quiz – human tasks

Q1. What are the outcomes of a human task?

1. Can be freely defined
2. Always `APPROVE` and `REJECT`
3. `APPROVE`, `REJECT`, and `ERROR`

Q2. A human task can be assigned to:

1. A specific user
2. A group
3. It cannot be assigned

Q3. What is escalation?

Q4. To add a human task to the BPEL process, we use:

1. `<assign>`
2. Special human task activity
3. `<invoke>`

Q5. Autogenerated task forms use:

1. ADF
2. ASP.NET
3. PHP

Summary

In this chapter, we have learned about human tasks and human interactions in BPEL processes. Support for human tasks is important, as it enables BPEL processes to include not only system-to-system interactions, but also human interactions.

To include a human task into the BPEL process, we first need to create a human task definition, where we have to specify various aspects of the human task, such as title and outcome, and human task payload that defines the data that is sent to human task and is received as an outcome. We need to assign the human task to a specific user or a group of users. We might also want to set the deadlines that will define when a human task must be completed. Finally, we can configure the notifications that will define who to notify if the human task is not completed in the specified time or if an error occurs.

Next, we have to add the human task invocation to the BPEL process with a specific human task activity. We also need to handle the outcomes and provide the corresponding activities to handle the various outcomes.

To be able to show the human task to the user, the task form is required. Oracle SOA Suite provides the ability to autogenerate task forms, which simplifies the development considerably.

After deploying the BPEL process and the task forms to the server, we have to use the worklist application to show and complete the human task.

Now that you have learned how to handle human tasks, we move ahead to learning events and event handlers in BPEL. We will see how BPEL processes can react to events, such as messages and timers. Stay tuned!

10
Events and Event Handlers

Business processes, particularly long-running processes that contain human interactions, often have to react to events. For example, let's imagine that a business process needs to provide a way to cancel the process while it is running. Or that we want to limit the maximum time in which a business process should finish. Or that a business process should start or stop on a specific date and time. All this can be achieved with events and Event Driven Architecture (EDA).

In this chapter, we will take a closer look at the events and event handlers in BPEL processes. We will do the following:

- Explain events and have a brief look at the EDA
- Understand how a BPEL process can react on events
- Get familiar with business, message, and alarm events
- Understand the difference between deadlines and durations
- Learn how to develop event-driven BPEL processes and how to invoke events from BPEL processes
- Learn how and when to use event handlers
- Get familiar with the `<pick>` activity
- Understand how the `<pick>` activity can be used with asynchronous callbacks

So let's get started...

Understanding events

So far we have talked about operation invocations. A BPEL process explicitly invokes an operation on a service or another BPEL process. Operation invocations are the most common interaction models used in software development. They require that the caller (service consumer) explicitly calls a service (also referred to as a service provider) by invoking a specific operation. This means that we need to know explicitly who we are calling. In cases where we would prefer a more loosely-coupled interaction, without explicitly stating who we are calling, operation invocations would be insufficient. This is where events come in.

An event represents an occurrence, something that happens or is regarded as happening, especially one of some importance. It enables a different interaction model, a model where it is not required to explicitly call a service. Rather, it is sufficient to trigger an event. Once the event is triggered, all services subscribed to this type of event will be invoked automatically.

An event-driven interaction model enables us to create a very loosely-coupled interaction. The one that triggers an event does not know which services are subscribed to that event. Therefore, it does not know which services will be invoked. Also, vice versa, the service subscribed to an event does not know who has triggered the event.

Events have become an important part of software architectures. EDA defines the concepts related to the production, detection, consumption, and reaction to events. EDA complements service-oriented architecture (SOA), as it enables SOA processes and services to react on events and to trigger events. Sometimes, SOA complemented with EDA is referred to as SOA 2.0. For more information on EDA, please refer to `http://en.wikipedia.org/wiki/Event-driven_architecture`. For more information on event processing, please refer to the book *Getting Started with Oracle Event Processing 11g, Packt Publishing*, or to the Oracle documentation at `http://docs.oracle.com/middleware/1213/eventprocessing/index.html`.

Business processes may be triggered by events. For example, let's imagine a process that takes care of book shelving. This process may be executed on different occasions, such as when the books arrive to the bookstore for the first time, after a customer has looked at the books, and during an inventory. Instead of explicitly invoking the process on each occasion, such a process could react on a corresponding event. A business process might also trigger an event. For example, the book warehousing process might trigger the event to bookshelf the books.

Business processes may have to react on events. Particularly long-running processes, which contain human interactions, often need to react on events. For example, in the previous chapter, we have added a human task to our book warehousing process where a user has to approve the selected bookstore. As it is usually not possible to foresee how long a user will need to complete a human task, we might want to add other measures to be sure that a certain BPEL process does not get stalled. For example, let's suppose that we would like to limit the total execution time of a specific BPEL process. We can achieve this using events and event handlers.

A second example would be a scenario where a business process has been initiated and is in progress; however, we would like to provide a possibility to cancel the process instance at any time. This is the case in many business processes, for example, in an ordering process, a client might place the order and change his or her mind after a certain time while the order is still being processed. In a bank, a client might apply for a loan and while the bank is deciding whether he is eligible for the loan, the client can change his mind.

Also, in our book warehousing process, where the processes select the appropriate bookstore to warehouse the books, we might have the need for handling events. In *Chapter 9, Human Tasks*, we have added a human interaction to the process. Therefore, we might handle both previously-described situations—limit the total execution time and handle cancelations (for example, if the books would be damaged during transport or similar situations).

Before we get to the example, let's just mention that events are also very useful with asynchronous invocations. In *Chapter 5, Interaction Patterns in BPEL*, we learned how to invoke services asynchronously. However, with events, we can wait for several incoming service calls simultaneously. Alternatively, we can limit the time waiting for an incoming call. We will talk more about this in the second half of this chapter.

Types of events

In BPEL processes, we can react on the following types of events:

- **Business events**: These are events with well-defined business meaning, explicitly triggered by a process, service, or other software component.
- **Message events**: These are triggered by incoming messages through operation invocations on port types.
- **Alarm events**: These are time related and are triggered either after a certain duration or at a specific deadline.

Please note that message and alarm events are part of the standard BPEL specification. Business events are part of EDA and Oracle event processing.

Business events

Business events represent occurrences with specific business meaning. For example, a business event could signal that the books have arrived and they require being sorted out to different bookstores. Or a business event could signal that the books have arrived to the bookstore and they need to be registered and shelved. We could find many more examples.

Business events contain a data payload, very similar to operations and their messages. For example, a business event signaling that a book has arrived to the bookstore would have an associated data payload containing the book data, such as title, ISSN, author name, and many others.

As we have already mentioned, business events need to be explicitly triggered by a process, service, or other software component. Once triggered, a business event will be delivered to all event-driven software components (processes, services, and others) that have subscribed to this type of event. In this sense, business events are one-way communications, which is asynchronous by its nature. Business events follow the fire-and-forget semantics, as the process or service that has triggered the event will not be notified about who has received the event.

Message events

Message events are related to operation invocations. In most cases, message events are triggered when the client or another service invokes an operation on the BPEL process. This makes sense in the following two scenarios:

- A BPEL process declares additional operations in WSDL, which can be invoked on the BPEL process
- In asynchronous invocations, where a BPEL process asynchronously invokes a partner link service and waits for the callback

Alarm events

Alarm events can be:

- Durations
- Deadlines

We usually specify a duration using a `<for>` duration expression. We specify a deadline using an `<until>` deadline expression.

To specify deadline and duration expressions, BPEL uses lexical representations of corresponding XML Schema data types. For deadlines, these data types are either `dateTime` or `date`. For duration, we use the `duration` data type. The lexical representation of expressions should conform to the XPath 1.0 (or the selected query language) expressions.

The evaluation of such expressions should result in values that are of corresponding XML Schema types: `dateTime` and `date` for deadline and `duration` for duration expressions.

All three data types use lexical representation inspired by the ISO 8601 standard, which can be obtained from the ISO web page `http://www.iso.org/iso/home/standards/iso8601.htm`. The ISO 8601 lexical format uses characters within the date and time information. Characters are appended to the numbers and have the following meanings:

- `C` represents centuries.
- `Y` represents years.
- `M` represents months.
- `D` represents days.
- `h` represents hours.
- `m` represents minutes.
- `s` represents seconds. Seconds can be represented in the `ss.sss` format to increase precision.
- `Z` is used to designate **Universal Time Coordinated** (**UTC**). It should immediately follow the time of day element.

For the `dateTime` expressions, there is another designator:

- `T` is used as a time designator to indicate the start of the representation of the time.

Examples of deadline expressions are shown in the following code excerpts:

```
<wait>
  <until>'2014-03-18T21:00:00+01:00'</until>
</wait>
<wait>
  <until>'18:05:30Z'</until>
</wait>
```

For duration expressions, the following characters can also be used:

- `P` is used as the time duration designator. Duration expressions always start with `P`.
- `Y` follows the number of years.
- `M` follows the number of months or minutes.

- `D` follows the number of days.
- `H` follows the number of hours.
- `S` follows the number of seconds.

To specify a duration of 4 hours and 10 minutes, we use the following expression:

```
<wait>
  <for>'PT4H10M'</for>
</wait>
```

To specify the duration of 1 month, 3 days, 4 hours, and 10 minutes, we need to use the following expression:

```
<wait>
  <for>'P1M3DT4H10M'</for>
</wait>
```

The following expression specifies the duration of 1 year, 11 months, 14 days, 4 hours, 10 minutes, and 30 seconds:

```
<wait>
  <for>'P1Y11M14DT4H10M30S'</for>
</wait>
```

Developing an event-driven BPEL process

Firstly, we will develop an event-driven BPEL process. This is a BPEL process triggered by a business event. We will develop a process for book shelving. As we have already mentioned, such a process can be executed on various occasions, such as when a book arrives to the bookstore for the first time, after a customer has looked at the book, or even during an inventory.

In contrast to a BPEL process, which exposes an operation that needs to be invoked explicitly, our book shelving process will react on a business event. We will call it a `BookshelfEvent`.

We can see that in order to develop an event-driven BPEL process, we will need to firstly declare a business event, the `BookshelfEvent`. Following this, we will need to develop the event-driven book shelving BPEL process.

Declaring a business event

We will declare the `BookshelfEvent` business event, which will signal that a book is ready to be book shelved. Each business event contains a data payload, which is defined by the corresponding XML schema type. In our case, we will use the `BookData` type, the same one that we used in the book warehousing process.

Time for action – declaring a business event

To declare the `BookshelfEvent` business event, we will go to the composite view. We will proceed as follows:

1. Right-click on the project in the **Application** window and select **New** and then **Event Definition**:

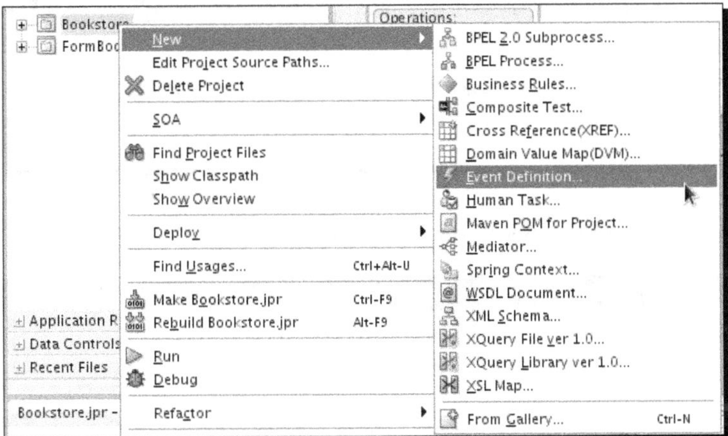

2. A **Create Event Definition** dialog box will open. We will specify the EDL filename. This is the file where all the events are defined (similar to WSDL, where the web service operations are defined). We will use the **BookEDL** for the EDL filename. For the **Namespace** field, we will use `http://packtpub.com/events/edl/BookEDL`, as shown in the following screenshot:

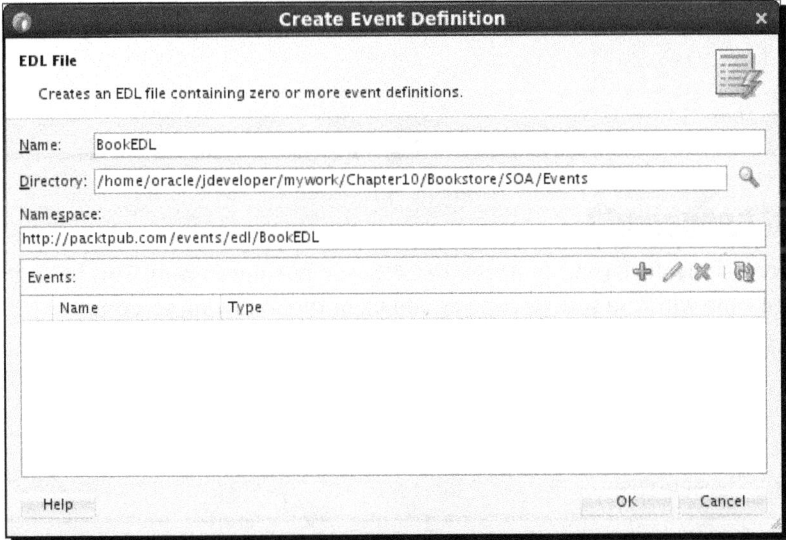

3. Next, we need to define the business events. We will use the green plus sign to declare the `BookshelfEvent` business event. After clicking on the green plus sign, the **Create Event** dialog box will open. We need to specify the event name, which is `BookshelfEvent`. We also have to specify the XML **Type**, which will be used for the event data payload. We will use the `BookData` from the **Book Warehousing** BPEL process schema, as shown in the following screenshot:

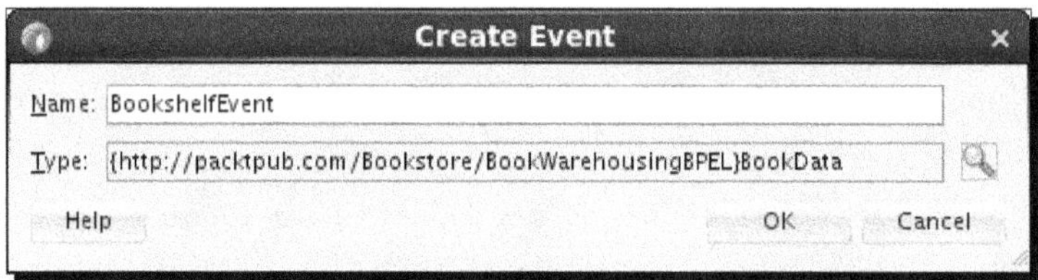

4. After clicking on the **OK** button, we should see the following:

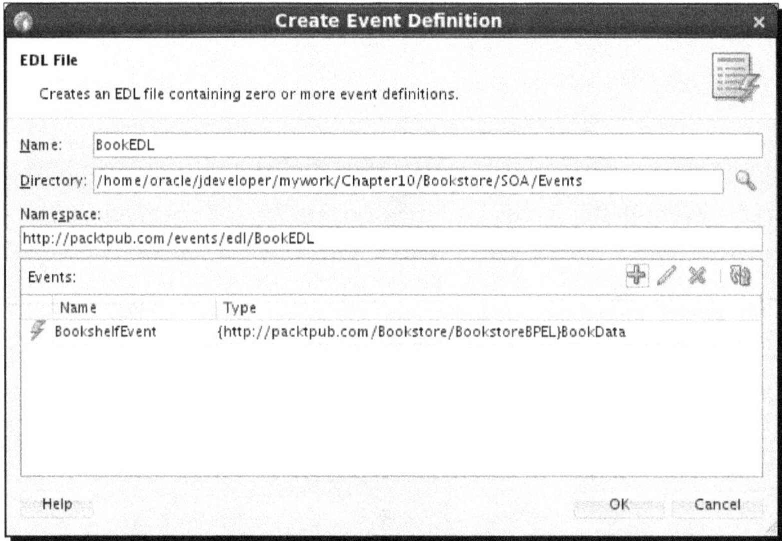

What just happened?

We have successfully declared the `BookshelfEvent` business event. This has generated the `BookEDL.edl` file with the source code as shown in the following screenshot:

```
<?xml version = '1.0' encoding = 'UTF-8'?>
<definitions xmlns="http://schemas.oracle.com/events/edl"
targetNamespace="http://packtpub.com/events/edl/BookEDL">
   <schema-import location="../Schemas/BookstoreBPEL.xsd"
   namespace="http://packtpub.com/Bookstore/BookstoreBPEL"/>
   <event-definition name="BookshelfEvent">
      <content xmlns:ns1="http://packtpub.com/Bookstore/BookstoreBPEL" element="ns1:BookData"/>
   </event-definition>
</definitions>
```

Developing a book shelving BPEL process

After declaring the business event, we are ready to develop the event-driven book shelving BPEL process. The process will be triggered by our `BookshelfEvent` business event. This means that the process will not have a classic WSDL with the operation declaration. Rather it will be triggered by the `BookshelfEvent` business event.

Time for action – developing an event-driven book shelving BPEL process

To develop the event-driven book shelving BPEL process, we will go to the composite view. We will carry out the following steps:

1. Drag-and-drop the **BPEL Process** service component from the right-hand side toolbar to the composite components area. We will do this the same way as in the previous examples in this book.
2. The **Create BPEL Process** dialog box will open. We will select the **BPEL 2.0 Specification**, type `BookShelvingBPEL` for the **Name** of the process, and specify the namespace as `http://packtpub.com/Bookstore/BookShelvingBPEL`. Then, we will select **Subscribe to Events** from the drop-down list for the **Template**:

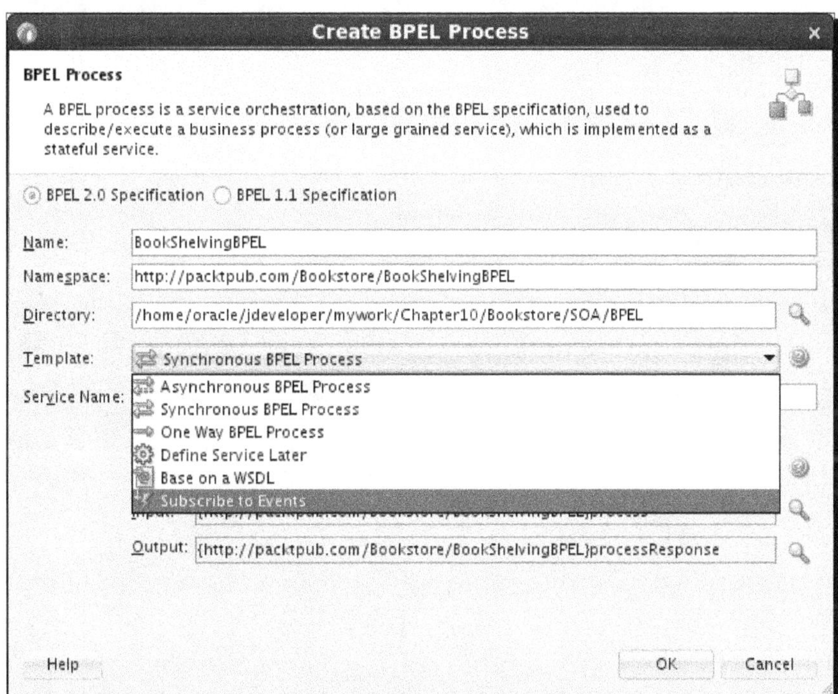

3. Next, we will need to specify the event to which our BPEL process will be subscribed. We will select the green plus sign and the **Event Chooser** dialog window will open. Here, we will simply select the `BookshelfEvent` business event:

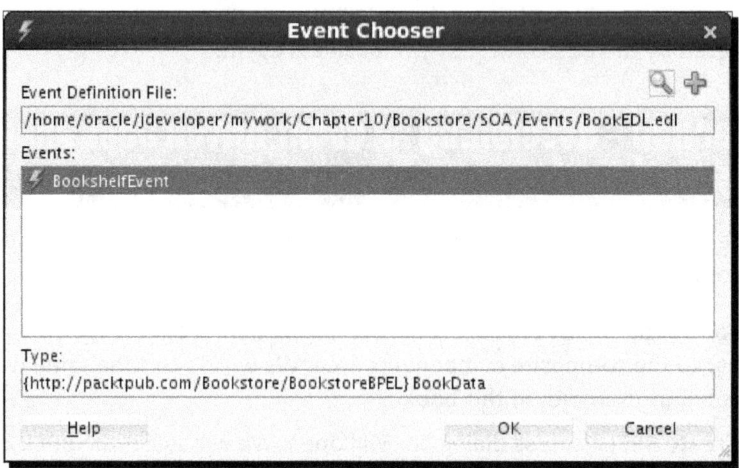

4. After clicking on the **OK** button, we should see the following screenshot:

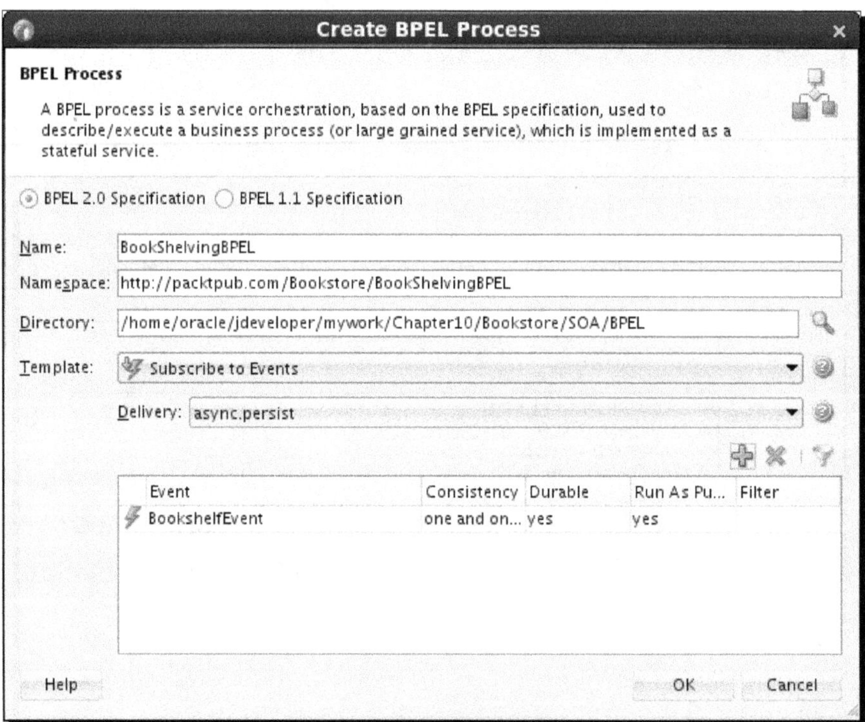

For event-driven BPEL processes, three consistency strategies for delivering events exist. The **one and only one** option delivers the events in the global transaction. **Guaranteed** delivers events asynchronously without a global transaction. **Immediate** delivers events in the same global transaction and the same thread as the publisher, and the publish call does not return until all immediate subscribers have completed processing.

5. After clicking on the **OK** button, we can find the new `BookShelvingBPEL` process on the composite diagram. Please note that the arrow icon denotes that the process is triggered by an event:

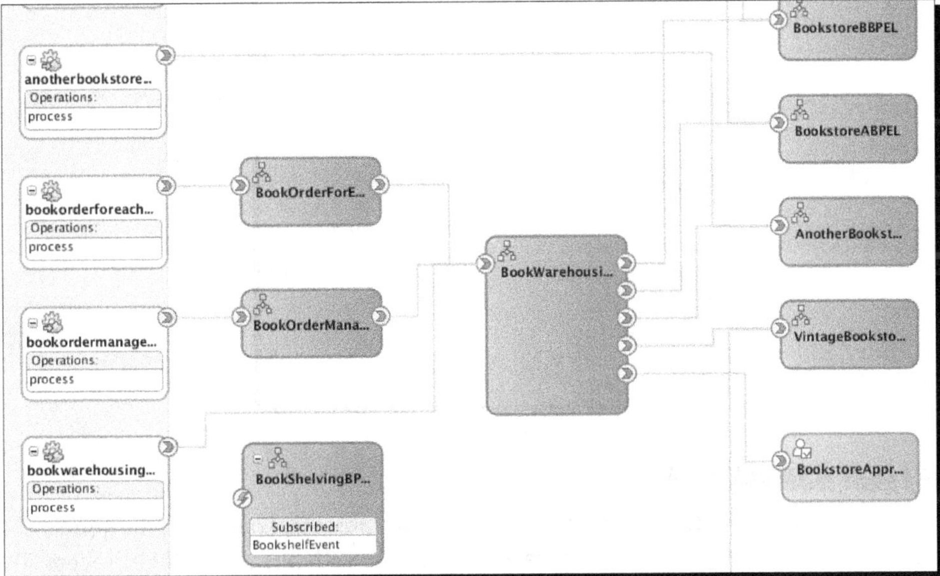

6. Double-clicking on the `BookShelvingBPEL` process opens the BPEL editor, where we can see that the BPEL process has a slightly different `<receive>` activity, which denotes that the process will be triggered by an event. Also, notice that an event-driven process does not return anything to the client, as event-driven processes are one-way and asynchronous:

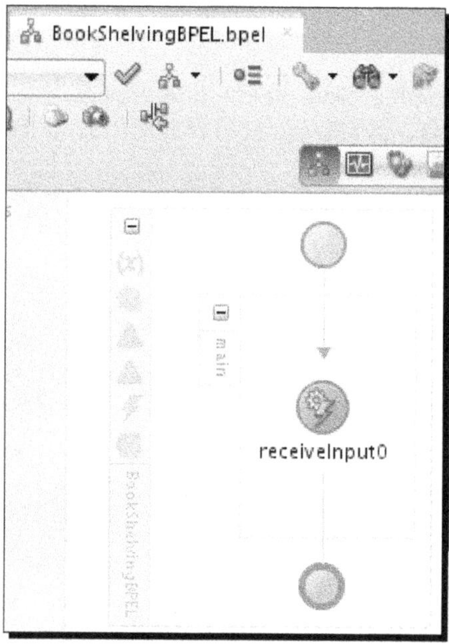

What just happened?

We have successfully created the `BookShelvingBPEL` process. Looking at the source code we can see that the overall structure is the same as with any other BPEL process. The difference is in the initial `<receive>` activity, which is triggered by the `BookshelfEvent` business event, as shown in the following screenshot:

```
<!--
  ////////////////////////////////////////////////////////////////////
   ORCHESTRATION LOGIC
   Set of activities coordinating the flow of messages across the
   services integrated within this business process
  ////////////////////////////////////////////////////////////////////
-->
<sequence name="main">
    <!-- Receive event from requestor. -->
    <receive name="receiveInput0"
             bpelx:eventName="ns1:BookshelfEvent"
             variable="inputVariable0"
             createInstance="yes"/>

</sequence>
</process>
```

Have a go hero – implementing the BookShelvingBPEL process

Implementing the event-driven `BookShelvingBPEL` process does not differ from implementing any other BPEL process. Therefore, it's your turn now. You should implement the `BookShelvingBPEL` process to do something meaningful. It could, for example, call a service which will query a database table. Or, it could include a human task.

Triggering a business event from a BPEL process

Let's now try to trigger a business event from a BPEL process. When a BPEL process triggers a business event, all processes, services, and other components that are subscribed to this event will execute.

Triggering a business event from a BPEL process is quite simple. It requires using the `<invoke>` activity where we specify the business event instead of a partner link and operation name.

Time for action – triggering BookshelfEvent from the book warehousing BPEL process

We will trigger the `BookshelfEvent` business event from the book warehousing BPEL process. This will result in executing the `BookShelvingBPEL` process, which we have created in the previous section.

We will trigger the `BookshelfEvent` business event using the `<invoke>` activity, which we will locate at the end of the book warehousing BPEL process, after the **BookStore Approval** human task and the corresponding `<if>` activity.

Let's start by performing the following steps:

1. Open the **Book Warehousing** BPEL process and scroll to the end of the process. We will drag the `<invoke>` activity from the right-hand side toolbar to the BPEL process and drop it after the **BookStore Approval** human task and the corresponding `<if>` activity.

2. Name the `<invoke>` activity `TriggerBookshelfEvent`, as shown in the following screenshot:

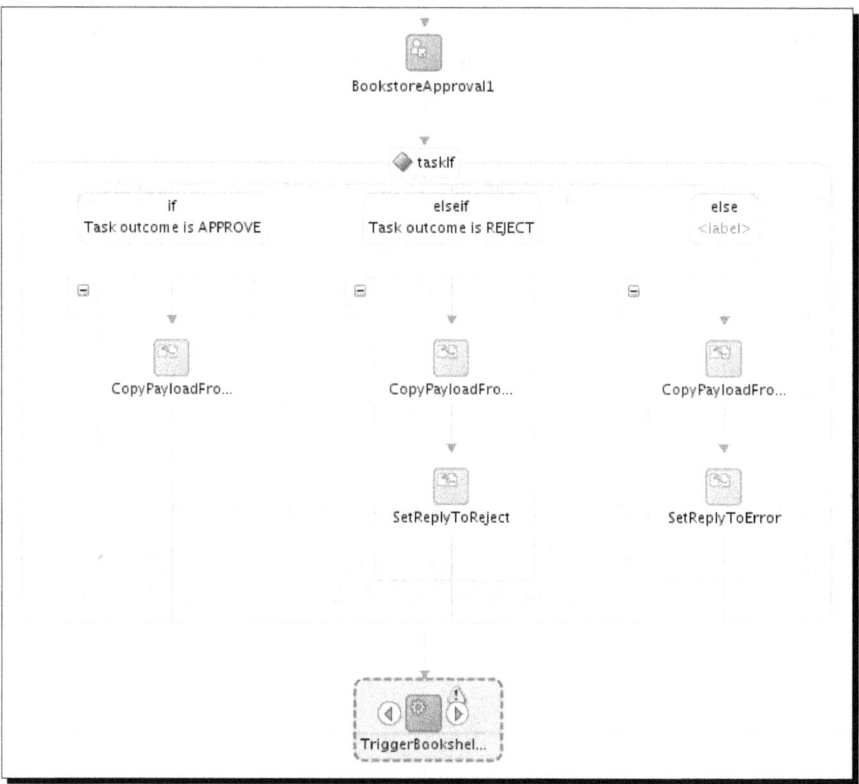

3. Double-clicking on the `<invoke>` activity will open the **Edit Invoke** dialog box, where we will select **Event** for **Interaction Type**:

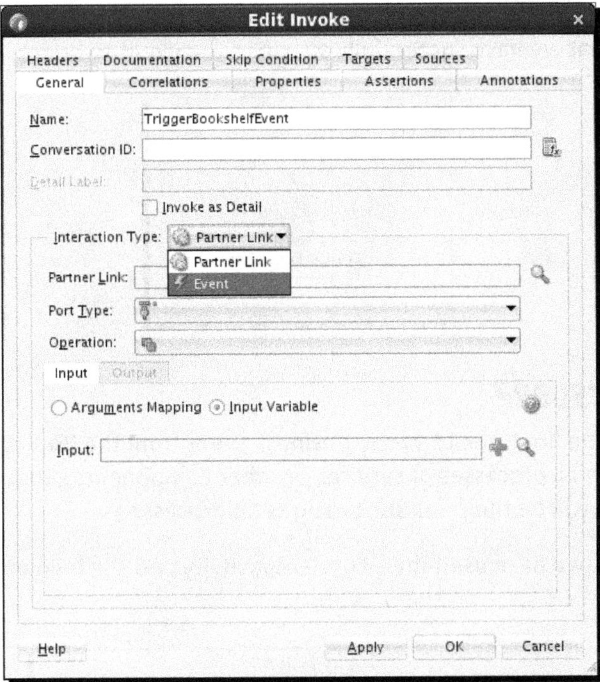

4. Select the `BookshelfEvent` business event under **Event**. We also need to specify the data payload—we need to specify a variable with the corresponding data type. We will select the `BookData` variable:

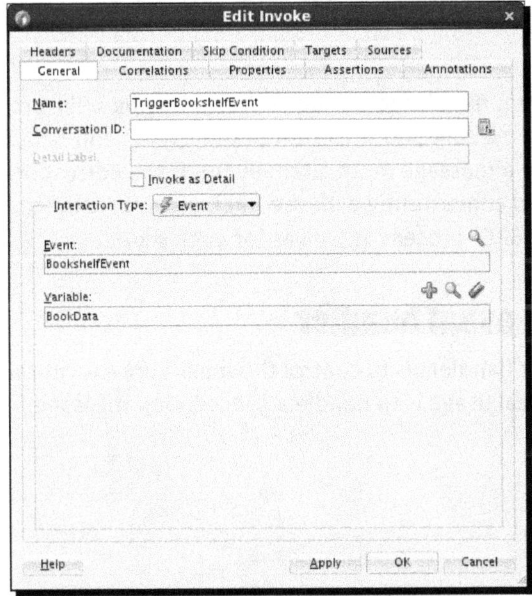

5. After clicking on **OK**, we should see an arrow on the `<invoke>` activity icon, denoting that we have successfully specified the event to be triggered:

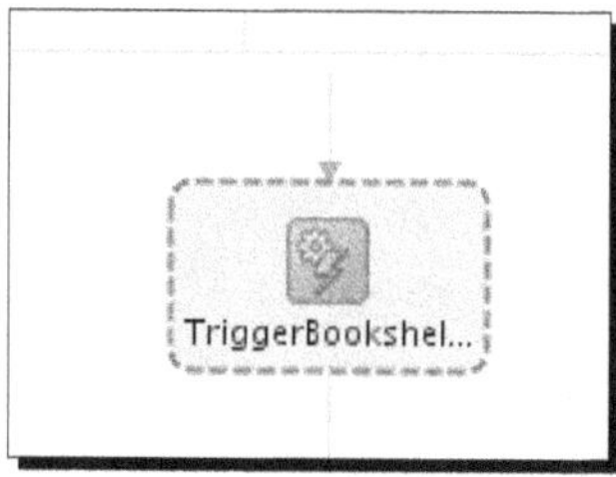

What just happened?

We have triggered the `BookshelfEvent` business event from the **Book Warehousing** BPEL process. This will fire all processes or services or other components subscribed to this event. In our example, this will be the `BookShelvingBPEL` process.

To trigger the event, we have used the `<invoke>` activity and the following source code has been generated:

```
<invoke name="TriggerBookshelfEvent"
        bpelx:invokeAsDetail="no"
        bpelx:eventName="ns8:BookshelfEvent"
        inputVariable="BookData"/>
```

Adding an event handler to the Book Warehousing BPEL process

We will now add an event handler to our **Book Warehousing** BPEL process. Event handlers allow a BPEL process to execute and still listen to the events and handle them whenever they occur. The event can be a message or an alarm event. If the corresponding events occur, an event handler is invoked concurrently with the BPEL process instance. We can specify event handlers for the whole BPEL process as well as for each scope.

Adding an alarm event handler

A typical usage of event handlers is to control the maximum execution time of a BPEL process. The other typical usage is to handle a cancellation message from the client.

Time for action – adding an event handler to the BPEL process

Let's now add an event handler to the main **Book Warehousing** BPEL process. First, we will add an alarm event handler for the maximal execution time of a BPEL process. Then, we will add a message event handler, which will allow the cancelation of a running BPEL process instance.

We will proceed as follows:

1. Open the `BookWarehousingBPEL.bpel` process.
2. On the left-hand side, we will select the **Add OnAlarm** icon, as shown in the following screenshot:

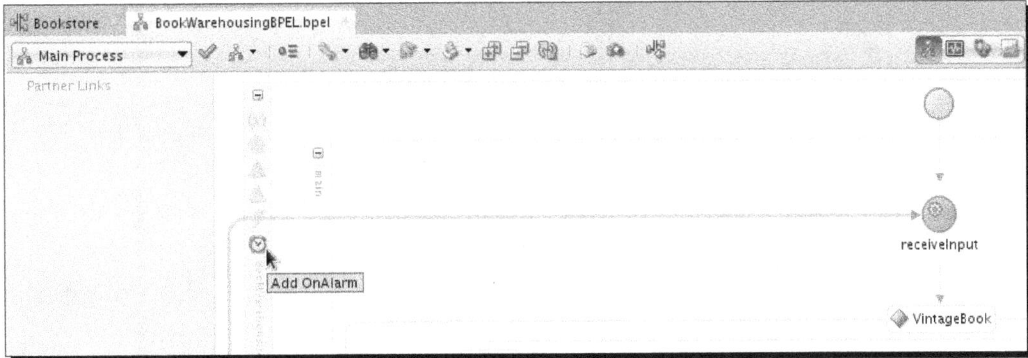

3. Scroll to the right-hand side of the BPEL process and you should see that an **OnAlarm** event handler has been added to the BPEL process flow:

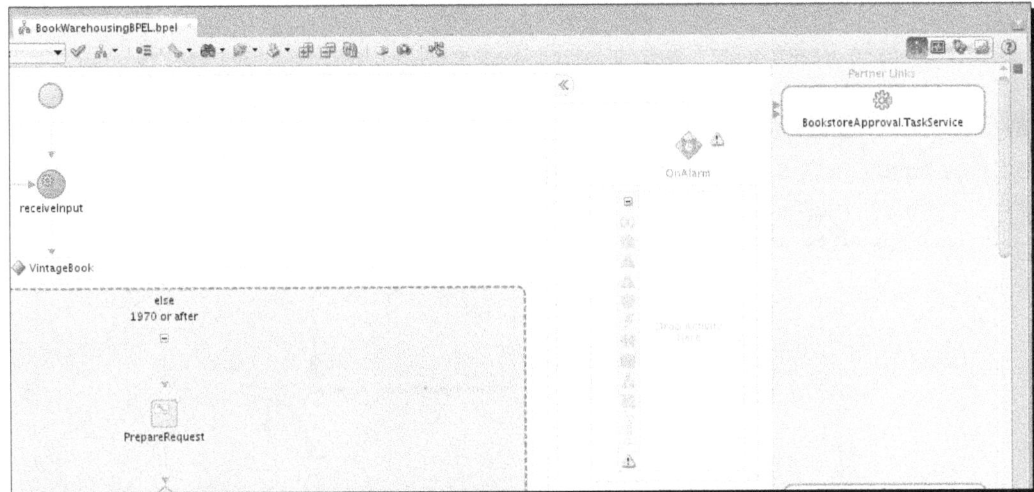

4. We need to specify the deadline or duration expression for the **OnAlarm** event handler. Let's double-click on the **OnAlarm** icon. A pop-up **EditOnAlarm** window will appear, where we can specify **For** durations or **Until** deadlines. We could also specify **Repeat Every** duration, in which case the event handler would repeat every specified duration.
5. Select the **For** duration and enter **15 Mins**. Also, name the **OnAlarm** handler as `Max Exec Time`. Click on **OK**:

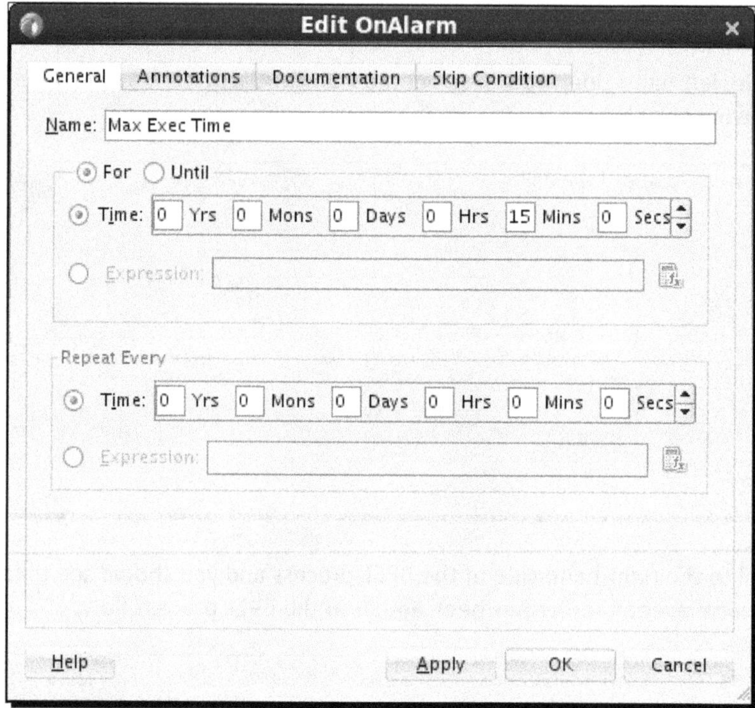

What just happened?

We have added an **OnAlarm** event handler to our BPEL process. We have specified that the alarm event will trigger 15 minutes after the BPEL process instance is initiated. The following code has been added to the BPEL process:

```
<onAlarm bpelx:name="Max Exec Time">
  <for>'PT15M'</for>
  <scope name="Scope1"></scope>
</onAlarm>
```

Specifying alarm event activities

Now that we have added the alarm event handler, we have to specify what will happen when the alarm event is triggered. We specify this by putting activities within the event handler scope.

For this example, we will notify the client that an event has occurred and then we will terminate the process. In a more sophisticated process, we could notify a user (for example, through a human task) or we could do a more sophisticated action.

To notify the client that an event has happened, we first have to decide how we will do the notification. As this is an asynchronous BPEL process, we will use the `<invoke>` activity to return the result through a callback. We have specified an `onResult` operation on the callback WSDL port, as shown in the following screenshot:

```
<wsdl:portType name="BookWarehousingBPEL">
    <wsdl:operation name="process">
        <wsdl:input message="client:BookWarehousingBPELRequestMessage"/>
    </wsdl:operation>
</wsdl:portType>
<wsdl:portType name="BookWarehousingBPELCallback">
    <wsdl:operation name="onResult">
        <wsdl:input message="client:BookWarehousingBPELResponseMessage"/>
    </wsdl:operation>
</wsdl:portType>
```

To notify the client that an event has occurred, we will add an `onEvent` operation on the callback interface.

In asynchronous callback scenarios, it is a common practice that we specify several different operations on the callback port type, through which the BPEL process notifies the client about the possible outcomes. Typically, we specify `onResult`, `onFault`, and `onEvent` operations.

Time for action – adding onEvent to the callback interface

To add the `onEvent` operation to the callback WSDL interface, we will proceed as follows:

1. Open the `BookWarehousingBPEL.wsdl` interface.

2. Scroll down to the declaration of the `BookWarehousingBPELCallback` port type. We can see that the port type specifies a single `onResult` operation:

```
<wsdl:portType name="BookWarehousingBPELCallback">
    <wsdl:operation name="onResult">
        <wsdl:input message="client:BookWarehousingBPELResponseMessage"/>
    </wsdl:operation>
</wsdl:portType>
```

3. We will add another operation, `onEvent`, which we will use to signal that an event has happened on the BPEL process. In our example, we will use the same input message as in the `onResult` operation. Let's add the `onEvent` operation declaration:

```
<wsdl:portType name="BookWarehousingBPELCallback">
    <wsdl:operation name="onResult">
        <wsdl:input message="client:BookWarehousingBPELResponseMessage"/>
    </wsdl:operation>
    <wsdl:operation name="onEvent">
        <wsdl:input message="client:BookWarehousingBPELResponseMessage"/>
    </wsdl:operation>
</wsdl:portType>
```

What just happened?

We have added an `onEvent` operation declaration to the WSDL callback interface of the BPEL process. We will use this callback operation to signal to the client that an event has happened on the BPEL process.

Time for action – specifying alarm event handler activities

Let's now add the activities that will execute within the alarm event handler. As we have already said, we will notify the client that an event handler has been invoked on the BPEL process.

To achieve this, we will perform the following steps:

1. Open the `BookWarehousingBPEL.bpel` process.
2. Before we can add the `<invoke>` activity, we will prepare the variable for the response message. To achieve this, we add the `<assign>` activity into the event handler body (using drag-and-drop).

3. Rename the `<assign>` activity as **AssignAlarmEventCallback**, as shown in the following screenshot:

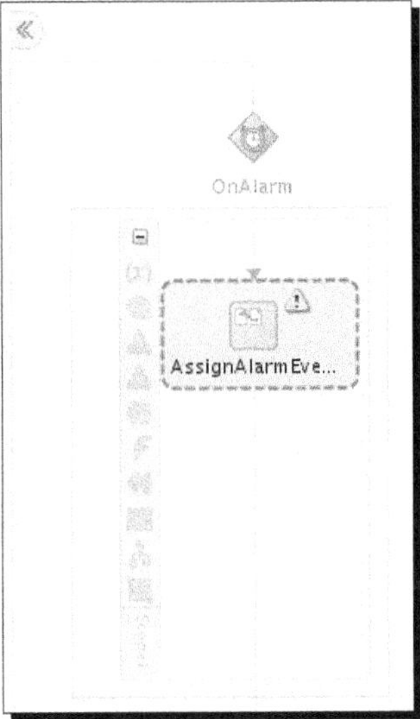

4. By double-clicking on the `<assign>` activity, we will copy the literal string **Alarm Event – 15 Minutes Timeout** into `outputVariable`. As some web services can take longer than expected to return a response, it is important that a BPEL process is able to take time out and continue with the rest of the flow after a period of time:

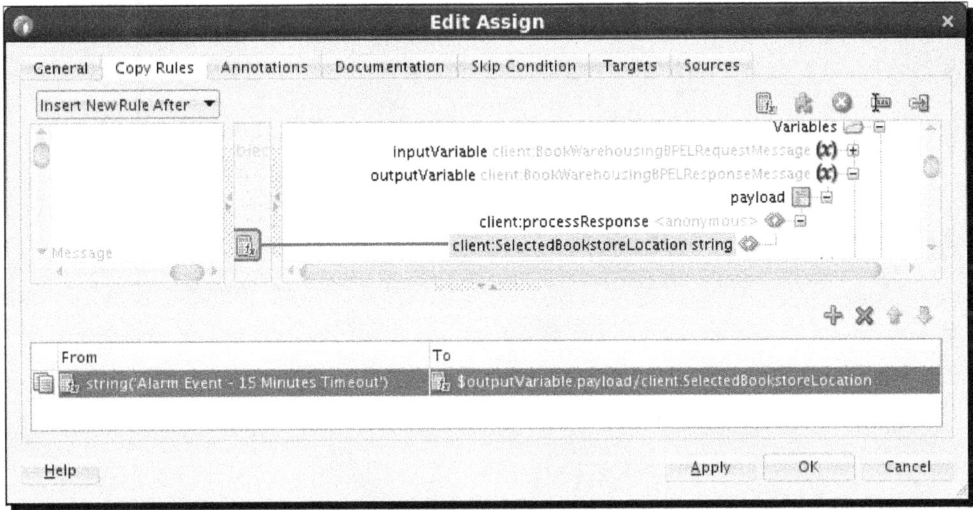

5. Next, we will drag-and-drop the `<invoke>` activity and place it after the `<assign>` activity. We will name the activity `callbackClientOnEvent`. Then, we will connect the `<invoke>` activity with the client partner link, which is located on the left-hand side of the BPEL process diagram.

6. A pop-up window will open, where we have to specify the partner link, port type, operation name, and input variable used for the callback. We will use the `BookWarehousingBPELCallback` port type and select the `onEvent` operation (which we have already added). We will select `outputVariable` as the input variable of the `<invoke>` activity, as shown in the following screenshot:

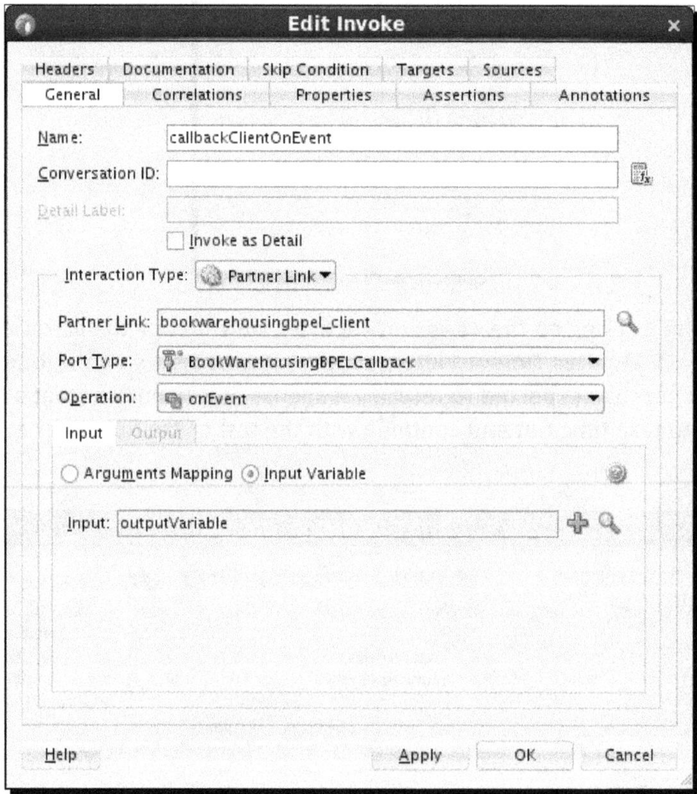

7. Finally, we will add the `<exit>` activity to terminate the execution of the BPEL process:

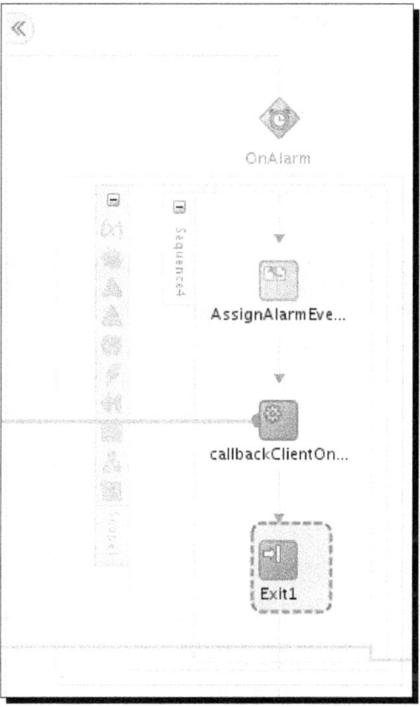

What just happened?

We have added an `OnAlarm` event handler to our BPEL process. We have specified that the alarm event will trigger 15 minutes after the BPEL process instance is initiated. The following code has been added to the BPEL process:

```
<eventHandlers>
  <onAlarm bpelx:name="Max Exec Time">
    <for>'PT15M'</for>
    <scope name="Scope1">
      <sequence name="Sequence4">
        <assign name="AssignAlarmEventCallback">
          <copy>
            <from>string('Alarm Event - 15 Minutes Timeout')</from>
            <to>$outputVariable.payload/client:SelectedBookstoreLocation</to>
          </copy>
        </assign>
        <invoke name="callbackClientOnEvent" bpelx:invokeAsDetail="no"
                partnerLink="bookwarehousingbpel_client"
                portType="client:BookWarehousingBPELCallback"
                operation="onEvent" inputVariable="outputVariable"/>
        <exit name="Exit1"/>
      </sequence>
    </scope>
  </onAlarm>
</eventHandlers>
```

Adding a message event handler

Let's now add another event handler. As we have mentioned earlier, a typical scenario is to provide a way to cancel the BPEL process instance in progress. Let's suppose that we would like to provide a way to cancel a BPEL process instance with an operation call.

To achieve this, we will add a message event handler to the BPEL process.

Time for action – adding a message handler to the BPEL process

Let's now add the event handler to the main book warehousing BPEL process. First, we will add an alarm event handler for the maximal execution time of a BPEL process. Then, we will add a message event handler, which will allow the cancelation of a running BPEL process instance.

We will proceed as follows:

1. Open the `BookWarehousingBPEL.bpel` process.
2. On the left-hand side, select the **Add OnEvent** icon, which is just above the **Add OnAlarm** icon, which we selected earlier.
3. Scroll to the right-hand side of the BPEL process, and you should see that an **OnEvent** event handler has been added to the BPEL process flow:

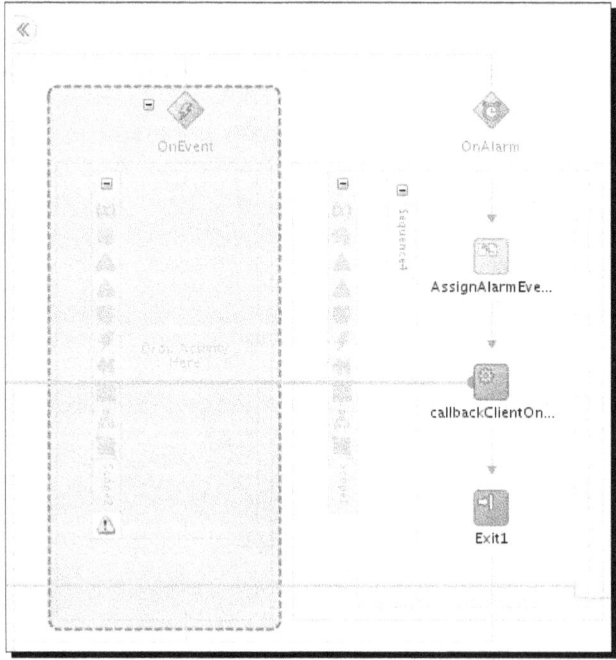

What just happened?

We have added an **OnEvent** event handler to our BPEL process. The following code has been added to the BPEL process:

```
<onEvent>
  <scope name="Scope2"></scope>
</onEvent>
```

Declaring a cancel operation on the BPEL interface

For the **OnEvent** event handler, we need to specify the partner link, port type, and operation name which will trigger the event. Similar to the alarm event, we need to add a new operation to the process interface. We will name the operation `cancel`.

We will add the `cancel` operation to the BPEL process WSDL interface. Namely, this time the client needs to call the BPEL process in order to cancel the process instance. This requires that we add a cancel operation to the BPEL process WSDL interface.

Time for action – declaring the cancel operation on the BPEL process interface

To add the `cancel` operation to the BPEL process WSDL interface, we will proceed as follows:

1. We will open the `BookWarehousingBPEL.wsdl` interface.
2. We will scroll down to the declaration of the `BookWarehousingBPEL` port type. We can see that the port type specifies a single `process` operation:

```
<wsdl:portType name="BookWarehousingBPEL">
    <wsdl:operation name="process">
        <wsdl:input message="client:BookWarehousingBPELRequestMessage"/>
    </wsdl:operation>
</wsdl:portType>
```

3. We will add the `cancel` operation, which the client will use to cancel the running BPEL instance. In our example, we will use the same input message as in the `process` operation:

```
<wsdl:portType name="BookWarehousingBPEL">
    <wsdl:operation name="process">
        <wsdl:input message="client:BookWarehousingBPELRequestMessage"/>
    </wsdl:operation>
    <wsdl:operation name="cancel">
        <wsdl:input message="client:BookWarehousingBPELRequestMessage"/>
    </wsdl:operation>
</wsdl:portType>
```

4. Next, we will add the `cancel` operation as the trigger for the **OnEvent** event handler. We will open the `BookWarehousingBPEL.bpel` process and double click on the **OnEvent** activity.

5. A window will pop up, where we will specify the partner link, port type, and operation name. We will specify the client partner link, the **BookWarehousingBPEL** port type, and the **cancel** operation. For the variable, we will type the `cancelInputMessage` name and select **Message Type** as `BookWarehousingBPELRequestMessage`, as shown in the following screenshot:

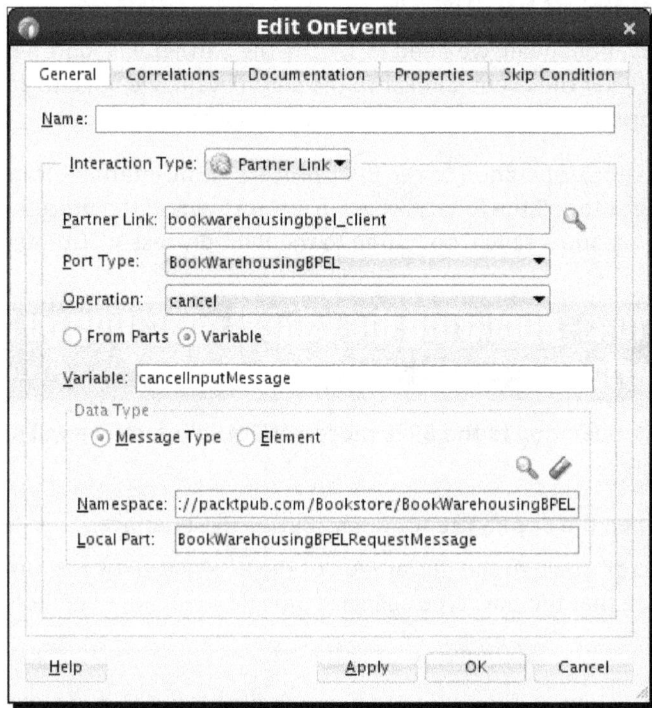

What just happened?

We have added the `cancel` operation declaration to the WSDL interface of the BPEL process. We will use this operation to cancel the current running process instance.

We have also specified that this operation is the trigger for the `OnEvent` message handler, which has generated the following code:

```
<onEvent partnerLink="bookwarehousingbpel_client" operation="cancel"
         portType="client:BookWarehousingBPEL"
         variable="cancelInputMessage"
         messageType="client:BookWarehousingBPELRequestMessage">
  <scope name="Scope2"></scope>
</onEvent>
```

Specifying message event activities

Next, we will add the message event activities. This means that we will specify the activities that should be performed once the `cancel` operation triggers our event handler.

We will throw a fault with the name `CancelInstance` and terminate the process instance. We have chosen to throw the fault, as this would allow a BPEL process to invoke compensation and termination handlers, if present. We will see more on compensation in *Chapter 11, Compensations*.

Time for action – specifying message event activities

To throw the fault and to exit the process, we will perform the following steps:

1. Open the `BookWarehousingBPEL` process. We will drag-and-drop the `<throw>` activity to the message event handler scope.
2. Name the `<throw>` activity `ThrowCancelInstance`.
3. Double-click on the `ThrowCancelInstance` activity and then specify the **Fault QName**. The **Namespace URI** is the same as for the BPEL process itself: `http://packtpub.com/Bookstore/BookwarehousingBPEL`. The **Local Part** name should be `CancelInstance`. We will not specify the **Fault Variable** as the BPEL faults do not require a variable:

4. Next, drag-and-drop the `<exit>` activity and place it after the `<throw>` activity. This way the process will terminate. We should see the following BPEL diagram:

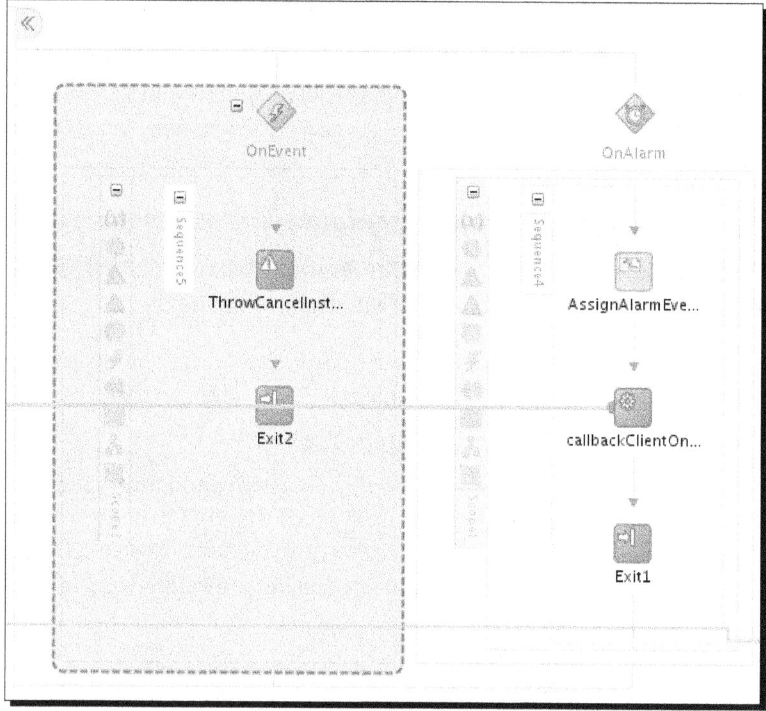

What just happened?

We have added activities that will execute once the `OnEvent` message handler is triggered. We have decided to throw a fault and to exit the process instance. The following code has been generated:

```
<eventHandlers>
  <onEvent partnerLink="bookwarehousingbpel_client" operation="cancel"
           portType="client:BookWarehousingBPEL"
           variable="cancelInputMessage"
           messageType="client:BookWarehousingBPELRequestMessage">
    <scope name="Scope2">
      <sequence name="Sequence5">
        <throw name="ThrowCancelInstance" faultName="client:CancelInstance"/>
        <exit name="Exit2"/>
      </sequence>
    </scope>
  </onEvent>
```

With this, we have concluded our discussion on event handlers. We are now ready to deploy and test the example.

Deploying and testing event handlers

We will deploy the example process the same way as we did in *Chapter 9, Human Tasks*. Please note, however, that you should either check the overwriting of any existing composites with the same revision ID, undeploy the previous example, or use a higher revision ID; otherwise, you will get an error stating that you cannot overwrite an existing version of an SOA composite.

After the deployment, initiate a BPEL process instance. The instance should wait at the human task, which you can see from **Flow Trace**:

After 15 minutes, you will see that the alarm event handler has been triggered and the process has been aborted:

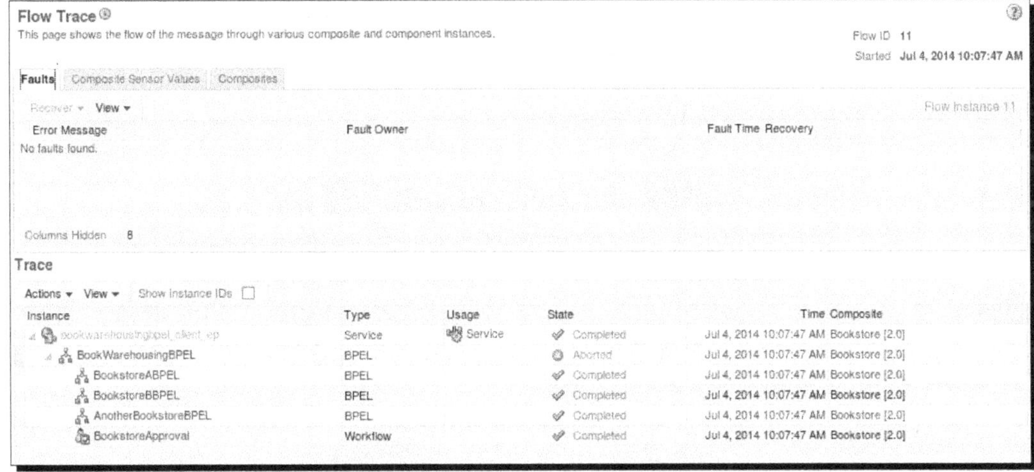

This confirms that our alarm event handler has been triggered. We can see that the termination happened exactly 15 minutes after the `BookWarehousingBPEL` process was invoked.

Asynchronous invocations and events

Now that we have explained the event handlers, let's look at another useful side of events. In real-world BPEL processes, a BPEL process often makes an asynchronous invocation of partner link services (as we already know from *Chapter 5, Interaction Patterns in BPEL*, these could be services or other BPEL processes). During an asynchronous invocation, the BPEL process first executes an `<invoke>` activity and then waits for the callback using `<receive>`.

However, the callback operation might not return a single operation call, such as `onResult`. Rather, the BPEL process should be able to wait for more than one callback operation, for example, `onResult`, `onFault`, and `onEvent`.

So far, we have seen how to define an event handler, which waits for incoming events parallel to the execution of the BPEL process flow. However, in scenarios where a BPEL process waits for the callback, using the event handler would make little sense. Therefore, BPEL provides another activity called `<pick>`.

We will learn how to use the `<pick>` activity to handle events related to callback invocations. To understand the `<pick>` activity, we will add another activity to our `Book Warehousing` BPEL process. So far, our process has queried the bookstores for stock quantity, selected the most appropriate bookstore, and asked a user to approve the bookstore selection using a human task.

We will task another activity to confirm that the books have been successfully warehoused. To achieve this, our `Book Warehousing` BPEL process will asynchronously invoke another service, which will respond to confirm whether the books have been successfully warehoused. This service, which we will call `WarehousingConfirmation`, will actually be another BPEL process, which will respond via a callback, confirming whether the books have been successfully warehoused. Let's start.

Implementing the WarehousingConfirmation service

To implement the `WarehousingConfirmation` service, we could use any programming language. However, as we are learning BPEL in this book, we will stick with BPEL and implement an asynchronous `WarehousingConfirmationBPEL` process. The BPEL process should make a callback using `onResult` for signaling successful or unsuccessful warehousing, but also provide `onFault` and `onEvent` callback operations.

The proposed WSDL port type declaration for the `WarehousingConfirmationBPEL` process is listed in the following screenshot:

```
<!-- portType implemented by the WarehousingConfirmationBPEL BPEL process -->
<wsdl:portType name="WarehousingConfirmationBPEL">
        <wsdl:operation name="confirmWarehousing">
                <wsdl:input message="client:WarehousingConfirmationBPELRequestMessage"/>
        </wsdl:operation>
</wsdl:portType>

<!-- portType implemented by the requester of WarehousingConfirmationBPEL BPEL process
for asynchronous callback purposes
-->
<wsdl:portType name="WarehousingConfirmationBPELCallback">
        <wsdl:operation name="onResult">
                <wsdl:input message="client:WarehousingConfirmationBPELResponseMessage"/>
        </wsdl:operation>
        <wsdl:operation name="onFault">
                <wsdl:input message="client:WarehousingConfirmationBPELResponseMessage"/>
        </wsdl:operation>
        <wsdl:operation name="onEvent">
                <wsdl:input message="client:WarehousingConfirmationBPELResponseMessage"/>
        </wsdl:operation>
</wsdl:portType>
```

Have a go hero – implementing WarehousingConfirmation

It's your turn now. You should implement the `WarehousingConfirmationBPEL` process in the same way as we did earlier in this chapter. You can also refer to *Chapter 5, Interaction Patterns in BPEL*, for more information.

Invoking the WarehousingConfirmation service

We will now add the asynchronous invocation of the `WarehousingConfirmationBPEL` service to the `Book Warehousing` BPEL process. We will use the `<invoke>` activity to initiate the invocation. Then, we will use the `<pick>` activity to handle different incoming events from the callback.

Time for action – invoking the WarehousingConfirmation service

To asynchronously invoke the `WarehousingConfirmationBPEL` service, we will do the following:

1. Open the `BookWarehousingBPEL.wsdl` interface.
2. Scroll to the bottom of the process. After the human task and before the callback (`callbackClient`), we will add a new scope, called `WarehousingConfirmationInvocation`.

3. Within the scope, first add an `<invoke>` activity to invoke the `WarehousingConfirmationBPEL` service invocation. Next, we will name the activity `WarehousingConfirmationInvoke`.
4. Connect the `<invoke>` activity to the **WarehousingConfirmationBPEL** partner link.
5. A window pops up, where we will specify the **Partner Link**, **Port Type** (`WarehousingConfirmationBPEL`), and **Operation** (`confirmWarehousing`), as shown in the following screenshot:

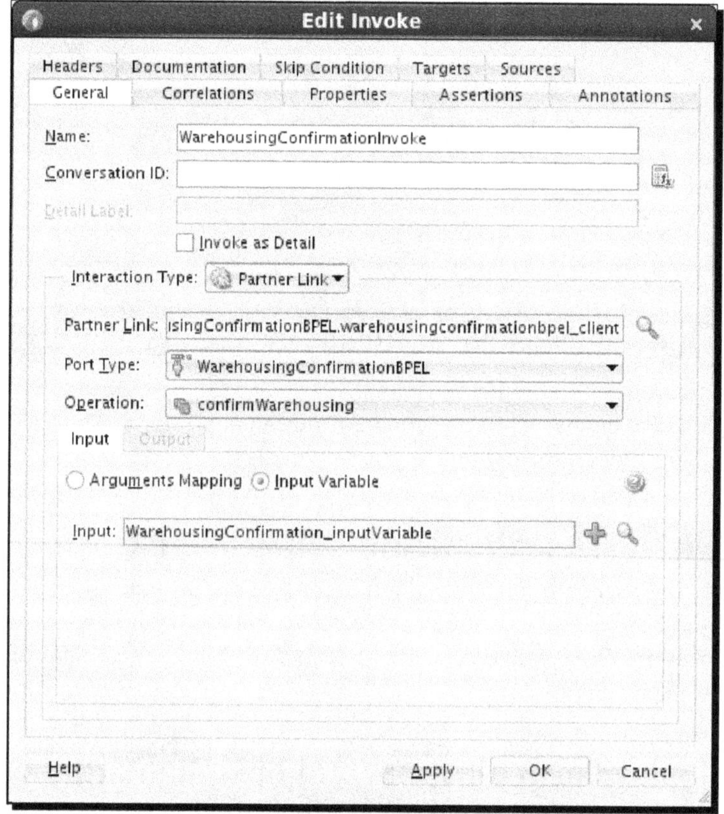

6. We do not have the input variable created yet; therefore, we will create this on the fly, using the green plus sign icon.
7. Pressing the green plus sign icon opens the **Create Variable** window. We will create a variable, local to the scope, and name it `WarehousingConfirmation_inputVariable`:

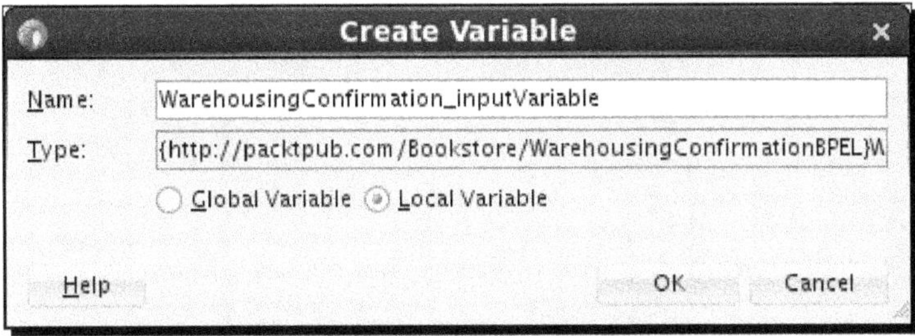

8. Next, we will add the <assign> activity. Place it before the <invoke> activity. In the <assign> activity, we will prepare the `WarehousingConfirmation_inputVariable` variable for the asynchronous invoke. Name the <assign> activity `AssignWarehousingConfirmation`.

9. To prepare the `WarehousingConfirmation_inputVariable` variable, we need to make assignments. Double-click on the <assign> activity and copy the data. Copy the `BookISSN`, `Title`, `Edition`, and `PublishingYear` from the `BookData` variable to the `WarehousingConfirmation_inputVariable` variable. Copy the `Bookstore` location from the `BookstoreLocationWithLowestStockQuantity` variable, as shown in the following screenshot:

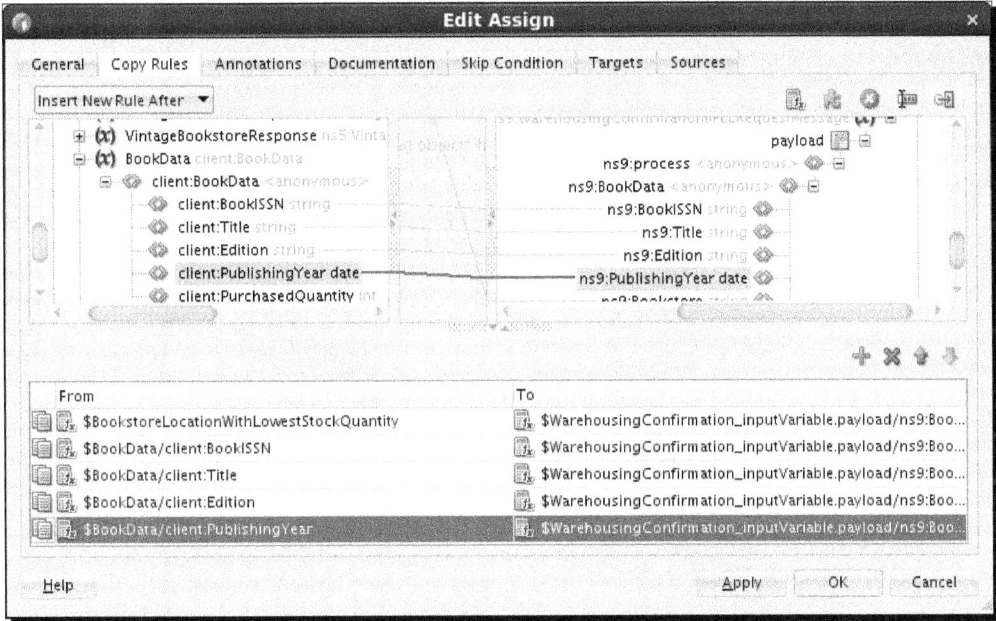

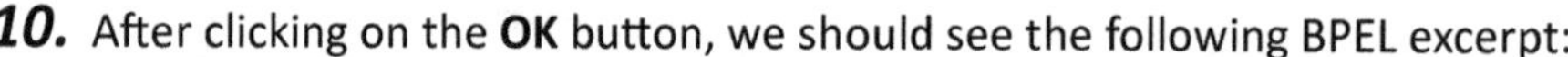

10. After clicking on the **OK** button, we should see the following BPEL excerpt:

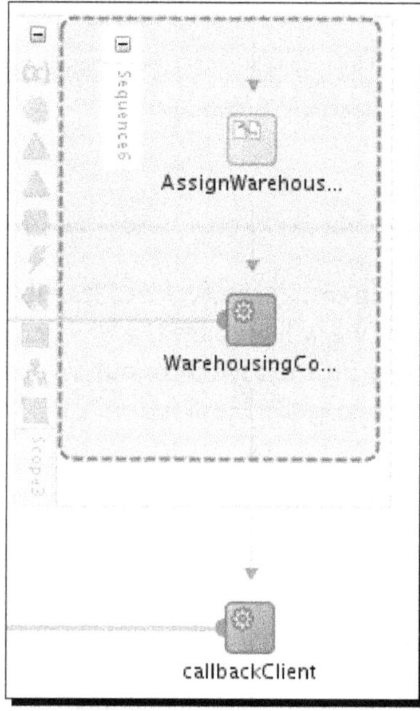

What just happened?

We have added the asynchronous invocation of the `WarehousingConfirmationBPEL` service with the corresponding assign. The following BPEL code has been generated:

```
<scope name="WarehousingConfirmationInvocation">
  <variables>
    <variable name="WarehousingConfirmation_inputVariable"
              messageType="ns9:WarehousingConfirmationBPELRequestMessage"/>
  </variables>
  <sequence name="Sequence8">
    <assign name="AssignWarehousingConfirmation">
      <copy>
        <from>$BookstoreLocationWithLowestStockQuantity</from>
        <to>$WarehousingConfirmation_inputVariable.payload/ns9:BookData/ns9:Bookstore</to>
      </copy>
      <copy>
        <from>$BookData/client:BookISSN</from>
        <to>$WarehousingConfirmation_inputVariable.payload/ns9:BookData/ns9:BookISSN</to>
      </copy>
      <copy>
        <from>$BookData/client:Title</from>
        <to>$WarehousingConfirmation_inputVariable.payload/ns9:BookData/ns9:Title</to>
      </copy>
      <copy>
        <from>$BookData/client:Edition</from>
        <to>$WarehousingConfirmation_inputVariable.payload/ns9:BookData/ns9:Edition</to>
      </copy>
      <copy>
        <from>$BookData/client:PublishingYear</from>
        <to>$WarehousingConfirmation_inputVariable.payload/ns9:BookData/ns9:PublishingYear</to>
      </copy>
    </assign>
    <invoke name="WarehousingConfirmationInvoke" bpelx:invokeAsDetail="no"
            partnerLink="WarehousingConfirmationBPEL.warehousingconfirmationbpel_client"
            portType="ns9:WarehousingConfirmationBPEL" operation="confirmWarehousing"
            inputVariable="WarehousingConfirmation_inputVariable"/>
  </sequence>
</scope>
```

Waiting for callback

To wait for the callback, we could use the <receive> activity. However, with the <receive> activity, we could only wait for a single operation callback. In our case, we have three possible operation callbacks.

Therefore, we will use the <pick> activity. With the <pick> activity, we can specify that the BPEL process awaits the occurrence of one of a set of events. Events can be message events handled using the <onMessage> activity and alarm events handled using the <onAlarm> activity. For each event, we then specify an activity or a set of activities that should be performed.

Within <pick>, we can specify several <onMessage> and <onAlarm> elements. The <onAlarm> elements are optional (we can specify zero or more), but we have to specify at least one <onMessage> element.

Time for action – waiting for callback

To wait for the callback using the <pick> activity, we will do the following:

1. Add the <pick> activity by dragging-and-dropping it to the `BookWarehousingBPEL` process. Place it immediately after the <invoke> activity within the `WarehousingConfirmationInvocation` scope. We should see the <pick> activity with a single `OnMessage` branch:

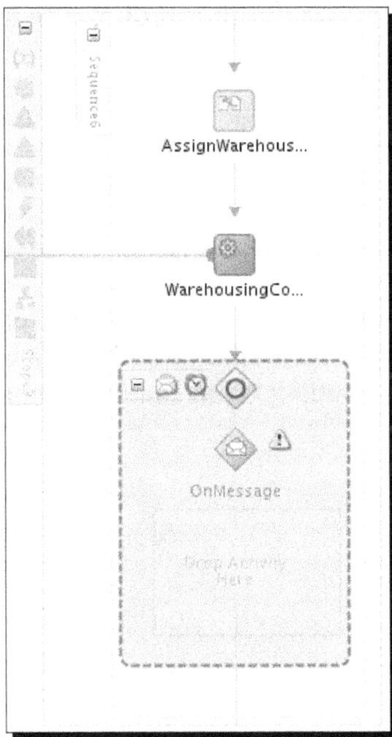

2. Double-clicking on the **OnMessage** icon opens the dialog box, where we need to specify the **Partner Link**, **Port Type**, and **Operation**:

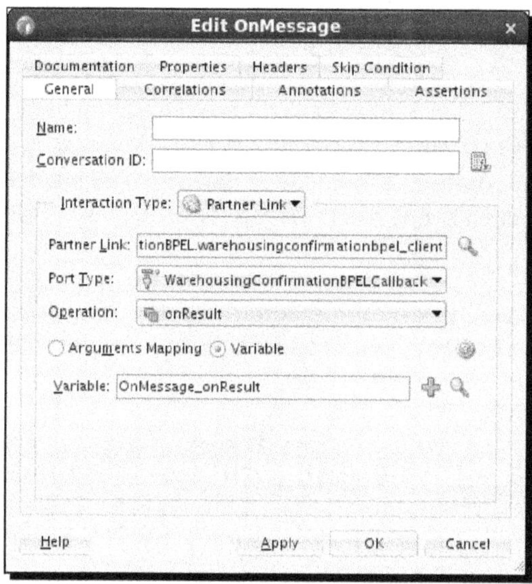

3. Similarly, we will create the variable on the fly, using the green plus sign icon. We will create a local `OnMessage_onResult` variable:

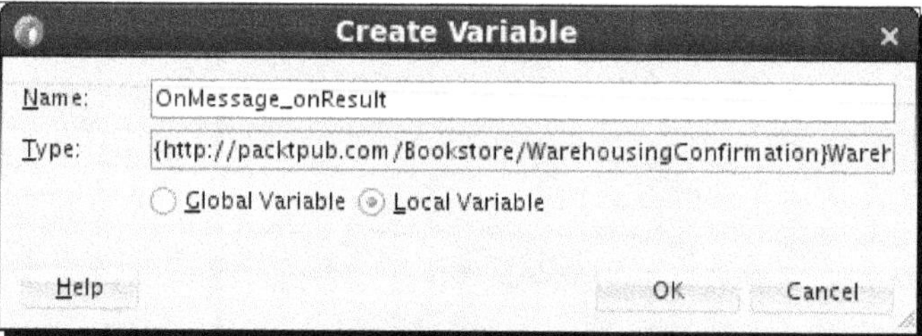

4. To handle the response, we will place an `<if>` activity within the `OnMessage` scope. Within the `<if>` activity, we will check whether the books have been successfully warehoused. The corresponding XPath condition should look as follows:

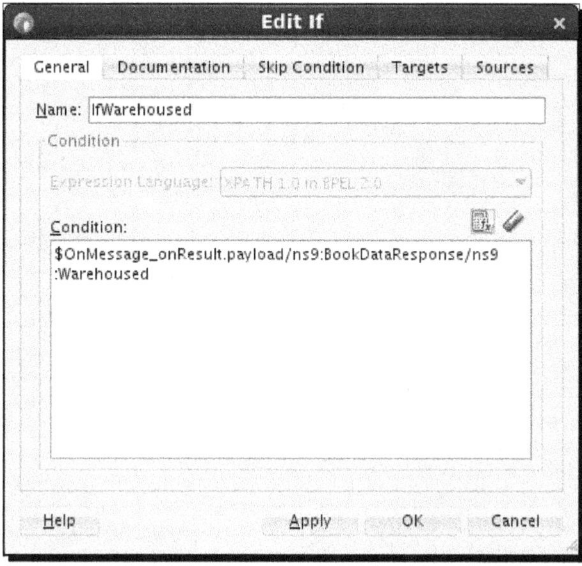

5. For each branch, we will use an `<assign>`, where we will assign a successful or unsuccessful warehousing to `outputVariable`.

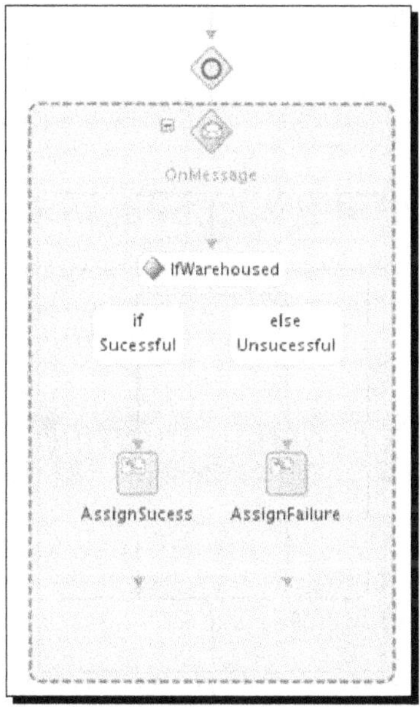

What just happened?

We have added the <pick> activity to wait for the `onResult` callback operation invocation from the `WarehousingConfirmationBPEL` service. The following BPEL code has been generated:

```
<pick name="Pick1">
  <onMessage variable="OnMessage_onResult"
             partnerLink="WarehousingConfirmationBPEL.warehousingconfirmationbpel_client"
             portType="ns9:WarehousingConfirmationBPELCallback" operation="onResult">
    <if name="IfWarehoused">
      <documentation>
        <![CDATA[Sucessful]]>
      </documentation>
      <condition>$OnMessage_onResult.payload/ns9:BookDataResponse/ns9:Warehoused</condition>
      <assign name="AssignSucess">
        <copy>
          <from>concat($outputVariable.payload/client:SelectedBookstoreLocation,'SUCESSFUL')</from>
          <to>$outputVariable.payload/client:SelectedBookstoreLocation</to>
        </copy>
      </assign>
      <else>
        <documentation>
          <![CDATA[Unsucessful]]>
        </documentation>
        <assign name="AssignFailure">
          <copy>
            <from>concat($outputVariable.payload/client:SelectedBookstoreLocation,'UNSUCESSFUL')</from>
            <to>$outputVariable.payload/client:SelectedBookstoreLocation</to>
          </copy>
        </assign>
      </else>
    </if>
  </onMessage>
</pick>
```

Waiting for onFault and onEvent callbacks

So far, we have specified the `<onMessage>` part of the `<pick>` activity for the `onResult` callback. We need to add the `onFault` and `onEvent` branches as well. We will proceed in a similar way as we did earlier.

Time for action – waiting for onFault and onEvent callbacks

To wait for the `onFault` and `onEvent` callbacks, we will do the following:

1. Add two additional `<onMessage>` branches to the `<pick>` activity. We will achieve this by clicking on the **Add OnMessage** icon next to the `<pick>` activity icon. To add two branches, we should click on it twice. We should see the following:

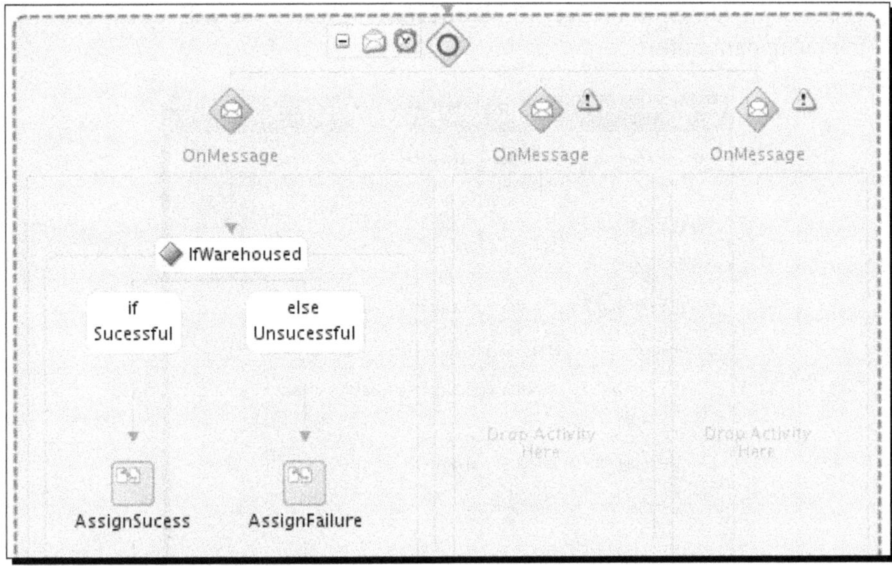

2. We need to configure each <onMessage> branch. The first branch will react on the **onFault** message. We will specify the following parameters:

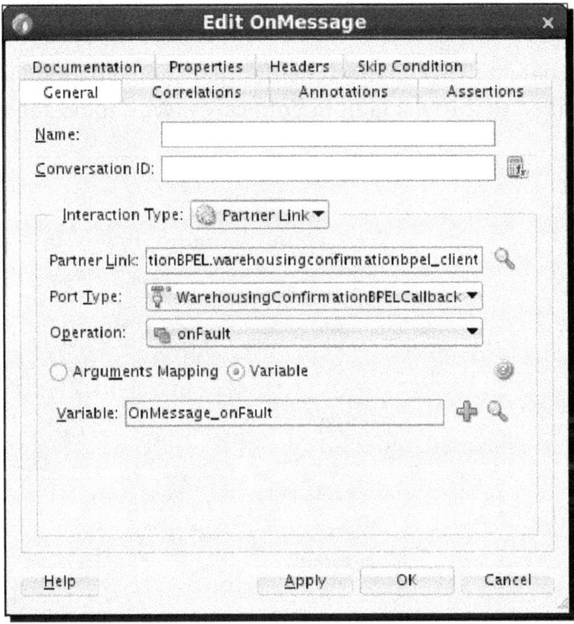

3. The second branch will react on the **onEvent** message. We will specify the following parameters:

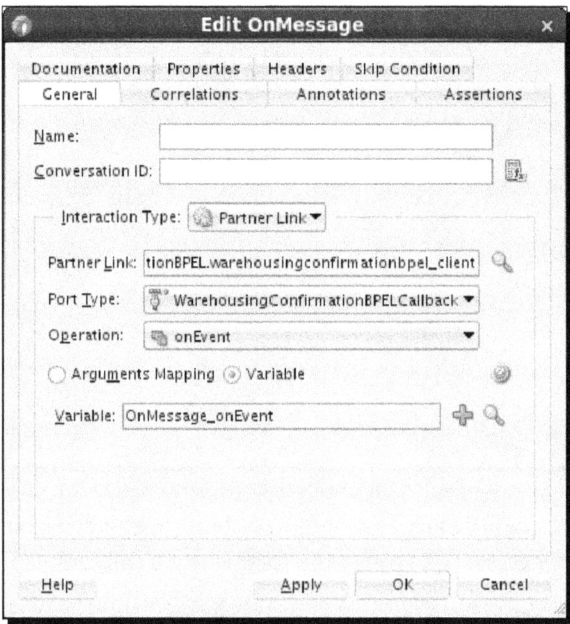

4. Next, we will need to specify the activities that should happen in both branches. We have decided to throw a fault in both cases. We should see the following:

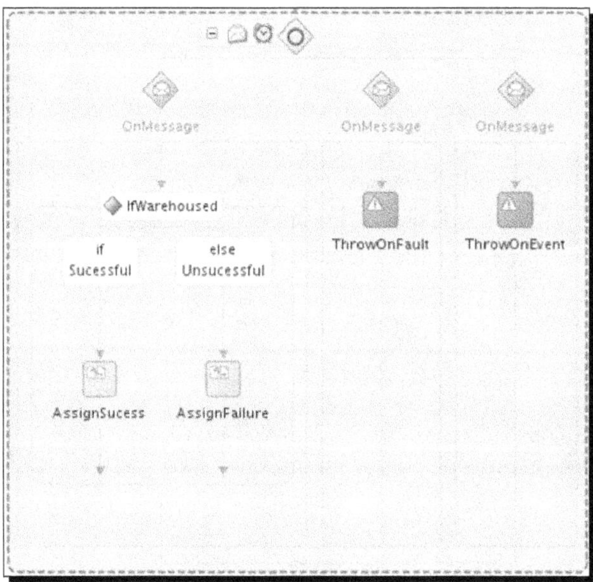

What just happened?

We have added the `<onMessage>` branches of the `<pick>` activity for the `OnFault` and `OnEvent` callbacks from the `WarehousingConfirmationBPEL` service. The following BPEL code has been generated:

```
<onMessage variable="OnMessage_onFault"
           partnerLink="WarehousingConfirmationBPEL.warehousingconfirmationbpel_client"
           portType="ns9:WarehousingConfirmationBPELCallback"
           operation="onFault">
  <throw name="ThrowOnFault" faultName="client:OnFault"/>
</onMessage>
<onMessage variable="OnMessage_onEvent"
           partnerLink="WarehousingConfirmationBPEL.warehousingconfirmationbpel_client"
           portType="ns9:WarehousingConfirmationBPELCallback"
           operation="onEvent">
  <throw name="ThrowOnEvent" faultName="client:OnEvent"/>
</onMessage>
```

Adding an alarm event for callback

To finalize our example, we will add an alarm event to our `<pick>` activity for the callback from the `WarehousingConfirmationBPEL` service. We will use a duration expression and limit the time for confirmation to 1 day. Similar to the event handlers earlier in this chapter, we will use an `<onAlarm>` branch.

Time for action – adding an alarm event for callback

To add an alarm event to our `<pick>` activity, we will do the following:

1. Add an `<onAlarm>` branch to the `<pick>` activity. We will achieve this by clicking on the **Add OnAlarm** icon next to the `<pick>` activity icon. We should see the following:

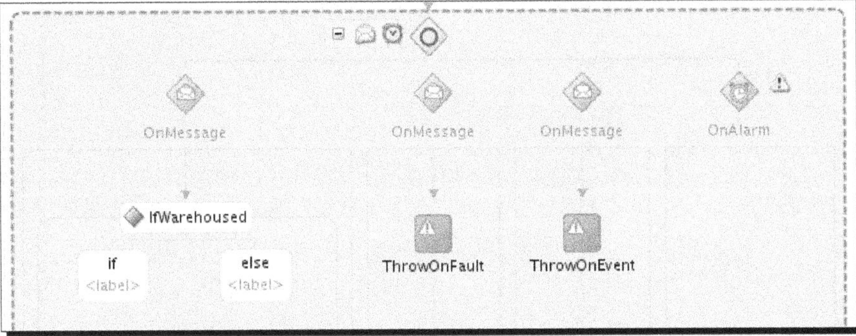

2. By double-clicking on the **OnAlarm** icon, we will specify the deadline to `1` day:

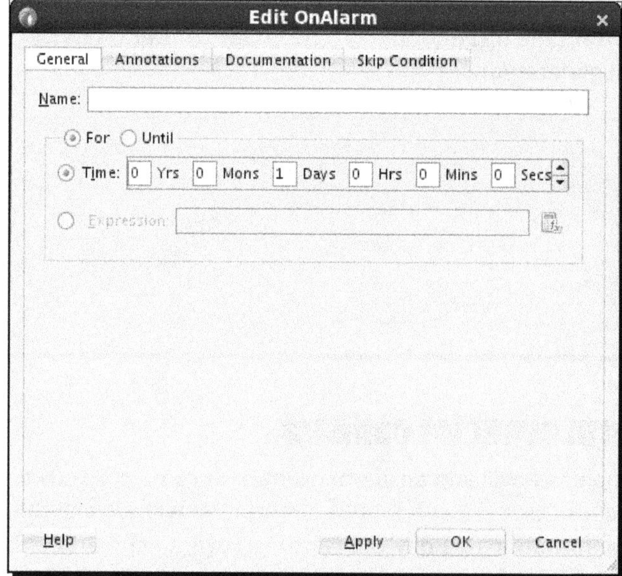

3. Next, we need to add the activity that will perform if the deadline is reached. In our example, we will simply throw a fault. We will name the fault **Timeout**. We should see the following:

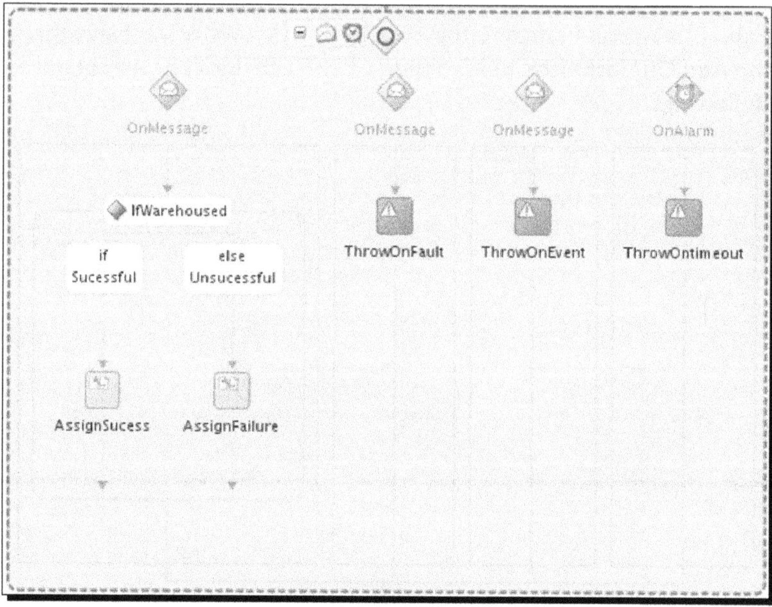

What just happened?

We have added the `<onAlarm>` branch of the `<pick>` activity for the timeout, which we have set to `1` day. This way we have limited the time our process waits for the book warehousing success confirmation callback. The following BPEL code has been generated:

```
<onAlarm>
  <for>'P1D'</for>
  <throw name="ThrowOntimeout" faultName="client:Timeout"/>
</onAlarm>
```

With this, we have concluded our discussion of the `<pick>` activity. We now understand how to handle events with asynchronous callbacks in BPEL processes.

Have a go hero – deploying and testing the example

It's your turn now. You should deploy and test the example. To deploy the example, proceed the same way as in the previous example. Then, invoke the BPEL process instance and wait for the message or alarm event to occur.

Pop quiz: events and event handlers

Q1. What type of events can a BPEL process react on?

1. Business events
2. Operation events
3. Alarm events
4. Callback events
5. Message events

Q2. Alarm events can be:

1. Deadlines
2. Durations
3. Stopwatches
4. Internet time

Q3. An event handler can be added to:

1. A scope
2. An individual activity
3. A process

Q4. A business event is declared by:

1. An event name
2. An event type
3. An XML element
4. A variable

Q5. What does the `PT4H10M` expression mean?

1. A duration expression of 4 hours and 10 months
2. A deadline expression of 4 hours and 10 months
3. A duration expression of 4 hours and 10 minutes
4. A deadline expression of 4 hours and 10 minutes

Q6. A `<pick>` activity can have:

1. Multiple `<onMessage>` activities and no `<onAlarm>` activities
2. One `<onMessage>` activity and no `<onAlarm>` activities
3. Multiple `<onMessage>` activities and multiple `<onAlarm>` activities
4. Multiple `<onAlarm>` activities and no `<onMessage>` activities

Summary

In this chapter, we have learned about different types of events and managing the events from BPEL processes within the SOA environment. We have explained the events and the difference between the event-driven approach and operation invocations. We have briefly mentioned the Event Driven Architecture. We have learned that a BPEL process can react on business events, message events, and alarm events. Business events are events with a well-defined business meaning, which are explicitly triggered by a process, service, or other software component. Message events are triggered by operation invocations on port types. Alarm events are triggered by deadline or duration expressions.

A BPEL process can be event-driven, which means that it will be triggered by a business event. A BPEL process can also trigger a business event, which will result in executing all processes, services, and other components subscribed to this type of event.

A BPEL process can react on events using event handlers. Event handlers monitor the specified message or alarm events simultaneously while the BPEL process is executing. This enables a BPEL process to react on events such as cancelation messages or timeouts.

A BPEL process can also react on events in asynchronous invocations. When waiting for callbacks, it is often useful to use the `<pick>` activity to be able to wait for different messages and for alarm events.

Now that you have learned how to handle events, we move ahead to learn about compensations.

11

Compensations

Suppose you need to write a book on ordering process. This might include two main tasks: order registration and charging the client's credit card.

Imagine there is not enough credit in the customer's credit card when initiating a credit card transaction. In this case, we need to rollback a "Register Book Order" activity in order to avoid financial losses to the bookseller. This is where we need to have compensations in the BPEL processes. The already completed tasks can be rolled backed. In the preceding example, the BPEL process should implement necessary activities to cancel the book order during the compensation.

When using a self-contained synchronous system, all information is available during a change to simply roll the change back if an error or unexpected situation occurs. However, in a BPEL environment, things are often not self-contained, and a change needs to be committed to move on. If any error or unexpected situation occurs after this commit, a new transaction is needed to "undo" the original, as a roll back to undo the original is no longer possible. We will talk more about compensation in this chapter.

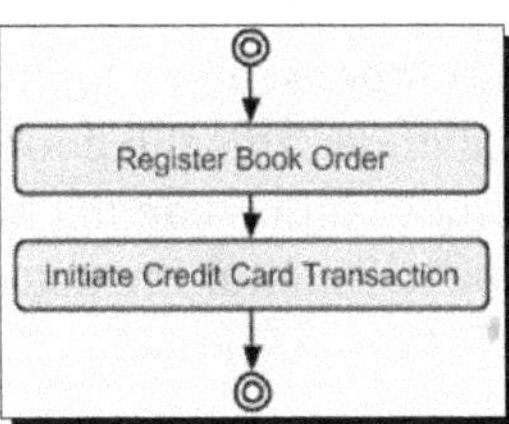

We will cover the following topics:

- Introduction to compensation in business processes
- Adding compensation handlers to a BPEL process
- Understanding long-running processes
- Understanding the concept of compensation
- How to implement a compensation in BPEL
- The structure of compensation handlers
- Compensating activities and default compensation handlers

Introducing compensation in business processes

In this section, we introduce a new sample BPEL process that models a compensation scenario. The high-level process execution is depicted in the following figure:

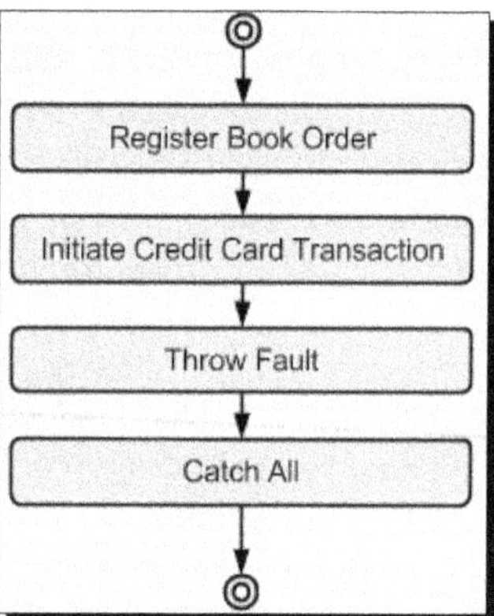

The `registerBookOrder` scope models the registration of a new book order. It includes an `<empty/>` activity called `dummyRegisterBookOrder` that simulates the registration behavior. Also, the scope contains a compensation handler, which will be discussed later in this chapter. This compensation handler discards the book order as the compensation logic. For demonstration purposes, the compensation handler also includes a `<wait/>` activity with a 30-seconds delay to allow time to monitor the activity, otherwise things might happen too fast to observe.

The `initiateCreditCardTransaction` scope models the credit card transaction related to the new book order. It includes an `<empty/>` activity called `dummyInitiateCreditCardTransaction` that simulates the credit card transaction. Similar to `dummyRegisterBookOrder`, this scope will also have a delay and a compensation handler (to reverse the credit card transaction).

The `throwFault` sequence models a fault generation within the BPEL process. For demonstration purposes, the BPEL process itself throws a fault called `TriggerCompensationFault` that is caught by the `catchAll` sequence. However, in real-life scenarios, the fault can be generated due to exceptional behaviors in the BPEL process itself, or from partner web services.

The `catchAll` sequence triggers the compensation logic for the `registerBookOrder` and `initiateCreditCardTransaction` scopes.

Defining the compensation logic for a <scope> activity with <compensationHandler>

WS-BPEL 2.0 allows you to define the compensation logic per `<scope>` activity or per `<invoke>` activity. Here, we will define the compensation logic within a `<scope>` activity. We add the aforementioned scopes (`registerBookOrder` and `initiateCreditCardTransaction`) in the sample BPEL process.

Time for action – adding compensation handlers

Let's perform the following steps of instructions to construct the book order process. First of all, let's create a new asynchronous BPEL 2.0 process named **Book_Order_Process**. We illustrated the process to create an asynchronous BPEL in *Chapter 5, Interaction Patterns in BPEL*. Perform the following steps:

1. Drag-and-drop a `<scope>` activity from the BPEL constructs palette in between the **receiveInput** and **callbackClient** activities. Name the `<scope>` activity `registerBookOrder`.
2. Drag-and-drop an `<empty>` activity to this `<scope>` activity, and name it `dummyRegisterBookOrder`. This is used to model the tasks related to book order registration, such as creating an entry in the order management system.
3. Now we will add a compensation handler to this `<scope>` activity. Click on the **Add Compensation Handler** icon on the scope, and it will create `<compensationHandler>` within the `<scope>` activity:

4. Now the <scope> activity looks as follows. Make sure to click on the + mark if you do not see the menu on the left:

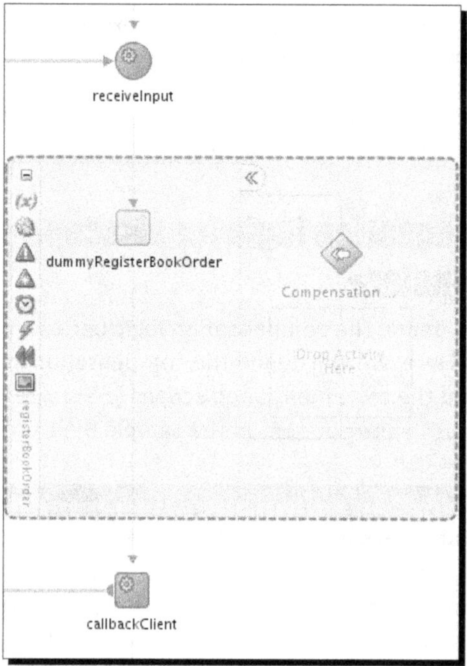

5. Let's add the compensation logic into <compensationHandler>. For demonstration purposes, we will add a <wait> activity with a 30-seconds break, so the user can monitor the status of the process before compensation starts. Drag-and-drop a <wait> activity inside the compensation handler and configure it to have a 30-seconds interval, as follows.

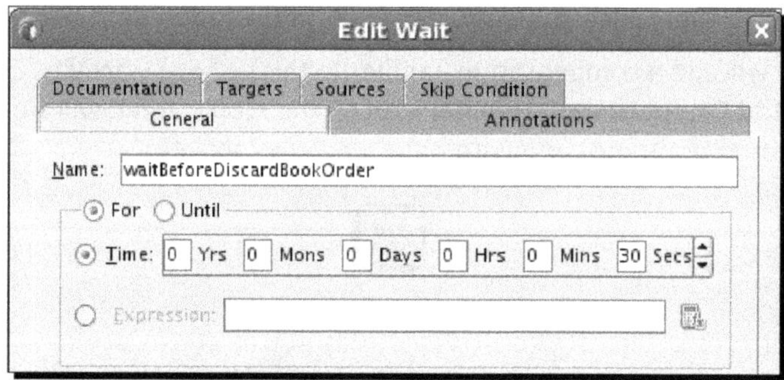

6. Drag-and-drop an `<empty>` activity after the previously added `<wait>` activity. Again, this `<empty>` activity is for demonstration purposes, so it represents the compensation logic to be executed. After this step, we finished adding `registerBookOrder`, the `<scope>` activity that models the book order registration. The scope looks as follows:

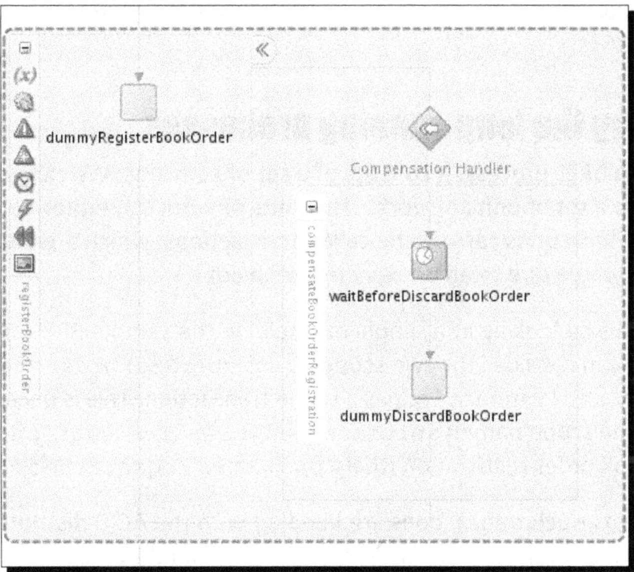

7. Likewise, we need to add an adjacent `<scope>` activity to model the credit card transaction. Repeat the steps from 1 to 5 to create a `<scope>` activity named `initiateCreditCardTransaction`. The outcome is as follows:

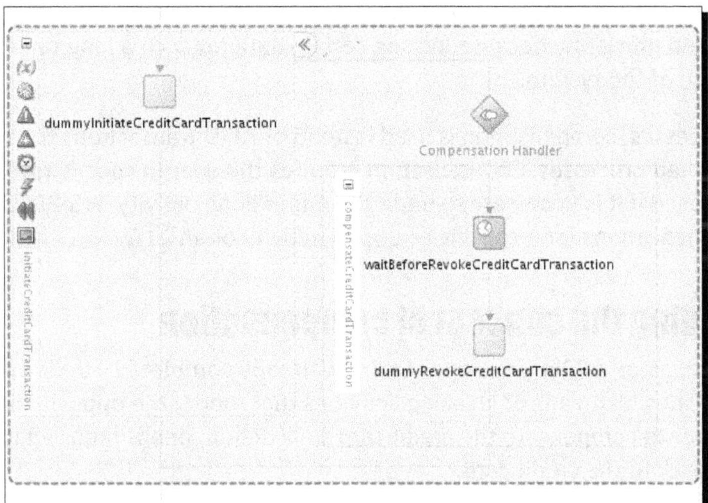

What just happened?

In the previous section, we created two scopes named `registerBookOrder` and `initiateCreditCardTransaction`, which model the book order registration process with `<compensationHandler>`. For demonstration purposes, we didn't add actual implementation specific activities; rather, we added `<empty>` activities and the `<wait>` activities in each `<compensationHandler>`, so the user can monitor the state of the BPEL process.

Understanding the long-running processes

When it comes to a BPEL process, it consists of a set of activities. We can generally categorize these activities into a set of units of works. The units of work can either be one activity or a set of activities. These units can also be called transactions, which are either executed or compensated as a whole due to an unexpected behavior.

Let's understand this by looking at a simple example. In the sample BPEL process in this chapter, we can consider the two scopes, `registerBookOrder` and `initiateCreditCardTransaction`, as a single transaction. This is because if the credit card transaction (the scope named `initiateCreditCardTransaction`) fails, we need to roll back the book order registration (the scope named `registerBookOrder`) as well.

In enterprise systems, such transactions are handled with the ACID distributed transaction model. ACID stands for atomicity, consistency, isolation, and durability. This model defines a transaction model that uses data locking and isolation. Such a model works perfectly well in trusted domains within enterprise. Also, it expects the transactions to be relatively short.

However, when it comes to business processes, they are typically long-running processes, sometimes several hours and sometimes several months. Also, they interact with loosely coupled partner web services. In such situations, the ACID distributed transaction model cannot be applied efficiently because locking certain data for such a long time will affect the performance of the system.

In business processes, compensation is used instead of ACID transactions to reverse the effect of unfinished processes. Compensation requires the user to specify reversing activities that can be invoked if it is necessary to undo the effect of an activity. WS-BPEL 2.0 supports specifying compensations for a specific `<scope>` activity or an `<invoke>` activity.

Understanding the concept of compensation

Compensation enables a BPEL developer to undo already completed `<scope>` and `<invoke>` activities by means of invoking activities that model the opposite behavior. For example, in order to compensate the credit card transaction, one is required to deposit the same amount back to the credit card.

The difference between fault handling and compensation

If we compare <faultHandlers> and<compensationHandler>, we see that they both address a somewhat similar issue. Both define an activity to be triggered to handle an exceptional situation. However, what <faultHandlers> does is act upon error messages or other exceptions returned by partner web services and exceptions thrown from the BPEL process and runtime. The thrown fault is caught by <faultHandlers> and is acted upon accordingly. So, <faultHandlers> tries to recover from an activity that did not finish normally. However, a <compensationHandler> tries to reverse an activity or a set of activities that was successfully finished as part of a business process that is being abandoned.

Time for action – triggering a fault within the BPEL process

So far, we implemented two <scope> activities that model the book ordering process. However, to trigger <compensationHandler> of the <scope> activities, we need to have either <catch>, <catchAll>, <compensationHandler>, or <terminationHandler>. We will use <catchAll>, and inside this, we will trigger <compensationHandler>. To trigger <catchAll>, we need to throw an explicit fault after the execution of the two scopes. Next, we learn how to throw this fault.

Carry out the following steps:

1. Add a <sequence> activity named `throwFault` after the <scope> activity named `initiateCreditCardTransaction`. Then, drag-and-drop an <if> activity within it and specify its condition, as shown in the following screenshot. This condition will check the content of `inputVariable` and check whether it contains the `compensate` value:

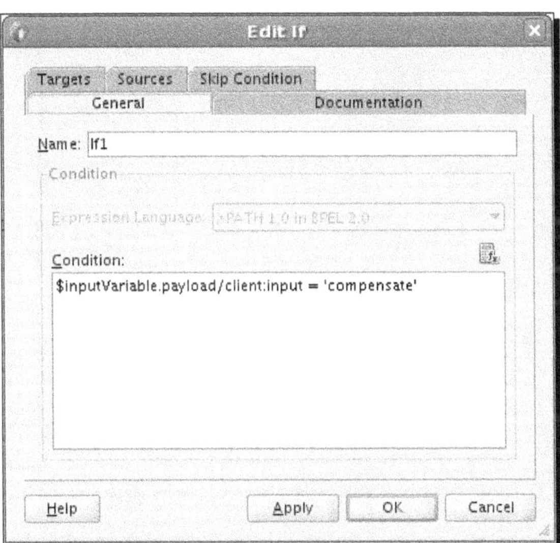

2. Add a `<throw>` activity inside it, so if the content of `inputVariable` contains the `compensate` value, it triggers the `<throw>` activity. Configure this activity to throw a fault named `TriggerCompensationFault`, as follows:

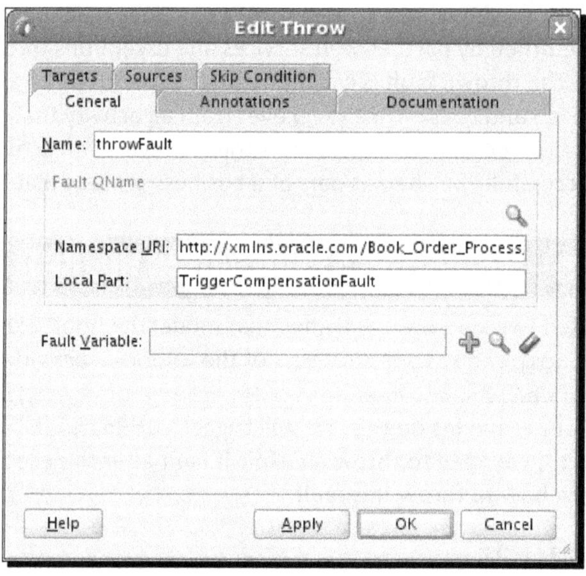

3. For `<else>`, add an `<empty>` activity, so if the content of `inputVariable` does not contain the `compensate` value, the fault is not thrown. Then the `<sequence>` named `throwFault` looks like what is shown in the following screenshot:

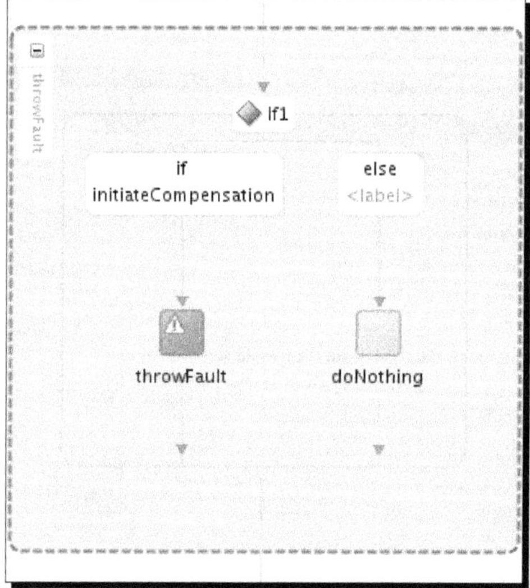

What just happened?

In the previous section, we throw a fault from the BPEL process if `inputVariable` contains a `compensate` value. This fault is used to trigger the compensation of the created scopes.

Initiating a compensation for scopes within a BPEL process

In the previous section, we throw a fault from the BPEL process if `inputVariable` contains the `compensate` value. Now we need to catch it and trigger `<compensationHandler>` for the `registerBookOrder` and `initiateCreditCardTransaction` scopes.
For this, we will add a `<catchAll>` activity to catch the thrown fault and trigger `<compensationHandler>` within the `<catchAll>` activity in the next section.

Time for action – triggering compensation for the BPEL process

Carry out the following steps:

1. Click on the BPEL process and then click on the following **Add CatchAll** icon:

2. Once this is done, the `<catchAll>` activity will be added to the BPEL process, as follows:

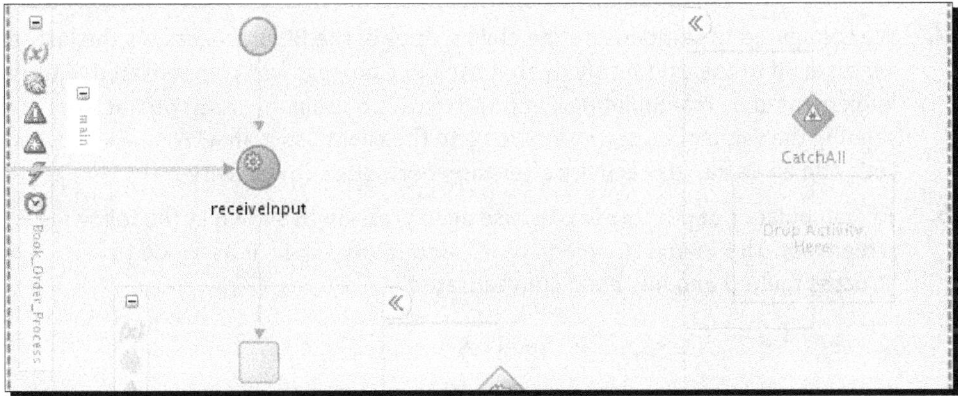

3. Within the `<catchAll>` activity, we can trigger `<compensationHandler>` for all the child scopes by using the `<compensate>` activity. However, before triggering it, add a `<sequence>` activity called **catchall**, and within it, add a `<wait>` activity with an interval of 30 seconds, so the user can monitor the status of the BPEL process before triggering `<compensationHandler>`, as follows:

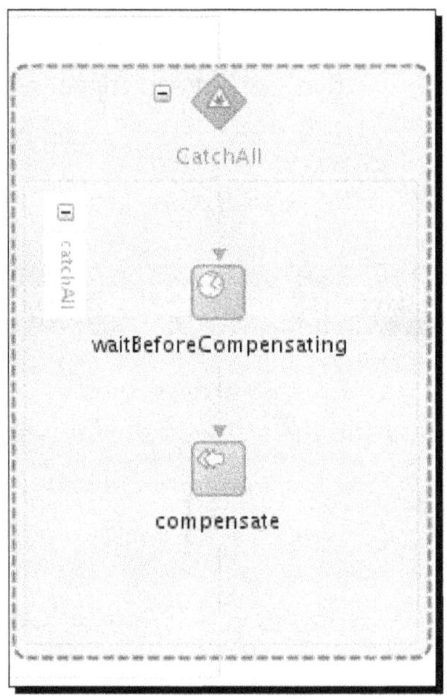

4. We configured to compensate the child scopes of the BPEL process. As the last step, we respond to the user notifying that the BPEL process was compensated. This is implemented by manipulating `outputVariable` using an `<assign>` activity and sending the value of `outputVariable` to the client using an `<invoke>` activity. Let's add an `<assign>` activity after the `<compensate>` activity.
5. To manipulate `outputVariable`, use an expression as shown in the following screenshot. The `<result>` element in `outputVariable` is assigned to **'Process faulted and has been compensated'**:

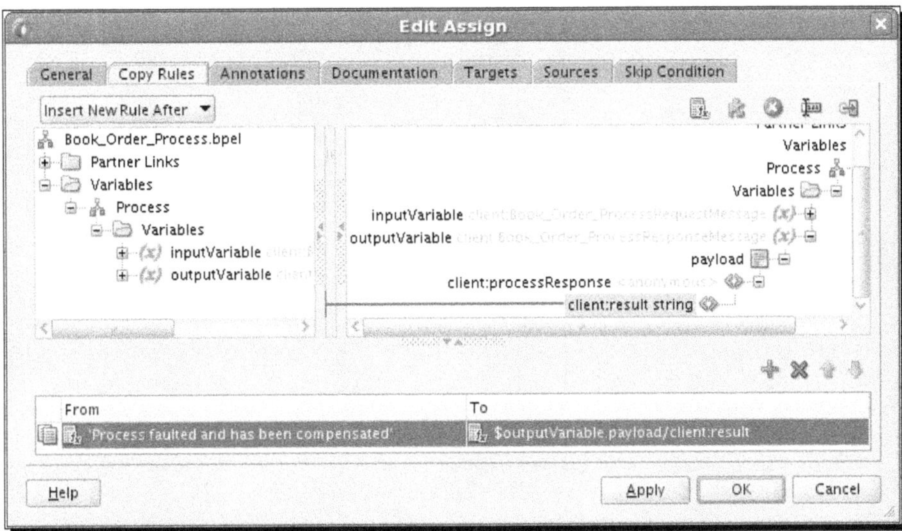

6. Add an `<invoke>` activity after the `<assign>` activity and configure it as shown in the following screenshot. It sends the modified value of `outputVariable` back to the client:

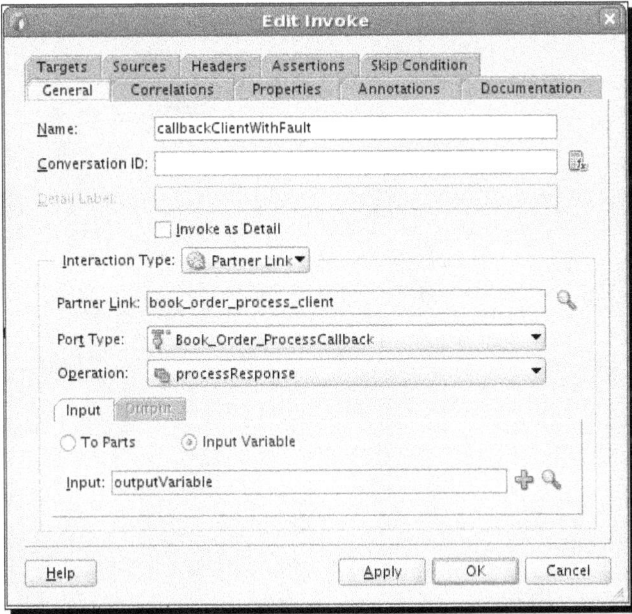

The final BPEL process looks like the following:

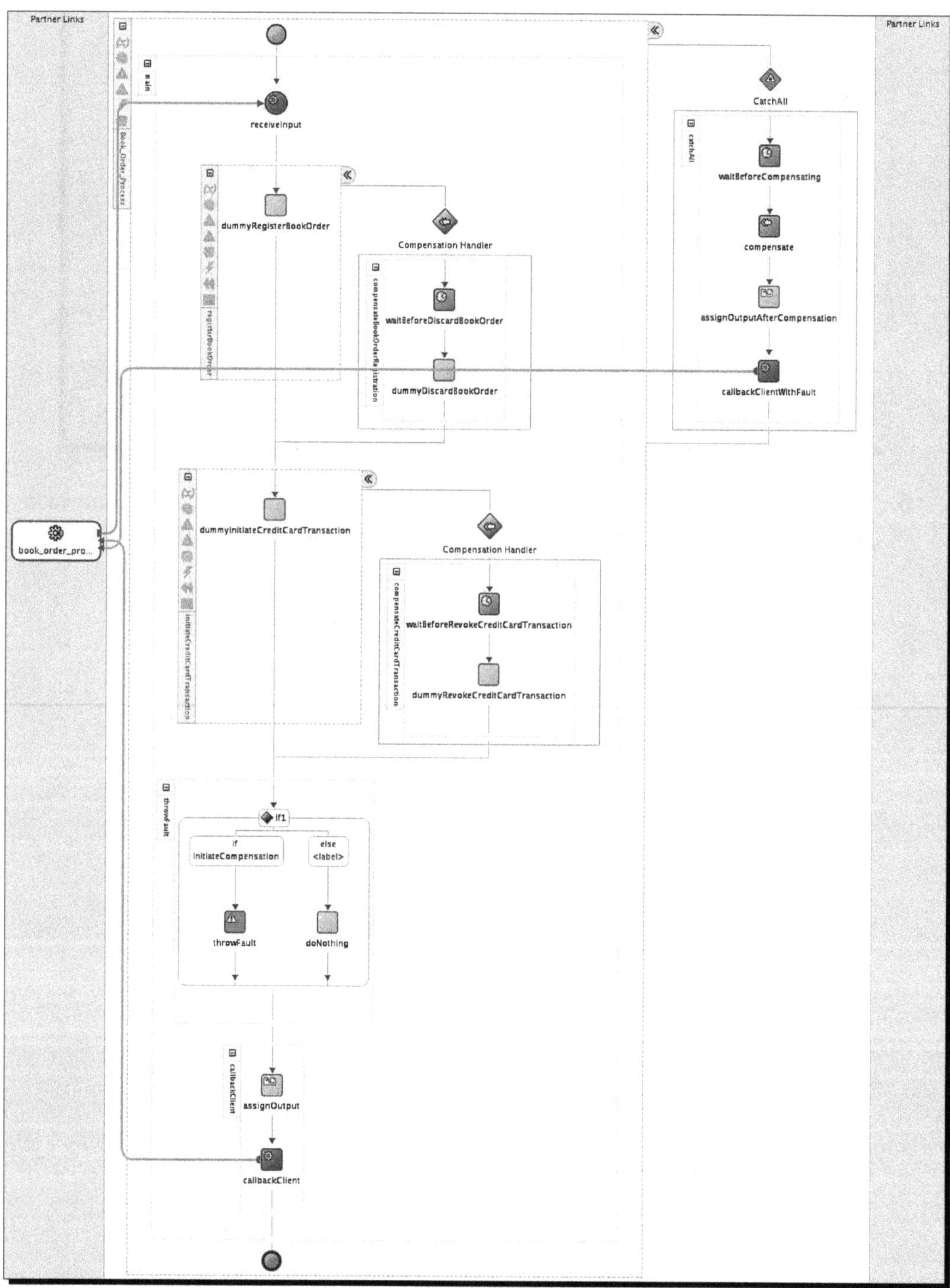

What just happened?

In the previous section, we completed the book ordering process. This BPEL process throws a fault from the `throwFault` sequence, and the fault is caught by the `catachAll` sequence. Then, within the `catachAll` sequence, `<compensationHandler>` of child scopes is triggered.

Implementing compensation handlers

To implement the compensation, WS-BPEL 2.0 provides the `<compensationHandler>` construct. Note that this construct can be defined only for a `<scope>` or an `<invoke>` activity.

This `<compensationHandler>` of the scope is defined immediately after `<faultHandlers>`:

```
<scope>
  <partnerLinks></partnerLinks>
  <messageExchanges></messageExchanges>
  <variables></variables>
  <correlationSets></correlationSets>
  <faultHandlers></faultHandlers>
  <compensationHandler>
    <!—Compensation activities -->
  </compensationHandler>

  <terminationHandler></terminationHandler>
  <eventHandlers></eventHandlers>
</scope>
```

The other option of defining `<compensationHandler>` is within an `<invoke>` activity. This is more like a shortcut that allows a BPEL developer to specify a compensation for an `<invoke>` activity without enclosing it in a `<scope>` activity for the sake of specifying the compensation. We call it as an inline compensation handler:

```
<invoke ... >
  <compensationHandler>
    <!—Compensation activities -->
  </compensationHandler>
</invoke>
```

Within `<compensationHandler>`, we can specify an activity that has to be executed for compensation. This activity can either be a basic activity such as `<invoke>`, or a structured activity such as `<sequence>` or `<flow>`. Consider the following code snippet:

```
<compensationHandler>
  <sequence>
    <assign>...</assign>
```

```
        <invoke ... />
        <assign>...</assign>
        <invoke ... />
    </sequence>
</compensationHandler>
```

Triggering compensation handlers

We have to use <compensationHandler> to undo an activity that has completed normally, whereas <faultHandler> is used to act upon an exception condition during the execution of an activity. The main purpose of a compensation is to undo a <scope> or an <invoke> activity.

WS-BPEL 2.0 provides two activities to trigger a compensation handler. They are as follows:

- <compensateScope>: This activity triggers <compensationHandler> of a specific child scope
- <compensate>: This activity triggers <compensationHandler> of all child scopes

The <compensateScope> activity is used to trigger the compensation of a specified child scope. The child scope is specified by the attribute named `target`. The following example triggers a child scope named `registerBookOrder`:

```
<compensateScope target="registerBookOrder"/>
```

The <compensate> activity is used to trigger the compensation of all child scopes. The following example triggers the compensation handler of each completed child scope in a particular order:

```
<compensate/>
```

Now, we know the activities that enable you to trigger and compensate <compensationHandler>, but where can we put them?

We can only use the <compensate> and <compensateScope> activities within the following constructs:

- <catch>
- <catchAll>
- <compensationHandler>
- <terminationHandler>

In the provided sample example, we used `<catchAll>` to put `<compensate>` to trigger the compensation:

```
<catchAll>
  <sequence name="catchAll">
    ...
    <compensate name="compensate"/>
    ...
  </sequence>
</catchAll>
```

The execution of multiple compensation handlers

If we trigger a compensation handler for a scope, then it triggers compensation handlers for the completed and immediately enclosed scopes in the reverse order of completion. For example, in the sample BPEL process provided for this chapter, there are two scopes named `registerBookOrder` and `initiateCreditCardTransaction`, which are defined within a sequence called `main`. The scope `initiateCreditCardTransaction` will complete its execution after `registerBookOrder`. Suppose we use a `<compensate>` activity in the global fault handler. Then, compensation handlers of both the scopes get triggered in the reverse order. This means that the scope named `initiateCreditCardTransaction` will compensate before the scope named `registerBookOrder`.

The default compensation handler

We can define `<compensationHandler>` only for an `<invoke>` and a `<scope>` activity. The visibility of `<compensationHandler>` in a scope is limited to the inner `<scope>`. If `<compensationHandler>` is not defined for a given `<scope>` activity, then the BPEL runtime cannot trigger all the compensation handlers defined within the enclosed `<scope>`. Hence, the BPEL runtime implicitly specifies a default compensation handler, as shown in the following code. A default compensation handler compensates all inner scopes in the reverse order of their completion and rethrows the fault to the parent scope:

```
<compensationHandler>
  <compensate />
</compensationHandler>
```

Have a go hero – compensating specific scopes

Update the sample BPEL process such that it compensates each specific scope (`registerBookOrder` and `initiateCreditCardTransaction`) one by one.

Pop quiz

Q1. What is the difference between fault handlers and compensation handlers?

Q2. Which construct does not support to specify `<compensate>` and `<compensateScope>`?

1. `<catch>`
2. `<catchAll>`
3. `<eventHandlers>`
4. `<compensationHandler>`
5. `<terminationHandler>`

Q3. What is the behavior of a compensation handler if it belongs to a scope that is not completed normally?

Q4. Which statement is true and which is false?

1. It is possible to define `<compensationHandler>` for `<process>`
2. A compensation handler of a scope should be defined immediately before `<faultHandlers>`

Summary

In this chapter, we learned about compensation in WS-BPEL 2.0 in detail. It lets us define a compensation logic as per a `<scope>` or an `<invoke>` activity and trigger it from `<catch>`, `<catchAll>`, `<compensationHandler>`, or `<terminationHandler>` using `<compensate>` or `<compensateScope>`. We used a book ordering process to explain the concepts in detail. Therefore, at the end of this chapter, the reader is capable of specifying compensation handlers and can trigger them in BPEL processes to undo activities in the business processes that have already completed normally.

A Pop Quiz Answers

Chapter 1, Hello BPEL

Pop quiz – BPEL basics

Q1	1, 4, 6
Q2	3
Q3	`<process>`
Q4	Yes
Q5	`<assign>`
Q6	5
Q7	2
Q8	2

Chapter 2, Service Invocation

Pop quiz – service invocation

Q1	2
Q2	2, 4, 5
Q3	The WSDL file
Q4	4

Chapter 3, Variables, Data Manipulation, and Expressions

Pop quiz – variables and data manipulation

Q1	2
Q2	type, element, messageType
Q3	`<variable name="BookStoreWithLowestQuantity"` `messageType="client:BookstoreBPELResponseMessage"/>`

Q4	`<assign>`
	`<copy>`
	`<from variable="BookstoreAResponse" />`
	`<to variable="BookStoreWithLowestQuantity" />`
	`</copy>`
	`</assign>`

Q5	2
Q6	1
Q7	2

Chapter 4, Conditions and Loops

Pop quiz – conditions and loops

Q1	2, 3
Q2	while, repeatUntil, forEach
Q3	repeatUntil
Q4	forEach
Q5	duration, deadline
Q6	2
Q7	3

Chapter 5, Interaction Patterns in BPEL

Pop quiz – labels

Q1	One-way
Q2	Content of the WS-Addressing based header can be used by the BPEL runtime for correlation purposes. WS-BPEL 2.0 also provides a standardized mechanism using correlation sets, where the correlation property of the outgoing and incoming message is compared.
Q3	1
Q4	Asynchronous invocation is useful for external services, which take a long time to process the request and respond back to the BPEL process. So if the BPEL process is synchronous, there is a possibility that its client may time out before the BPEL process responds back.

Chapter 6, Fault Handling and Signaling

Pop quiz

Q1	`<throw>` is used to signal faults explicitly from the BPEL process. But `<rethrow>` is used only within a fault handler like `<catch>` or `<catchAll>` to propagate the caught fault to the enclosing scope explicitly.
Q2	A pair of `<receive>` and `<reply>` is used to propagate a fault back to a synchronous client where a pair of `<receive>` and `<invoke>` is used to propagate a fault back to an asynchronous client.

<table>
<tr><td>Q3</td><td>

```
<catch faultName="fltns:faultName" >
   ...
</catch>

<catch faultVariable="fltns:faultVariable" >
   ...
</catch>

<catch faultName="fltns:faultName" faultVariable="fltns:faultVariable" >
   ...
</catch>

<catch faultName="fltns:faultName" faultVariable="fltns:faultVariable"
faultMessageType="xmlns:faultMessaheTypefaultMessageTypefaultMessaheType">
   ...
</catch>

<catch faultName="fltns:faultName"
faultMessageType="xmlns:faultMessaheTypefaultMessageTypefaultMessaheType" >
   ...
</catch>

<catch faultName="fltns:faultName" faultElement="xmlns:faultElement" >
   ...
 </catch>
```

</td></tr>
<tr><td>Q4</td><td>

```
<catch><!--with no attributes-->
   ...
</catch>

<catch faultName="fltns:faultName" faultElement="xmlns:faultElement"><!-
-faultElement or faultMessageType attributes cannot exist without
faultVariableattibute-->
   ...
</catch>

   <catch faultVariable="fltns:faultVariable"
   faultMessageType="xmlns:faultMessaheTypefaultMessageTypefaultMessaheType"
   faultElement="xmlns:faultElement"><!--Either one attribute that is
   faultMessageType or faultElement can exist with faultVariable attribute.
   Not Both-->
   ...
</catch>
```

</td></tr>
</table>

Chapter 7, Working with Scopes

Pop quiz – playing audio

Q1	3
Q2	2, 4
Q3	2, 3
Q4	3

Chapter 8, Dynamic Parallel Invocations

Pop quiz

Q1	2, 3
Q2	The loop is not executed.
Q3	The completion condition is not triggered, in other words, all the possible iterations will be executed.
Q4	3

Chapter 9, Human Tasks

Pop quiz – human tasks

Q1	1
Q2	1, 2
Q3	An escalation means that the human task will be assigned to the user or group which is higher in the hierarchy after a certain period of time. We can configure how many escalation levels should be used for our human task and who is the highest approver title that can get the human task assigned.
Q4	2
Q5	1

Chapter 10, Events and Event Handlers

Pop quiz – events and event handlers

Q1	1, 3, 5
Q2	1, 2
Q3	1, 3
Q4	1, 3
Q5	3
Q6	1, 2, 3

Chapter 11, Compensations

Pop quiz

Q1	Compensation handler tries to rollback an activity that is completed normally. But a fault handler tries to recover from an activity that could not completed normally due to an exceptional situation occurred.
Q2	3
Q3	Nothing is suppose to happen, as compensation handler only tries to rollback an activity that is completed normally.
Q4	1. False 2. False

Index

Symbols

A

B

C

D

E

I

J

K

L

M

N

O

P

Q

R

S

T

U

V

W

X

Thank you for buying

WS-BPEL 2.0 Beginner's Guide

About Packt Publishing

Packt, pronounced 'packed', published its first book "*Mastering phpMyAdmin for Effective MySQL Management*" in April 2004 and subsequently continued to specialize in publishing highly focused books on specific technologies and solutions.

Our books and publications share the experiences of your fellow IT professionals in adapting and customizing today's systems, applications, and frameworks. Our solution-based books give you the knowledge and power to customize the software and technologies you're using to get the job done. Packt books are more specific and less general than the IT books you have seen in the past. Our unique business model allows us to bring you more focused information, giving you more of what you need to know, and less of what you don't.

Packt is a modern, yet unique publishing company, which focuses on producing quality, cutting-edge books for communities of developers, administrators, and newbies alike. For more information, please visit our website: `www.PacktPub.com`.

About Packt Enterprise

In 2010, Packt launched two new brands, Packt Enterprise and Packt Open Source, in order to continue its focus on specialization. This book is part of the Packt Enterprise brand, home to books published on enterprise software – software created by major vendors, including (but not limited to) IBM, Microsoft and Oracle, often for use in other corporations. Its titles will offer information relevant to a range of users of this software, including administrators, developers, architects, and end users.

Writing for Packt

We welcome all inquiries from people who are interested in authoring. Book proposals should be sent to `author@packtpub.com`. If your book idea is still at an early stage and you would like to discuss it first before writing a formal book proposal, contact us; one of our commissioning editors will get in touch with you.

We're not just looking for published authors; if you have strong technical skills but no writing experience, our experienced editors can help you develop a writing career, or simply get some additional reward for your expertise.

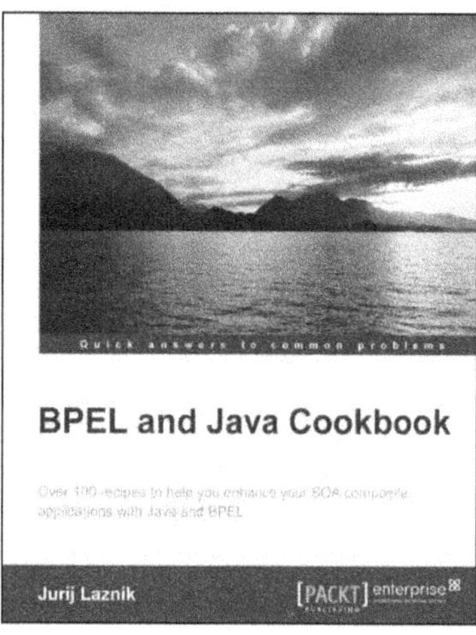

BPEL and Java Cookbook

ISBN: 978-1-84968-920-5   Paperback: 382 pages

Over 100 recipes to help you enhance your SOA composite applications with Java and BPEL

1. Easy to understand recipes for integrating Java and BPEL.
2. Covers a wide range of integration possibilities for orchestrating business processes.
3. Provides step-by-step instructions on examples stretching throughout the chapters, covering all phases of development from specification to testing.

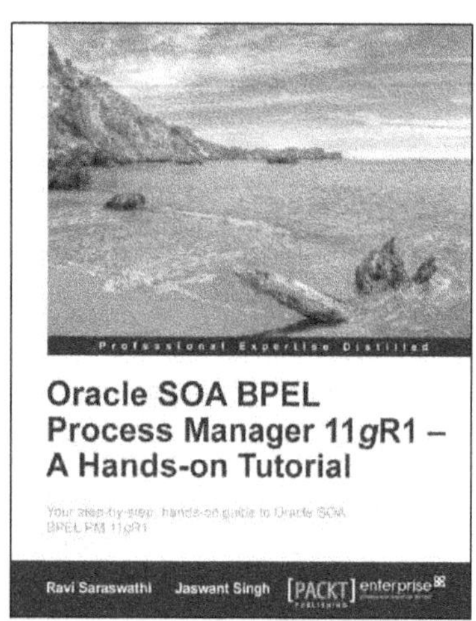

Oracle SOA BPEL Process Manager 11*g*R1 – A Hands-on Tutorial

ISBN: 978-1-84968-898-7   Paperback: 330 pages

Your step-by-step, hands-on guide to Oracle SOA BPEL PM 11*g*R1

1. Learn by doing, with immediate results.
2. Create, integrate, and troubleshoot BPEL services with Oracle BPEL Process Manager and JDeveloper step by step.
3. Design, develop, test, deploy, and run a full SOA composite application using industry leading practices.

Please check **www.PacktPub.com** for information on our titles

Applied SOA Patterns on the Oracle Platform

ISBN: 978-1-78217-056-3 Paperback: 572 pages

Fuse together your pragmatic Oracle experience with abstract SOA patterns with this practical guide

1. Demonstrates how to approach the Big Problem, decompose it into manageable pieces, and assess the feasibility of SOA methodology to build the entire solution using real-life examples.

2. Explores out the links between SOA Principles, Open Standards, and SOA Frameworks with clear standards implementation roadmaps.

3. A collection of lessons learned from various implementations undertaken over the years, but the book can also be used as a textbook of preparation for SOA Professional/Architect exams (from SOA school).

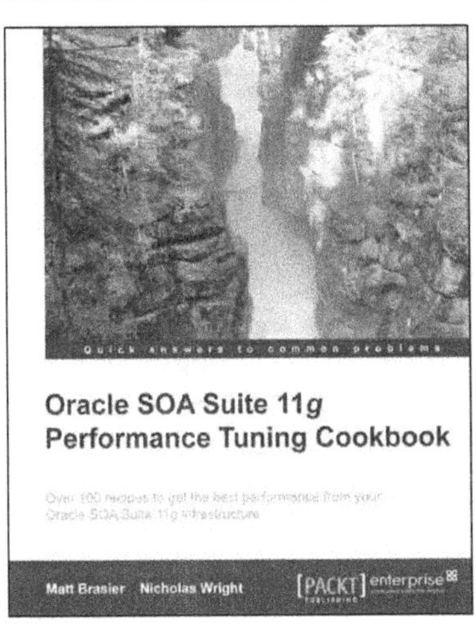

Oracle SOA Suite 11*g* Performance Tuning Cookbook

ISBN: 978-1-84968-884-0 Paperback: 328 pages

Over 100 recipes to get the best performance from your Oracle SOA Suite 11*g* infrastructure

1. Tune the Java Virtual Machine to get the best out of the underlying platform.

2. Learn how to monitor and profile your Oracle SOA Suite applications.

3. Discover how to design and deploy your application for high-performance scenarios.

4. Identify and resolve performance bottlenecks in your Oracle SOA Suite infrastructure.

Please check **www.PacktPub.com** for information on our titles

www.ingramcontent.com/pod-product-compliance
Lightning Source LLC
Chambersburg PA
CBHW080707220326
41598CB00033B/5340

* 9 7 8 1 8 4 9 6 8 8 9 6 3 *